Reformation
and Scholasticism

Texts and Studies in Reformation and Post-Reformation Thought

General Editor
Prof. Richard A. Muller, Calvin Theological Seminary

Caspar Olevianus, *A Firm Foundation: An Aid to Interpreting the Heidelberg Catechism,* translated, with an introduction by Lyle D. Bierma.

John Calvin, *The Bondage and Liberation of the Will: A Defence of the Orthodox Doctrine of Human Choice against Pighius,* edited by A. N. S. Lane, translated by G. I. Davies.

Law and Gospel: Philip Melancthon's Debate with John Agricola of Eisleben over Poenitentia, by Timothy J. Wengert.

Martin Luther as Prophet, Teacher, and Hero: Images of the Reformer, 1520–1620, by Robert Kolb.

Melancthon in Europe: His Work and Influence beyond Wittenberg, edited by Karin Maag.

Reformation and Scholasticism: An Ecumenical Enterprise, edited by Willem J. van Asselt and Eef Dekker

Reformation
and Scholasticism

An Ecumenical Enterprise

Edited by
Willem J. van Asselt
and Eef Dekker

Baker Academic
A Division of Baker Book House Co
Grand Rapids, Michigan 49516

©2001 by Willem J. van Asselt and Eef Dekker

Published by Baker Academic
a division of Baker Book House Company
P.O. Box 6287, Grand Rapids, MI 49516-6287

Printed in the United States of America

Library of Congress Cataloging-in-Publication Data

Reformation and Scholasticism / [edited by] Willem J. van Asselt and Eef Dekker.
    p.   cm. — (Texts and studies in Reformation and post-Reformation thought)
    Includes bibliographical references and index.
    ISBN 0-8010-2242-8 (pbk.)
    1. Protestantism. 2. Scholasticism. I. Asselt, W. J. van II. Dekker, E. III. Series.
BX4817.R44 2001
230′.044—dc21   2001016163

For information about academic books, resources for Christian leaders, and all new releases available from Baker Book House, visit our web site:

http://www.bakerbooks.com

Contents

Series Preface

The heritage of the Reformation is of profound importance to the church in the present day. Yet there remain many significant gaps in our knowledge of the intellectual development of Protestantism in the sixteenth century, and there are not a few myths about the theology of the Protestant orthodox writers of the late sixteenth and the seventeenth centuries. These gaps and myths—frequently caused by ignorance of the scope of the particular thinker's work, by negative theological judgments passed on the theology of the Reformers or their successors by later generations, or by an intellectual imperialism of the present that singles out some thinkers and ignores others regardless of their relative significance to their own times—stand in the way of a substantive encounter with this important period in our history. Understanding and appropriation of that heritage can occur only through the publication of significant works—monographs and sound, scholarly translations—that present the breadth and detail of the thought of the Reformers and their successors.

Texts and Studies in Reformation and Post-Reformation Thought proposes to make available such works as Casper Olevianus's *Firm Foundation*, Theodore Beza's *Table of Predestination*, and Jerome Zanchi's *Confession of Faith*, together with significant monographs on traditional Reformed theology, under the guidance of an editorial board of recognized scholars in the field. Major older works, like Heppe's *Reformed Dogmatics,* will be reprinted or reissued with new introductions. These works, moreover, are intended to address two groups: an academic and a confessional or churchly audience. The series recognizes the need for careful, scholarly treatment of the reformation and of the era of Protestant orthodoxy, given the continuing presence of misunderstandings particularly of the later era in both the scholarly and the popular literature as well as the recent interest in reappraising the relationship of the Reformation to Protestant orthodoxy. In addition, however, the series hopes to provide the church at large with worthy documents from its rich heritage and thereby to support and to stimulate interest in the roots of the Protestant tradition.

Richard A. Muller

Contributors

DR. WILLEM J. VAN ASSELT is lecturer in Church History, Utrecht University.

PROF. DR. CORNELIS AUGUSTIJN is professor emeritus in Church History at the Free University, Amsterdam.

DRS. ANDREAS J. BECK is Ph.D. researcher in Church History, and is working on a thesis on Gisbertus Voetius's doctrine of God.

DR. FRITS G. M. BROEYER is lecturer in Church History, Utrecht University.

PROF. DR. LUCO J. VAN DEN BROM is professor in Systematic Theology, Groningen University.

DR. EEF DEKKER is lecturer in Philosophical Theology, Utrecht University.

DR. HARM GORIS is research fellow in Systematic Theology at the Catholic Theological University, Utrecht.

DR. BERT LOONSTRA (1956) is minister of the Christian Reformed Churches in Hoogeveen, the Netherlands.

PROF. DR. RICHARD A. MULLER is P. J. Zondervan Professor in Church History at Calvin Theological Seminary, Grand Rapids (U.S.A).

DR. SEBASTIAN REHNMAN is lecturer in Systematic Theology at the Johannelund Theological Institute, Uppsala, Sweden.

PROF. DR. WILLEM VAN'T SPIJKER is professor emeritus in Church History at the Theological University of the Christian Reformed Churches, Apeldoorn, the Netherlands.

DR. CARL TRUEMAN is lecturer in Church History at the University of Aberdeen.

DR. ANTONIE VOS is lecturer in Systematic Theology, Utrecht University.

The editors gratefully acknowledge the services of Susan Schmurr, administrative assistant at the H. Henry Meeter Center for Calvin Studies, and Brian Lee, teaching assistant and Ph.D. candidate at Calvin Theological Seminary. Their work of copyediting, producing camera-ready copy, and indexing this volume is greatly appreciated.

Abbreviations

CO   *Ioannis Calvini Opera Quae Supersunt Omnia.* Edited by Wilhelm Baum, E. Cunitz, and E. Reuss. 59 vols. Brunswick: A. Schwetschke, 1863–1897.

CR   Philip Melanchthon. *Corpus Reformatorum. Philippi Melanchthonis opera quae supersunt omnia.* Edited by Karl Bretschneider and Heinrich Bindseil. 28 vols. Halle: A. Schwetschke and Sons, 1834–60.

CTJ   *Calvin Theological Journal.*

DNB   *Dictionary of National Biography.* Edited by Leslie Stephen and Sidney Lee. London, 1885–1901.

KD   Karl Barth. *Die Kirchliche Dogmatik.* Zollikon: Verlag der Evangelischen Buchhandlung, 1939–1967.

LW   *Luther's Works.* Edited by Conrad Bergendorff. Philadelphia: Muhlenberg, 1958.

PMA   L. M. de Rijk. *La philosophie au moyen âge.* Leiden, 1985. Translation of *Middeleeuwse wijsbegeerte. traditie en vernieuwing.* Assen, 1981.

PRRD   Richard A. Muller. *Post-Reformation Reformed Dogmatics.* 2 vols. to date. Grand Rapids, 1987– .

SCES   Sixteenth Century Essays and Studies [series]. Sixteenth Century Journal Publishers: Kirksville, Missouri.

StA   Philip Melanchthon. *Melanchthons Werke in Auswahl.* Edited by Robert Stupperich. Gütersloh, 1951–1975.

WA   Martin Luther. *Luther's Werke. Kritische Gesamtausgabe.* 65 vols. Weimar: H. Böhlau, 1883–1993.

WABr   Martin Luther. *Luther's Werke. Kritische Gesamtausgabe. Briefwechsel.* 18 vols. Weimar: H. Böhlau, 1930–1985.

Introduction

I. Introduction

Research into the history of Reformed Protestantism could, until recently, generally be characterized by a profound lack of interest in the phenomenon of "Reformed scholasticism."[1] The research was mainly oriented to the history of the piety (*pietas*) and spirituality commonly indicated with the term "second Reformation."[2] In our view, there are two reasons for the limited interest among researchers.

First, this limited interest derives from the presupposition that post-Reformation scholasticism was not much more than a rigid and inflexible complex of dogmas involving a regression to outdated medieval patterns of thought. The vital kerygma of the reformers, it is claimed, was replaced by the dead letter of a dogmatic system, which, as a Procrustean bed, obscured the gospel.[3] A second factor is the predominantly negative judgement with regard to the use of the scholastic method itself, appropriated anew by these orthodox theologians in their explication of doctrine. Because of this, it is claimed, orthodox theology got caught up

1. Many thanks to our colleagues Andreas J. Beck, Richard A. Muller, and Carl R. Trueman, who helped us in various stages of this project.
2. In the Netherlands, the theme of Reformed scholasticism has recently received only incidental attention. See the article series "Gereformeerde Scholastiek" in *Theologia Reformata* 29 (1986) and 30 (1987). Cf. also W. van't Spijker, "Orthodoxie en Nadere Reformatie," in T. Brienen et al, ed., *Theologische aspecten van de Nadere Reformatie*, (Zoetermeer, 1993), 12–13. For a positive appreciation, see F. G. Immink, *Divine Simplicity* (Kampen, 1987), 146–57.
3. See W. van't Spijker, "Gereformeerde Scholastiek II: Scholastiek, Erasmus, Luther, Melanchthon," *Theologia Reformata* 29 (1986): 27: "Reformed scholasticism is by definition always post-Reformation. It can only originate to the detriment of the cause." By this "cause" van't Spijker means "the gospel of free grace"; in "Gisbertus Voetius (1589–1676)," in T. Brienen et al, ed., *De Nadere Reformatie, Beschrijving van haar voornaamste vertegenwoordigers*, (The Hague, 1986), 83, van't Spijker characterizes Voetius' theology as follows: "Predestination, piety and church are central tenets. But they stand solidified in the forms of scholasticism"; idem, "Orthodoxie en Nadere Reformatie" in Brienen et al, ed., *Theologische aspecten*, (Zoetermeer, 1993), 22. C. Graafland, "Gereformeerde Scholastiek V: De invloed van de scholastiek op de Gereformeerde Orthodoxie," *Theologia Reformata* 30 (1987): 24, submits that Reformed scholastics like Beza and Zanchi, by employing the philosophical method of Aristotle, incorporated the Scriptural witness into a distorting hermeneutical process, which eventually resulted only in alienation from the Bible.

in the dangerous rationalistic tide, thereby resulting "inevitably" in the rationalism of the Enlightenment. This view has been defended by, among many others, Basil Hall,[4] who argues that, already at the time of Calvin, the scholastic method was being introduced into Reformed circles by some theologians, thereby beginning to dominate the scene in a way not foreseen by its users.

Recent scholarship has, however, brought to light a number of theological misconceptions and historical inaccuracies in the standard evaluation of Reformed scholasticism from the period of post-Reformation orthodoxy.[5]

This collection of essays may be regarded in part as a specimen of the newer approach, focusing on the relationship between Reformation and Scholasticism. This relationship, of course, is at least a double one. We may not only ask for a backward-looking account of continuities and discontinuities between Reformation and Medieval scholasticism, but also, for a forward-looking one concerning the relationship of Reformation and Protestant scholasticism. These two approaches, moreover, point toward other questions, notably, that of the way Protestant Scholasticism relates to its Catholic contemporary, Contra-reformational Scholasticism.

The contributions in this volume, therefore, all bear testimony to the ongoing debate regarding the so-called continuity hypothesis—the hypothesis that there is continuity between Medieval Scholasticism and Reformation on the one hand and between Reformation and Reformed Scholasticism on the other. Most of the contributions arose out of a symposium dedicated to this theme, which was held at Utrecht, in the Netherlands, in May 1997.

In the remainder of this introduction, we would like to make some terminological remarks (section 2), and to sketch a rather detailed, but by no means complete account of the history of earlier and recent research (sections 3, 4, and 5, respectively). We then summarize and juxtapose all

---

4. B. Hall, "Calvin against the Calvinists," in G. E. Duffield, ed., *John Calvin*, Courtenay Studies in Reformation Theology 1 (Appleford, 1966), 12–37.

5. See among many other works, Olivier Fatio, "Orthodoxie II: Reformierte Orthodoxie," in Gerhard Müller, ed., *Theologische Realencyclopädie*, vol. 25, (Berlin/New York: Walter de Gruyter, 1995), 485–97; Christoph Strohm, *Ethik im frühen Calvinismus: Humanistische Einflüsse, philosophische, juristische und theologische Argumentationen sowie mentalitätsgeschichtliche Aspekte am Beispiel des Calvin-Schülers Lambertus Danaeus*, Arbeiten zur Kirchengeschichte 65 (Berlin: De Gruyter, 1996), 17–18, and the works by Donnelly, Fatio, Klauber, Meijering, Muller, Platt and Sinnema mentioned below.

the different approaches in three models (section 6), followed by a broader outline of the motifs and driving forces behind the new research (sections 7–8). In the last section we summarize the essays themselves (section 9).

II. Some Preliminary Remarks on "Orthodoxy," "Scholasticism," and "Reformed"

The term "orthodoxy" basically refers to a certain period in the history of Protestantism after the Reformation, relating to developments in both Lutheran and Reformed circles.[6] This period continues into the 17th and 18th centuries. With regard to the original meaning, various nuances can be discerned in the term.[7] In the sense of "the right doctrine" or "opinion," the word refers to a certain content, which was to be defended in confrontation with deviating views. Here, the term orthodoxy also has a normative meaning closely related to the teaching of the church through the ages. Furthermore, the term orthodoxy formulates a strong linkage between systematic theology and ecclesiastical confessions. During the period of orthodoxy theologians were motivated by their desire to work for and in the church. The difference with the term "scholasticism" lies especially in the fact that orthodoxy refers to the proper content of theology, while scholasticism indicates a form of scientific practice (below we shall extensively come back to scholasticism). The two terms therefore do not coincide. About our use of the term "Reformed," we regard it as more appropriate to refer to the theologians from this period and the tradition in which they stood, with this term, rather than with the name "Calvinists" or "Calvinism." Thereby we seek to indicate that the term Reformed has a broad scope. We are dealing with a complex movement: the designation of this movement as Calvinism is suggestive, rather than illuminating, and denies the progressive character of this theology.[8] Furthermore, the word Calvinist has its background in the sociology of religion, rather than in theology.[9]

6. Parts of sections 2–6 have been published as "Studie van de gereformeerde scholastiek. Verleden en toekomst," *Nederlands Theologisch Tijdschrift* 50 (1996): 290–312.

7. Cf. Richard A. Muller, *Christ and the Decree: Christology and Predestination in Reformed Theology from Calvin to Perkins*, 2nd. ed., (Grand Rapids, 1988), 12–13; Graafland, "Gereformeerde Scholastiek V," 5–7.

8. Cf. J. P. Donnelly, *Calvinism and Scholasticism in Vermigli's Doctrine of Man and Grace*, (Leiden, 1976), 1: ". . . to designate this complex movement Calvinism obscures almost as much as it illuminates."

9. See Alister McGrath, *The Intellectual Origins of the European Reformation* (Oxford,

In addition we may say that during the period after the Reformation a theology developed in Protestant circles, which sought to justify the newly acquired ecclesiastical and theological positions over against opponents. These positions were formulated in such a way to bring to expression continuity with the Reformation, as well as with the age-old tradition of Christian theology since the apologists.[10]

III. Previous Research

Discussions about the relation between the Reformation and later developments—Reformed scholasticism in particular—gained momentum especially after the second world war. At this time various researchers defended the view that the post-Reformation theologians had broken the equilibrium of Calvin's theology, thereby bringing it to ruin. They were not the first to make this claim, which had already been propounded in the 19th century. We shall first discuss these older results[11] while passing over Lutheran scholasticism, because with some variations, the same applies to this form of scholasticism as does to Reformed scholasticism.[12]

A. The school of Schleiermacher and Hegel: Schweizer, Baur and Gass

The first scholar to concern himself explicitly with the question of the significance of scholastic orthodoxy as an historical phenomenon was the Swiss theologian Alexander Schweizer (1808–1888). He was a student of Schleiermacher, and the latter's views on faith and religion played an

1987), 6: "The introduction of the term "Calvinist' appears to have been an attempt to stigmatize Reformed theology as a foreign influence in Germany."

10. Cf. E. P. Meijering, *Reformierte Scholastik und patristische Theologie: Die Bedeutung des Väterbeweises in der Institutio Theologiae Elencticae F. Turrettins unter besonderer Berücksichtigung der Gotteslehre und Christologie* (Nieuwkoop, 1991), 420: "Post-Reformation orthodoxy is no regression to the dark age of scholasticism (which exists only in the minds of anti-speculative, or more accurately: differently speculative Protestant theologians), but it concerned itself anew with the questions that Christian theology has always been posing and answering ever since the time of the apologists."

11. Cf. also R. Scharlemann, *Aquinas and Gerhard: Theological Controversy and Construction in Medieval and Protestant Scholasticism* (New Haven, 1964), 13–18; Muller, *Christ and the Decree*, 1–13.

12. A good overview of the Lutheran tradition is provided by C. H. Ratschow, *Lutherische Dogmatik zwischen Reformation und Aufklärung* (Gütersloh, 1964/1966). Cf. also Robert D. Preuss, *The Theology of Post-Reformation Lutheranism: A Study of Theological Prolegomena* (St. Louis, 1970).

important role in his evaluation of orthodoxy.[13] He was of the opinion that Reformed scholasticism had constructed a theology in which a complete system could be deduced from the absolute divine decision of predestination. The idea of a divine predestination corresponded, in Schweizer's judgement, with Schleiermacher's notion of the "feeling of absolute dependence." Thus Schweizer could see predestination as a "Centraldogma" of Protestantism, and that in a positive sense. From this anthropological perspective, post-Reformation developments could therefore be positively appreciated.

A second important figure in the early phase of the older research was Ferdinand Christian Baur (1792–1860). He was also a student of Schleiermacher, but as his studies progressed he found in Hegel's philosophy an explanatory principle which seemed to make sense of the diversity of phenomena he was studying. Individuals, epochs, and nations were according to Hegel necessary steps in the progression of history. The necessity consists therein that facts, individuals and nations are, at each moment, exactly what the world reason requires. Thus Baur also regarded developments in the Protestant world after the Reformation in a positive light. After all, these developments were reasonable. They had not been brought about by individuals or schools of thought, but had unfolded themselves according to an "inner principle." Just as the inner principle of the early church was constituted by the interpretation of the person of Christ, the inner principle of Reformed scholasticism was the concept of divine predestination.[14]

An important but forgotten author who gave a detailed description of the whole historical development of Protestant theology was Wilhelm Gass (1813–1889). He took over from Schweizer and Baur the thesis concerning the central place of predestination in the theology of Reformed orthodoxy. However, as a Hegelian, he emphasized even more strongly than Baur the idea that the eventual shape of the developing Protestant theology had been the result of the realization of

---

13. Schweizer, *Die Glaubenslehre der evangelisch-reformierten Kirche*, 2 vols. (Zürich 1844–1847); Schweizer, *Die Protestantischen Centraldogmen in ihrer Entwicklung innerhalb der reformierten Kirche* (Zürich, 1853). See for Schweizer's theological views, Brian A. Gerrish, *Tradition and the Modern World: Reformed Theology in the Nineteenth Century* (Chicago, 1978), 119–36. In the Netherlands J. H. Scholten was influenced by Schweizer.

14. F. C. Baur, *Lehrbuch der christlichen Dogmengeschichte*, 3d ed. (Tübingen, 1867), I:314 ff.

the inner principle of predestination.[15] This principle had provided the orthodox theologians of the 17th century with a basis for taking over metaphysical structures into their theological conception, and for the use of the scholastic method in its further elaboration. The latter development, according to Gass, was not due to the leading example of Beza, but took place under the influence of the work of Suárez.

Thus a glance at the views of Schweizer, Baur and Gass shows that they positively appreciated the development of Reformed theology. From a Schleiermacherian perspective, continuity was discerned between Calvin's theology and that of his followers. However, the views of these 19th century researchers were not so much the result of critical historical research as they were illustrations of their own theological convictions. Their philosophical-theological position determined to a great extent their understanding of the history of dogma.

B. Ebrard, Schneckenburger, Scholten, Bavinck, and Heppe

The views of Schweizer, Baur and Gass were subjected to criticism from various quarters. Johannes Heinrich August Ebrard (1818–1888) immediately attacked Schweizer in his *Das Verhältniss der reformirten Dogmatik zum Determinismus*[16] and his *Christliche Dogmatik*.[17] Ebrard judged Schweizer not only to be inadmissibly biased, but also to have based his studies on too small compendia instead of the main works, and to have been eclectic. Ebrard himself wanted to study the sources in their own context, and to make use of detailed studies, like, for example, those of Voetius. He concluded that there was no determinism in Reformed Scholasticism and that even for supralapsarians like Voetius, God could not be the author of sin. Unfortunately, the studies of Ebrard were judged to be wrongheaded by his opponents, and that judgment seemed to have had the most impact. Ebrard became a forgotten author.

Matthias Schneckenburger (1804–1848) focussed in his research especially on the confessional differences between Lutheran and Reformed writers. On this subject, he wrote a comparative Dogmatics,

---

15. See W. Gass, *Geschichte der Protestantischen Dogmatik in ihrem Zusammenhange mit der Theologie überhaupt* (Berlin, 1854–1859), esp. 1:7–9.

16. Johannes Heinrich August Ebrard, *Das Verhältniss der reformirten Dogmatik zum Determinismus* (Zürich, 1849). See *also Vindiciae theologiae reformatae a laude determinismi immunis* (1848).

17. Johannes Heinrich August Ebrard, *Christliche Dogmatik* (Königsberg, 1851–52), 2d ed. (Königsberg, 1862–63).

which, because of its thorough study of the sources, is still of considerable importance.[18] Also within Reformed theology itself, he discerned a far greater variety in theological approach than had hitherto been granted. Contra Schweizer and Baur he maintained that Calvin and his followers had not given pride of place to the doctrine of predestination, but had followed the order of the Apostolicum. The more scholastic form of theology, which treated predestination as part of the doctrine of God, was in Schneckenburger's opinion as characteristic of Lutheran as of Reformed orthodoxy.

While in the Netherlands C. Sepp and especially J. H. Scholten[19] remained more or less dependent on Schweizer in their study of Reformed theology, Herman Bavinck (1854–1921) was more ambivalent toward Schweizer's "philosophical reworking" of Reformed theology and its history. He applied the historical-critical method to the dogma-historical *aperçu* of Reformed theology, and in the preface to the first edition of his *Gereformeerde Dogmatiek* of 1895 he wrote that he had given more attention to patristic and scholastic theology "than is usually the case with Protestant dogmaticians." He added: "Men like Irenaeus, Augustine and Thomas do not belong exclusively to Rome. They are *patres* and *doctores* to whom the entire church owes a great debt."[20] On the one hand, he knew how the Reformed Scholastics themselves regarded scholastic theology, but on the other, he saw their theology as a less pure version of Reformed theology.[21]

Contemporaneously with Schweizer, Baur and Gass, the Marburg professor Heinrich Heppe (1820–1879) published his views. He was also a student of Schleiermacher, but he explained the central position of the doctrine of predestination as the result of *external* factors. In contrast with the aforementioned historians of dogma, however, he evaluated these developments negatively rather than positively. He turned Schweizer's hypothesis on its head and saw Beza in particular as the one responsible for placing predestination at the beginning of Dogmatics - that is before

18. M. Schneckenburger, *Vergleichende Darstellung des lutherischen und reformierten Lehrbegriffs* (Stuttgart, 1855).

19. J. H. Scholten, *De Leer der Hervormde Kerk in hare grondbeginselen, uit de bronnen voorgesteld en beoordeeld,* 4th ed. (Leiden, 1870); C. Sepp, *Het godgeleerd onderwijs in Nederland gedurende de 16e en 17e eeuw* (Leiden, 1873/74).

20. H. Bavinck, *Gereformeerde Dogmatiek* (Kampen, 1895), 1:3. We use mainly the 4th edition of 1928. Vol. 1, 150–79 contains an overview of the history and literature of Reformed Dogmatics.

21. Cf. *Gereformeerde Dogmatiek* 1:60 with 1:154, and with page iv of the 1895 edition's preface.

the doctrines of creation and salvation. According to Heppe, Beza's *Tabula praedestinationis* formed the metaphysical foundation for the development of the later Reformed theology. This view had implications, of course, for his understanding of the development of Reformed theology during the 16th and 17th centuries.[22]

Heppe's presentation of the facts has been very influential for a long time, and is widely prevalent even today. Yet, serious objections have been raised against his presentation of Reformed orthodoxy.[23] The order of the *loci*, as Heppe describes it in his textbook, often does not reflect the order of the systems he cites. Moreover, he regards what he claims to find in Beza, as representative for the whole of Reformed theology after Calvin. In the light of the considerable influence of Heppe's textbook, it comes as no surprise that the errors indicated are still around today.

It is noteworthy, in addition, that Heppe in fact published a whole range of textbooks, of which *Reformierte Dogmatik* is just one. Heppe's view was that on two sides of the spectrum, a "wrong" type of theology was to be found: the Bezan, predestinarian type formed one side of the spectrum—to which he devoted a volume—while the other side consisted of what he described in his *Geschichte des deutschen Protestantismus*[24] as the "wrong" Lutheran approach. The correct, middle position was to be found, according to Heppe, in the Melanchthonian branch of Lutheranism, to which he devoted his book *Dogmatik des deutschen Protestantismus im sechzehnten Jahrhundert*.[25]

---

22. H. Heppe, *Die Dogmatik der evangelisch-reformierten Kirche: Dargestellt und aus den Quellen belegt* (1861); ed. Ernst Bizer (Neukirchen, 1958). Among the many scholars who followed Heppe with regard to Beza are: Johannes Dantine, "Das christologische Problem im Rahmen der Prädestinationslehre von Theodor Beza," *Zeitschrift für Kirchengeschichte* 77 (1966): 81–96; Johannes Dantine, "Les Tabelles sur la doctrine de la prédestination par Théodore de Bèze," *Revue de théologie et de philosophie* 16 (1966): 365–77; Michael Jinkins, "Theodore Beza: Continuity and Regression in the Reformed Tradition," *Evangelical Quarterly* 64 (1992): 131–54.

23. See e.g. Muller, *Christ and the Decree*, 3–4; Muller, *Post-Reformation Reformed Dogmatics*, 2 vols. to date (Grand Rapids, 1987–), henceforward *PRRD*, 1:86.

24. 4 vols., Marburg 1852–1859.

25. 3 vols. Fr. A. Perthes: Gotha, 1857. A sketch of this trifurcation in Protestant theology with the correct middle branch is found in Heppe's programmatic article "Der Charakter der deutsch-reformirten Kirche und das Verhältniss derselben zum Luthertum und zum Calvinismus," in *Theologische Studien und Kritiken*, Heft 3 (1850): 669–706.

C. Weber and Althaus

When we turn to the 20th century, we see how the results of the 19th century research continue to have their impact. The views of Hans Emil Weber (1882–1950) and Paul Althaus (1888–1966) are significant in this regard. Although Weber was no adherent of the Hegelian philosophy of history, he nevertheless followed Baur's theory concerning the inner principle. He reduced the two main streams of Protestantism to two inner principles.[26] Lutheranism, in his eyes, was characterized by the inner principle of justification, and Calvinism by that of predestination. Weber universalized this typology, and tended to disregard the variations within Lutheran and Reformed theology. He even took his view of predestination as the inner principle of Calvinism so far as to claim that supralapsarianism was the unavoidable consequence of the doctrine of predestination.

The views of Paul Althaus confirmed those of Weber. Althaus, who is especially well-known for his Luther studies, and who, together with Karl Holl, pioneered the Luther renaissance in Germany in the nineteen-twenties, wrote a doctoral dissertation at Göttingen in 1913 with the title *Vernunft und Offenbarung in der deutschen reformierten Dogmatik um 1600*.[27] In it, he accepted Weber's thesis that the doctrine of predestination had provided grounds for speculation and had led, via the scholastic method, to a "rigid" system controlled by the doctrine of the decrees. Like Weber, Althaus limited his analysis to the problem of the relation between revelation and reason, and regarded the theology of Maccovius as a representative model of the whole development of Reformed scholasticism on the basis of the doctrine of predestination.[28]

D. Barth and Bizer

The rise of dialectical theology after the first world war partly meant a continuation of Heppe's interpretation of Reformed scholasticism. In his

---

26. H. E. Weber, *Reformation, Orthodoxie und Rationalismus*, 3 books in 2 volumes, (Gütersloh, 1937–1951). See also the earlier works by the same author, then called E. Weber: *Die philosophische Scholastik des deutschen Protestantismus im Zeitalter der Orthodoxie* (Leipzig, 1907), and *Der Einfluß der protestantischen Schulphilosophie auf die orthodox-lutherische Dogmatik* (Leipzig, 1908).

27. Published in an expanded form as *Die Prinzipien der deutschen reformierten Dogmatik im Zeitalter der aristotelischen Scholastik* (Leipzig, 1914; reprint, Darmstadt, 1967).

28. A balanced view on Maccovius' theology is given in Martin I. Klauber, "The Use of Philosophy in the Theology of Johannes Maccovius (1578–1644)," *CTJ* 30 (1995): 376–91.

foreword to Bizer's republication of Heppe's *Dogmatik*, Karl Barth wrote that he regarded the latter's work as a more reliable guide than the works of Schweizer, even though Heppe's presentation also contained shortcomings and weaknesses. In Barth's judgement, Heppe regarded Melanchthon, rather than Calvin, as the "father of Reformed theology," and took no notice of the breaks brought about by the federal theology of Cocceius and his students.

In his *Kirchliche Dogmatik* Barth devoted large sections of his many dogma-historical excursions to Reformed orthodoxy. These show that he was well aware of the fact that Reformed orthodoxy did not constitute a monolithic structure, but exhibited a great diversity. Furthermore, he explicitly rejected the claim that the Reformed theology of the 17th century was exclusively a predestinarian system controlled by the doctrine of the decrees.[29] His own criticisms concerned mainly the important place that had been allocated to natural theology. While Calvin had rejected it, his followers had resuscitated the *"Unfug"* of natural theology, thereby departing radically and fatally from Calvin.[30] Barth was convinced, nevertheless, that no theologian could practice his profession satisfactorily without some knowledge of scholasticism: "Hostility against scholasticism is the mark of the false prophet. The true prophet would not shy away from submitting his message also to this test."[31] Ernst Bizer, who published a new edition of Heppe's *Dogmatik* in 1958 along with an historical introduction, went along with Barth's understanding. He saw the acceptance of natural theology, together with the use of a rational method, as well as an historical interpretation of Scripture, followed by the growth of pietism, as the one decisive cause that had led to "rationalism," which he regarded as characteristic of the Reformed theology of the 17th century.[32] Even the *"Frühorthodoxie"* had

---

29. K. Barth, *Kirchliche Dogmatik*, II/2, 38: "Precisely in loyalty to Calvin, we ought not to assume, without further ado, that the doctrine of predestination was the 'palladium' of the old Reformed church, especially not in the specific form in which it was then presented." See also ibid., 65–74; 120–23; 359–75.

30. Barth, *KD* II/1, 140–41.

31. Barth, *KD* I/1, 296.

32. Bizer, "Frühorthodoxie und Rationalismus," *Theologische Studien* 71 (Zürich, 1963). In "Die reformierte Orthodoxie und der Cartesianismus," *Zeitschrift für Kirche und Theologie* 55 (1958): 306–72, Bizer took more account of the diversity in Reformed theology. We could also point to this approach in Walter Kickel, *Vernunft und Offenbarung bei Theodor Beza: Zum Problem des Verhältnisses von Theologie, Philosophie und Staat* (Neukirchen-Vluyn 1967), and Heiner Faulenbach, *Die Struktur der Theologie des Amandus Polanus von Polansdorf* (Zürich 1967).

already fallen victim to this rationalism. Bizer investigated the theology of Beza, Ursinus, Danaeus and Zanchius with regard to their rational quality, and came to the conclusion that these theologians had derived the doctrines of creation and salvation with logical necessity from the conception of God. At the same time, they had thought that they could make the concept of God transparent to reason, since the existence of God could be proved. Even though these divines had stated that Scripture was superior to reason, they were also convinced that one could prove rationally that Scripture is the Word of God. Thus the revelatory content of the Bible was not opposed to reason: it simply proclaimed the factuality of that which could be inferred, through reason, from "nature." The origin of this "two sources doctrine" lay, according to Bizer, already in the theology of Melanchthon and his student Ursinus. The most important research problem, in Bizer's judgement, concerned the determination of the relation between reason and revelation, and the determination of the concept of "nature."

The objections to Bizer's presentation can be summarized as follows. First, his definition of rationalism is unclear and ambiguous, since he makes no distinction between rational argumentation and rationalistic philosophy. A second objection is that he does not select one specific doctrine for the purpose of investigating its course of development, but considers predestination and christology in Beza, the problem of "necessity" in Ursinus, and the doctrine of creation in Danaeus. In this way, an image is constructed which is not representative of every theologian of this period.

E. Balance

From our consideration of these positions in the older research, two things become clear. In the first place, none of the researchers gives a wholly accurate account of post-Reformation developments. In some instances this is due to their philosophical background, in others to their theological position, and in yet others to the refusal to take alternative views into account. A very common handicap of all the research thus far, has been the tendency to over-hastily generalize certain positions, regarding them as representative of the whole development. In the second place, one is struck by how often the term scholasticism is used in a pejorative sense, namely in the sense of "speculative," "rigid," "dead and dry." However, all these predicates are value judgements, and are therefore unacceptable. Lastly, it may be stated that, in the older research, little account was taken of the variation of the systematic patterns within Reformed orthodoxy. They were too easily presented as a monolithic bloc.

IV. First traces of an Alternative Appreciation: Armstrong, Donnelly, and Bray

Although the outlook of Brian Armstrong is still strongly colored by a negative evaluation of the influence of medieval theology on Reformed scholasticism, his achievement was to demonstrate that the scholastic approach to theology had occupied a place within Reformed theology right from the start.[33] Like the Renaissance, which was characterized by both humanistic and Aristotelian revivals, humanistic and scholastic trends can also be discerned within the Reformation, and from its inception. The first trend was more anthropological and empirical in nature, and was oriented towards rhetoric; the second was more theocentric in nature, and was oriented towards dialectics. However, both traditions shared the same reformational assumptions. According to Armstrong, French Calvinism in particular exhibited humanistic trends.

Parallel to this humanistically oriented Calvinism, the scholastic trend gained momentum especially in Italy, in and around Padua. Here, Aristotle was being studied in the original language.[34] The pioneers of Reformed scholasticism, the former Augustinian monks Petrus Martyr Vermigli (1500–1562) and Girolamo Zanchi (1516–1590), came from this North-Italian tradition.[35] As Donnelly argued, these scholars brought a

33. B. G. Armstrong, *Calvinism and the Amyraut Heresy: Protestant Scholasticism and Humanism in Seventeenth-Century France* (London, 1969), 31–42.

34. The most prominent scholar in Padua was the philosopher Jacopo Zabarella (1532–1589). He developed a methodology based on the concepts of *resolutio* and *compositio,* in which he employed Aristotle's distinction between two classes of science: contemplative and practical sciences. He regarded the compositive order the most appropriate for the contemplative sciences. In it, one argues from cause to effect. The practical sciences, for their part, take their point of departure in the aim or purpose of something, and therefore employ a resolutive order. See J. H. Randall, "The Development of Scientific Method in the School of Padua," in P. O. Kristeller & P. P. Wiener, eds., *Renaissance Essays* (New York, 1968), 217–51. Cf. B. P. Copenhaver & C. B. Schmidt, *Renaissance Philosophy,* A History of Western Philosophy 3 (Oxford, 1992), 117–21. See for the significance of this methodology for Reformed theology G. P. Hartvelt, "Over de methode der Dogmatiek in de eeuw der Reformatie: Bijdrage tot de geschiedenis van de gereformeerde theologie," *Gereformeerd Theologisch Tijdschrift* 62 (1962): 97–149.

35. See for Zanchius, O. Gründler, *Die Gotteslehre Girolamo Zanchis und ihre Bedeutung für seine Lehre von der Prädestination,* Beiträge zur Geschichte und Lehre der Reformierten Kirche, Bd. 20 (Neukirchen-Vluyn, 1965). See for Vermigli, in addition

well-defined knowledge of medieval theology and its methods into the service of the Reformation.

John S. Bray followed Armstrong in explicating the essence of Reformed scholasticism in terms of six characteristics.[36] First, this theology was characterized by "basic assumptions and principles," upon which a logical belief system was erected, which was regarded as rationally justifiable, and which, for a large part, took the form of syllogistic argumentation. Secondly, Bray highlighted the heavy dependence on the methodology and philosophy of Aristotle. The third characteristic, which he identifies, is the emphasis on the role of reason and logic in religion, which in practice amounted to an equal status being given to revelation and reason (the two sources doctrine already claimed by Bizer). Fourthly, Reformed scholasticism distinguished itself by a great interest in speculative and metaphysical thought, concentrated especially on the doctrine of God, specifically on questions relating to the will of God. As a fifth characteristic, Bray mentions the interpretation of Scripture as a "body of propositions," which God had revealed once and for all. This gave rise to an a-historical and timeless element in Protestant scholasticism. Lastly, Bray pointed to what he regarded as the emergence of a new conception of faith, which differed significantly from the reformational conception. The Reformed scholastics understood faith as a *habitus*, which is caused to exist within a person.

The conclusion of this strand of scholarship was that the influence of the Italian tradition on Protestant scholasticism had hitherto been seriously underestimated. In the older research, specifically in the case of Althaus (although he was familiar with the Italian tradition), it had been assumed that the scholastic method had been introduced primarily by Melanchthon and the Danzig theologian Bartholomaeus Keckermann (1571–1609).[37] This older research had not been capable, however, of explaining the earliest forms of scholasticism within Reformed theology, an issue resolved, to a certain extent, by Donnelly and Bray.

Nevertheless, the positions of Armstrong and Bray are themselves not

---

to Donnelly, *Calvinism and Scholasticism* also his article "Italian Influences on the Development of Calvinist Scholasticism," *Sixteenth Century Journal* 7 (1976): 81–101, and Mariano Di Gangi, *Peter Martyr Vermigli, 1499–1562: Renaissance Man, Reformation Master* (Lanham/New York/London: University Press of America, 1993).

36. J. S. Bray, *Theodore Beza's Doctrine of Predestination* (Nieuwkoop, 1975), 12–15.

37. See for Keckermann, W. H. Van Zuylen, *Bartholomaeus Keckermann: Sein Leben und Wirken* (diss., Tübingen, 1934); R. A. Muller, "Vera Philosophia cum sacra Theologia nusquam pugnat: Keckermann on Philosophy, Theology, and the Problem of Double Truth," *Sixteenth Century Journal* 15 (1984): 341–65.

without their difficulties. We do not regard their six characteristics as particularly helpful. Some of them are just false, while others are dubious and must be qualified before being of any use.[38] Moreover, in the judgement of Armstrong and Bray, the use of the scholastic method inevitably implies a clearly defined doctrinal content. They offered no explanation of the fact that, within the framework of the scholastic method, divergent, and in some cases even mutually exclusive, types of theology could emerge. We could easily point at some examples of this phenomenon, e.g. the conflict between the scholastic Gomarus, and the equally scholastic Arminius,[39] or the controversies between Voetius and Cocceius. While they differed fundamentally about salvation history and the order of salvation, both nevertheless made use of scholastic concepts as well as their associated argumentative techniques and methods of disputation.[40]

V. Recent research

There is a growing consensus among researchers of the last decades that scholasticism was too vaguely defined by the earlier research, and that the definitions which were ascribed to it were often loaded with value-judgements.[41] Moreover, recent research has shown that the earlier research often approached the reformers and their heirs as if they had worked in an intellectual vacuum. We need, however, to take into account all the intellectual forces that were at work during the late

---

38. See the extensive discussion in Richard A. Muller, "Calvin and the 'Calvinists': Assessing Continuities and Discontinuities Between the Reformation and Orthodoxy," part I, in *CTJ* 30 (1995): 345–75; ibid., part II, in *CTJ* 31 (1996): 125–60.

39. See Richard A. Muller, "Arminius and the Scholastic Tradition," *CTJ* 24 (1989): 263–77; Muller, *God, Creation, and Providence in the Thought of Jacob Arminius. Sources and Directions of Scholastic Protestantism in the Era of Early Orthodoxy* (Grand Rapids, 1991); Eef Dekker, *Rijker dan Midas. Vrijheid, genade en predestinatie in de theologie van Jacobus Arminius (1559–1609)* (Zoetermeer, 1993).

40. See W. J. van Asselt, *Amicitia Dei: Een onderzoek naar de structuur van de theologie van Johannes Cocceius (1603–1669)* (Ede, 1988), 42–44; and Van Asselt's contribution in this collection below. Cf. also Stephen Strehle, *Calvinism, Federalism, and Scholasticism: A Study of the Reformed Doctrine of the Covenant* (Bern, 1988), 222–46; he exaggerates somewhat the scholastic element in Cocceius, when he says: "In fact, if any tradition of federal theology merits to be disparaged as Scholastic, it would be Cocceius and his constituency" (246).

41. The term "Reformed scholasticism" is therefore regarded by J. Platt to be "a somewhat slippery phenomenon to grasp." See his *Reformed Thought and Scholasticism: The arguments for the existence of God in Dutch Theology, 1575–1650* (Leiden, 1982), 7.

Middle Ages, the Renaissance, and the Reformation if an adequate evaluation of the phenomenon of Reformed scholasticism is to be achieved.[42] This theology cannot be studied apart from this context. Too often, scholasticism was associated solely with the Middle Ages, without incorporating into the research its modified form, which had flourished during the Renaissance in the Italian universities. Furthermore, it is now generally agreed that the opposition of scholasticism and humanism is an outdated product of an *ideeengeschichtliche* (history of ideas) conception, in which these phenomena were studied in abstraction from the context.

L. M. de Rijk has offered a good attempt at a clearer definition of scholasticism in his book on medieval philosophy, in which he consistently interprets scholasticism as no more than a method. He defines it as an "approach, which is characterized by the use, in both study and teaching, of a constantly recurring system of concepts, distinctions, definitions, proposition analyses, argumentative techniques and disputational methods,"[43] a definition which will be found in many contributions in this collection. Although de Rijk writes on medieval scholasticism, his definition of scholasticism as a method applies equally to Reformed (and Lutheran) scholasticism.

Richard Muller has offered a complementary account of the discussions concerning the place and significance of Reformed scholasticism in the history of theology. In his judgement, the central problem is the question of the continuity or discontinuity between, on the one hand, the Reformation and orthodoxy, and on the other hand, between orthodoxy and the whole tradition of western theology as such.[44] According to Muller, the core of the scholastic method, in every period, consists in the so-called *quaestio* technique, in which four aspects can be discerned:

42. See for the Middle Ages H. A. Oberman, *The Harvest of Medieval Theology: Gabriel Biel and Late Medieval Nominalism,* 3rd ed., (Durham, N.C., 1983); for the Renaissance P. O. Kristeller, *Renaissance Thought and Its Sources* (New York, 1979); Kristeller, "Renaissance Aristotelianism," *Greek, Roman and Byzantine Studies* 6 (1965): 157–74; Erika Rummel, "The Conflict between Humanism and Scholasticism Revisited," *Sixteenth Century Journal* 23 (1992): 713–26; Rummel, *The Humanist-Scholastic Debate in the Renaissance and Reformation*, (Cambridge: Harvard University Press, 1995). More literature in McGrath, *The Intellectual Origins*, 204–17.

43. See L. M. de Rijk, *Middeleeuwse wijsbegeerte. Traditie en vernieuwing*, 2nd ed. (Assen, 1981), 25 and 111. French edition: *La Philosophie au moyen Age* (Leiden: E. J. Brill, 1985), 20–21, 85, henceforth cited as PMA.

44. Muller, *PRRD*, 1:15, 21–39; 2:6-11.

1. the presentation of a thesis or *quaestio*, a thematic question;
2. the indication of the subjects that stand to be discussed in that *quaestio*, the so-called *status quaestionis*;
3. the treatment of a series of arguments or objections against the adopted positions, the so-called *objectiones*;
4. the formulation of an answer (*responsio*), in which account is taken of all available sources of information, and all rules of rational discourse are upheld, followed by an answer to the objections, which is as comprehensive as possible.

When this structure, or some form of it, is not found in a work, in Muller's judgement one ought not to refer to it as scholastic.[45]

The definitions offered by de Rijk and Muller are argued or presupposed by many other scholars.[46] Furthermore, both de Rijk and Muller take the fact into account that Medieval and, respectively, Reformed, scholasticism exhibit far greater variety than was suggested by the earlier research. Against this background, the most adequate and useful definition of scholasticism seems to be the one which takes the term primarily as indicative of a method, which supplied the broad framework within which doctrines could be developed, and which was not bound, in terms of both method and content, to any one philosophy, such as the Aristotelian.[47] This definition also guards against the idea that one particular doctrine or concept is necessarily moved to the foreground merely by the use of the scholastic method, thereby assuming the status of an inner principle, which would then serve as a key to the understanding of the whole system.

We would like to mention some other researchers here who have worked to clarify problems in the study of Reformed Scholasticism—without, of course, pretending to be exhaustive. John Platt has shown conclusively that the Barthian accusation, to the effect that the *Unfug* of

45. See Richard A. Muller, "Scholasticism and Orthodoxy in the Reformed Tradition: An Attempt at Definition" (Inaugural Address, Grand Rapids, 1995), 4–5.

46. See, for example, Calvin G. Normore, "Scholasticism," in R. Audi, ed., *The Cambridge Dictionary of Philosophy* (Cambridge, 1995), 716–17; David Burrell, "Scholasticism," in Alan Richardson and John Bowden, *A New Dictionary of Christian Theology* (London, 1983), 524–26; Ulrich G. Leinsle, *Einführung in die scholastische Theologie* (Paderborn, etc., 1995), 5–15, and cf. the scholars mentioned or cited in Muller, "Calvin and the 'Calvinists,'" part I, 367, including Weisheipl, Knowles, Maurer, and Steinmetz.

47. Otherwise, one would be obliged to say that the scholastic method is as such Aristotelian. But that is not true.

natural theology and rationalism had found a way into Reformed theology via a scholastic "two sources doctrine" was unfounded.[48] He, too, defines scholasticism as "a system of instruction" which had already flourished in Wittenberg under the leadership of Melanchthon, and was emulated by other Protestant universities, both Reformed and Lutheran. In this regard, Platt is of the opinion that one may rightly speak of continuity with the medieval tradition. The alleged aversion against the scholastic tradition on the part of the reformers ought therefore not to be exaggerated.[49] It is not insignificant that Calvin never uttered a negative statement against the work of Beza, nor did Luther object to Melanchthon's teaching.[50]

According to Olivier Fatio, who has done detailed research into the influence of Calvin during the era of Reformed orthodoxy, the latter did indeed exert a strong influence during the post-Reformation period through the *Institutio*.[51] His ideas were summarized and adapted to the needs of the systematic theology of the time, for pedagogical purposes, but he was never intentionally or consciously misrepresented. The insights of this reformer were guarded and further developed with the help of methods dating from the medieval theology of the 13th, 14th and 15th century.

Donald Sinnema has recently payed attention to Antoine de la Roche Chandieu (1534–1591, pseudonym: Sadeel) and his work *De Verbo Dei Scripto* (1580), on the "true method by which to dispute theologically as well as scholastically *(theologice et scholastice)*."[52] In this work De Chandieu argued that neither reason, nor the church, but the Bible alone, could serve as *principium theologiae*. He also distinguished between a scholastic

---

48. Platt, *Reformed Thought and Scholasticism*, 239.

49. Cf. section 3 of Muller's contribution to this volume.

50. On Melanchthon's view, see also the study of Günter Frank, *Die theologische Philosophie Philipp Melanchthons (1497–1560)*, Erfurter theologische Studien 67 (Leipzig: Benno, 1995).

51. O. Fatio, "Présence de Calvin à l'époque de l'orthodoxie réformée: Les abrégés de Calvin à la fin du 16e et au 17e siécle," in Neuser, ed., *Calvinus Ecclesiae Doctor: Die Referate des internationalen Kongresses für Calvinforschung* (Kampen, 1978), 171–207. See also his *Méthode et Théologie: Lambert Daneau et les débuts de la scolastique réformée* (Geneva, 1976).

52. Donald Sinnema, "Antoine De Chandieu's Call for a Scholastic Reformed Theology (1580)," in W. Fred Graham, ed., *Later Calvinism: International Perspectives*, Sixteenth Century Essays & Studies, vol. 22 (Kirksville, Miss., 1994), 159–90. Chandieu was a French aristocrat, who studied in Geneva under Calvin and converted, under the latter's influence, to the Reformed religion. His entry into the ministry, in Paris in 1557, was followed by a turbulent life.

and a rhetorical approach to a theological topic. He regarded both approaches as equally legitimate, even though he preferred the use of syllogisms because of their precision and their economy: "res ipsas quaeramus, verborum multitudine neglecta."[53] De Chandieu compared the rhetorical treatment of a topic with an open hand, and the scholastic approach with a fist. These analyses of Chandieu are ample evidence of the early presence in Reformed theology of the scholastic approach next to that of rhetoric. From this, Sinnema draws the conclusion that, what was at stake in the use of the scholastic method, was "an orientation," rather than "a set of doctrines or matter of theological content."[54] The use of either one of the two methods depended, in his view, on the situation more than on anything else. The rhetorical approach is found mainly in homiletic and popular-theological writings, and the scholastic approach in an academic and polemical context.

VI. Three Theories

When we look back over 150 years of research into the development of Reformed scholasticism, taking particular note of the place allotted to the latter in the history of Protestant theology, we can reduce the various positions to three theories or interpretative models. We shall designate the two primary theories simply the discontinuity theory and the continuity theory. In both the reference point is the Reformation. The discontinuity theory postulates a sharp break between the Reformation and the Middle Ages on the one hand, and the Reformation and orthodoxy on the other. The continuity theory denies any such sharp breaks and clear lines of demarcation, and emphasizes the continuous development within the history of theology. The continuity theory comes with two evaluations, one negative and one positive (or neutral). We shall therefore distinguish two forms of the continuity theory: the negative continuity theory and the positive continuity theory.[55] Let us first sketch

---

53. De Chandieu described both approaches by means of the metaphor of the human body, as it is observed, and as it is anatomically analyzed. See Antonius Sadeel, "De Verbo Dei Scripto adversus Humanas Traditiones, Theologica et Scholastica Tractatio," in *Opera Theologica* (Geneva, 1592), 2–3 and 11–12. On the influence of Sadeel on Sibrandus Lubbertus: C. van der Woude, *Sibrandus Lubbertus* (Kampen, 1963), 36, 72, 82, 374. Sinnema, "De Chandieu," 186–87, also claims an influence of Sadeel on Lucas Trelcatius Jr. and Johann Heinrich Alsted, pioneering Reformed theologians of the early 17th century.

54. Sinnema, "De Chandieu," 188.

55. On the use of "positive" and "negative," see also below, footnote .

the theories and then evaluate them.

A. The Discontinuity Theory

Adherents of the discontinuity theory consider scholastic orthodoxy a fatal deviation from the Reformation. If one seeks to grasp the pure Reformed Protestantism of Reformers like Calvin, one has to bypass orthodoxy completely. One could also characterize the discontinuity theory as the "two sources doctrine."[56] According to this interpretation, scholasticism put very heavy emphasis on human rationality. Initially, reason had taken its place next to the revelation in Holy Scripture, but towards the final stages of the development, reason even became the most important principle in the theological undertaking, to the extent of more or less replacing revelation as the source of the knowledge of God. Since reason belonged to the domain of so-called natural theology, this primacy of reason had the result that Reformed dogmaticians increasingly gave more space to natural theology, viewing it as a separate source of knowledge next to the revealed knowledge of God. Following these developments, the history of orthodoxy became the chronicle of the inroad of rational argumentation into the practice of theology. The *loci* of revealed theology came to be treated within the borders drawn by natural reason.[57] The use of the synthetic method in the explication of doctrine (which does not begin with God's work of salvation, but argues towards it, whereas the analytical method works the other way around) further strengthened the rationalistic element in this system.[58] Having come thus far, only a small step was required in order to arrive at the rationalism of the Enlightenment.[59]

56. See G. van den Brink, *Oriëntatie in de filosofie I* (Zoetermeer, 1994), 147–53.

57. Thus already E. Troeltsch, *Vernunft und Offenbarung bei Johann Gerhard und Melanchthon* (Göttingen, 1891).

58. Weber, *Reformation*, 106, speaks of a "rational construction, which moves from the objectivity of the decrees, to the subjective outworking in living faith or, vice versa, which works back from the latter to the former. And even within this rational construction of predestination, both became dubious, and that turned out to be the judgement upon the thought which it had created."

59. N. T. Bakker, *Miskende Gratie: Van Calvijn tot Witsius: Een vergelijkende lezing, balans van 150 jaar gereformeerde orthodoxie* (Kampen, 1992), defends this theory; he states that things went "completely wrong" with orthodoxy, and that, "after more or less 150 years of Reformed Protestantism, barely one stone of Calvin's initial effort was left upon another" (15). Here, the contrast between Reformation and orthodoxy has been maximized.

B. The Negative Continuity Theory

Central in this theory is the view that the scholastic element can already be discerned in some of the Reformers themselves, and thus, there is continuity. Since, however, scholasticism is viewed negatively, continuity between Reformation and Reformed Scholasticism is also viewed negatively. Thus it is maintained that "in the Reformation itself (especially in Calvin and Bucer) a scholastic element had already been present, which was taken up later by orthodoxy, this time with a much more conscious systematization and rationalization of the faith, and with an equally conscious employment of scholastic modes of thought."[60] An Aristotelian-philosophical conceptual framework, it is claimed, increasingly determined the hermeneutic of this kind of orthodoxy. This philosophy was much more than just a formal-instrumental apparatus. Its use also had important consequences with regard to content. In practice, it turned out that Scripture had been distorted in a rationalistic fashion by orthodoxy.

C. The Positive Continuity Theory

Representatives of this position argue that it is a mistaken assumption to suppose that the Renaissance, humanism and the Reformation were by definition anti-scholastic.[61] Reference is made to the views of that major expert on the Renaissance, Paul Oskar Kristeller, who has made a persuasive case for the claim that scholasticism had maintained a gradual

---

60. Graafland, "Gereformeerde Scholastiek V," 7 n.6; cf. his comment: "By applying this method, from analysis to synthesis, from the concrete Scriptural data to the all-determining general truths, by then proceeding to read the whole Scripture in a levelling fashion, from the perspective of those general truths, the point was eventually reached where Dogmatics reigned supreme over Scripture, without this being noticed by those involved, who lived with the unshaken conviction that they followed a thoroughly Biblical approach," ibidem, 24. Somewhat difficult to place is Stephen Strehle, *The Catholic Roots of the Protestant Gospel. Encounter Between the Middle Ages and the Reformation*, Studies in the History of Christian Thought 60 (Leiden: Brill, 1995), who sometimes seems to embrace the discontinuity thesis, but at other moments opts for a moderate version of the "negative" continuity thesis.

61. We want to emphasize here that "positive" continuity includes "neutral" continuity. A juxtaposition of "neutral" and "negative" theories, however, sounds a bit strange. The point is that, historically spoken, a continuity may be discerned between Reformation and Reformed Scholasticism, whether or not this is viewed as welcome. Some of the contributors in this collection of essays view Scholasticism as an acceptable and viable way of doing theology, but that does not obliviate the vital historical point: is there continuity, and if so, in what ways exactly?

development throughout the 14th century, until this scientific method reached its summit during the 16th, and the beginning of the 17th, century. With regard to method, a number of elements that were elaborated in 17th century scholasticism had already appeared in the work of the very first Reformed theologians. Furthermore, it is pointed out that, with regard to the reception of Aristotle by Reformed theologians, one should be careful to distinguish between formal aspects and aspects related to content. Appropriation did occur, but so did antithesis. Even Aristotle's logic was only received from the medieval tradition in a not very aristotelian form,[62] while his concept of God and his views on the eternity of the world were sharply denounced by Reformed theologians.[63]

Moreover, representatives of the "positive" continuity theory place the emphasis on a double continuity,[64] whereby attention is drawn, not

62. Very important is the fact that even when the 16th and 17th century academics used "aristotelian," "Peripatetic" or the like in their logic instruction books, it almost never meant that they were, in a strict sense, following Aristotle. See Joseph S. Freedman, "Aristotle and the Content of Philosophy Instruction at Central European Schools and Universities during the Reformation Era (1500–1650)," *Proceedings of the American Philosophical Society* 137 (1993): 213–53. There is ample evidence that when the Reformed scholastics rejected Ramism, they did so not because they disliked Ramus, but rather because they were convinced that "Aristotle" had a far better instrument for correct thinking to offer than Ramism. See Donald Sinnema, "Aristotle and Early Reformed Orthodoxy: Moments of Accomodation and Antithesis," in Wendy E. Helleman, ed., *Christianity and the Classics. The Acceptance of a Heritage* (Lanham/New York/London, 1990), 119–48, esp. 123–28. Cf. also the literature mentioned in note below.

63. See Muller, *PRRD*, 1:94, 234.

64. Of course, important work has been done with regard to the continuity between the medieval and the Reformation period by Oberman, Steinmetz and others. See Heiko A. Oberman, *Forerunners of the Reformation* (New York: Holt, Rinehart and Winston, 1966); Oberman, *Harvest of Medieval Theology*; Oberman, *Masters of the Reformation: Emergence of a New Intellectual Climate in Europe*, trans. Dennis Martin (Cambridge University Press, 1981); and Oberman, "The Shape of Late Medieval Thought: the Birthpangs of the Modern Era," in C. Trinkaus and H. A. Oberman, eds., *The Pursuit of Holiness in Late Medieval and Renaissance Religion* (Leiden: Brill 1974), 3–25; David C. Steinmetz, *Misericordia Dei: The Theology of Johannes von Staupitz in its Late Medieval Setting* (Leiden: Brill, 1968). Muller underlines the double continuity; see *PRRD*, 1:39: "It is not only an error to attempt to characterize Protestant orthodoxy by means of a comparison with one or another of the Reformers . . . It is also an error to discuss Protestant orthodoxy without being continually aware of the broad movement of ideas from the late Middle Ages, through the Reformation, into post-Reformation Protestantism"; also *PRRD*, 2:88f. and 93ff.; he warns against "the fallacy of identifying a 'Golden Age' of Protestant theology." Cf. also Martin I. Klauber, "Continuity and

only to continuity with the theology of the reformers, but also with that of the (late) medieval theologians. However, this theory also recognizes a certain discontinuity: obviously, Reformed scholasticism was no duplicate of the medieval systems, and no repetition of the Reformation. An identification, which denies any historical, literary and methodological development, and places the statements of Reformed scholasticism on one timelessly normative level, is rejected.[65] Reformed scholasticism is seen as a form of Protestant-Catholic theology bearing a distinctive stamp.

D. Evaluation of the Theories

Both the discontinuity and the negative continuity theory are vulnerable to criticism. They have given extremely negative connotations to the terms scholasticism and rationalism, while using them in an unnuanced manner with reference to the whole of 17th century Reformed dogmatic thought. Also with reference to the concept of rationalism, we should bear in mind that a distinction must be made between rational argumentation and rationalistic philosophy as a worldview. The former is characteristic of Reformed scholasticism, which employed argumentative techniques, distinctions, and proposition analyses, all within a framework determined by revelation. That, however, is something rather different from the use of the categories of a specific worldview as a basis for Christian theology. The use of rational argumentation in Reformed scholasticism does not amount, therefore, to the acceptance of a rationalistic worldview. Viewed historically, it would seem that systematic reflection is unavoidable for every form of theology. That use is then made of conceptual frameworks not derived directly from the Bible seems obvious enough. The influence of philosophy on

---

Discontinuity in Post-Reformation Reformed Theology: An Evaluation of the Muller Thesis," *Journal of the Evangelical Theological Society* 33–34 (1990): 467–75. Also Muller's and Vos' contributions in this volume provide further details of the double continuity thesis.

65. Such an identification of scholastic orthodoxy and Reformation is, according to Graafland, already encountered in the 18th century in Comrie. See C. Graafland, "Alexander Comrie (1706–1774)," in T. Brienen et al, ed., *De Nadere Reformatie: Beschrijving van haar voornaamste vertegenwoordigers* (The Hague, 1986), 329f. Graafland also points out that a similar identification occurred in neo-Calvinist theology, as the latter was propounded during the 19th century at the Free University of Amsterdam, under the leadership of A. Kuyper. He refers to dissertations by A. Honig, *Alexander Comrie* (Utrecht, 1892), and A. Kuyper Jr., *Johannes Maccovius* (Leiden, 1899). See also Graafland, "Gereformeerde Scholastiek V," 7 n.7.

theology becomes more dangerous, the less one is aware of it (H. Dooyeweerd).[66]

The positive continuity theory is rather recent in its present form, and has to be further corroborated. However, a few points are quite well established. For example, the new research shows clearly that it is a mistake, both historically and systematically, to appeal to Calvin as the sole standard against which later developments in Reformed theology are to be measured. Apart from Calvin, cognizance should be taken of the theology of, among many others, Bullinger, Musculus, Vermigli, and Zanchi. An evaluation of Reformed scholasticism in the light of Calvin alone cannot do justice to the variety and the multi-faceted nature of early reformational theology and, by the same token, to the general problems associated with the complexity of the channels through which theological themes are transmitted. Moreover, this approach took too little account of the factors that had motivated Reformed orthodox theologians to approach the subject as they did.

In addition, it may be stated that two positions are, in any case, not adequate: (1) a radical discontinuity model, which regards the development of post-Reformation theology as a break with the reformers; (2) an unnuanced continuity model, which assumes an identity between Reformation and orthodoxy, and which disregards the fact that orthodoxy drew inspiration not only from the theology of the reformers, but (like the reformers themselves) also from patristic and medieval sources. We may ask specifically, therefore, whether or not continuity with patristic and medieval sources implies discontinuity with the Reformation.

Also the more general question of the significance of methodological changes needs to be addressed. Do changes in methodology necessarily imply corresponding changes in content?[67] Or is it possible that changes in method are precisely what are required in order to formulate the same content in a new context? Muller has remarked, in this regard, that methodological changes can cause material changes, if a theological system moves its adherents to eliminate tensions and paradoxes in the

---

66. See Van den Brink, *Oriëntatie*, 152.

67. C. van der Woude grants that scholasticism, during and after the synod of Dordt, had a formal, rather than a material, character, but he also poses the question whether the "scholastic yeast" did not also have a material impact. See his *Op de Grens van Reformatie en Scholastiek* (Kampen, 1964), 18–19. He agrees with Weber that "rational constructions and rational thought" in the predestinarian teaching of Dordt cleared the way for the Enlightenment.

original (unsystematic) formulation.[68] In our view, the terminology of continuity and discontinuity itself should be used with care. After all, continuity is not the same as static reproduction, and discontinuity implies the presence of a continuum. The developments in the two centuries following the Reformation are part and parcel of a living tradition, characterized by a quest for alternative ways of doing theology, for the sake of meeting the demands of the time, while simultaneously guarding the continuity with the past. The tradition of Reformed theology was a highly dynamic process. The Reformed theologians persisted with exegesis,[69] preaching and the writing of catechisms. Certainly, they added a new genre to their writings: the theological system. In doing so, they employed a technical apparatus, which differed from the techniques in the areas of homiletics and catechetics.

VII. More Traits and Tenets of the Newer Approach

If anything has become clear so far, it is that the theme of (dis)continuity between Reformation and (Reformed) Scholasticism is a central tenet in this collection of essays. But there is more to say. In addition to the positive continuity theory, there are two other hypotheses at stake, which mutually reinforce each other.

The first additional hypothesis is that the faith of the Church does not only have its own view of life, but also its own frame of thought. This becomes clear, for instance, in the way in which Christianity developed crucial concepts like that of the will (invented by Augustine!), which is absent in Antiquity.[70] We may also think of the notion of radical contingency, an invention of the Christian Medieval thinkers. Also the independent development of Medieval logic could be mentioned here. It is easily shown that Aristotelian logic was not only expanded far beyond

---

68. Muller, *PRRD*, 1:23.

69. It is a widely held misconception that the scholastics quoted Bible verses as proof texts, without any exegetical justification. The *dicta probantia* were drawn from a generally accepted exegetical tradition. They formed the link between Bible text and theological system, which was developed via the procedure of the so-called "legitimate conclusions," that were based on the doctrine of the analogia Scripturae and the *analogia fidei*. All these elements formed part of the hermeneutics current at the time. See Gisbertus Voetius, *Exercitia et Bibliotheca studiosi Theologiae* (Ultrajecti, 1644), 36–80. Cf. also Muller, *PRRD*, 2:522, 525 and 537.

70. Cf. A. Dihle, *The Theory of the Will in Classical Antiquity* (Berkeley/Los Angeles/London, 1982); Nico W. den Bok, "Freedom of the Will. A Systematic and Biographical Sounding of Augustine's Thoughts on Human Willing," *Augustiniana* 44 (1994): 237–70.

the boundaries at which Aristotle had left it—and even in part independently of the body of Aristotelian writings[71]—but also that its inner structure was transformed. Moreover, the occurrence of a syllogism as such is no indication of Aristotelianism. The history of medieval logic makes very clear that what was studied in connection with syllogistic reasoning, goes beyond the original Aristotelian syllogistic. This is even more true in the case of the Reformation era. Although under the influence of an emphasis on rhetoric, a large portion of genuine medieval contributions to logic and semantics fell into oblivion, the part in which syllogistic reasoning was addressed functioned completely.[72] The seventeenth-century theologians could manage quite complex pieces of reasoning under the heading of syllogism, while in fact a kind of predicate logic was at stake.[73] And, to drive the point home, syllogistic reasoning is often just an explicit form of everyday inference, which every rational being performs.

The second additional hypothesis is that Scotism is as least as important as Thomism, both in the medieval and in the post-reformation period. If it is true that Christian thought has its own framework, we may wonder whether it is a coincidence that Aquinas's way of incorporating Aristotelian elements in his thought was initially rejected, and that his thought was only much later recognized as being within that Christian framework.[74] In the later medieval period, we find Scotism as a rival

71. De Rijk has shown that many developments in logic had already taken place before Aristotle's complete writings became available. See his *Middeleeuwse Wijsbegeerte*, 92, 101 (PMA, 70, 77), and also his *Logica Modernorum. A Contribution to the History of Early Terminist Logic*, 3 vols. (Van Gorcum: Assen 1962–1967), esp. vol. 1, 13–20; vol. 2, 11. Cf. the essays 7–18 in Norman Kretzmann, Anthony Kenny, Jan Pinborg, eds., *The Cambridge History of Later Medieval Philosophy* (Cambridge, 1982), which all bear testimony to the addition of many issues to the established, aristotelian logic.

72. Jennifer E. Ashworth, "The Eclipse of Medieval Logic," in Kretzmann, et al, eds., *The Cambridge History of Later Medieval Philosophy*, 787–96. Cf. also Ashworth, "Traditional Logic" in C. B. Schmitt, general ed., *The Cambridge History of Renaissance Philosophy*, (Cambridge, 1988), 143–72 with Lisa Jardine, "Humanistic Logic," ibid., 173–98.

73. See for example, Gisbertus Voetius' reasoning with respect to the universality of Christ's death, explained in W. J. van Asselt en E. Dekker, ed., *De scholastieke Voetius. Een luisteroefening aan de hand van Voetius' Disputationes Selectae* (Zoetermeer, 1995), 161–66.

74. See the 219 propositions, many of them containing Aristotelian tenets, condemned by the Church in 1277. They are edited by H. Denifle and Aemile Chatelain, *Chartularium Universitatis Parisiensis,* vol. 1 (Paris, 1889), 543–58, and translated in Ernest L. Fortin and Peter D. O'Neill, "The Condemnation of 1277," in Ralph Lerner and Muhsin Mahdi, eds., *Medieval Political Philosophy: A Source Book*

school, combating precisely the Aristotelian elements in the Thomist school. There is increasing evidence available that Scotism plays a role in Reformed Scholasticism.[75] One of the reasons why older scholars were so willing to point out Thomism in Reformed Scholasticism is perhaps that later medieval scholasticism was very easily, but incorrectly, identified with Thomism. It is also worth noting that even in cases when a reformed scholastic uses at first sight Thomistic *terms*, he conveys in fact Scotistic *concepts*.[76]

When it comes to the content rather than the method of scholasticism, we can easily see that in fact a wide variety of thoughts are available. Nevertheless, there is a remarkable continuity here as well. A mainstream Augustinianism may be discerned, which runs through theologians like Anselm, Bonaventure and Duns Scotus to Luther, Calvin, Voetius and Turretin. The basic opposition of Luther and Calvin to scholasticism is often confined to late medieval nominalism in its semi-pelagian form.[77] What is more—although its sources are notoriously difficult to identify—scholars have long found Scotistic elements in Calvin's thought.[78]

(Toronto: Collier-Macmillan, 1963), 335–54 (the reprint in A. Hyman and J. J. Walsh, eds., *Philosophy in the Middle Ages* [New York: Harper and Row, 1967], 540–49 is only an abridged version). See also Roland Hissette, *Enquête sur les 219 articles condamnés à Paris le 7 mars 1277* (Louvain/Paris, 1977), who provides a helpful discussion of the relevance of the propositions.

75. Which is not to say that all Scotist tenets are evidenced. See A. Goudriaan, "Over historisch onderzoek van de zeventiende-eeuwse systematische theologie," in *Kerkhistorische Studiën*, ed.. C. E. Brons-Alberti, et al. (Leiden, 1996), 63–73. Note that seventeenth-century metaphysics—available to the theologians of that century, of course—bears scotistic traits: "Mehr als vom thomanisch-aristotelischen . . . Seinsbegriff ist für die Betrachtung der Schulmetaphysik des frühen 17. Jahrhunderts vom Seinsbegriff der skotistischen Tradition auszugehen." Ulrich Gottfried Leinsle, *Das Ding und die Methode. Methodische Konstitution und Gegenstand der frühen protestantischen Metaphysik,* 2 vol., (MaroVerlag: Augsburg, 1985), 63.

76. This point is argued in Vos's contribution. Cf. also the first section in Beck's contribution.

77. Josef Lortz understood Luther's thought as a reaction against a problematic late medieval theology. See Josef Lortz, *The Reformation in Germany*, transl. Ronald Walls, 2 vols, (London/New York: Herder and Herder, 1968), 1:67–77, 193–210.

78. See for instance, David C. Steinmetz, *Calvin in Context* (New York/Oxford: Oxford University Press, 1995), 40–52; Heiko A. Oberman, "Initia Calvini: The Matrix of Calvin's Reformation," *Mededelingen van de Afdeling Letterkunde, nieuwe reeks* 54/4 (Amsterdam: Koninklijke Nederlandse Academie van Wetenschappen, 1991), 10–19; Alexandre Ganoczy, *Le jeune Calvin: Genèse et évolution de sa vocation réformatrice* (Wiesbaden: Steiner, 1966), 40; cf. also Beck's contribution below, section 1 (with more

It is arguable that Luther in fact opposed a new strand of thought in his immediate predecessors and contemporaries. If this line of argument is correct, Luther was in fact a defender of the genuine, medieval Augustinian position against a "modern" paradigm.[79]

In addition, we could point at the way in which Roman catholic theologians like Suárez were widely read by the Protestant scholastics and were taken over in matters about which there was no significant dispute, i.e. for example large portions of the doctrine of God, or almost a complete agreement on christology (in so far as the Reformed are concerned; the Lutherans walk another route here—but perhaps on minor questions). The fact that writings of people like Suárez were used tells us two things: first, there is not an absolute schism between Roman Catholic and Protestant in the scholarly sense, and second, if the Protestant theologians were not already aware of the great medieval theologians, they would definitely become aware of them by reading their Roman Catholic colleagues.

There is also a very interesting continuity in discontinuity. For we

---

literature in his footnote 11).

79. This amounts to the important thesis of Henri de Lubac, developed in his *Surnaturel* and later works. See also J. H. Walgrave, *Geloof en theologie in de crisis* (Kasterlee, Belgium, 1966), who portrays Luther and Calvin as medievals reacting against the new paradigm! Its background is this: in the augustinian, medieval anthropology, man is essentially made for and directed toward God, i.e. cannot find his fulfilment in the creaturely realm. This picture was almost all-pervasive from Augustine onward. Somewhere in the transition from Middle Ages to Renaissance a new way of looking at reality arose. Nature was seen now as an independent, autonomous "basement," upon upon which a first floor might be built. Nature's finality is not seen any longer as aimed at a transcendent grace, but aimed at an immanent, natural fulfillment. So grace is no longer essential, but accidental to human nature. Nature can supply its own, autonomous, fulfillment in this "divorce" model.

One of the first straightforwardly applying this divorce between nature and grace is Cajetanus (1469–1534), the cardinal before whom Luther was to appear in 1518. Many theologians were to follow him. He takes it for granted that every nature can reach its natural goal, and is equipped to reach that goal effectively. References can be found in Walgrave, *Geloof en theologie*, 140. Walgrave thus draws our attention to a phenomenon which may strike one as surprising: seen from the perspective of the two models of nature and grace, it is quite plausible that Luther and Calvin are in fact medieval reactions to the new "divorce" model. Luther and Calvin adhered to the Augustinian picture of mankind as essentially, not only accidentally, related to God. In reaction to the model of divorce, their claim is that sin does not only affect one independent area, but the complete person. Walgrave, *Geloof*, 148–58. See on the "divorce" model also Arvin Vos, *Aquinas, Calvin, and Contemporary Protestant Thought* (Washington D.C./Grand Rapids: Christian University Press/Eerdmans 1985), esp. 123–60.

should also emphasize the aforementioned fact that already in the Medieval period itself Aristotelian theses were condemned by the Church. In this respect, Luther was hardly alone. The Christian outlook did shy away from influences alien to it, be it in the thirteenth or in the sixteenth century.

The Protestant theologians themselves were quite aware of a double meaning of the term scholasticism. On the one hand, they could use it to describe and appreciate a method, as explained above, on the other hand, it was used to refer to a certain type of late medieval, speculative theology or even contemporary theology. In this latter sense, for example, Calvin used it when referring to the "scholastics."[80]

All these remarks can be set in the context of the question: In which way is scholasticism oecumenical? We note the following partial answers.

1. At least in its general applicability. If people see reason to take a different stance on a topic, they can still understand what the other says. This shows for the post-reformation period: Lutheran, Reformed and Roman Catholic theologians make use of the same scholastic method.

2. In its historical dimension: the period in history in which scholasticism was simply the method by which one engaged in academic discourse is extremely long.

3. In contemporary research. Scholars of different denominational and ecclesiastical backgrounds explore together the richness of the scholastic material (as evidenced here as well as in other writings).

4. We may see a thorough occupation with scholasticism as an exercise in precisely and pointedly applying theological categories. It does not help churches if they try to just forget to search for truth and to approach oecumenical issues with unsound pieces of reasoning. Of course, scholasticism is not identical with sound reasoning. It remains, however, a *conditio sine qua non*.

VIII. What, Then, Are the Claims of the "New" School?

It is probably useful to gather in the form of statements what the position of those adhering to the new type of research consists of. We have listed 10 characteristics, which are not all equally extensively elaborated on in

80. See Richard Muller's contribution to this volume.

this volume.[81]

1. Scholasticism is a scientific method of research and teaching, and does as such not have a doctrinal content, neither does it have reason as its foundation.
2. There is a continuity between the Medieval, Reformation and Post-reformation Era (which is of course, not to deny that there are many differences).
3. "Aristotelianism" is exceedingly problematic when applied with a broad brush, and should rather be avoided if used unspecified.
4. Syllogisms are used by any person in a reasoning process (but not always consciously and explicitly), and are therefore, in themselves, not a sign of anything beyond that reasoning process, let alone of Aristotelianism.
5. The scornful way in which Luther and Calvin treated scholasticism is not to be taken as an overall hermeneutical principle to read scholasticism.
6. Let the scholastics themselves define scholasticism.
7. Protestant scholasticism does not proceed by abstracting proof texts out of Scripture, nor does Medieval scholasticism avoid or neglect Scripture and scriptural language.
8. Christian faith, and therefore, Christian theology, has its own view of life, its own frame of thought and is not to be identified with any philosophical system.
9. Parts of that unique Christian frame of thought are the concepts of will and contingency.
10. The relative placement of a *locus* in a system of doctrine does not as such change its content.

IX. Overview of the Contributions to This Volume

The various contributions are divided into five sections. In the first section we have three essays which set up a general discussion of the field. In the opening piece Richard A. Muller takes issue with a Alister McGrath's wrongheaded historical picture, in which Beza is portrayed as starting from general principles, unlike Calvin who began with the specific historic phenomenon of Jesus Christ. Muller gives ample

81. See also R. A. Muller who discusses complementary traits in "Calvin and the Calvinists: Assessing Continuities and Discontinuities between Reformation and Orthodoxy," parts 1 and 2, *CTJ* 30 (1995): 345–75; 31 (1996): 125-60.

evidence that this picture does not meet the facts. He goes on to show that Calvin himself has many scholastic traits, and that Calvin's scorn regarding the "Scholastics" really turns out to be addressed to some contemporary Sorbonne theologians, and not to scholasticism in general. He then investigates how the Reformed scholastics saw their own way of doing theology and shows that they regarded the scholastic method as applicable to the *genre* of classroom disputes, systematic teaching and the like, and not readily applicable to exegesis, preaching, oration, catechesis, piety, etc.

C. Augustijn's contribution deals with the way in which Luther and Melanchthon dealt with scholasticism. He takes his point of departure in their own perception of scholasticism. It is very clear that Luther saw Aristotle as the main problem in theology, which name he took to stand for any synergistic model of theology. Melanchthon's rejection of scholasticism has, in part, a different background: he is quite humanist in his approach, and follows the Humanists in their disdain for scholasticism in favor of the *bonae litterae.*

W. van't Spijker gives an overview of the four different short stages in which the Reformation period may be subdivided. He notes a gradual return to Scholasticism. The refutation of Bellarmine characterizes the last period, from 1586 onwards, and shapes the method of Reformed scholasticism. Three main theological issues were at stake between the Protestant and the Catholic: Scripture, grace, and the church. van't Spijker warns us not to judge the Scholastics from our all too easy retrospective point of view, and to treat both Reformers and Scholastics together like friends.

The essays in the second section explicitly take the relationship between Middle Ages and Reformation into account. Antonie Vos defends the thesis that Reformed Scholasticism is only to be understood in the broader movement of the history of the university, whereas the university is in fact "the cradle of a new Christian philosophy." The university thus creates a basic continuity in learning and method from 1100 until about 1800. It is therefore incorrect and even damaging to a good understanding of both Reformation and scholasticism to suppose a sharp contrast between the periods before and after 1517. Vos also argues that the nineteenth-century interpretation of Reformed scholasticism as a determinism is due to the breakdown of the university learning around 1800, when scholasticism becomes an ill-understood phenomenon.

Harm Goris provides evidence for the claim that it is never simply a matter of taking one outstanding or famous scholastic writer as the mould of subsequent developments. In earlier research there has been a tendency to emphasize the role of Aquinas as the major influence in Reformed Scholasticism. Goris points out that, at least in the case of Zanchi, it is a simplification to do so. A strong case can be made that Duns Scotus' thoughts are at least as important for this major Protestant voice.

Our third section is devoted to the relationship of Counter-reformational and Reformed Scholasticism. Eef Dekker provides a sample of the debate between Catholic and Protestant in the persons of Bellarmine and Ames, and concentrates on the doctrine of free will. Here, the dividing lines do not run exactly along the Protestant-Catholic divide. Ames is quite capable of pointing at problems in Bellarmine's text. One of the main problematic points is, perhaps surprisingly, the way in which Bellarmine wrestles with his arguments for and against Thomism and Scotism, respectively. Ames seems to be in sympathy with a Scotist position.

Frits G.M. Broeyer provides a second sample of the oecumenical debate, and throws light upon the discussion between Bellarmine and Whitaker concerning some of the major points of debate, like the doctrine of Scripture, sin and grace, the Church, and justification. Whitaker was the first Protestant theologian to write against Bellarmine. Broeyer argues that Aquinas was a major Medieval source for Whitaker, and that he was quite capable to make use of the apparatus of scholasticism. He may be regarded as a transitional figure in the rise of Reformed Scholasticism.

In the fourth section we have gathered some samples of Reformed scholasticism: Owen, Voetius, Cocceius and, from a different perspective, Owen again. Sebastian Rehnman takes issue with the older portraits of John Owen, and characterizes him in contrast to these as a scholar of his days, i.e. a Reformed Scholastic, very well entrenched in not only biblical studies, but also in Patristic, Medieval and contemporary writers, in pagan philosophy as well as in Reformation authors. Rehnman finds the evidence for his claims in a careful scrutiny of the quotations Owen provides in his writings.

Andreas J. Beck defends the thesis that in the case of Gisbertus Voetius we encounter a representative Reformed scholastic, in whose work a Scotist background is clearly visible. Beck evidences this by pointing at the way in which Voetius handles both a contingent and a necessary dimension in the divine attributes, at his use of synchronic contingency and at the pivotal role of the divine will. Furthermore, he argues that these characteristics allow for the *contingent* relationship of God's necessary being to his contingent creation while avoiding the extremes of necessitarianism and voluntarism.

Willem J. van Asselt's contribution questions the traditional thesis that Cocceius should be viewed as a thoroughgoing anti-scholastic theologian. Although Cocceius argues against "scholastic theology," close inspection shows that he did not have in mind scholasticism as a method, but rather, certain contents of late medieval, semi-pelagian theology and certain forms of seventeenth century Reformed scholasticism which left no room for the new exegetical insights which he wanted to apply.

Carl R. Trueman shows that if one applies Quentin Skinner's plea for a linguistic approach to the history of ideas to the study of Puritan thought, it becomes evident that English Puritanism was an international intellectual phenomenon, shaped as much by medieval and Renaissance antecedents and by European university culture as any other seventeenth century movement. It is not, therefore, to be viewed as a sectarian and destructive force. This analysis also shows the ecumenical dimension of Puritan thought. Trueman shows this approach to apply in the case of John Owen, who makes as much use of "Aristotelian" language in his attack on Arminius as any other seventeenth-century theologian.

Two essays on contemporary relevance make up our last section. Luco J. van den Brom offers an analysis of Karl Barth's comments on scholasticism, from which he makes clear that one should distinguish between scholastic method and theological content. Van den Brom then continues to show that there is no contradiction between the vast reasoning skills of the medieval scholars and their way of dealing with authorities. Scholasticism, then, is a reasonable methodology, which bears striking resemblance to much what we would nowadays be prepared to call "good method," and put to use in contemporary theology, as a kind of rational laboratory.

Bert Loonstra's contribution deals with the significance that Reformed Scholasticism might have for the present-day hermeneutical debate about the interpretation of the Bible and for the current practice of Reformed dogmatic theology. After having pointed out that in several ways the views of the Reformed Scholastics have been superseded (for example, the view on the vowel points in the Masoretic text of the Old Testament), he argues that their hermeneutical views may correct the modern ones on the aspect of truth-claims. The same applies to modern systematic theology: they still must and can lay claim to universal validity of what Scripture has to say. However, modern systematics is more aware of the cultural-historical nature of all language—which may make us more modest.

1

The Problem of Protestant Scholasticism —A Review and Definition

Richard A. Muller

I. The Problem

Any attempt to review the study of Protestant scholasticism during the last twenty-five years must come to the conclusion that the field has altered drastically, both in terms of interest in the phenomenon itself and in matters of approach and definition. Twenty-five years ago there was very little interest in the subject at all, largely because of the existence of a theologically-motivated stereotype of Protestant scholasticism as an undifferentiated, doctrinaire, Aristotelian, metaphysical monolith at odds with the heritage of the Reformation. I do not think that I exaggerate when I say that, at that time, most Protestants viewed "Protestant scholasticism" as a historical surd or as an unpleasant theological oxymoron: to be Protestant and scholastic at the same time was to be a living contradiction. It was deemed sufficient to define the problem, isolate the phenomenon, and then leap over it in an attempt to recover the Reformation from the clutches of recrudescent scholasticism.[1]

II. The Older Definition, Unfortunately Still Cited

The distaste for scholasticism that characterized the literature also tended to determine approach and definition. Approach to the materials was largely negative and was characterized by a series of theological contrasts between the Reformation and the post-Reformation eras that was suspiciously like the rigid contrast once made between the Middle Ages and the Reformation and, equally suspiciously, redolent of the

---

1. For an extended survey of earlier scholarship and relevant collateral literature see R. A. Muller, "Calvin and the Calvinists: Assessing Continuities and Discontinuities between Reformation and Orthodoxy," parts 1 and 2, *CTJ* 30 (1995): 345–75; 31 (1996): 125-60.

theological categories of mid-twentieth-century neo-orthodoxy. To wit, the Reformation understood God's revelation as "personal" or as an "event" while scholastic Protestantism understood it as "propositional"; the Reformation was "dynamic," scholasticism, "static"; the Reformers held that Christ alone was "God's Word" and that Scripture was a witness to it, the scholastics assumed ("rigidly," of course) that Scripture was Word and, indeed, verbally dictated by God; the Reformers partook of the gentle spirit of humanism, the scholastics were immersed in the rigors of Aristotelian logic and metaphysics.[2] This approach produced definitions of Protestant scholasticism that were geared primarily toward the identification of post-Reformation Protestant thought as a deductive rationalism.

It may be useful, if only by way of a scholastic *via negativa* approach, identifying first what the phenomenon is not before passing on to what it is, to offer one of these standard definitions. The form taken in Alister McGrath's *Reformation Thought* is illustrative of his immersion both in twenty-five year old secondary sources and in the above-noted dogmatic categories: as distinct from the Reformation, Protestant scholasticism "assigned" a "major role" to "human reason" in order to present "Christian theology . . . as a logically coherent and rationally defensible system, derived from syllogistic deductions." According to this scholasticism, "theology was understood to be grounded in Aristotelian philosophy" and produced a "philosophical, rather than biblical" theology "concerned with metaphysical and speculative questions." In summary, McGrath notes,

> The starting point of theology thus came to be general principles, not a specific historic event. The contrast with Calvin will be clear. . . . Calvin focused on the specific historical phenomenon of Jesus Christ and moved out to explore its implications. . . . By contrast, Beza began from general principles and proceeded to deduce their consequences for Christian theology.[3]

---

2. Cf. e.g., J. K. S. Reid, *The Authority of Scripture: a Study of Reformation and Post-Reformation Understanding of the Bible* (London: Methuen, 1962).

3. Alister McGrath, *Reformation Thought: An Introduction*, second edition (Grand Rapids: Baker, 1993), 129–30; the definition derives, without citation but with clear verbal reliance, from Brian G. Armstrong, *Calvinism and the Amyraut Heresy: Protestant Scholasticism and Humanism in Seventeenth Century France* (Madison: University of Wisconsin Press, 1969), 32.

If one asks, moreover, the identity of the fundamental principle from which Beza "deduced" all of theology, McGrath has a simple answer, the eternal decree of God, used as a "controlling principle" for the entire theological system.[4] This definition, in short, is a nearly perfect summary of all that was wrong about the older scholarship.

I cannot do more here than to note that the work of a series of scholars has shown this judgment of Beza's theology to be quite unfounded, both in its own content and in its consequences for the Reformed tradition. If central dogmas and systems deduced from a single principle are the primary indicators of scholasticism, then there were no Protestant scholastics in any of the orthodox confessional traditions of the sixteenth and seventeenth centuries. Beza certainly does not fit this description.[5] Nor can I do more than point to the documentation of a continuity of Aristotelianism, variously understood and differently appropriated by a vast number of thinkers, in theology and philosophy extending from the thirteenth through the seventeenth centuries.[6] So too, would it be impossible even to list, in a presentation this brief, the Protestant exegetes and philologists who produced biblical commentaries, critical texts, translations, hermeneutical studies, and who pioneered the use of Judaica in the study of Scripture.[7] Concerning the

4. McGrath, *Reformation Thought*, 130.

5. Thus, Jill Raitt, "Beza, Guide for the Faithful Life," in *Scottish Journal of Theology* 39/1 (1986): 83–107; idem, *The Eucharistic Theology of Theodore Beza: Development of the Reformed Doctrine* (Chambersburg, Pa., 1972); idem, "The Person of the Mediator: Calvin's Christology and Beza's Fidelity," *Occasional Papers of the Society for Reformation Research*, I (Dec. 1977): 53–80; idem, "Beza, Theodore," s.v. in *Encyclopedia of the Reformation*, ed. Hans J. Hillerbrand, et al. 4 vols. (New York: Oxford University Press, 1996); Tadataka Maruyama, *The Ecclesiology of Theodore Beza: The Reform of the True Church* (Geneva: Droz, 1978); Robert Letham, "Theodore Beza: A Reassessment," in *Scottish Journal of Theology* 40 (1987): 25–40; Richard A. Muller, "Calvin and the Calvinists . . . Part I," 345–75; "Part II," 125–60; idem, *Christ and the Decree: Christology and Predestination in Reformed Theology from Calvin to Perkins* (Durham, N.C.: Labyrinth Press, 1986; paperback edition, Grand Rapids: Baker, 1988), 79–96; and idem, "The Myth of 'Decretal Theology,'" in *CTJ* 30/1 (April 1995): 159–67.

6. See Charles B. Schmitt, *Aristotle and the Renaissance* (Cambridge, Mass.: Harvard University Press, 1983); idem, *John Case and Aristotelianism in Renaissance England* (Montreal: MicGill-Queen's University Press, 1983); and idem, *The Aristotelian Tradition and Renaissance Universities* (London: Variorum Reprints, 1984); also see Peter Petersen, *Geschichte der aristotelischen Philosophie im protestantischen Deutschland* (Leipzig, 1921; repr. Stuttgart, 1964).

7. E.g., Junius, Tremellius, Drusius, Rivetus, Lightfoot, Walton, Wheelocke, Pococke, Castell, Glassius, Weemes, Cappel, Buxtorf Sr. and Jr., de Dieu, Ainsworth.

definition itself, its view of Reformation theology as "focused on the specific historical phenomenon of Jesus Christ and . . . its implications," irrepressibly Barthian in its anachronism, biases the case from the start with a false dichotomy between Reformation and post-Reformation theology.

Furthermore, one might wonder how it is possible to ground an entire Christian theology on Aristotle while at the same time deducing the entire theology from the divine decree of predestination, a concept that presumably never crossed the mind of Aristotle. One might also ask whether a Lutheran or an Arminian theology of the seventeenth century, one that, barring the confessional differences, was organized and argued in virtually the same way as the Reformed theologies, must fall short of being "scholastic" given the fact that it does not hold to the Reformed doctrine of predestination. (Of course, the notion that "scholasticism" is rigidly Aristotelian and intensely predestinarian would also render large numbers of the medieval scholastics something less than scholastic as well.) And one ought to question the identification of Protestant scholasticism as "deductive rationalism" given both the failure of such a definition suitably to describe medieval scholasticism and the presence of a genuine deductive rationalism in the seventeenth century, namely, Cartesian philosophy, alongside of and often in fundamental conflict with Protestant scholasticism.

The definition simply does not fit the historical evidence. The reason for this failure of the definition is clear when one reconstructs its own historical pedigree.[8] The entire notion of "central dogmas" belongs to the nineteenth century. Not only did various nineteenth-century theologians assume that an entire system of Christian doctrine not only could but ought to be constructed around a single principle (viz., a "central dogma" or "material principle"),[9] these same writers also

---

For further detail, see Richard A. Muller, "Biblical Interpretation in the Sixteenth and Seventeenth Centuries" s.v. in *Historical Handbook of Major Biblical Interpreters*, ed. Donald K. McKim (Downers Grove, Ill.: InterVarsity Press, 1998).

8. The point is argued in some detail in Muller, "Calvin and the Calvinists, Part I," 345–58.

9. See the discussion in Claude Welch, *Protestant Thought in the Nineteenth Century*, 2 vols. (New Haven: Yale University Press, 1972–85), I:65, 68–69 (Schleiermacher), 164–65 (Biedermann), 223–27 (Hofmann and Thomasius); II:13, 17–18 (Ritschl); Brian A. Gerrish, *Tradition in the Modern World: Reformed Theology in the Nineteenth Century* (Chicago: University of Chicago Press, 1978), 121–27, 145–47 (Schweizer). Also note Richard A. Muller, "Emanuel V. Gerhart on the 'Christ-Idea' as Fundamental Principle a Study of Late-Nineteenth-Century Christocentrism," in *Westminster Theological Journal*

typically concluded that every age of the church, even those ages that did not write theological systems, constructed their doctrines around a distinct central dogma. Their histories of Christian doctrine, moreover, reflect this assumption: "Along with the 'central dogma' of every age," wrote Seeberg, "there comes to view, not indeed a peripheral system of doctrine (Thomasius), but a general conception of Christianity dependent upon and involved in the central, dominating thought."[10] Very much like the earlier, topical method used by historians like Neander and Hagenbach, this method imposed a theological grid on the materials of history in order to render them doctrinally cohesive. As several late nineteenth-century historians and theologians pointed out, the explicit concept of a "material principle" or central dogma was not used to describe the theological enterprise before the early nineteenth century.[11]

It is, therefore, understandably difficult to find any theologian who developed his system on the basis of an explicit central dogma or deductive principle before the nineteenth century. And the exceptions tend to "prove the rule" that this was not normative procedure for the orthodox Reformed of the sixteenth and seventeenth centuries: the one use of predestination as a fundamental deductive principle that I have located is Pierre Poiret's *L'Oeconomie divine, ou système universel* (1687), and, although its author was nominally Reformed, the work arose out of a confluence of French Roman Catholic mysticism with Cartesian philosophy, not out of the main stream of Reformed theology.[12] There were, admittedly, a few more or less Cartesian writers among the

---

48 (1986): 97–117.

10. Reinhold Seeberg, *Text-book of the History of Doctrines*, trans. Charles Hay, 2 vols. (repr. Grand Rapids: Baker Book House, 1977), I, 23.

11. See Carl Beck, "Das Princip des Protestantismus. Anfrage in einem Schreiben an *D*. Ullmann," in *Theologische Studien und Kritiken* 24 (1851): 408–11; Albrecht Ritschl, "Über die beiden Principien des Protestantismus," in *Zeitschrift für Kirchengeschichte,* 1 (1876): 397–413; and Karl Stange, "A Ritschls Urteil über die beiden Principien des Protestantismus," in *Theologische Studien und Kritiken* (1897): 599–621. Cf. Heppe, *Geschichte des deutschen Protestantismus,* 1:25–32; idem., "Der Charakter der deutsch-reformirten Kirche und das Verhältniss derselben zum Luthertum und zum Calvinismus," in *Theologische Studien und Kritiken*, Heft 3 (1850): 669–706; Dorner, *History,* 1:220–64; Schaff, *History,* 7:16–26, adding a third principle, the social or ecclesiastical; and O. Ritschl, *Dogmengeschichte,* 1:42–64; also note Welch, *Protestant Thought in the Nineteenth Century,* 1:270.

12. See Richard A. Muller, "Found (No Thanks to Theodore Beza): One 'Decretal' Theology," in *CTJ* 32/1 (April 1997): 145–51.

Reformed in the second half of the seventeenth century, but they were a rather small minority and they were all hesitant to recast Reformed theology according in a deductive pattern. The only other deductive models that I have located in the older tradition are Wolffian systems of the eighteenth century, like Daniel Wyttenbach's *Tentamen theologiae dogmaticae methodo scientifico pertractatae* (1747–49) and *Theses theologicae praecipua christianae doctrinae capita ex primis principiis deducta continentes* (1747), which attempt to derive theology from the principle of "sufficient reason."

The actual notion of the divine decree of predestination as the fundamental or material principle and central dogma of the older Reformed theology probably cannot be found before Alexander Schweizer's *Glaubenslehre* (1844–47) and *Protestantischen Centraldogmen* (1854–56)—and there it appears as part of Schweizer's attempt to show that all useful Protestant theological roads led to Schleiermacher.[13] In short, the concept of a deductive system is not the product of Reformed scholasticism, certainly not of the work of Theodore Beza; the notion of predestination as a deductive principle has no clear association either with seventeenth-century Reformed theology or with the older Aristotelianism; and the understanding of predestination as an explicitly identified "central dogma" is most probably a nineteenth-century development. The proponents of the definition, in other words, never raised the seemingly obvious questions concerning the sixteenth and seventeenth-century writers understanding of their own theology that ought rather naturally to occur to a historian.

III. Calvin and Scholasticism: L'École des sophistes vs. l'école de Dieu

The problematic character of the older definition and the inherent difficulty of coming to terms with the problem of Reformation and scholasticism or, indeed, Reformation, humanism, and scholasticism is perhaps nowhere more evident than in the work of John Calvin. For at the same time that Calvin polemicized bitterly against the "scholastics,"

---

13. Alexander Schweizer, *Die Glaubenslehre der evangelisch-reformirten Kirche dargestellt und aus den Quellen belegt*, 2 vols. (Zürich: Orell, Füssli, 1844–47); idem, *Die protestantischen Centraldogmen in ihrer Entwicklung innerhalb der reformierten Kirche*, 2 vols. (Zürich: Orell, Füssli, 1854–56); also note, idem, "Die Entwicklung des Moralsystems in der reformirten Kirche," in *Theologische Studien und Kritiken* 23 (1850): 5–78, 288–327, 554–80; and idem, "Moses Amyraldus: Versuch einer Synthese des Universalismus und des Partikularismus," in *Theologische Jahrbücher* 11 (1852): 41–101, 155–207.

one of his colleagues identified Calvin's own lecture style as "scholastic." Calvin himself wrote of training "scholastics"—*scholastici* or *scolastiques*—in logic and in the methods of disputation at the Academy of Geneva, and Beza praised the Academy as a *respublica scholastica*. Add to this the "humanist" practice of writing *Colloquia scholastica* and the subject of Melanchthon's 1536 address to the University of Wittenberg, *De laude vitae scholasticae oratio*.[14] Contrary to much of what has been claimed about the Reformers and the humanists, the mention of "scholastics" and their cultivation of "scholasticism" were not invariably associated with polemic. Indeed, as these references indicate, "scholastic" and related terms were used by Reformers and humanists alike as references to the academic culture of their own and of the preceding eras—sometimes with positive, sometimes with negative connotation, and often in a neutral manner, with reference to the methods employed in an academic context.

As can be demonstrated from the text of the *Institutes*, Calvin's response to medieval scholasticism was not entirely negative—and even the negative response varied in degree.[15] Calvin could speak of "Lombard and the scholastics" without any great rancor and he could even, on occasion, indicate that a definition or distinction made by the "scholastics" was useful. Inasmuch, moreover, as he rendered into French his most negative references to *scholastici* as attacks on the *theologiens Sorbonniques*, his polemic often takes on the color of a highly specific contemporary attack rather than a generalized assault on the entire academic culture of the Middle Ages. So too, are there instances in the *Institutes* where attacks on the "scholastics," if taken as a general point of disagreement with the medieval doctors, would indicate only Calvin's ignorance of the diversity of medieval opinion: in the case of his claim that the scholastics wrongly understood God *in se* as the object of faith, the point stands better as a diatribe against a specific, perhaps contemporary, abuse than against medieval scholasticism as a whole.[16]

---

14. *CR* 11, col. 298–306.

15. See Muller, "Scholasticism in Calvin: a Question of Relation and Disjunction," in *Calvinus Sincerioris Religionis Vindex: Calvin as Protector of the Purer Religion*, ed. Wilhelm H. Neuser and Brian Armstrong (Kirksville, MO: *Sixteenth Century Journal* Publishers, 1997), 247–65.

16. A similar point can and must be made concerning Calvin's overt distaste for Aristotle: there is, certainly, ample evidence that Calvin, like Luther and Melanchthon, associated elements of Aristotelian philosophy with the scholastic theology that he saw as problematic and dangerous—yet there are numerous positive uses of Aristotle in

Calvin was also in the habit of identifying the church and the office of preaching as *l'école de Dieu*.[17] As Parker and more recently, Steinmetz, have pointed out, there is a strong resemblance between the method of Calvin's preaching and the medieval scholastic practice of glossing the entire text of Scripture in a running commentary as the basic course in the theological curriculum.[18] So also was it in the context of his examination of the exegetical tradition that Calvin most probably found positive access to scholastic distinctions—given not only the fact that large numbers of the standard distinctions had arisen out of exegetical meditations but also the fact that Calvin's use of many of the distinctions is directly connected with his discussion of biblical texts.[19] There was, in other words, much in Calvin's work that maintained strong parallels with medieval patterns of exposition, specifically those associated with the scholastic theological curriculum.

It is crucial here to recognize that Calvin was no more against *scholastici* in general (this is what he called his own students in the Academy) than he despised the concept of a *schola*. Calvin's own language tells us as much: he bitterly attacks the *scholastici* or "academics" who have lost their way in sophisms. He surely had a generalized sense of the problematic nature of the school theology that belonged to the centuries before the Reformation and he shared with his humanistic teachers and colleagues an aversion to academic speculation and academic barbarism, the former in theology and philosophy, the latter in the use of language. Yet, it was the *théologiens Sorbonniques* in their *école sophistique* who received his greatest anger and scorn for their useless speculations and "devilish blasphemies."[20] Calvin sought not a rejection

---

Calvin's theology, both explicit and implicit. See John Calvin, *The Bondage and Liberation of the Will: A Defense of the Orthodox Doctrine of Human Choice against Pighius*, ed. A. N. S. Lane, trans. G. I. Davis, Texts and Studies in Reformation and Post-Reformation Thought 2 (Grand Rapids: Baker Book House, 1996), 115, 149–50, 226.

17. See John Calvin, *Vingt deux sermons sur le Pseaume cent dix-neuvième*, in *CO* 32, col. 453–54. Cf. the extended discussion of this and related issues in Raymond A. Blacketer, "L'École de Dieu: Pedagogy and Method in Calvin's Interpretation of Deuteronomy" (Ph.D. dissertation: Calvin Theological Seminary, 1998) and cf. Parker, *Calvin's Preaching*, 25–29.

18. Cf. Mülhaupt, *Die Predigt Calvins*, 17–18 with Parker, *Calvin's Preaching*, 80, 132.

19. Thus, e.g., Calvin approved of scholastic distinctions concerning different levels of necessity, Calvin, *Institutes*, I.xvi.9; II.xii.1; he also approved of the distinction between the "sufficiency" and "efficiency" of Christ's satisfaction, Calvin, *Commentarius in Iohannis Apostoli epistolam*, *CO* 55, col. 310.

20. Calvin, *Sermons sur le Livre de Iob*, *CO* 34, col. 339: "Et de fait, quand ces docteurs

but a reform of school theology in the service of the church. Humanist and Reformer alike sought, perhaps before anything else, curricular change as an engine of broader reforms. The *scolastiques* in Calvin's own Academy of Geneva, preparing to gloss the Word in *l'école de Dieu*, were protegeés of the Calvin who had become an instructor, indeed, a *magister* in Strasbourg and Geneva.[21] This is not to minimize Calvin's hatred of scholasticism—rather it is to define it and focus it in terms of Calvin's own theological and political context against the anti-reformatory theology of the Sorbonne and, by extension, against any contemporary theology at the foundation of counter-Reformation.

IV. Letting Protestant Scholasticism Define Itself

If we are to define the phenomenon of "Protestant scholasticism" we ought, at very least, to ask the theologians of the time, in and through their writings, for *their* understanding of what the term "scholastic" might mean when applied to their work; for *their* understanding of the nature and object of the theological discipline; for *their* understanding of the principles or *principia* and *axiomata* of their own theology; for *their* understanding of the method and order of theological system. So too, if we are to raise the issue of the continuities and discontinuities between earlier models of theology and theological education (whether medieval or Reformation) and the Protestant scholastic era, we ought to look in detail to the language of the time rather than apply global generalizations that do not comport with the details of history.

The term "scholastic" was used by sixteenth and seventeenth-century Protestant theologians to indicate both the setting and the method of their theology, with fairly careful distinction between the positive and the negative connotations of the word. It is of the greatest importance, in the first place, that we recognize the presence of a positive use of the term "scholastic" throughout the eras of the Renaissance and Reformation. Humanists and Reformers did not invariably use the term to refer to a problematic method or context for teaching or writing theology and philosophy. Their writings frequently used the term in a positive way to indicate their own academic setting or method. The adjective *scholasticus/a/um* appears, thus, as an indicator of the academic setting and it refers specifically to the methods used in classroom disputation or in

---

Sorboniques disent, que le Dieu a une puissance absolue, c'est un blaspheme diabolique qui a esté forgé aux enfers."

21. Cf. Calvin to Farel, 27 October 1540, in *CO* 11, col. 91–92 (*Letters*, I, 212).

written works arising out of that context.[22] By extension, "scholastic" refers to academic forms that are syntactically brief, clear, and logical, as distinct from forms of discourse less suited to the classroom, such as oration, which would tend to be syntactically complex, ornate, and rhetorically persuasive.[23]

This usage implied a differentiation between theological works that employed different methods for the sake of different settings. Although, with some justice, the larger academic theological enterprise of the late sixteenth and the seventeenth century can be called "scholastic," not all theological works by these nominally "scholastic" theologians fit the description, followed the method, or were intended for the academic setting. A biblical commentary might not be scholastic in method (although, given the academic audience or origin of some of the commentaries, it certainly could be); a catechism or a work of piety would only very rarely follow scholastic method or belong to the scholastic setting; and a hymn would, surely, never do so. Yet works in all of these forms were written by the so-called Protestant scholastic theologians. In the seventeenth century, a theological work was identified as "scholastic" when it belonged to the classroom, echoed the patterns of disputation then typical of education, and employed a refined method of argument to define the terms of debate, the *status quaestionis*, and the resolution of debate with various clearly identified opponents.[24]

Finally, on the negative side of the usage, the term "scholastic"

22. Cf. the usage in *Leges Academiae Genevensis* (Geneva: Stephanus, 1559; facsimile repr. Geneva: J. G. Fick, 1859), fol. c.i, verso; also *L'Ordre du College de Geneve*, in ibid., fol. c.i, verso with the similar understanding in Mathurin Cordier, *Colloquiorum scholasticorum libri IIII, ad pueros in sermone Latino paulatim exercendos* (Geneva: Stephanus, 1564); note also Aloys Bömer, *Die lateinischen Schülergespräche der Humanisten*, 2 vols. (Berlin, 1897–99; repr. Amsterdam: P. Schippers, 1966) with L. Massebieau, *Les colloques scolaires de seizième siècle, et les auteurs, 1480–1570* (Paris: J. Bonhoure, 1878; repr. Geneva: Slatkine, 1968).

23. Cf. Andreas Hyperius, *De theologo, seu de ratione studii theologici, libri III* (Basel, 1556), 398; with Jean Budé's preface to John Calvin, *Praelect. in proph. minores, CO* 42, col. 187–88 (*CTS Minor Prophets* I, xxvi–xxvii) and with the *Acta ofte handelingen der Versamelingen der Nederlandsche Kerken, die onder 't Crius sitten . . . gehouden tot Wesel, den 3 Novembris . . . M.D.LXVIII*, cap. I.4, "anstellinge van Collegien, Leraars, haar onderhout, ampt, ontzag, de Scholastyke oeffeningen . . ." in C. Hooijer, *Oude Kerkordeningen der Nederlandsche Hervormde Gemeenten (1563–1638) . . . verzameld en met Inleidingen voorzien* (Zalto-Bommel: Joh. Noman en Zoon, 1865), 31; and note the comments in T. H. L. Parker, *Calvin's Preaching*, 132.

24. Cf. the citations of seventeenth-century definitions in Richard A. Muller, *PRRD*, 1:258–63.

continued, throughout the seventeenth century, to be used as a pejorative term for theology that had gone too far in the academic or speculative direction to be useful to the church. Protestant theologians of the era continued, despite their own acknowledged "scholasticism," to refer to medieval theology, particularly late medieval theology, as scholastic in the negative sense, and they often accused their own Protestant opponents of scholasticism when the occasion arose. In other words, the theologians of the late sixteenth and seventeenth centuries consciously differentiated their own academic or scholastic theology from the excessively academic and therefore, in their view, problematic, theology of the later middle ages. In no way did they understand their scholasticism as a recrudescence of medieval models. With some justice, they recognized that their scholasticism was rooted in the academic practice of their own times, which, from our historical perspective, can be identified as a product of the Renaissance as much as it was also an heir to the medieval heritage. The weight of this latter point will become particularly apparent when, below, we note something of the method and order of Protestant scholastic theology.

The nature and object of the theological discipline was also discussed at length by the Reformed scholastics. Drawing on the models found in medieval theology, the late sixteenth and seventeenth-century Protestant writers asked whether theological *scientia* was speculative or practical. The point of the questions was to define theology either as a discipline the content of which ought to be known or, better, contemplated, as a goal in and of itself or as a discipline the content of which was to be known as leading to a goal beyond itself. Although the occasional Reformed theologian, like De Moulin, identified theology as a speculative or contemplative discipline, by far the majority of Reformed writers identified theology as mixed discipline, both speculative and practical, contemplative and active, while a significant minority, many of them associated with covenant theology, argued that theology as we know it is primarily practical or active.[25]

As for the object of theology, the Reformed scholastics, like the medieval models that they consulted, recognized that God *in se* could not be the object of theology. It was characteristic of the Reformed scholastics to assert that the object of theology was God as he has chosen to reveal

---

25. See Muller, *PRRD*, 1:215–26; and, of course, even DuMoulin's understanding of theology as "speculative" did not intend "speculation" in the modern sense but rather contemplation of theological knowledge as legitimate end.

himself.[26] These definitions also correlate with the clear distinction between theology and metaphysics made by Reformed writers of the early seventeenth century. Keckermann and Maccovius defined the object of metaphysics as "being in general" or "being understood as being" (*Ens in genere* or *Ens, quatenus Ens*) and therefore refused categorically to allow metaphysics to take God as its proper object.[27] Alsted, who differed with them on the point, restricted metaphysical consideration of God to the discussion of God as *prima causa* and *ens nobilissimum*, or as *ens per essentiam* as distinct from *ens per participationum*.[28] The claim that Protestant scholastic theology was primarily concerned with metaphysical speculation flies in the face of the basic definitions offered by the scholastic theologians themselves.

So too did the Reformed scholastics offer detailed discussions of their theological *principia* and *axiomata*. Suffice it to say, in the first place, that these discussions *do not* identify predestination or the divine decrees either as a *principium* or as a fundamental *axiom* of theology. Nor, when the Reformed scholastics discuss the topic of "fundamental doctrines" do they depart from the topics of the creed in order to identify predestination as "fundamental." *Principia* were defined, in the Protestant scholastic systems of the seventeenth century, either as the ultimate essential and cognitive foundations of theology or as the basic *axiomata* or *aphorismi* of argument from which conclusions might be drawn.[29]

In the former sense of the term, the *principia* of theology were identified as God, the *principium essendi* or essential foundation, and Scripture, the *principium cognoscendi* or cognitive foundation of theology.

26. E.g., Alsted, *Praecognita theologica*, I.ix; Turretin, *Inst. Theol. Elenct.*, I.v.4

27. Bartholomaus Keckermann, *Scientiae metaphysicae brevissima synopsis*, in *Opera*, I, col. 2015; Johannes Maccovius, *Metaphysica, ad usum quaestionum in philosophia ac theologia* (Leyden, 1658): 2–3, 6.

28. Alsted, *Methodus metaphysica*, 24, 32–33.

29. Cf. Sibrandus Lubbertus, *De principiis Christianorum dogmatum* (Franecker, 1591), I.i with Antoine de la Roche Chandieu, *De verbo Dei scripto*, in *Opera theologica* (Geneva, 1593): 7–10, and with Johannes Cloppenburg, *Aphorismi theologiae christianae, ex scriptura prophetica et apostolica demonsrtati*, in *Opera Theologica*, 2 vols. (Amsterdam, 1684); Johannes Cocceius, *Aphorismi per universam theologiam breviores*, and *Aphorismi per universam theologiam prolixiores*, in *Opera omnia theologica, exegetica, didactica, polemica, philologica*, 12 vols. (Amsterdam, 1701–1706), 7:3–16 and 17–38, respectively. And see Donald W. Sinnema, "Antoine De Chandieu's Call for a Scholastic Reformed Theology (1580)," in *Later Calvinism: International Perspectives*, ed. W. Fred Graham (Kirksville: Sixteenth Century Journal Publishers, 1994), 176–79; *PRRD*, 1:76, 297–98.

Neither of these *principia* were understood as propositions or axioms from which doctrine could be deduced. Rather, each in its own way is a *sine qua non* of Christian theology: Christian theology could not exist without God, its essential foundation, and it could not be known apart from the special revelation provided in Holy Scripture, its cognitive foundation.[30] Now, of course, the Protestant scholastics did develop doctrinal expositions of these two *principia* and place them at the beginning of their theological systems, usually placing the *locus de Scriptura Sacra* second in order after a prolegomenon and the *locus de Deo* third.[31] Neither of these doctrinal *loci* was, moreover, deduced from a single principle; rather both were composed on the basis of analysis of biblical texts in what might be called the context of a fairly traditional churchly exegesis and of an equally traditional Christian philosophical background.

In the latter sense, according to which *principia* are identified as the *axiomata* or *aphorismi* on which arguments are based, the Reformed orthodox assume that these basic statements are available either from

---

30. Cf. Johannes Wollebius, *Compendium theologiae christianae* (Basel, 1626), I.iii with Johannes Hoornbeeck, *Antisocinianismus*, I.i.1, in *Summa controversiarum religionis, cum infidelibus, haereticis, schismaticis* (Utrecht, 1653); and *PRRD*, 1:295–304.

31. Thus, e.g., Amandus Polanus von Polansdorf, *Syntagma theologiae christianae* (2 pts., quarto, Hainau, 1609; folio, Geneva, 1617); Samuel Maresius, *Collegium theologicum sive systema breve universae theologiae comprehensum octodecim disputationibus* (Groningen, 1645); Johannes Cocceius, *Summa theologiae ex Scriptura repetita* (Amsterdam, 1665); Franciscus Turretinus, *Institutio theologiae elencticae*, 3 vols. (Geneva, 1679–85); Petrus van Mastricht, *Theoretico-practica theologia* (Utrecht, 1714). It is important to note that, contrary to much received opinion, Cocceius' actual system of doctrine, the *Summa theologiae*, proceeds in the same manner as the "scholastic" theologies of his opponents, beginnning with definitions of theology, moving on to a *locus de Scriptura* and then to a *locus de Deo*. It is certainly a "covenant theology" given its massive emphasis on the historically-ordered series of covenantal dispensations, but it also follows the typical Reformed scholastic usage in its extensive discussion of the divine essence and attributes and in its doctrine of predestination. It is, thus, quite anachronistic to pose this presumed covenantal, biblical theology against scholastic orthodox dogmatics: see Willem J. van Asselt, *Amicitia Dei: een Onderzoek naar de Structuur van de Theologie van Johannes Coccejus, 1603–1669* (Ede: Grafische Vormgeving, 1988); and idem, "The Doctrine of the Abrogations in the Federal Theology of Johannes Cocceius" in *CTJ* 29/1 (April, 1994): 101–16; contra the much-cited Charles S. McCoy, "The Covenant Theology of Johannes Cocceius" (Ph.D. Dissertation, Yale University, 1956); idem, "Johannes Cocceius: Federal Theologian," in *Scottish Journal of Theology*, XVI (1963): 352–70; and more recently, Charles S. McCoy, and J. Wayne Baker, *Fountainhead of Federalism: Heinrich Bullinger and the Covenantal Tradition* (Louisville, KY: Westminster/John Knox Press, 1991).

revelation or from reason and, in the former case, are found either as express statements in Scripture or as statements constructed on the basis of the biblical revelation.[32] Even so, Cocceius could write short synopses of theology entitled *Aphorismi per universam theologiam*.[33] From this perspective, the *principia* or *axiomata* of theology are as numerous as the sub-points of the various *loci* of the theological system, and it was never a matter of deducing an entire theology from any particular one of them, rather the theologian's task was to use each of them as the basis for arguing and/or developing the details of a given topic.[34] The identification of *axiomata*, therefore, points to yet another characteristic of the Protestant scholastic theology, the concern for method and order.

The method and order of these theologies, whether they fell within the bounds of what the sixteenth or seventeenth century would have deemed "scholastic," was defined by the use of biblically-derived *loci* and their arrangement in a suitable order. As might also be said of the Middle Ages, the primary text of sixteenth and seventeenth-century Protestant scholastic theology was most certainly the Bible. The work of constructing dogmatic theology presumed the task of exegesis, as perhaps most notably instanced by Van Mastricht's *Theoretico-practica theologia* (1714) in which each theological *locus* began with a sustained exegesis of text in the original language and the basis for further dogmatic, polemical, and practical discussion.[35] Here too, we see a significant continuity in method with the Reformation, inasmuch as the task of finding a proper order for biblically-derived theological *loci* and for doctrinal disputations was outlined for Protestantism by Melanchthon and followed out not only in his own *Loci communes* but also in the doctrinal works of Calvin, Musculus, and Hyperius. One might even argue that Melanchthon's humanistic view of the *loci* and the right *methodus* or *ordo* lay at the heart of Protestant orthodox dogmatics.

The task of the dogmatic theologian, throughout the sixteenth and seventeenth centuries, consisted in the identification and elicitation of

---

32. Thus, *Westminster Confession*, I.vi, vii, ix.

33. Cf. Cocceius, *Aphorismi per universam theologiam breviores*, in *Opera*, 7:3–16; and idem, *Aphorismi per universam theologiam prolixiores*, in *Opera*, 7:17–38.

34. Cf. Donald W. Sinnema, "Antoine De Chandieu's Call for a Scholastic Reformed Theology (1580)," in *Later Calvinism: International Perspectives*, ed. W. Fred Graham (Kirksville, MO: Sixteenth Century Journal Publishers, 1994): 176–79.

35. For further description of Van Mastricht's work, see Richard A. Muller, "Giving Direction to Theology: the Scholastic Dimension," in *Journal of the Evangelical Theological Society* 28/2 (June, 1985): 183–93.

the basic theological topics or *loci* from the text of Scripture, the arrangement of these *loci* in a suitable order, and the explication of their contents in terms of the implications of the biblical text, the traditionary development of the doctrine (with specific recourse to the patristic materials),[36] and the contemporary issues and adversaries of orthodoxy. Given the grounding of Protestant "scholastic" theology in Scripture and their specific limitation of the role of reason to an instrumental function,[37] it should come as no surprise that the reputed "Aristotelianism" of the Protestant scholastics was not a matter of wholesale appropriation. Rather their Aristotelianism was the modified Aristotelianism of the scholastic tradition which excluded such features of Aristotle's philosophy as the eternity of the world and the finitude of God, and which had, in addition, been filtered through the debates of the Reformation and Renaissance.[38]

The usual *methodus* or "way through" the topics was the so-called "synthetic" order which began with first causes, proceeded to examine means, and concluded with final causes or goals. This model, however, was not a matter of logical deduction: as Paul Helm has pointed out this would be to confuse "a logically necessary condition, consistency, with a logically sufficient condition, deducibility."[39] The doctrines of creation and redemption were not, for example, inferred from the essence and attributes of God. Rather, they were set forth because they were understood to be biblical teachings or, indeed, doctrinal *loci* drawn from Scripture—and placed after the doctrine of God inasmuch as God is

---

36. See Irena Backus, "The Fathers in Calvinist Orthodoxy: Partistic Scholarship" in Backus, ed., *The Reception of the Church Fathers in the West: From the Carolingians to the Maurists*, 2 vols. (Leiden: Brill, 1997), 2:839–66; and E. P. Meijering, "The Fathers in Calvinist Orthodoxy: Systematic Theology," in ibid., 2:867–88.

37. Cf. the discussion in Muller, *PRRD*, 1:236–49.

38. See here *The Cambridge History of Renaissance Philosophy*, ed. Charles B. Schmitt, et al. (Cambridge and New York: Cambridge University Press, 1988), and Donald W. Sinnema, "Aristotle and Early Reformed Orthodoxy: Moments of Accommodation and Antithesis," in *Christianity and the Clasics: The Acceptance of a Heritage*, ed. Wendy Helleman (Lanham, MD: University Press of America, 1990): 119–48; Leroy E. Loemker, "Leibniz and the Herborn Encyclopedists," in *Struggle for Synthesis: The Seventeenth Century Background of Leibniz's Synthesis of Order and Freedom* (Cambridge, Mass.: Harvard University Press, 1972): 276–77; and Martin I. Klauber, "Reason, Revelation, and Cartesianism: Louis Tronchin and Enlightened Orthodoxy in Late Seventeenth-Century Geneva," in *Church History* 59 (1990): 326–39.

39. Paul Helm, "Calvin (and Zwingli) on Divine Providence," in *CTJ* 29/2 (1994): 391.

prior to both as the necessary condition for any creation or redemption. The standard order of Reformed orthodox theology, moreover, that begins with God, moves on to creation, human nature, the fall, sin, covenant, Christ, the order of salvation, the church, and the last things, is fundamentally reflective of the canonical order of the biblical narrative which, on the assumption of God, moves to creation, through the history of sin and redemption, to the last things.

Something must be said, in addition, concerning the larger task of the Protestant scholastic theologian. The school-theology of the late sixteenth and the seventeenth century was, in marked contrast to its rumored rationalism, highly biblical and exegetical. This point has already been available to us from consideration of the foundation of the *locus* method of theological formulation, but it is worth drawing out into the broader context of the Protestant theological faculty, in which biblical studies occupied so prominent a place. Over against, moreover, the often-heard modern objection that this was a purely dogmatic biblicism for the sake of theological system, we can only note here that the era of Protestant orthodoxy was an age of vast linguistic and textual expertise on the part of theologians: it was not only the age of Protestant scholastic theological system, it was also the age of the great polyglot Bibles and of the beginnings of Christian targumic and talmudic study. Many of the systematic or dogmatic theologians of the era—perhaps most notably Voetius and Witsius—were skilled not only in the basic biblical languages, Greek and Hebrew, but also in the ancient cognate tongues, Aramaic, and Syriac.[40]

V. By Way of Conclusion: The Sources, Antecedents, and Resultant Character of Protestant Scholasticism

Having offered some fairly contextualized definition of the phenomenon of Protestant scholasticism, we may finally provide some account of its sources and antecedents. The older scholarship tended to identify two grounds for the rise of Protestant scholasticism—the outward, pragmatic need for defense of Protestant doctrine in the face of polemic and the more inward, positive concern for the systematic development of ideas.[41]

40. On Voetius, see: Arnoldus Cornelis Duker, *Gisbertus Voetius*, 3 vols. (Leiden: Brill, 1897–1914); and Jan Anthony Cramer, *De theologische faculteit de Utrecht ten tijde van Voetius* (Utrecht: Kemink, 1932); on Witsius see J. van Genderen, *Herman Witsius: bijdrage tot de kennis der gereformeerde theologie* (s'Gravenhage: Guido de Bres, 1953).
41. Thus, Ernst Troeltsch, *Vernunft und Offenbarung bei Johann Gerhard und*

Whereas there is some truth in this view, it remains, like the definition of Protestant scholasticism cited at the outset, far too immersed in theological concerns and far too little based on examination of the historical context of the phenomenon. Certainly, Protestant orthodoxy felt the need to answer the polemics of a highly developed Roman Catholic scholastic theology. The careful critique leveled by Bellarmine, for example, resulted in a demonstrable refinement of Protestant orthodox theology and, as one aspect of the refinement, an explicit recourse to the older scholastic tradition and its theological distinctions.

The claim of an inner logic of systematic development, however, founders on the central dogma theory that spawned it. In the absence of any identifiable inner dogmatic principles on which to base the development, it becomes quite difficult to claim it. What is more, the development of Protestant scholasticism did not bring about the creation of a wide variety of new doctrinal concepts: the basic topics of the Reformed orthodox theologies remained the same as the basic topics of the medieval summas and commentaries on Lombard and as the basic topics of the theologies of Reformation era codifiers like Calvin, Vermigli, Musculus and Bullinger. What might be called "new" doctrinal topics, like the covenant of nature or works, the covenant of grace, and the *pactum salutis*, arose as much out of exegetical considerations as out of any inner logic of system.

In addition, there were forces at work in the development of scholastic Protestantism other than these purely doctrinal pressures. Much of the development of Protestant scholasticism and/or orthodoxy can be traced to the varied pressures of institutionalization—varied inasmuch as the institutionalization of Protestantism progressed on several fronts. We must speak, certainly, of the broad process that has been called "confessionalization,"[42] although, I think that the term must be taken beyond its more recent socio-political or cultural usage to include what it once almost exclusively would have indicated, namely the solidification of the confessional standards of the branches of the magisterial Reformation between the time of the Council of Trent and

---

Melanchthon (Göttingen, 1891).

42. See Heinz Schilling, ed., *Die reformierte Konfessionalisierung in Deutschland: das Problem der "Zweiten Reformation": Wissenschaftliches Symposion des Vereins für Reformationsgeschichte 1985* (Gutersloh: Gutersloher Verlagshaus G. Mohn, 1986); and idem, *Civic Calvinism in Northwestern Germany and the Netherlands: Sixteenth to Nineteenth Centuries*, Sixteenth Century Essays & Studies 17 (Kirksville, Mo.: Sixteenth Century Journal Publishers, 1991).

the Synod of Dort. On the more theological side, Protestant scholasticism represents the academic answer to a demand that Christian doctrine be elaborated within the bounds of a body of dogmatic norms, the churchly confessions. In addition, this scholasticism represents a closely defined academic culture of the late Reformation that parallels the socially broader definition of Protestant life and culture that has come to be known as confessionalization. In other words, Protestant scholasticism is, in part, the result of the educational as well as the theological-confessional institutionalization of the Reformation.

Next, the rise of scholastic orthodoxy evidences the increasing interest of Protestant theologians in claiming overtly the catholic past through the incorporation of the larger tradition of the church, both patristic and medieval into the theological and spiritual thought-forms of Protestantism. It is not a matter of accident that the invention of the term "patrology" to describe a historical and theological sub-discipline came from the Protestant side of early seventeenth-century theological education, just as it ought not to be a great surprise that Protestant academics increasingly looked in an overt and positive way to the theological and philosophical debates of the middle ages for insight into the details and problems of academic theology. And, of course, this process was gradual: the Reformers themselves drew strongly on the church fathers and insisted that the *saniores scholastici* of the middle ages often supported the Protestant cause against Rome. Protestant scholasticism represents a broader and more detailed encounter with and grasp of these materials.

Furthermore, and equally importantly, Protestant scholasticism is the form taken by the academic culture of the Protestant universities in the wake of the development and modification of logic, rhetoric, and philosophy in the fifteenth and early sixteenth centuries.[43] We are not speaking here of a modification specifically related either to the Protestant content of the theology or to the institutionalization of specifically Protestant models in the university, but rather of a late Renaissance development shared by Protestant and Roman Catholic faculties alike. Thus, the method of Protestant scholasticism, with its concentration on the exegetical identification of theological *loci*, reflects the impact of the Renaissance, specifically of Agricolan dialectic, on the disciplines of logic and rhetoric as they impinged on the order and

---

43. See William T. Costello, *The Scholastic Curriculum at Early Seventeenth-Century Cambridge* (Cambridge, MA: Harvard University Press, 1958).

arrangement of the various academic disciplines. So too, the philosophical views of the Protestant scholastics reflect not only the older materials examined in the Protestant reassessment of the church's tradition but also the developing Aristotelianism of the late Renaissance: Protestant treatises on metaphysics cite Aquinas, Albert the Great, and Duns Scotus—but they also cite Zabarella and Suàrez.[44]

Finally, scholastic Protestantism was a fundamentally biblical movement that drew both on the principial *sola Scriptura* of the Reformation and on the burgeoning Protestant exegetical tradition for the heart of its theology. The Protestant theologian of the seventeenth century was assumed to be fluent in Latin and highly competent in classical Greek and Hebrew. Many of the major theologians of the era added to this linguistic paraphernalia a fair ability in the ancient cognate languages, Aramaic and Syriac. The scholastic era of Protestantism produced massive examination of the biblical text and the ancient versions and paraphrases, major lexical efforts, and significant philological advance: the humanist model triumphed in the scholastic context. This linguistic and exegetical ability, moreover, was far more closely tied to the dogmatic task by the scholastic orthodox of the seventeenth century than it has been since that time. Discussions of the era have often missed this point, inasmuch as they have paid even less attention to the so-called "pre-critical" exegesis of the era than they have to the dogmatic theology itself.

In sum, the sources and antecedents of Protestant scholasticism or scholastic orthodoxy include the theology, philosophy, logic, rhetoric, and general academic culture of the later middle ages, Renaissance, and Reformation. If it is inconceivable to imagine Protestant scholasticism without the antecedents of Reformation Protestantism and medieval scholasticism, it is also quite inconceivable to imagine it apart from the Renaissance, indeed, the humanistic development of logic and rhetoric and the humanistic emphasis on classical languages and philology. The resultant phenomenon, Protestant scholasticism, was no mere recrudescence of medieval categories, nor was it a phenomenon necessarily characterized by commitment to particular elements of

---

44. Cf. Karl Eschweiler, "Die Philosophie der spanischen Spätscholastik auf dem deutschen Universitäten des siebzehnten Jahrhunderts," in H. Finke, ed., *Gesammelte Aufsätze zur Kulturgeschichte Spaniens* (Münster: Aschendorff, 1928) and Ernst Lewalter, *Spanisch-jesuitisch und deutsch-lutherische Metaphysik des 17. Jahrhunderts* (Hamburg, 1935; repr. Darmstadt: Wissenschaftliche Buchgesellschaft, 1968).

Aristotelian philosophy or to a particular formulation of the doctrine of predestination. And, most certainly, it was not a theological system developed on the basis of the notion of a single "central dogma." Rather it was the academic theology of the later sixteenth and seventeenth-century Protestant universities—and whatever virtues or faults it may have been identified as embodying by its practitioners and critics in the seventeenth century were the faults and virtues of the academic culture of the age.

2

Wittenberga contra Scholasticos

Cornelis Augustijn

In what follows, I shall address the question of how the reformers thought about scholasticism during the period before Calvin's first activity as a theologian. For this purpose, I have chosen the Wittenberg theologians, leaving the Swiss theologians out of consideration. I have given my contribution the programmatic heading *Wittenberga contra scholasticos*.

It is essential to provide some clarification of both the terms that have now been mentioned. I shall limit *Wittenberga* biographically to Luther and Melanchthon, and chronologically to the period before 1536. These limitations are well justified. It would naturally have been possible to include Karlstadt as well, but the basic picture would not have been greatly changed by that. However, Melanchthon, next to Luther, cannot be left out of account. He represents a somewhat different approach to scholasticism than that of Luther. I limit myself to the first twenty years of the reformation, partly because I want to highlight the background to Calvin's views on scholasticism. Furthermore, neither in the case of Luther, nor in that of Melanchthon, do I notice any change at a later time. As far as the term "scholastics" is concerned, it is actually quite simple. I have in mind the theology and theologians of the universities from around the year 1000 until the time of Luther and Melanchthon. I have, therefore, excluded monastic theology and its representatives. I am, furthermore, going to be just as unfair to the scholastics as were Luther and Melanchthon; the account of their opinion of scholasticism, rather than the question of what scholasticism itself was, will take priority.

The structure of my paper has, in this way, already been hinted at. First, I shall treat Luther's view of scholasticism, then Melanchthon and the new way of doing theology, after which I shall comment on the background to Melanchthon's views, and then close by drawing some conclusions.

I. Luther and Scholasticism

The most important sources for this section are Luther's *Disputatio contra scholasticam theologiam* [1] of September 1517, the *Heidelberg Disputation* [2] of April 1518, and some letters written to Georg Spalatinus during those months. [3] The Danish theologian Leif Grane has written an important book on this material. [4]

During this period, in the months during which the famous ninety-five theses originated, Luther concerned himself mainly with the question of how one should properly engage in theologizing. This is for him a question of method; he is in search of a *modus loquendi theologicus* for doing theology. However, he is not primarily interested in theological methodology as such. He continually poses the question of how it is possible that, in terms of content, theology could have deteriorated so drastically during the preceding centuries. Not only in the *Disputation against Scholastic Theology*, but certainly there in particular, his answer exhibits the character of a veritable litany. Many theses end with *contra scholasticos, contra omnes scholasticos, contra Gabrielem*; in the latter phrase Gabriel Biel is to be understood as the embodiment of all the evil done by the scholastics.

Which evil does he have in mind? Stated briefly: through the immense impact of Aristotelianism on scholastic theology, theology has deteriorated into anthropology. The right theology would see the human being primarily as a sinner; scholastic theology takes its point of departure in Aristotle's view of humanity—that is, in the natural endowment of human nature. It then proceeds to pose the question of how much of the salvation of humanity is to be ascribed to the grace of God. Grace, and therefore God Himself, has thereby become secondary—they complete that which is lacking in the natural abilities of humanity. Luther's black sheep is the *facere quod in se est*. "Whoever does what lies within his ability, and believes that he does something good, does not believe that he is nothing at all, and does not despair of his own

---

1. D. Martin Luther's *Werke. Kritische Gesam(m)tausgabe* (Weimar, 1883–), 1:221–28, henceforth abbreviated WA; cf. Melanchthon's *Werke in Auswahl*, ed. Robert Stupperich, (Gütersloh, 1951–1975), 1:163–72, henceforth abbreviated StA.

2. WA 1:221–28; cf. StA 1:186–218.

3. Especially the letter of 22 February 1518; D. Martin Luther's *Werke. Kritische Gesamtausgabe. Briefwechsel* (Weimar 1930–), 1, No.61, henceforth abbreviated WA.B.

4. Leif Grane, *Modus loquendi theologicus. Luthers Kampf um die Erneuerung der Theologie (1515–1518)*, Acta Theologica Danica 12 (Leiden, 1975).

strength, yes he imagines so much, that he strives with his own strength towards grace."[5] And somewhat more pronounced: "The person who intends to acquire grace by doing what lies within his power, heaps sin upon sin, thereby becoming doubly guilty."[6] Luther answers the objection that, with this theology, he only drives human beings to despair, with the statement: "To say that we are nothing, and that we still sin, even when we do what is in our power, does not mean that one drives humanity to despair, but that one drives them to the grace of our Lord Jesus Christ."[7] In 1536, in his *Disputatio de homine*, Luther still draws a contrast between the two views of human nature. Philosophy views the human being as "animal rationale," a being endowed with reason, and reason always strives for what is highest. Theology sees him as a "creature of God" who, since the fall, is subject to the power of the devil, also with regard to his reason, which is, after all, the very best element in human nature.[8]

This attack on the Aristotelian view of human nature in scholasticism is accompanied, in Heidelberg, with an attack on the view of God which is characteristic of scholasticism. The *theologus gloriae* seeks to gain knowledge of God's wisdom, righteousness, goodness, and everything that is invisible in God, his glory and majesty, from created reality. The *theologus crucis* dares to seek knowledge of God in the suffering, in the humiliation and shame of the cross, in Christ, that is.[9] Here lies the origin of Luther's notion of the hidden God, the God who is to be found only in the form of the suffering Christ. Summarized in one sentence: "Therefore the true theology and knowledge of God is to be found in the crucified Christ."[10]

With both of these disputations we stand at the beginning of the reformation. It is clear that this beginning is characterized by a relentless attack on scholasticism. The attack is aimed at the content of

5. Luther, *Disputatio Heidelbergae habita*, thesis 18, probatio; WA 1:361, 28–30; cf. StA 1:207, 21–24.

6. Luther, *Disputatio Heidelbergae*, thesis 16, WA 1:360, 25–26; cf. StA 1:206, 13–14.

7. Luther, *Disputatio Heidelbergae*, thesis 17, probatio; WA 1:361, 19–21; cf. StA 1:207, 13–15.

8. Luther, *Disputatio de homine*, WA 39[I]:174–80; cf. StA 5:126–33, especially thesis 1, 4, 21, 22, 28; cf. the literature referred to in StA, especially the works of G. Ebeling.

9. Luther, *Disputatio Heidelbergae*, thesis 19–21 with probationes; WA 1:361, 31–362, 33; cf. StA 1:207, 25–209, 5.

10. Luther, *Disputatio Heidelbergae*, thesis 20, probatio; WA 1:362, 18–19; cf. StA 1:208, 17.

scholasticism, not at its form, and only occasionally at its method. This content concerns the doctrine of sin and grace, more specifically, it is aimed against any attempt to formulate a Pelagian understanding of salvation.

Method is not left out of consideration altogether. Of the one hundred theses of the *Disputatio contra scholasticam theologiam*, five deal with the scholastic method. They are aimed against Aristotle, and against the use of logic in theology. The harshest of the theses is certainly: "The statement that a theologian, who is not a logician, is a monstrous heretic, is itself monstrous and heretical."[11] I shall return to the question of what is precisely meant here by a "logician," but it does not require much argument to establish that what is being referred to is the logic and dialectics deriving from Aristotle, as it had been developed in scholasticism, and applied in the exegesis of the Bible. Luther is convinced that, when this method is applied, anything at all can be defended with an appeal to the Bible, even the most absurd claim. In the *Resolutiones*, also of 1518, he gives a fine example, and during the course of the exposition, he exclaims: "And then I am not even considering the grammar. That alone could have taught them that their view could not be supported with this biblical statement. But they would rather follow the new dialectic than the true grammar."[12]

Half a year earlier, Spalatinus had enquired from Luther whether he regarded dialectics as necessary, or at least useful, for theology. Luther's answer[13] was unambiguous: unqualifiedly harmful! The trouble is that dialectics uses the same words in a different way from theology and the Bible. Just like the jurist, the theologian may not "speak without a text."[14] Just as the claims of the jurist have value only insofar as he can appeal to a legal text, the claims of a theologian are significant only insofar as he can appeal to a biblical statement. Scholastic theology transgresses this rule: even when it uses biblical statements, it makes the Bible say whatever it wishes it to say, for its language is forced into the categories

---

11. Luther, *Disputatio contra scholasticam theologiam*, thesis 45 (47); WA 1:226, 17–18; cf. StA 1:169, 7–8.

12. Luther, *Resolutiones disputationum de indulgentiarum virtute*, conclusio 26; WA 1:577, 36–38; cf. Grane, *Modus loquendi theologicus*, 176.

13. Luther to Spalatinus, 22 February 1518; WA.B 1:No. 61, 10–11; 24–25; cf. Grane, *Modus loquendi theologicus*, 141–43.

14. Luther to the bishop of Brandenburg, [13 February 1518]; WA.B 1, No. 58, 29–30.

of dialectics. The conceptual tools of the logician then dominate the language of the Bible. Luther regards as sufficient what he calls "the innate dialectic," by which one compares statements of faith to one another, thus arriving at truth.[15]

In the introduction to the *Resolutiones*, Luther refers to the public statement which was customary in academic theological disputations, and which he now repeats. He does not wish to teach or defend anything which cannot be inferred, first from Holy Scripture, then from the church fathers accepted by the western church and from the *Corpus iuris canonici*.[16] However, the familiar words acquire a new meaning. Quoting is not sufficient, grammar must be the judge of the meaning of a statement. The contrast with the scholastic practice of theology is sharp. The Bible ought to be treated primarily just like any other literary work we have inherited.

Does this mean that Luther, in his opposition to scholastic theology and its method, takes the side of the humanists? He was of course familiar with them.[17] It is known that he had used Erasmus' *Annotations to the New Testament* in his lectures soon after its appearance. Luther's own *Commentary on the letter to the Galatians* of 1519 refers often, and repeatedly positively, to Erasmus' *Annotations*, although one should keep in mind that this partly had a political background. Luther also studied and used *Lefèvre d'Etaples*. Yet, undeniably, Luther's use and exegesis of the Bible is very different from that of the biblical humanists.

I shall give one example. In *De servo arbitrio* Luther deals, among others things, with the Bible texts put forward by Erasmus in support of a certain degree of human freedom of choice. Erasmus had begun by letting his prime witness, Jesus Sirach 15, speak for itself extensively: "Since the beginning, when He (God) made man, He has subjected man to his own decisions. If you wish to observe the commandments, they will preserve you. Before man lies life and death, and whatever man desires will be given to him."[18] Luther explained that the first sentence, "God has

---

15. Luther to Spalatinus, 22 February 1518; WA.B 1, No. 61, 16.

16. Luther, *Resolutiones disputationum de indulgentiarum virtute*; WA 1:529, 33–530, 3.

17. See for the following Cornelis Augustijn, "Erasmus im Galaterbriefkommentar Luthers von 1519," in Cornelis Augustijn, *Erasmus. Der Humanist als Theologe und Kirchenreformer*, Studies in Medieval and Reformation Thought 59 (Leiden, New York, Cologne, 1996), 53–54.

18. Erasmus, *De libero arbitrio diatribe*, in *Opera omnia emendatiora et auctiora* 9 (Lugduni Batavorum, 1706), 1221 A-C.

subjected man to his own decisions," meant that God had appointed man as lord over all creatures, and that the second sentence, "if you wish to keep the commandments," was conditional and therefore said nothing about the possibility of man observing the commandment.[19] Such an exegesis is, of course, mistaken. Furthermore, Luther appeals to the dialecticians in order to prove his statement about the meaning of a conditional sentence. He vehemently attacks Erasmus' view that according to normal language usage the statement "if you wish to observe the commandments" would be meaningless if human beings did not have a real freedom of choice. Luther exclaims, "Erasmus apparently measures God's word according to the yardstick of human language usage; oh yes, human reason sits enthroned!"[20] Erasmus did not deserve such an accusation, and it is indeed pointless. It goes to show, however, that Luther does use the kind of dialectic, which he condemns in principle, when it suits him. It is more than a polemical trick.

I have presented this example rather extensively, because it eloquently demonstrates the fact that Luther, in spite of his plea that one should follow the grammar, often acts directly contrary to it, and that he is more bound to the old dialectic than he realizes. Those who are familiar with his work, will know that Luther, not just sometimes, but frequently, deals with the biblical text in a very arbitrary manner.

II. Melanchthon and the New Way of Theologizing

Melanchthon shares Luther's judgement of the content of scholasticism as a theology, which detracts from God's grace, and ascribes to human beings a contribution to the attainment of their salvation. The first chapter of the first edition of the *Loci communes* of 1521[21] is crystal clear. It deals with "the powers of man and his free will," is extensive in comparison to the other chapters, and exhibits agreement with Luther's view. It is unnecessary to examine it in any more detail here.

Melanchthon's statements about the method of systematic theology give a different impression. On this topic he has explicit views of his own, much more consistent than is the case with Luther, he adopts a new way

19. Luther, *De servo arbitrio*; WA 18:671, 19–674, 12.
20. Luther, *De servo arbitrio*; WA 18:673, 6–7, 16–18; 674, 13.
21. Melanchthon, *Loci communes rerum theologicarum* (1521) in *Corpus Reformatorum, Philippi Melanthonis Opera quae supersunt omnia*, Karl Bretschneider and Heinrich Bindseil ed., 28 vols. (Halle: A. Schwetschke and Sons, 1834–1860), henceforth abbreviated CR, 21:86–97; cf. StA 2/1:21–31.

of theologizing, and argues in support of it. He does the latter especially in the *Loci communes*. I shall use the revised edition of 1535,[22] not only to avoid transgressing my time limit, but also because this edition deals clearly and explicitly with questions of method, more so than the introduction of the 1559 edition.

The title of the book already draws the attention: *loci communes*, general concepts. The term *locus* derives from Latin rhetoric, especially from Cicero and Quintillian, and can have different meanings: a certain subject which is dealt with, but also the grounds on which a claim rests.[23] Already in the first sentence, Melanchthon indicates its importance:

> In education it is very useful to divide the main topics into a logical sequence, to put them together into a whole, and to impress them on the memory. Therefore I have also brought together the most important subjects of Christian teaching that can, in my view, make the greatest contribution to the nurture of faith, and that are useful in the exercises of the pious, that ought, furthermore, to be present in the churches and to be emphasized in the sermons.[24]

It should now be clear what Melanchthon has in mind, the *loci* are the important subjects that ought to be dealt with. In many places he states the demand that they must be related to "pietas."[25] In the above quotation, I have translated this word with "faith"; this is an unsatisfactory translation, but piety or some such word would have caused even more misunderstanding. What Melanchthon has in mind is doctrine insofar as it is directly relevant to people.

It is now time to pay some special attention to Melanchthon's

22. Melanchthon, *Loci communes theologici* (1535); the preface consists of a letter to Henry VIII, and a piece addressed "piis et studiosis scholasticis," thereafter the introduction to the *loci*; CR 21:333–49.

23. See for this S. Wiedenhofer, *Formalstrukturen humanistischer und reformatorischer Theologie bei Philipp Melanchthon*, 2 vols., Regensburger Studien zur Theologie 2 (Bern, Frankfurt M., Munich, 1976), 1:373–76.

24. Melanchthon, *Loci communes theologici*; CR 21:333. I give this central quotation in Latin: "Cum in docendo magnopere prosit, tenere summas rerum ordine et ratione distributas et in methodum contractas, collegi et ego praecipuos locos doctrinae christianae eosque quos arbitrabar maxime ad pietatem alendam conducere et in vita et in exercitiis piorum usum habere, denique qui extare in ecclesiis et in concionibus inculcari maxime debent."

25. Melanchthon, *Loci communes theologici*, CR 21:334: "locos ad pietatem necessarios"

statement that the main topics must be "put together into a whole." Here we have a second keyword. In Latin, the term *methodus* is used as a term which can be rendered as "concise summary," or "short route to arrive at knowledge as fast as possible."[26] In his own definition, Melanchthon especially emphasizes the order that is imposed upon it namely that it is essential to grasp the beginning, continuation, and end.[27]

I summarize. In the *Loci*, Melanchthon wishes to summarize the most important subjects of Christian doctrine in an ordered sequence. The emphasis is on those subjects that are directly relevant to living faith.

Melanchthon is convinced that, in doing so, he is following in the footsteps of many others. Paul in the letter to the Romans, Origen's *De principiis*, Cyprian, the confessions of the early church, John of Damascus in the eastern church, Peter Lombard in the western church, each of them had the same purpose in mind.[28] Yet Scripture precedes all these. "The best summary is provided," according to Melanchthon, "by the prophetic and apostolic books." They provide all the important constituents of the doctrine, and the historical books provide examples of what is taught in the biblical *loci*.[29] Why, then, is something else still required next to these? "Because most of these things have disappeared through the traditions of the clergy and the new kind of doctrine of the monks, the studies of the church must be called back to the sources, the dirt must be wiped from the holy writ, and the direction shown, as it were. Through this teaching, the simple ones will find it easier to recognize the heavenly doctrine, which is presented to us in the writings of the apostles and prophets."[30] That is, God wants the voice, which shows the way to the heavenly writings, to be heard in the church. The old ideal, expressed anew by the biblical humanists, is clearly discernible here: back to the source, to scripture.

It is in this context that Melanchthon also brings scholasticism into the picture. We are being accused, says Melanchthon, of deviating from the church, while in fact we identify wholeheartedly with the *consensus catholicae ecclesiae*, with everything that the church has taught unanimously throughout the ages. But we do not want to have anything to do with that bunch of innovators, who "have added labyrinths of

26. See Wiedenhofer, *Melanchthon*, 368–70.
27. Melanchthon, *Loci communes theologici*, CR 21:341, 347.
28. Melanchthon, *Loci communes theologici*, CR 21:333–34.
29. Melanchthon, *Loci communes theologici*, CR 21:341.
30. Melanchthon, *Loci communes theologici*, CR 21:341.

questions to Peter Lombard. Therein they have mixed philosophy and gospel with each other in a foolish manner, and at the same time they have defended the superstition and veneration of images accepted by the people."[31] The summary of everything Thomas Aquinas, and others like him, have perpetrated does not mix words: justification through faith is destroyed; no distinction is made between law and gospel; one evil follows another: the doctrine of penance, the ceremonies of the monks, celibacy, the worship of the eucharistic bread, the veneration of the saints.[32]

What demand does Melanchton insist on as an antidote? He is in favor of a *liberalis eruditio*, that is a good education in the *artes liberales*, including philosophy. Such an education not only gives glory to the church, but it even makes the doctrine more transparent. Nothing is worse than the "uncivilized and barbaric theology of the anabaptists."[33] Development contributes not only to sound judgement and good education, but also to a good way of life.[34] On the other hand, he also warns strongly against the confusion between philosophy and theology; there is an enormous difference between the two.[35]

But let us return to the *Loci*, as Melanchthon would like to see them. The most important, but also the most difficult, is to explicate the doctrine *dextre et perspicue*,[36] that is: in a suitable, appropriate and clear way. Especially the demand of *perspicuitas* is stated repeatedly.[37] The following statement is a shining example: "The pursuit of clarity of expression is useful in the whole of life, and is furthermore a sign of sincerity and honesty."[38] Close to this ideal is that of the *diligentia*, that is precision, and the *simplicitas*, simplicity. "I myself," writes Melanchthon, "have always exerted myself in order to speak *appropriately and rightly in setting forth the dogmas*."[39] He abhors *perplexa, paradoxa, absurda*;[40] it bewilders the conscience, and nothing is learnt from it. If one reflects on these demands, one realizes how much Melanchthon owes to Cicero and

31. Melanchthon, *Loci communes theologici*, CR 21:342.
32. Melanchthon, *Loci communes theologici*, CR 21:343.
33. Melanchthon, *Loci communes theologici*, CR 21:338.
34. Melanchthon, *Loci communes theologici*, CR 21:338.
35. Melanchthon, *Loci communes theologici*, CR 21:347.
36. Melanchthon, *Loci communes theologici*, CR 21:341.
37. Melanchthon, *Loci communes theologici*, CR 21:335, 337, 341, 346.
38. Melanchthon, *Loci communes theologici*, CR 21:346.
39. Melanchthon, *Loci communes theologici*, CR 21:346.
40. Melanchthon, *Loci communes theologici*, CR 21:333.

Quintillian. They remain his prime examples. Could one not also say: Thus speaks the born schoolmaster, who knows exactly what is essential in education? There is an interesting passage, in which he says that it would be splendid if *splendor et lumen orationis*, that is magnificent, decorative language, were also added, just as the images of Phidias exhibit dignity and eminence. He himself is no more, however, than a potter who produces small pots; said without imagery: he does not pursue charming eloquence.[41] Thus speaks the schoolmaster, but also the man who knows what is important in church. Repeatedly he even says explicitly that the church would be well advised to compile a concise summary of the doctrine, as the church had often done in antiquity.[42] But in the final analysis, he is first of all a man of the school. Twice he speaks of the *militia scholastica*,[43] the school as a kind of military service. He calls upon the scholastics—here of course meant in the sense of: the people of the school, of education—to guard the post to which God has assigned them.

I shall now offer an evaluation. Luther's famous saying, that the *Loci* deserve to be added to the canon, is certainly very Lutheran. But it is just as certainly true that, with this explication, and its further outworking in the *Loci communes* itself, we stand at the dawn of a new system of practicing systematic theology. Those who have read some sections from Aquinas, for example, would immediately note the difference. There the one question leads to the next, and the questions are solved by the system, in itself clear, of the *quaestio*, in which the *auctoritates* are placed over against one another, and a conclusion is finally drawn. That means that the tree branches out increasingly wide, for one always has to enter into discussion with one's predecessors. Even regardless of the content, Melanchthon wants to know nothing of this system of theologizing. He wants to refer directly to the Bible. A splendid example is offered by the beginning of the *Loci* in the second edition, where de *Deo* is treated. In the very first sentence Melanchthon reminds the reader of Christ's warning. When Thomas poses the most difficult question of all, that of the nature of God, "Christ calls him away from an investigation into the secret nature" and points to himself: whoever sees me, sees the Father.[44]

---

41. Melanchthon, *Loci communes theologici*, CR 21:336–37.
42. Melanchthon, *Loci communes theologici*, CR 21:334–36, 341.
43. Melanchthon, *Loci communes theologici*, CR 21:345, 348.
44. Melanchthon, *Loci communes theologici*, CR 21:351.

III. The Background to Melanchthon's Views

Melanchthon's views concerning the system of *loci* do not stand by themselves. On the one hand, they are embedded in the whole of his philosophy of science and his historical views; on the other, they stand in direct relation to the new scientific method, which had been developing for some decades. I can treat none of these extensively, but I would like to make one comment on it.

Melanchthon has given clear expression to his view in his inaugural oration in Wittenberg in 1518, *De correctione studiorum*.[45] For him the darkest epoch was the period from 1200 onwards. In it he sees three fatal developments.[46] The first is the brutal manner of commenting and philosophizing, the second is that thereby the personal and ecclesiastical life, and the studies, are deformed. A third is the continual strife between the adherents of the different schools. The deformation of the studies also affected grammar and dialectics or rhetoric. Stated briefly, this means that he lays the blame for all evils at the door of scholasticism. Now, however, the tide has turned, now is the time of the *renascentes litterae*, the revival of letters. That means for the students of Wittenberg: *fontes ipsos artium ex optimis auctoribus hauritis*: you derive the sciences from the sources, the best authors.[47] This is indeed the turnabout of scientific method in the 16th century stated as briefly as possible. For the natural sciences the new method did not hold much promise, for theology it was a different matter. Melanchthon briefly offers a new syllabus: knowledge of Greek and Hebrew—for we westerners drink from their wells—, a quick overview of the content of theology, an end to *glossulae, concordantiae, discordantiae*. "But when we come with our heart to the sources, we begin to taste Christ, and his commandment will be clear as the day to us."[48] In this, not only the Bible plays a role however. "We take up Homer, as well as Paul's letter to Titus. Here you will discover how much the unique character of a word contributes to the understanding of the mysteries of the holy teaching, and how great the difference is between exegetes who do, and who do not, know Greek."[49] Such pronouncements show clearly that Melanchthon takes over

---

45. Melanchthon, *De corrigendis adolescentiae studiis*; StA 3:29–42.
46. Melanchthon, *De corrigendis*, StA 3:33, 3–31.
47. Melanchthon, *De corrigendis*, StA 3:38, 19–20.
48. Melanchthon, *De corrigendis*, StA 3:40, 19–21.
49. Melanchthon, *De corrigendis*, StA 3:41, 35–42, 1.

Erasmus' program, and that in a double sense: via the languages to theology, and: true theology is also, in the language of mysticism: tasting Christ. The "via the languages" leads Erasmus to the *loci* method – here meant in the narrower sense of a reasoned concordance—, in which biblical passages, but also old biblical exegetes and passages from non-Christian authors, are incorporated in order to arrive, by means of comparison, at the meaning of obscure passages.

Within this whole, the new scientific method also plays a role. The formalised language of dialectics had evoked strong resistance. Interesting in this regard is the first appearance in 1520 of Juan Luis Vives' invective, *In pseudodialecticos*.[50] It consists, for a great part, of various examples of the absurdities at which the dialectics of the day had arrived. However, there are also passages in which the precise problem is carefully pointed out. "Who does not realise that dialectics is the science, which concerns language? With which language does your dialectics actually deal? French? Spanish? That of the Vandals? Certainly not with Latin. The dialectician should use words and concepts that are familiar to everyone who knows the language in which he speaks."[51] This attack struck home with particular force, since Vives had taught dialectics in Paris for years. Dialectics was closely associated with scholasticism, which used this conceptual apparatus. Vives relates how, during his student days, one of his teachers had warned him: "the better you are as a grammarian, the worse you will be as a dialectician and a theologian."[52] The resistance against this form of dialectics is a struggle against a scientific method, which was regarded by many as outdated. The new theological method propagated by Melanchthon, thus stood in the context of two opposing methods in general.

IV. Some Conclusions

The conclusions following from the foregoing are so self-evident that I shall formulate them very briefly.

The most prominent feature in Luther is his insight that, in scholasticism, Aristotle occupies the most important place. "Aristotle" is for him, in this regard, quite simply the rejection of total dependence on

---

50. Juan Luis Vives, *In Pseudodialecticos. A critical edition*, ed. Charles Fantazzi, Studies in Medieval and Reformation Thought 27 (Leiden, 1979).

51. Vives, *In Pseudodialecticos*, 35, 4, 6–10.

52. See Vives, *In Pseudodialecticos*, 14.

God, an anthropology that takes no account of sin, and a theology that does not look for God in Jesus. He is convinced that dialectics should be no part of a curriculum for theological studies, as he says in his letter to Spalatinus, it is "a game or exercise of childlike souls."[53] He even says: "I used to take account of the doctrines and rules of scholastic theology, and exerted myself to treat scripture and the church fathers according to these. I retreated in shock from a confusion worse than that of the inferno."[54] Such pronouncements do not, however, mean that he positively opted for the new method of theologizing. Many traces of a scholastic mode of theologizing are to be found in his work. Probably one could count him principally among the representatives of a *Frömmigkeitstheologie*. In order to avoid misunderstanding, I must add that I do not, with this qualification, seek to detract in the least from Luther's genius, but rather to emphasize it.

In Melanchthon, the contempt for scholasticism is just as pronounced as in Luther. More so than in Luther however, it fits into the general picture of the course of history in the last few centuries. That is also why "scholasticism" acquires such a broad meaning in his thought; he even puts the blame for the deterioration of values during the preceding three centuries onto "scholasticism." Furthermore, his rejection of scholasticism has a different background. Melanchthon is inspired by the ideal of the humanists, the idea of a *renascentia litterarum* is dear to him. As "a man of the school" he strives for a new mode of theologizing, and the way in which he pictures this is derived from the humanists, especially from Erasmus. This is not to deny that he has wholeheartedly given himself over to Luther's doctrine of sin and grace, and has, in his own way, put in into words in the *Loci*.

---

53. Luther to Spalatinus, 22 February 1518; WA.B 1, No. 61, 11–12.
54. Luther to Spalatinus, 22 February 1518; WA.B 1, No. 61, 44–47.

3

Reformation and Scholasticism

Willem van't Spijker

I. Introduction

The theme of this volume requires of its contributors a twofold limitation in scope, which I would like to introduce as follows. First, I intend to focus on the way in which the Reformation is supposed to have been generally presented within the Reformed tradition. Secondly, I shall limit myself by not going beyond the end of the sixteenth century.[1]

It should be acknowledged at this point that this subject involves certain ecumenical dimensions. In addition to the Reformed, both Lutheran and Roman Catholic theologians used scholasticism as well.[2] We could go even further by claiming that the movement from Reformation to scholasticism as such reflects broad and deep cultural concerns. It would, therefore, be most interesting to trace the line from Reformation, via scholasticism to the eighteenth century, when the movement seems to be swallowed up by pietism and Enlightenment. It would take us too far afield, however, to investigate these aspects of the subject, and so, though we must always keep them in mind, we shall not in this paper address them directly. Our focus here will be simply this: *the Reformation from a Reformed perspective until the beginning of the seventeenth century.*

I would first like to present some lines of historical analysis and then examine theological themes, before concluding with some critical observations.

II. Historical Analysis

Roughly speaking, one can distinguish four short periods in the

---

1. The distinctive marks of reformed scholasticism have been clearly set forth in the preceding chapters.

2. This is implied by the title of the symposium held on May 29, 1997 in Utrecht, from which the present collection of articles is derived: "Reformation and Scholasticism. An ecumenical enterprise?"

development of Reformation theology. The first of reaches as far as the middle of the 1530s, the second one as far as the 1550s, and the third one begins during the time of publication of the Lutheran *Konkordienbuch* (1580). The last period started before the beginning of the seventeenth century and was characterized by a strong Roman Catholic offensive initiated by Bellarminus.

We can deal very briefly with the *first two decades* of the Reformation. They are characterized by a radical reaction against scholastic theology[3] and against the Roman Catholic hierarchy.[4] Both reactions belong together to some extent, as they are both rooted in the rejection of a certain rational and ethical optimism based upon an optimistic view of man.[5]

3. *Disputation against Scholastic Theology,* in *Luther's Works,* Conrad Bergendorff, ed. (Philadelphia: Muhlenberg, 1958), henceforth abbreviated LW, 31:5–16; *Heidelberg Disputation, 1518,* LW 31:37–76; cf. Theses 42ff. in the *Disputation against Scholastic Theology*: "It is an error to maintain that Aristotle's statement concerning happiness does not contradict Catholic doctrine. This in opposition to the doctrine on morals. 43. It is an error to say that no man can become a theologian without Aristotle, This in opposition to common opinion. 44. Indeed, no one can become a theologian unless he becomes one without Aristotle," LW 31:12; W. Link, *Das Ringen Luthers um die Freiheit der Theologie von der Philosophie* (München, 1955); L. Grane, *Contra Gabrielem. Luthers Auseinandersetzung mit Gabriel Biel in der Disputatio Contra Scholasticam Theologiam 1517* (Gyldendal, 1962); L. Grane, *Modus loquendi theologicus. Luthers Kampf um die Erneuerung der Theologie (1515–1518)* (Leiden, 1975); H. A. Oberman, "Headwaters of the Reformation: Initia Lutheri-Initia Reformationis," in *The Dawn of Reformation. Essays in Late Medieval and Early Reformation Thought* (Edinburgh, 1986), 39–83; H. N. Hagoort, *Wijsheid van het vlees. Over 97 onbekende stellingen van Maarten Luther* (Gouda, 1992); K. H. Zur Mühlen, "Luthers Kritik am scholastischen Aristotelismus in der 25. These der Heidelberger Disputation von 1518," in *Reformatorisches Profil. Studien zum Weg Martin Luthers und der Reformation* (Göttingen, 1995), S. 40–65; E. G. Schwiebert, *The Reformation,* Vol. II: *The Reformation as a University Movement* (Minneapolis, 1996).

4. A. Darquennes, *De Juridische Structuur van de Kerk volgens Sint Thomas van Aquino* (Leuven, 1949). Luther's opposition to this ecclesiastical structure in the Roman Catholic Hierarchy: *An den christlichen Adel deutscher Nation von des christlichen Standes Besserung* (1520), in *Luthers Werke. Kritische Gesamtausgabe [Schriften],* henceforth abbreviated WA, 6:404–65; *Von den Papsttum zu Rom wider den hochberühmten Romanisten zu Leipzig,* (1520), WA 5:285–324. Cf. S. H. Hendrix, *Ecclesia in Via. Ecclesiological Developments in the Medieval Psalms Exegesis and the Dictata super Psalterium (1513–1515) of Martin Luther* (Leiden, 1974); K. Hammann, *Ecclesia spiritualis. Luthers Kirchenverständnis in den Kontroversen mit Augustin Alveldt und Ambrosius Catharinus* (Göttingen, 1989); G. Neebe, *Apostolische Kirche. Grundunterscheidungen an Luthers Kirchenbegriff unter besonderer Berücksichtigung seiner Lehre von den notae ecclesiae* (Berlin, New York, 1997).

5. H. A. Oberman, *The Harvest of medieval Theology. Gabriel Biel and Late Medieval Nominalism* (Cambridge, 1963), 120–84; W. Ernst, *Gott und Mensch am Vorabend der*

Luther was intimately involved in this rejection of scholasticism and of the Roman hierarchy. His fight against the scholastics and their theology led to his condemnation by both Louvain and Paris.[6] This was the time of the young Luther and, hence, of the adolescent Reformation. Aristotle was ferociously attacked and Thomas Aquinas, too, came in for heavy criticism.[7] Luther's discovery of justification by faith had led him to mount a radical resistance to the governing church and to its theology, a theology which pervaded the intellectual culture of the university.

Something similar took place in the wider areas which could also be included within the Reformation's sphere of influence. The Reformation was in no way compatible with the scholasticism which had been practiced within the universities up till then.[8] During this time, the evangelical movement was predominantly concerned with preaching and counseling. This does not, of course, imply that theology was neglected. On the contrary, it was central to the Reformation concern for rebuilding the church and reforming society in a completely new way.[9]

In the meantime the educational institutions had difficulty keeping up with the changes. For a number of universities, the Reformation implied a total transformation of curriculum and pedagogy, a transformation which was perceived to entail a serious threat of diminishing quality in both education and research.[10]

Reformation. Eine Untersuchung zur Moralphilosophie und Theologie bei Gabriel Biel (Leipzig, 1972).

6. H. de Jongh, *L'ancienne faculté de théologie de Louvain au premier siècle de son existence (1432–1540). Ses débuts, son organisation, son enseignement, sa lutte contre Érasme et Luther, Avec documents inédits* (Louvain, Paris, 1911), 213ff.; F. T. Bos, *Luther in het oordeel van de Sorbonne. Een onderzoek naar ontstaan, inhoud en werking van de Determinatio (1521) en naar haar verhouding tot de vroegere veroordelingen van Luther* (Amsterdam, 1974).

7. U. Kühn, O. Pesch, *Rechtfertigung im Gespräch zwischen Thomas und Luther* (Berlin, 1967); D. R. Janz, *Luther on Thomas Aquinas. The Angelic Doctor in the thought of the Reformator* (Wiesbaden, 1989); O. H. Pesch, *Martin Luther, Thomas von Aquin und die reformatorische Kritik an der Scholastik. Zur Geschichte und Wirkungsgeschichte eines Mißverständnisses mit weltgeschichtlichen Folgen* (Hamburg, Göttingen, 1994).

8. E. Rummel, *The Humanist-Scholastic Debate in the Renaissance and Reformation*, Cambridge (London, 1995).

9. W. Maurer, *De junge Melanchthon zwischen Humanismus und Reformation*, Band 2, *Der Theologe* (Göttingen, 1969); A. Pettegree, ed., *The reformation of the parishes. The ministry and the Reformation in town and country* (Manchester, New York, 1993).

10. "Zu schweren Bedenken freilich schien in Wittenberg eine Wahrnehmung Anlass zu geben: der Rückgang der gelehrten Studien an der Universität und die Verödung der Hörsäle. Dass die Wittenberger Studenten in Menge die Universitätsstudien aufgaben und in die Heimat zurückkehrten, daran kann nicht gezweifelt werden ... In Wahrheit ist die rapide Abnahme der Studierenden in der

In addition, the emergence of the anabaptist movement with its strong criticism of anything which vaguely resembled scholarship, required a reorientation of both the method and the content of study. Karlstadt, who was Luther's supervisor, had made it known that he was never again prepared to admit anyone to the degree of doctor of philosophy.[11] Students did not see the point of studying anymore and left the lecture-halls *en masse*.[12] This ultimately made necessary a strong reformation of the university itself, which also included the return of Aristotle to the curriculum, as was the case in Wittenberg.[13]

During the 1530s, *the second period*, the reformation of education continued in several towns in Germany. One can think of the reformation of the university of Tübingen as proposed by the theologians from Strasbourg and under the leadership of Ambrosius Blaurer and Simon Grynaeus (1534–1535).[14]

In the very same year the reinstitution of the university of Basel took

---

Zeit seit 1521 eine an allen Universitäten zu beobachtende Tatsache . . ." H. Barge, *Andreas Bodenstein von Karlstadt*, 2 vols. (Leipzig, 1905; reprint, Nieuwkoop, 1968), 1:418f.; "Die Zusammenbruch der gelehrten Studien im Jahrzehnt von 1520–1530 gehört zu jenen Erschütterungen, welche die plötzliche Veränderung der geistigen Gesamtstruktur eines Zeitalters notwendig mit sich bringt." ibid., 420. R. J. Sider, *Andreas Bodenstein von Karlstadt. The Development of his Thought* (Leiden, 1974), 148–53; C. A. Pater, *Karlstadt as the Father of the Baptist Movements: The Emergence of Lay Protestantism* (Toronto, Buffalo, London, 1984). On the relation between academic Theology and the movement of the Reformation: L. Grane, ed., *University and Reformation. Lectures from The University of Copenhagen Symposium* (Leiden, 1981).

11. Barge, *Karlstadt*, 2:12.

12. Barge, *Karlstadt,* 2:13, n. 24.

13. P. Schwarzenau, *Der Wandel im theologischen Ansatz bei Melanchthon von 1525–1535* (Gütersloh, 1956); A. Sperl, *Melanchthon zwischen Humanismus und Reformation* (München, 1959); S. Wiedenhofer, *Formalstrukturen humanistischer und reformatorischer Theologie bei Philipp Melanchthon*, 2 vols. (Bern, Frankfurt, München, 1976); M. Beyer, G. Wartenberg, eds., *Humanismus und Wittenberger Reformation. Festgabe anläßlich des 500. Geburtstages des Praeceptor Germaniae Philipp Melanchthon am 16. Februar 1997, Helmar Junghans gewidmet* (Leipzig 1996); T. J. Wengert & M. P. Graham, *Philip Melanchthon (1497–1560) and the Commentary* (Sheffield, 1997). See Melanchthon's writings on this subject in: R. Nürnberger, *Melanchthon Werke in Auswahl*, 3 vols. (Gütersloh, 1961); Philip Melanchthon, *A Melanchthon Reader, Translated by Ralph Keen* (New York, Bern, Frankfurt am Main, Paris, 1988); J. Knape, *Philipp Melanchthons "Rhetoric."* (Tübingen, 1993); O. Berwald, *Philipp Melanchthons Sicht der Rhetorik* (Wiesbaden 1994).

14. H. A. Oberman, *Werden und Wertung der Reformation. Vom Wegestreit zum Glaubenskampf*, 2d ed. (Tübingen, 1979); M. Brecht, H. Ehmer, *Südwestdeutsche Reformationsgeschichte. Zur Einführung der Reformation im Herzogtum Württemberg 1534* (Stuttgart, 1984), 255ff.; *Urkunden zur Geschichte der Universität Tübingen aus den Jahren 1476–1550* (Tübingen: R. von Roth, 1877; repr., Aalen, 1973).

place, where, remarkably enough, Karlstadt played a vital part.[15] Here, both Bucer's and Capito's influence are clearly noticeable as well. Karlstadt, who was not prepared to grant anyone a doctorate in Wittenberg during the 1520s, appeared to be such a convincing defender of the doctorate in Basel only ten years later, that both Grynaeus and Myconius were forced by him to acquire doctorates. Both of them strongly resisted this as they had been professors in Basel for years.[16] Capito acted as mediator in this affair by presenting an essay on the doctorate in Christ's church.[17] A solution was found in the creation of separate chairs for both Myconius and Grynaeus. I refer to this example, because it makes clear that in Basel in 1535 the scholarly nature of theology was assessed in terms of the theological degree a professor had obtained. With that, a professional standard was applied which one could not claim to have been directly derived from the subject matter of the educational system itself.

During the 1530s the organization of university education in Strasbourg entered a new phase.[18] The grammar school was basically transformed into a university in personal formation. Bucer strongly encouraged the pursuit of scientific education, and managed to employ Johannes Sturm at the grammar school. His insights were rooted in a

15. U. Bubenheimer, *Consonantia Theologiae et Jurisprudentiae. Andreas Bodenstein von Karlstadt als Theologe und Jurist zwischen Scholastik und Reformation* (Tübingen, 1977), 257ff.; E. Bonjour, *Die Universität Basel von den Anfängen bis zur Gegenwart 1460–1960* (Basel, 1971); 121ff.

16. W. van't Spijker, "Bucer en de twist over het doctoraat in Bazel," in *Theologia Reformata* XXVI (1983): 98–112, also in C. Augustijn, W. H. Neuser, H. J. Selderhuis, eds., *Geest, Woord en Kerk. Opstellen over de geschiedenis van het gereformeerd protestantisme voor dr. W. van't Spijker* (Kampen, 1991), 48–62.

17. W. van't Spijker, "Une disputation au sujet du Doctorat par le D. Wolfgang Capiton où est soulevée la question de savoir si le nom ou le titre d'un Docteur peut exister dans l'Église de Dieu," in M. de Kroon, M. Lienhard, eds., *Horizons Européens de la Réforme en Alsace, Mélanges offerts à Jean Rott pour son 65e anniversaire* (Strasbourg, 1980), 95–106.

18. W. Sohm, *Die Schule Johann Sturms und die Kirche Straßburgs in ihrem gegenseitigen Verhältnis 1530–1581. Ein Beitrag zur Geschichte deutscher Renaissance* (München, Berlin, 1912); A. Schindling, *Humanistische Hochschule und freie Reichsstadt. Gymnasium und Akademie in Strassburg 1538–1621* (Wiesbaden, 1977); J. Rott, "Jean Sturm, le premier recteur du Gymnase et de l'Academie de Strasbourg (1507–1589)," in G. Livet, F. Rapp, J. Rott, *Strasbourg au coeur religieux du XVIe siècle. Actes du Colloque international de Strasbourg (25–29 mai 1975)* (Strasbourg, 1977), 185–88; 189–96: R. Faerber, "La pensée religieuse et théologique de Jean Sturm," in *Schriften der Jahre 1538–1539,* Martin Bucers Deutsche Schriften 7, (Gütersloh, Paris: Robert Stupperich, 1964).

synthesis of piety and eloquence. Sturm fervently defended the *eloquens pietas* and he himself was responsible for a considerable share of teaching, in which he paid all possible attention to rhetoric and dialectic.[19]

Bucer's teaching role mainly consisted of defending the scientific character of theology. He first and foremost asked for special attention for the early church fathers.[20] According to him scientific theology was rooted in a long patristic tradition, in which St. Augustine was given specific attention. His understanding of grace functioned more or less as a bench-mark for determining what was orthodox and what was not.

Secondly, Bucer fervently defended the thesis that classical authors, too, like Aristotle and Plato, should play a role in improving the quality of education. Here again we can notice a direct assault on the view of the anabaptists in Strasbourg. Bucer made this clear in the exhaustive *Praefatio* of his commentary on the Epistle to the Romans. One could regard this as a strong argument for the quality of the university.[21]

In the third place, we ought to note the use of scholastic method, in particular in terms of the use of the syllogism. According to Bucer, the first and the last word was to be given to Scripture, the *primum principium theologiae*.[22] But he did not despise the cogency of rational reasoning at

19. Jean Sturm, *Classicae epistolae sive scholae Argentinenses restitutae*, ed. J. Rott (Paris, Strasbourg, 1938); L. Spitz, B. S. Tinsley, *Johann Sturm on Education. The Reformation and Humanist Learning* (St. Louis, 1995).

20. W. van't Spijker, "Reformatie tussen patristiek en scholastiek: Bucers theologische positie," in: J. van Oort, ed., *De kerkvaders in Reformatie en Nadere Reformatie* (Zoetermeer, 1997), 45–66.

21. *Metaphrasis et Enarratio in Epist. D. Pauli Apostoli ad Romanos* (Basel 1562): "An insit in Philosophia quod cum doctrina Pauli congruat," 27–39; W. van't Spijker, "De relatie tussen filosofie en theologie bij Bucer en haar betekenis voor zijn spiritualiteit," in *Theologia Reformata* XXII (1979), 6–23.

22. Bucer in: *Praelectiones doctiss. in Epistolam D. Pauli ad Ephesios* (Basel, 1561), 14, speaking about his hermeneutical principle: "Ex quo perspicitis facile, optimi auditores, in officio esse meo, ut in Epistola proposita, explicare omnia studeam ex ipso Apostoli verbo, quae cum in hac, tum in aliis suis epistolis nobis prodidit, tum si quid elucidatum probe sit ab aliis, illos quidem laude sua et mentione honorifica non fraudare, tamen simul ea Dei verbo quo illorum nititur enarratio, cum primis commemorare, sive ea interpretatio conclusa sit necessario, sive tantum probabiliter. Nam et probabilia in Theologia, dum non possunt necessario, debent tamen probabiliter, ad primum Theologiae principium referri, quod est: Deus dixit." J. Sturm wrote about Bucer's method: "quam erudite probabilia à necessariis disiungat, quam argumentose quae probanda sunt confirmet, quam subtiliter adversaria diluat, ita non acrimonia in vituperando, sed veritatem in docendo sit elencicos; neque ullum sit Dialecticorum praeceptum, idque Aristotelicum, cuius hic scriptor non plurima atque perspicua exempla habeat." *Martini Buceri Scripta Anglicana fere omnia* . . . (Basel, 1577), b 1 verso.

all. By using this method, Bucer intended to defend the catholicity of Reformation theology in relation to that of Rome. As to the anabaptists, he stood by his belief that God's truth is and will always be the same, whether it is spoken by Plato, by Aristotle or by Cicero or whoever.[23] He wanted to stress the reasonableness of theology by means of the instruments with which the Dominicans had made him familiar with during his youth in the monastery of Schletstadt.[24]

Thus, Bucer's Commentary to the Epistle to the Romans (1536) shows all characteristics of what appeared to him as the ideal of scientific theology during the thirties. In the meantime he linked this vision of the scientific character of theology to a survey of its practical character as well. Theology is the art of teaching people to live piously and happily. It is a difficult art indeed, the most difficult of all, because one has to learn to lead a godly life, while still being in the flesh. Nevertheless, this remains the requirement. It is not the amount of knowledge we possess which is at stake. We know enough if we know how to put into practice that which we know. In this way, scholarship and piety go hand in hand.[25]

Sturm wrote about Bucer's method in a letter to L. Hertel: "Martinum Bucerum, dum viveret, semper sum admiratus propter industriam, doctrinam, usum, judicium in omni disceptatione religionis. Ille in caeteris virtutibus istud quoque habuit laudabile quod imitandum est: res quas ad disputandum proposuit, in duas dividebat partes, et propositiones necessarias separabat a probabilibus, et hac ratione condocefaciebat *ta anankaia* a probabilibus distinguere adolescentes, ut scirent, quae retinenda et defendenda essent fortiter in Ecclesia et Republica, et in quibus largiendum aliquid temporibus necessariis." Sturm, *Classicae epistolae*, 104.

23. Praefatio *Ad Romanos*, 31: "Adeo nihil in philosophia praeteritum est, quod Dei metu animos replere, inque solido religionis studio conservare valeat. Porro Philosophia non solum unde petenda iustitia sit, et in quo summa bonorum nobis reposita, tam luculenter docet, subducens religione ad Deum, a quo sunt bona omnia, et cuius solius favoris persuasio, animis nostris veram tranquillitatem, certumque gaudium adducit, sed vitae quoque officia, veraeque religionis fructus, tam tradidit absolute, ut in hac quoque stupendum plane, quam congruat cum divinis literis." Comp. 35: "Nunc ita videndum quatenus quae in Philosophia insunt, cum his quae doctrina sacra habet, congruant et quousque ista Philosophiae cum Theologia consonantia progressa sit. Quod non de ipsa dogmatum natura quaeritur, eadem enim sunt, quae vera docentur, sive in sacris, sive in Philosophorum libris, nec recipit verum, magis et minus, ita neque inter vera, aliud vero magis, aliud minus consonat. Veritas simplex et unius modi est. Ad rationem pertinet administrationis, quod quaeritur."

24. L. Leijssen, "Martin Bucer und Thomas von Aquin," in *Ephemerides Theologicae Lovanienses* 55 (1979): 266–96; J. V. Pollet, "Le couvent dominicain de Sélestat (XIIIe-XVIIIe siècles). Étude d'Histoire et de Sociologie religieuses," in *Annuaire de las Societe des amis de la Bibliotheque de Sélestat* (n.d.): 17–55.

25. "In vera theologia tantum quisque rite novit quantum vita exprimit," Bucer to

I wish to remind us here that these ideas were Bucer's, because they serve as a model for what was believed to be ideal with regard to the link between piety and scholarship, *pietas* and *eloquentia*, in Strasbourg during the thirties. The one and only aim of *eloquentia* was to establish communication between science and the church, and between the church and society. Scholasticism should not be the science of the ivory tower, but should be the servant of preaching and dialogue; hence it is a communicative discipline.[26]

It was this ideal which was clearly recognizable from the 1530s till the mid–1550s, *the third period*. In the next period, from around the mid–1550s to the end of the 1570s, a number of changes were to take place. First of all, within the political spectrum, the religious peace of 1555 meant that the Lutherans gained more freedom, whereas the Reformed believers had difficulty obtaining positions within the establishment. Their position thus required a defensive retrenchment and further clarification of their stance with regard to the Lutherans.[27]

Ever since 1529, and the discussions at Marburg about the Lord's Supper, the two Reformation traditions had been more or less independent. The dispute concerning the Supper had led to fierce theological discussions, during which all kinds of scholastic mechanisms had once again come to the fore.[28] Oecolampadius confided to Zwingli, after having had a confidential chat with Luther at Marburg, that he had met Eck for the second time. This get-together had reminded him of the

---

Blaurer, T. Schiess, *Briefwechsel der Brüder Ambrosius und Thomas Blaurer* (Freiburg, 1908), 1:648; Bucer in *Enarratio in Evv.* 753: "Vera theologia non est theoretica et speculativa, sed activa et practica est, hoc est vitam vivere deiformem"; ibid., 1:549: "Vera theologia scientia est, pie et beate vivendi. Sine quo multa nosse, et variis de rebus posse disserere, etiam daemonum est"; *Ad Romanos*, 464: "Theologi veri est fugere argutias et logomachias, res vero ipsas sectari iuxta domini verbum quam simplicissime, omniaque huc referre, ut in fide in promissiones Dei, et studio in iuvandis proximis proficiamus." In *De vi et usu sacri ministerii, Tom Angl.*, 563: "scientia omnium ut divinissima, ita et difficullima, scientia vivendi Deum cum sis homo." Ibid., 485: "Iam hac arte vivendi Deum, cum sit natus perditus peccatis homo, nulla omnium est difficilior."

26. Spitz, Tinsley: *Johann Sturm on Education*, 45–58; J. Ficker, *Die Anfänge der akademischen Studien in Strassburg* (Strasbourg, 1912), 12ff.

27. E. Walder, ed., *Religionsvergleiche des 16. Jahrhunderts* (Bern, 1945), 41–54; C. Mirbt/K. Aland, *Quellen zur Geschichte des Papsttums und des römischen Katholizismus*, I, (Tübingen, 1967), 587ff.; cf. W. Hollweg, "Das Problem der reichsrechtliche Stellung des Pfälzer Calvinismus," in *Der Augsburger Reichstag von 1566 und seine Bedeutung für die Entstehung der Reformierten Kirche und ihres Bekenntnisses* (Neukirchen, 1964).

28. E. Bizer, *Studien zur Geschichte des Abendmahlsstreits im 16. Jahrhundert* (Gütersloh, 1940).

scholastic distinctions, which had been used by Eck in the religious discussions at Baden.[29] Indeed, the disputes concerning the Supper did lead to revivals in scholasticism from time to time. During the 1550s and later, after Luther's death, the return to debates about the eucharist not only signified the confrontation between the two mainstreams traditions of Reformation theology but also meant that the theological arsenal of yesteryear was opened again.[30]

A second important factor during this period is evident in the actions of two key figures within the Reformed tradition: Petrus Martyr Vermiglius and Jerome Zanchius, two Italians who brought a completely unique Thomistic influence within the reformed tradition.[31] Together with Beza, Ursinus and Olevianus[32] these two men can be seen as

---

29. Zwingli to Vadian *H. Zwinglis sämtliche Werke,* 10:316: "Hic Lutherus Oecolampadium ita excepit, ut ad me veniens clam quereretur se denuo in Eccium incidisse."

30. J. V. Pollet, *Martin Bucer, études sur la correspondance*(Paris, 1958–), 1:42, 48, 51, 139; 2:298, 495, 512.

31. J. C. McLelland, *The Visible Words of God. An Exposition of the Sacramental Theology of Peter Martyr A.D. 1500–1562* (Grand Rapids, 1957); Ph. McNair, *Peter Martyr in Italy. An Anatomy of Apostasy* (Oxford, 1967); M. W. Anderson, *Peter Martyr. A Reformer in Exile (1542–1562). A Chronology of Biblical Writings in England and Europe* (Nieuwkoop, 1975); J. P. Donnelly, *Calvinism and Scholasticism in Vermigli's Doctrine of Man and Grace* (Leiden, 1976); R. M. Kingdon, *The political thought of Peter Martyr Vermigli. Selected Texts and Commentary* (Geneva, 1980); J. C. McLelland, ed., *Peter Martyr and Italian Reform* (Waterloo, 1980); J. C. McLelland, G. E. Duffield, *The Life, Early Letters and Eucharistic Writings of Peter Martyr* (Appleford, 1989); J. P. Donnelly, R. M. Kingdon, *A Bibliography of the Works of Peter Martyr Vermigli, with a Register of Vermigli's Correspondence by W. Anderson,* SCES 13 (Kirksville, Missouri, 1990); *The Peter Martyr Library,* SCES 1-4 (Kirksville, Missouri, 1994-). On Hier. Zanchi: O. Gründler, *Die Gotteslehre Girolamo Zanchis und ihre Bedeutung für seine Lehre von der Prädestination* (Neukirchen, 1965).

32. H. Heppe, *Theodor Beza. Leben und ausgewählte Schriften* (Elberfeld, 1861); F. Gardy, *Bibliography des oeuvres théologiques, littéraires, historiques et juridiques de Théodore de Bèze, publiée avec la collaboration d'Alain Dufour* (Geneva, 1960); P. F. Geisendorf, *Théodore de Bèze* (Geneva, 1967); W.Kickel, *Vernunft und Offenbarung bei Theodor Beza. Zum Problem des Verhältnisses von Theologie, Philosophie und Staat* (Neukirchen, 1967); J. Raitt, *The Eucharistic Theology of Theodore Beza. Development of the Reformed Doctrine* (Chambersburg, 1972); J. S. Bray, *Theodore Beza's Doctrine of Predestination* (Nieuwkoop, 1975); C. van Sliedrecht, *Calvijns opvolger Theodorus Beza. Zijn verkiezingsleer en zijn belijdenis van de drieënige God* (Leiden, 1996). About Ursinus: K. Sudhoff, *C. Olevianus und Z. Ursinus. Leben und ausgewählte Schriften* (Elberfeld, 1857); E. K. Sturm, *De junge Zacharias Ursin, sein Weg vom Philippismus zum Calvinismus* (Neukirchen, 1972); D. Visser, *Zacharias Ursinus. The Reluctant Reformer. His Life and Times* (New York, 1983); L. D. Bierma, *German Calvinism in the Confessional Age. The Covenant Theology of Caspar Olevianus* (Grand Rapids, 1996); see also the several contributions on Olevianus in: *Monatshefte für*

spokesmen for Reformed Protestantism. But it is arguable that their theological contributions are, in their own way, unique. Their approach can be regarded as a kind of monastic theology, which does not grant a vital and central role to the congregation. For them, theology enjoys a certain independence in relation to the congregation. Both of them are rooted in the tradition of Thomism and adhere to the formal significance of Aristotle.[33] Both also had a great influence on the formation of the typical Reformed Protestantism, which developed alongside and contra Lutheranism.

In particular, Zanchius enjoyed the confidence of almost the whole of western European Reformed Christendom. He was given the task of designing a general reformed confession as opposed to the Lutheran *Formula Concordiae*.[34] This work was completed, though it was not accepted. Instead, the *Harmonia Confessionum* was published in Geneva, a document which did not gain general acceptance either.[35]

This period, however, is distinguished by the way it presents Reformed Protestantism in this confessional way. Behind this phenomenon was the conviction that it was not only possible for schools, but also for churches to supply a reformational survey of belief. This attempt already proves how strong the belief was in the vitality of a Reformed theology presenting itself in the forms of scholastic thinking. These are the years which can be regarded as being fundamental to the movement which was to emerge onto the stage of European culture from the centers of the Reformed Reformation.[36]

The *fourth period* follows on from this rather harmoniously, without any drastic changes or radical discontinuities. Nevertheless, this period is mentioned specifically, as it provides us with a document from Roman Catholic theology, which was to occupy the theological world for many

---

Evangelische Kirchengeschichte des Rheinlandes 37/38 (1988/89).

33. F. G. Immink, *Divine Simplicity* (Kampen, 1987), 146ff.

34. J. N. Bakhuizen van den Brink, "Het Convent te Frankfort en de Harmonia Confessionum," in *Ned. Arch. v. Kerkgesch.* 32 (1941): 235ff.

35. A. Bernus, "Jean-Francois Salvard," *Bulletin historique et litteraire de la Société de l'histoire du protestantisme francais* 36 (1887): 498–503; O. Labarthe, "Jean-Francois Salvard. Ministre de l'évangile. Vie, oeuvre et correspondance," in M. C. Junod, M. Droin-Bridel, O. Labarthe, *Polémiques religieuses. Études et textes* (Geneva, Paris, 1979), 345–470.

36. See O. Fatio, *Méthode et Théologie. Lambert Daneau et les débuts de la scolastique réformée* (Geneva, 1976); C. Strohm, *Ethik im frühen Calvinismus. Humanistische Einflüsse, philosophische, juristische und theologische Argumentationen sowie mentalitätsgeschichtliche Aspekte am Beispiel des Calvin-Schülers Lambertus Danaeus* (Berlin, New York, 1996).

years: Bellarminus' *Disputationes de controversiis* (1586).[37]

In this work, Bellarminus fought the Reformation, its representatives, and its dogmas in such a thorough manner, that Reformed theologians were still trying to refute his work years afterwards.[38] Intended as an answer to the theology of Reformation, it differs from previous polemic and apologetic documents, such as those written by Pighius and Tapper[39], mainly by presenting a new system, a *Summa*, which was meant to replace the older scholastic works. It was Rome's answer to Reformed theology, as this had gradually developed into a scholastic theology. In this way they mirrored each other as doctrinal systems, in which their respective and complete visions of belief and theology were counterparts. Was this scholasticism an ecumenical enterprise? Or were they two separate worlds? The answer to that question can only be given when we take a closer look at the theological themes which are decisive for the relationship between Rome and scholasticism.

III. Theological Themes

The first issue which is at stake is the confession of the authority of Scripture. As far as this is concerned, the Reformation shows a great deal of unanimity. In a certain sense it is born from Scripture. Luther's discovery did not in fact signify anything else but that Scripture was opened up to him. To him this was a basic hermeneutical principle, and was closely connected to justification by faith alone.[40]

With Calvin we come across the very same principle. We become

---

37. R. Bellarminus, *Disputationes de controversiis christianae fidei, adversus huius temporis haereticos* (Ingolstad 1586–1593). See also the contributions of Broeyer and Dekker, elsewhere in this volume.

38. Bellarminus found his opponents in Chemnitz, Gerhard, Chamier, Lubbertus, Junius, Amesius and numerous other theologians. See on Amesius also the contribution by Dekker, elsewhere in this volume.

39. R. Tapper, *Explicationis articulorum venerandae facultatis sacrae theologiae generalis studii Lovaniensis circa dogmata Ecclesiastica ab annis triginta quatuor controversa, una cum responsione ad argumenta adversariorum*, 2 vols. (Leuven 1555–1557); A. Pighius, *Controversiarum praecipuarum, in comitiis Ratisponensibus tractatum, et quibus nunc potissimum exagitatur Christi fides et religio, diligens, et luculenta explicatio* (Paris, 1549); cf. P. Polman, *L'Élement Historique dans la Controverse religieuse du XVIe Siècle* (Gembloux, 1932); H. Jedin, *Studien über die Schriftstellertätigkeit Albert Pigges* (Münster, 1931).

40. W. van't Spijker, *Luther en Calvijn. De invloed van Luther op Calvijn blijkens de Institutie* (Kampen, 1985), also in: *John Calvin's Institutes, his Opus Magnum. Proceedings of the Second South African Congress for Calvin Research July 31–August 3, 1984* (Potchefstroom, 1986), 106–32.

students of Scripture, something which is identical to becoming Christ's followers. The *docilitas*, which was existential to him ever since his *subita conversio*, remained for him the starting-point of his exegesis.[41]

Nevertheless, one can note a difference in emphasis. For Luther, Scripture functioned by means of a theological grammar.[42] Where Luther finds Christ, there Scripture is opened. Calvin too listens to the voice, the teaching, the doctrines of Christ Himself, but he perceives this voice mainly by means of the careful way in which he scans the text. It is respect for the text which is characteristic of his approach and which reveals him as an exegete who was shaped by humanism.[43]

To Luther the authority of Scripture functions in terms of our gracious God meeting the sinner who is to be cleared of sin. The element of actual justification always plays a part in this process. For Calvin, it is the *testimonium* of the Spirit, who convinces us in such a way that all other ways to security are apt to fail, which is vital when the authority of Scripture is at stake.

Both did defend the authority of Scripture towards Rome, though different issues were highlighted. These elements remained alive during later theological developments. Within their respective traditions. Nevertheless, a shift took place concerning the question of Scripture functioning as a *principium theologiae*.

Bucer already uses the Bible in that sense: to him it is the *primum principium theologiae*.[44] This does not, however, imply that a biblical principle can be used as the starting point from which all kinds of conclusions can be drawn. He continued to discern very carefully between that which can be concluded from a text evidently and that

---

41. Calvin's *docilitas* made him a disciple of Scriptures. *Doctrina* and *disciplina* belong for him together, as concepts they complement one another.

42. S. Raeder, *Grammatica Theologica. Studien zu Luthers Operationes in Psalmos* (Tübingen, 1977), 29: "Der von Luther als ausschließlich erkannte literale oder legitime Sinn ist nichtdestoweniger geistlich gemeint und geistlich zu verstehen ... Im Geist hören bedeutet für Luther aber dasselbe wie im Glauben hören;" 36: "Zur sprachlichen Form gehört ihr theologisch verstandener Sinn."

43. Raeder, *Grammatica Theologica,* 38: "So sehr Luther und der Humanismus in der Wertschätzung der Philologie und der Forderung nach Rückkehr zu den Quellen übereinstimmen, so kann man doch Erasmus oder Reuchlin nicht zu den Anhängern einer Grammatica Theologica rechnen, wenigstens nicht in den Sinne, wie Luther sie versteht." Cf. Calvin's characterisation of Luthers exegetical method: "Lutherus non adeo anxius de verborum proprietate aut historiae circumstantia satis habet fructiferam aliquam doctrinam elicere," CO 9:36.

44. Bucer. *Ad Ephesios* (1562), 14.

which is more or less likely. Johannes Sturm praised him for this approach. In that way room was created for a dialogue around an open Bible.[45]

Developments, however, led in a direction in which Scripture was mainly handled as a principle on the basis of which one could draw all sorts of conclusions with the help of logic. With Petrus Martyr the underlying idea is immanent, that truth is always and everywhere the same, though he acknowledged that the truth is not in essence a matter of a logical conclusion. To him the ultimate certainty is the use which the Holy Spirit makes of Scripture in order to lead into the truth.[46]

With Zanchius matters already appear to be more sensitive. He makes particular use of the syllogism, which is given the power of a means to convince in his broad theological essays. Otherwise, he clearly states that our belief cannot be founded on anything else than the Word of God which has been passed down in Holy Scripture: faith comes from hearing the message, and the message is heard through the word of Christ.[47]

A very clear example of using Scripture in such a way that it can be called paradigmatic for Reformed scholasticism, is found with Ant. Sadeel, better known under the name of Chandieu who introduced his *Opera theologica* (1592) with an essay on treating the Bible in a scholastic way.[48] He strongly rejected the medieval scholastics, first of all because these scholars used principles from logic, secondly because they started from doubt, thirdly because they made things even more complex by their contrived arguments and last but not least, because they kept themselves occupied with idle and curious questions, which had no significance whatsoever for building up the congregation.[49]

45. See note 22.

46. P. Martyr Vermigli, *Loci Communes* (Frankfort, 1622), 2 b; 140–47; J. C. McLelland, ed. and trans., *Peter Martyr Vermigli, Philosophical Works. On the Relation of Philosophy to Theology*, SCES 39 (Kirksville, Missouri, 1996), xxvii-xxxiii.

47. Hier. Zanchi, *Opera Theologica* VIII (Geneva, 1649), 296–452; *De religione Christiana fides* (Neustadt, 1586), 1–8.

48. *Dn. Antonii Sadeelis Chandei nobilissimi viri Opera Theologica* (Geneva, 1592), Praefatio "De verbo Dei scripto. Adversus humanas traditiones. Theologica et Scholastica Tractatio," 5–13. About Antoine de Chandieu: A. Bernus, in: *Bulletin historique et littéraire du Société de l'histoire du Protestantisme Francais* (Paris, 1888–).; W. Neuser, in C. Andresen, ed., *Handbuch der Dogmen- und Theologiegeschichte*, 2 vol. (Göttingen, 1980), 2:309–11; D. Sinnema, "Antoine De Chandieu's Call for Scholastic Reformed Theology," in W. F. Graham, ed., *Later Calvinism. International Perspectives*, SCES 22 (Kirksville, Missouri, 1994), 159–90.

49. Chandieu, "Praefatio," 7ff.

On the other hand, Chandieu stated that only that appeal to Scripture could be made in theology which started from the axiom that Scripture only, as opposed to *ratio*, should be the leading principle. Exegesis should take that rule as its starting point, but should distinguish itself as the explanation of Scripture as such. Chandieu defended the authority of Scripture, the *sola scriptura* by means of this rule.[50]

It is clear that with him a further shift can be noticed as well, in that his criticism of scholastics, especially of Duns Scotus, mainly concerns the use of *ratio*, which operates independent of exegesis.[51]

In refuting Bellarminus, Reformed scholasticism comes to an end in a certain sense. It presents itself as a theological method which starts from Scripture in a concise and succinct way. It distinguishes itself from the rhetorical profusion of words, by means of which the simple-minded are taught and the slow are urged. This last matter should be taught from the pulpit[52]. Theology which comes from the pulpit should be stripped of the robe of oratorical trimmings. It should explain things in a simple and straightforward way by using clear arguments, in such a manner that the truth of the matter can be seen as with one's own eyes and can be touched with one's own hands. By using this description Chandieu refers to the apostolic function of theology: "That which we have seen with our eyes, which we have looked at and our hands have touched—this we proclaim concerning the Word of life" (1 John 1:1).[53]

The question arises as to how the doctrine of grace functions within

50. Chandieu, "Praefatio," 10.

51. "Humana autem ratio non potest esse principium Theologiae. Nam conciliaret auctoritatem Scripturae sacrae, atque ita ratio humana esset superior et verior quam S. Scriptura, at hoc esset non iam ratiocinari, sed insanire, sed blasphemare . . . Nihil potest esse Theologiae principium quod S. Scripturae repugnat, aut ab ea condemnatur. Inter humanam rationem autem et doctrinam sacram, saepius antithesis intercedit . . . Hinc fit ut non omnes ii, qui sunt ratione humana praediti agnoscant et probent veram Religionem Christianam, sed saepius ei contradicant. Humana igitur ratio non est Principium Theologicum." Chandieu, "Praefatio," 10.

52. Chandieu, "Praefatio," 11.

53. "Quod ad tractandi rationem attinet, duplicem esse statuo Theologicam tractationem: unam plenam et uberiori stylo compositam, quae et rudes doceat, et tardos excitet ad veritatis doctrinam amplectandam. Alteram autem accuratam quidem sed contractam, et quae sepositis iis quae ad commovendos animos adhibentur, detractaque orationis veste, res ipsas simpliciter et enucleate nobis explicet, atque argumenta nuda proponat, ita ut ipsa rerum veritas oculis propemodum conspici et digitis attrectari possit. Haec fortasse minus erit iis grata, qui orationis splendore delectantur, sed certe non minus utilis iis omnibus qui ut simplicitatis amantes, ita sunt veritatis studiosi." Chandieu, "Praefatio," 11.

this scholastic context. This is the second point of comparison between the Reformation and the scholastics. *Sola gratia* functioned in a convincing way, both with Luther and Calvin. Luther further developed this theme for Erasmus in his writing *De servo arbitrio*. He considered this treatise to be an account of his point of view on this subject which he was never to repudiate. Indeed, in the Strasbourg archives a letter of Luther has been preserved in which he wrote to Capito that he did not see any reason for publishing all his works, except for his catechism and his writing against Erasmus.

When Zanchius got himself into a heavy conflict with the fierce Lutherans under the leadership of Marbach in the sixties, he reminded them of this important letter in order to prove that his point of view as to predestination was in total agreement with Luther's opinion.[54] But Marbach was not impressed, nor were the other Lutherans.

Calvin, too, held the opinion that the doctrine of grace was best protected in the confession of election. His account of what he found in Scripture was formulated in a way that was in no way antithetical to that of Luther. One could say that Calvin's formulations were more polished, but that the contents of what he had to say in this respect were in agreement with what Luther meant when referring to *sola gratia*. For both of them the gratuity of grace was at stake, the complete undeserving character of God's work to and within man.[55]

The problem was not with the matter in itself but with the question of whether one could portray the truth in such a way that it could be seen with the eyes and touched with the hands. When it comes to the crunch, both had theological commitments which prevented them from looking into the abyss of the *mysterium tremendum*, though one should note that some nevertheless transgressed the boundaries here.[56]

54. W. van't Spijker, "Bucer als Zeuge Zanchis im Strassburger Prädestinationsstreit," in: H. A. Oberman, E. Saxer, A. Schindler, H. Stucki, *Reformiertes Erbe. Festschrift für Gottfried W. Locher zu seinem 80. Geburtstag*, 2 vols. (Zürich, 1993), 327–42, 331, n. 19.

55. On Calvin's doctrine of election, see W. H. Neuser: "Die Erwählungslehre dient der Glaubensgewissheit und umschliesst auch das Beharren im Glauben (perseverantia sanctorum). Die systematische Einordnung im III. Buch der "Institutio" verbietet eine Überwertung der Prädestinationslehre. Sie hat seelsorgerliche Ziele und soll nicht die Gottes- und Heilslehre bestimmen," in C. Andresen, *Handbuch*, 2:255.

56. Neuser, "Die Erwählungslehre," 256: "Calvin steht in einem Systemzwang, den er nicht bewältigt. Das 'decretum aeternum' vor der Zeit läßt das Christusereignis nicht als das entscheidende Heilsereignis erscheinen, sondern als Heilsdurchführung. Christus ist lediglich 'Spiegel' der Erwählung."

This was certainly demonstrated when the Lutherans got annoyed with the propositions which Zanchius had drawn up during the Strasbourg dispute about, amongst other things, predestination.[57] These propositions hardly left any room for preaching the promises of the Gospel. They were a summary of what Beza tried to express in his famous *Summa totius Christianismi* by means of a table.[58]

Almost all Reformed universities, however, reacted in a positive way when Zanchius' propositions were sent to them. Zanchius was considered to be Bucer's heir. Hyperius from Marburg expressed his surprise at the fact that this very confession encountered resistance in Strasbourg.[59] Apparently the theological climate within the whole Reformed world had changed, at least in when we look back in retrospect. Whether the Reformed scholastic world itself experienced it in this way is a question we leave aside for the time being. It is a fact that during the time of this fight a small book was published consisting of an anthology of Bucer's commentaries on predestination, the origin of sin, the nature of free will, and the hardening of the godless. The title page contained the text: 'Ask for the ancient ways'. Apparently, the publisher had no other intention but proving that Zanchius' opinions were in agreement with those of Bucer and the other reformers of the first hour.[60]

A third point of theological interest touches the confession with regard to the church. It is striking how much the doctrine of grace goes together with a strict view of the church in the Reformed tradition, as it had done in the theology of St. Augustine. Building the church is one of the most central and original elements of the Reformed tradition. Luther would have liked to write a book on justification by faith, but he did not find the time to do so. Bucer wrote a broad study on the church in the 1540s, but the magistrate of Strasbourg prevented it from being published. Most likely, we find his thoughts most clearly in *De Regno Christi* which he wrote in England.[61]

It was the church which Calvin had in mind in the midst of all his

---

57. J. Moltmann, *Prädestination und Perseveranz. Geschichte und Bedeutung der reformierten Lehre "de perseverantia sanctorum"* (Neukirchen, 1961).

58. Van Sliedrecht, *Calvijns opvolger*, 75–161.

59. W. van't Spijker, "Die Prädestination bei Hyperius," in *Calvin. Erbe und Auftrag. Festschrift für Wilhelm Neuser zu seinem 65. Geburtstag* (Kampen, 1991), 291–304.

60. *Doctrina M. Buceri De Praedestinatione, Causa Peccati, Libero Arbitrio, Excaecatione Impiorum [1562]*.

61. *Martini Buceri Opera Latina*, Vol. 15, *De Regno Christi, Libri Duo 1550*, ed. F. Wendel (Paris, Gütersloh, 1955).

activities in Geneva. 'When I arrived here', he said on his death-bed, 'there were only sermons. Now there is a well-formed congregation'.[62] How that congregation should ideally be structured, we can read in his writings, his church order, his liturgy and his confessions and cathechism. The influence of Bucer may be recognized in these structures. And it has remained a point of continuous interest for almost all Reformed theologians who have been prominent in the tradition.

The proposition can be defended that there is a close relationship between Reformed scholasticism and the vision of a strictly ordered presbyterian church with its offices and meetings. Beza had a decisive voice with regard to these developments. His fight with "the fanatic democrat from Paris," Jean de Morély,[63] and his influence on the conflicts in Heidelberg with which Erastus was associated, were all highly significant within the Reformed world.[64]

A Reformed church model eventually came into existence, the contours of which we can find in the writings of almost all spokesmen of Reformed scholasticism: Beza, Zanchius, Ursinus, Junius and many others.[65] This model showed a structure in which the progress of the Word could be guaranteed. As a structure was applied in scholastic theology as such, which could clarify, guarantee and support the truth, so the church form served no other means but letting the Word of truth sound. The scholastic church structure was very clearly and widespread

62. CO 9:891.

63. Th. Beza, *Ad tractationem de ministrorum Evangelii gradibus, ab Hadriano Saravia Belga editam* (Geneva, 1603), 5: "Ordinationis autem nomine, si electionem ipsam ministrorum intelligis, ministris non recte tribuis quod totius est Ecclesiae, eo tamen ordine servato, quem suo loco explicabimus, ne quis nos arbitretur illi nuper istic mortuo phantastico Morellio Parisiensi in Democratica politia revehenda assentiri." See W. van't Spijker, *Democratisering van de kerk anno 1562. Het conflict-Morély in de begintijd van de Gereformeerde Kerk in Frankrijk* (Kampen, 1975); Ph. Denis, Jean Rott, *Jean Morély (ca 1524– ca 1594) et l'utopie d'une democratie dans l'église* (Geneva, 1993).

64. R. Wesel-Roth, *Thomas Erastus. Ein Beitrag zur Geschichte der reformierten Kirche und zur Lehre der Staatssouveränität* (Lahr, 1954); R. C. Walton, "Der Streit zwischen Thomas Erastus und Caspar Olevian über die Kirchenzucht in der Kurpfalz in seiner Bedeutung für die internationale reformierte Bewegung," in *Monatshefte für evangelische Kirchengeschichte des Reinlandes* (1988/89): 205–46.

65. T. Beza, *Tractatus pius et moderatus de vera Excommunicatione, et christiano Presbyterio* (Geneva, 1610); Hier. Zanchi, *De Religione*, 137–91; "De Ecclesia," in *Opera Theologica*, 7:51–167; Z. Ursinus, "Judicium de Disciplina ecclesiastica en excommunicatione," in *Opera Theologica*, 3:802–12; F. Junius, "Ecclesiastici, sive de natura et administrationibus ecclesiae Dei," in *Opera Theologica* (Geneva, 1613; reprint, 1921–1978).

recorded by the later master of Utrecht scholastics, Gisbertus Voetius.[66]

Had the secret of theology, the secret of the Word, the secret of grace and the secret of the congregation, too, disappeared behind and within the structures as a result of this? That had never been the intention and it was not actually the case.

This can be tested by what is regarded by many as the center of Calvin's theology (it had also been a central and vital idea in Bucer's theology): the reality of the communion with Christ.[67] To Calvin this was indeed the secret of the Word, of grace and of the church. That secret has not at all disappeared in scholastic theology. It is there, as a central thought with Zanchius and with Martyr as well. Zanchius discussed it at length in his very personal *De religione christiana fides*.[68] We only receive complete salvation in the *koinonia* with Christ. Petrus Martyr confessed this mystic union with Christ as well, like in the footsteps of Calvin,[69] as a secret which is not to be seen with the eyes nor can be touched with the hands. It is the secret of which Calvin had said he could experience rather than actually comprehend. Yet both of them, Zanchius and Martyr, wrote about it by using scholastic terminology. Has the mystery, as a result of this, been robbed of its essence?

IV. Some Critical Reflections

The first one concerns labeling scholastic theology as an ecumenical enterprise. Lutheran and Roman Catholic theologians practiced this scholasticism during the time after the Reformation as well.

First and foremost, the question is whether they did such from a real ecumenical conviction, convinced of the ideal of the unity of the church. Not at all, in fact, one gets an impression of just the opposite: scholasticism in the service of polemics and apologetics. What influence this setting has on theology itself is not clear. Both in apologetics and in polemics we can easily distort things. Indeed, both with Lutheran, Reformed and Roman Catholic theologians this manner of practising theology happened almost simultaneously. In this way they tried to act on the era they were alive and also to pass on the message of

---

66. G. Voetius, *Politica Ecclesiastica* (Utrecht, 1663–1676).

67. D. E. Tamburello, *Union with Christ. John Calvin and the Mysticism of St. Bernard* (Louisville: Westminster, 1994; W. van't Spijker, *Gemeenschap met Christus. Centraal gegeven van de gereformeerde theologie* (Kampen, 1995).

68. Zanchi, *De religione*, 59–72.

69. Peter Martyr, *Loci communes*, 394–96.

Reformation or Counter Reformation.

I now come back to the question I raised at the beginning: To what extent do they all carry the stamp of their times? Is their way of practising theology characterized and stamped by the juncture in which European culture found itself? Theology as a discipline can, just like arts and science, adopt the conventions of expression of the era in which it is being practiced. Which factors played a part in this manifestation of what can be said to be a general cultural phenomenon?

Another question is the one of the nature of the return to Aristotle. Was it the same Aristotle with whom Thomas Aquinas worked, the philosopher, who played the part of first witness in the fields of ethics and dogmatics apart from or after Scripture? Luther held the opinion that he knew a different Aristotle than did Thomas and his scholastics.[70] Also Melanchthon[71], Sturm[72] and Hyperius[73] should be mentioned here: they were the ones who were inspired by Rudolf Agricola in their own *Topica theologica*. His work cannot be regarded as a straightforward interpretation of Aristotle. Agricola was heavily influenced by humanism and modern devotion.[74] Hence, one can question to what extent it is right to speak of a return to Aristotle.

A third remark concerns the variety which is, no doubt, found with all those who judged positively the application of philosophy to theology. They were no straightforward followers of one and the same school of philosophy. Scholasticism does not imply the end of variation. The problems only increase when one bears in mind that both Aristotelians and Ramists[75] could cooperate in one project without being hampered by discord or controversy. Ursinus and Olevianus can serve as examples, like Johannes Sturm and Martin Bucer.

70. G. Ebeling, *Luther. Einführung in sein Denken* (Tübingen, 1964), 95.

71. CR, vol. 9 and 13: "Elementa rhetorices," "Erotemata dialectices."

72. Sturm, *De amissa dicendi ratione*, see Spitz, Tinsley, *Johann Sturm*, 119–32.

73. *Topica theologica conscripta a clarissimo viro gravissimoque theologo, doctore Andrea Hyperio* (Wittenberg, 1565); W. van't Spijker, *Principe, methode en functie van de theologie bij Andreas Hyperius* (Kampen, 1990).

74. R. Agricola, *De inventione dialectica lucubrationes*, facsimile of the Cologne, 1539 editon (Nieuwkoop, 1967); F. Akkerman, A. J. van der Jagt, eds., *Rodolphus Agricola Phrisius (1444–1485). Proceedings of the International Conference at the University of Groningen 28–30 October 1985* (Leiden, New York, Kopenhagen, Köln, 1988); W. Kühlmann, ed., *Rudolf Agricola 1444–1485, Protagonist des nordeuropäischen Humanismus zum 500. Geburtstag* (Bern, 1994).

75. N. Bruyère, *Méthode et dialectique dans l'oeuvre de La Ramée. Renaissance et âge classique* (Paris, 1984).

When judging the relationship between the Reformation and scholasticism, the question arises whether we will not easily slip back into the mistake of following history only from a retrospective point of view. Thus, we can easily draw conclusions from facts and events which were far ahead for both Reformers and Scholastics. In that sense, Beza and Calvin would have to have been strangers to one another, as would Luther and Melanchthon, which no one would like to say. Presumably, it is most appropriate for us to try to treat them all together like friends and to follow the command of charity towards those who are only separated from us in time by history.

4

Scholasticism and Reformation

Antonie Vos

I. Introduction

The simple division of Western history into *antiquity*, the *Middle Ages* and the modern period—the *new age*—hides an enigma by setting aside (and overlooking) the Middle Ages. Likewise, the history of Western thought is very complicated, in spite of its simple classification in *ancient, medieval and modern* thought. In particular, there is the riddle of *modern scholasticism* since the Renaissance, in contrast with *medieval* scholasticism. For three centuries, many universities during the sixteenth, seventeenth, and eighteenth centuries engaged in enormous intellectual activity. Then we may distinguish between a catholic and a reformational branch of scholasticism. In particular, reformational scholasticism constitutes a rather forgotten world. One knows *that* it was, but scarcely *what* it was. It does still exist, but as a *terra incognita* of the past. Within this broad context of reformational scholasticism we have to ask about the place of *reformed* scholasticism in Western thought. In spite of a long tradition of neglecting this type of scholastic theology and philosophy there are now signs of rediscovering this past.[1] In order to repair this oversight we have to ask for the wider context of this historical phenomenon. A historical phenomenon deserves a historical interpretation. Much older research generally adopts a rather ahistorical approach.

The evolution of Western thought coincides with the history of Western philosophy and this philosophy boasts its own rationality. It even identifies *rationality* with its own way of thinking. Nevertheless, we have to pay attention to a remarkable paradox. Philosophical rationality

---

1. See Richard A. Muller, *Post-reformation Reformed Dogmatics*, 2 vols. to date (Grand Rapids: Baker, 1987–); E. P. Meijering, *Reformierte Scholastik und patristische Theologie. Die Bedeutung des Väterbeweises in der Institutio theologiae elencticae F. Turrettins unter besonderer Berücksichtigung der Gotteslehre und Christologie* (Nieuwkoop, 1991); E. Dekker, *Rijker dan Midas* (Zoetermeer, 1993), and E. Dekker and W. J. van Asselt, eds., *De scholastieke Voetius* (Zoetermeer, 1995), 3, 33, 34–54 and 55ff.

is proud of its knowledge and scientific approach, but is philosophy in general familiar with her own history?

The European mind presupposes that intellectual history sharply changed about 1500. Then a new world of thought was born with the advent of the Renaissance and Humanism. The main idea is that the keener minds of the Renaissance were precisely disturbed on the question of how fruitful the traditional premises were. "By the middle of the sixteenth century the New World had been discovered and partly explored . . . . The Copernican system was replacing that of Ptolemy. Printing had been invented. The story had been told too often to need repeating."[2]

According to this presumption of the breakdown of medieval scholasticism this breakdown is not a hypothesis to be verified, but a self-evident starting-point of Western culture and is considered to be so complete that we are now able to understand modern thought without its past. After the decline of ancient thought in the "Middle Ages" the Enlightenment of a new age dawns. This presumption leads to the practice of studying the philosophy and theology of the sixteenth, seventeenth, and eighteenth centuries without much recourse to medieval thought. General introductions and introductory courses to the history of philosophy mainly skip the medieval phase and in this vein they still jump from Augustine to Descartes, only looking reverently to Thomas Aquinas for a short while. The effect of this procedure is that historical research into sixteenth, seventeenth, and eighteenth century thought mainly takes place without any tradition-historical link with medieval thought. Thus the continuity of scholastic thought at the universities of these centuries is ignored and we are deprived of the possibility of explaining their theories from their own immediate past. This paradox of the Enlightenment approach clearly mirrors itself in the *Dogmengeschichte* tradition of Protestant theology.[3] However, the continuity of the history of the European universities and their sciences and humanities asks for leaving aside *a priori* periodizations.

In this essay, we shall look upon reformed scholasticism within the context of the history of the European university (section 2). Medieval university thought is the cradle of a new Christian philosophy, mainly put forward by the great theologians of the Middle Ages. Within this

2. George Boas, "French Philosophy," *The Encyclopedia of Philosophy* (New York/London, 1967), 3:238, 238–49.
3. See Richard Muller, chapter 1.

context the phenomenon of scholasticism has to be sketched (section 3) and in this light it can be shown that the key to understanding methodological and analytical continuity and discontinuity of Western philosophy and theology is the history of the European university (section 4). Against this background we look at the contribution of Franciscus Gomarus and pay some more attention to the medieval background (section 5). Then we consider the dilemma's of continuity and discontinuity reformed theology is beset with (section 6). The *Epilogue* offers a final perspective.

II. The Problem of the Wider Context of Reformed Scholasticism

According to this Renaissance view of the development of Western philosophy there is a *breakdown of traditional thought* about 1500. This traditional hypothesis means that English and French, German and Italian, Spanish and Dutch, Scandinavian and Middle- and East-European philosophy only start *after about 1500* and thus modern European philosophy is not much older than American thought. This widespread characterization of the history of critical learning and thought might not be compatible with the history of the European university which shows a remarkable continuity between its birth *about 1200* until *about 1800*. Only the nineteenth-century university takes a rather different route. The first six centuries of the history of the Western university, consisting of two blocks of three centuries, have to be seen as a whole and the development of the philosophy and the theology of these centuries have to be studied as a whole. This research asks for tradition-historical diagnostics in order to be able to evaluate agreements and differences.

Modern history of philosophy pays much attention to the great individual philosophers outside the universities. Hobbes and Descartes, Locke and Berkeley, Spinoza, and Leibniz are the privileged ones. This approach, however, begs the question. Can university thought be neglected so easily and naively? Can systematic thought of the sixteenth, seventeenth, and eighteenth centuries be understood without paying much attention to university thought and can the thought of the universities of these centuries be understood without interpreting it in the light of university thought of the thirteenth, fourteenth and fifteenth centuries? Is a realistic approach to the history of Western philosophy possible without seeing and taking into account the continuity of scholasticism from the beginning of the eleventh century until the end of the eighteenth century? A general understanding of the analytical

101

techniques, the methods and the ways of thinking which medieval theology and philosophy have developed, is essential to its elementary understanding.

The phenomenon of *science/Wissenschaft* rests on *methodological revolutions*. It is also co-operative. Critical and scientific thought cannot be an individual affair and therefore it needs *institutions* and not only talented scholars and individuals of genius. Such scientific institutions in the broad sense of *scientific* are very complex and the outcome of extremely inventive processes.

The decisive new institutions for higher and critical teaching and education were only invented during the eleventh and twelfth centuries. At the same time they enjoyed an enormous growth and some centers became influential and large. This achievement was made possible by two impressive innovations: the phenomenon of *monastic education* (*monastery schools*) and the phenomenon of *cathedral schools* or *church schools*. Famous examples of the first type of schools are the monastery schools of Cluny and Le Bec (Lanfranc and Anselm) and famous examples of the second type are the cathedral schools of Chartres and Paris (the school of the Notre Dame). The best schools of both types developed a unique dynamics of their own and became centers of higher learning, unique in sociological structure, unique in the power of theory formation taking place there. Being dependent on the process of mission and Christianization and on the Church they are somewhat isolated from the point of view of cultural history. In the eleventh century the best monastery schools and the best cathedral schools are still rivals of one another, but the near future will belong to the cathedral schools. In the twelfth century the best cathedral schools dethrone the hegemony of the monastic tradition. Here the academic patterns of *team formation* and *specialization* have been invented. In this world of learning lie the foundations of the internal structures of modern university life. Before the twelfth century *science/Wissenschaft* was the affair of a brilliant scholar or an individual of genius, apart from an exception to this rule, e.g. Plato's Academy during its short initial period.[4]

About 1200 a new institutional and educational revolution takes place: the university is born in Bologne, Paris, and Oxford. These universities are not only the oldest universities, but they are also the first universities in the world. The *medieval university* is the first kind of university. The first stage in the history of this university lasts until about

4. See A. Vos, *Johannes Duns Scotus*, (Leiden, 1994), 1–9.

1800 and in a natural way these first six centuries are to be divided in two sets of three centuries: the general Christian university of the first three centuries (c. 1200–c. 1500) and the so-called "confessional" university from the beginning of the sixteenth century until about 1800 (the Catholic, Lutheran, Reformed and Anglican university in Europe and the Dissenter university in New England). From the organizational and structural point of view, this university is the "medieval" university, both in its medieval and its early modern form. Without this university the phenomenon of scientific/wissenschaftlich discovery and research cannot be explained. In the thirteenth century we meet a small number of excellent universities. During the fourteenth and fifteenth centuries most countries of Europe see the birth of a university. In the sixteenth, seventeenth and eighteenth centuries this tradition continues in a confessional-Christian way.

An institutional revolution has given rise to university education and research and this type of the medieval university is the scene of a fundamental *paradigm change of thought*. The theoretical way of thought itself changed. At the thirteenth-century university the battle between Christian thought and ancient philosophy (Aristotelianism) was fought out and decided.[5] Christian contingency thought replaces ancient necessitarian thought.[6] New modalities of thought, like scotism and nominalism, do not have a counterpart in ancient philosophy and medieval Jewish thought. University theology is in the lead and in company of logic and philosophy of language, general philosophy and law; all these branches of learning were flourishing.

Before the Renaissance it was not only an ontological and philosophical revolution which revealed itself in contingency thought and creation theology, but this new way of thinking also paved the way to the new sciences. This process starts with discovering new types of experiments in the thirteenth century and the beginning of mathematical physics in the fourteenth century (the *Mertonians* of Oxford). The critical tendencies of the fourteenth century pull down Aristotle's physicist approach of nature. The sixteenth century sees a continuous renewal of theology and philosophy. During the seventeenth

5. See Vos, *Scotus,* 9–14; A. Vos, "Duns Scotus and Aristotle," in E. P. Bos, ed., *John Duns Scotus. Renewal of philosophy (1265/6–1308)* (Amsterdam, forthcoming); and Vos, "Knowledge, certainty and contingency," in ibid.

6. Details on the characterization of these types of thought: John Duns Scotus, *Contingency and Freedom. Lectura I 39*, transl., comment. and intro. by A. Vos Jaczn et al., (Dordrecht/Boston/London, 1994).

and eighteenth centuries great Christian thinkers build the new sciences of astronomy, physics and chemistry. Modern science is a harvest of Christian thought. The critical attitude of the exact sciences could not have been the fruit of ancient Greek and Hellenistic philosophy. The reason is quite simple: The nature and structure of modern science are excluded by the type of thought embodied in the Greek way of doing philosophy *(philosophia)*. One had still to wait for the true scientific spirit for centuries, because it took an enormous effort to pull down all kinds of fundamental errors of ancient philosophy and to construct a totally new way of thought. Contingent reality has to be approached in terms of contingency. The hypothetical-deductive structure of scientific explanations asks for acknowledging contingency and not an absolutely closed system of physicist phenomena. The medieval phase had an articulated function, even in the development of the physicist method. The modern scientific revolution (Thomas Kuhn) is no fruit of ancient thought; it is the harvest of medieval thought. Not only the new theology and the new philosophy of revelation, but also the exact sciences are invented and developed by faithful scholars.[7]

In sum, early modern thought from about 1500 until about 1800 in general, and early modern scholasticism during these centuries in particular, have to be placed within the whole of the history of about eight centuries of scholasticism. Scholasticism is essentially a method, as will be shown in the next section. The tradition of logical and linguistic analysis, which already had a long history behind it in the sixteenth century, is the methodological *Sitz im Leben* of university thought in the sixteenth, seventeenth and eighteenth centuries in general. In particular, this tradition of logical analysis has to be viewed as the bed of the scholastic theology of the Reformation. With help of the historical method, reformed scholasticism has not to be condemned, but has to be set within the whole of more than eight centuries of scholasticism and without these centuries of scholasticism there is no chance to discover and to be familiar with Western thought.

III. The Phenomenon of Scholasticism

Scholasticism shows a long tradition in many countries and during many

---

7. See A. C. Crombie, *Robert Grosseteste and the Origins of Experimental Science 1100–1700* (Oxford, 1953); David C. Lindberg, *John Pecham and the Science of Optics: Perspectiva communis* (Madison, 1970); R. Hooykaas, *Religion and the Rise of Science,* 2d ed. (Edinburgh/London, 1973).

centuries. For many centuries European thought was very much dependent on Church and theology and thus the tradition of scholasticism is closely interwoven with the tradition of Church and theology. So on the one hand, *reformational scholasticism* is of course a kind of scholasticism, and, on the other hand, it has its institutional roots in the reformation of Church and theology. The Reformation is a moment in the tradition of the Church.[8] The theology of the Reformation is a moment in the tradition of the theology of the Church. On the contrary, the "counter-reformational" theology of the Renaissance (c. 1450–c. 1600),[9] being the modern theology of a new era, constitutes a sharp caesura in the continuous development of theology and therefore, it creates an incisive discontinuity with respect to the Augustinian theology of the Middle Ages.[10] The problem of continuity and discontinuity is also a major problem in studying the scholasticism of the Reformation.[11]

From the beginning of the Western university, the theological faculty was the most advanced and creative faculty and, therefore, we have to try to understand *theological scholasticism* and *scholastic theology* within the orbit of the subjects of the university. The history of the university is the context of the history of theology and so in understanding scholastic

8. A. A. van Ruler, *Reformatorische opmerkingen in de ontmoeting met Rome* (Hilversum, 1965), 16; and compare van Ruler, "De noodzakelijkheid van een trinitarische theologie," *Verwachting en voltooiing* (Nijkerk, 1978), 9–28; and van Ruler, "Perspectieven voor de gereformeerde theologie," *Theologisch Werk* II (Nijkerk, 1971): 78–100.

9. See Charles B. Schmitt and Quentin Skinner, eds., *The Cambridge history of Renaissance Philosophy* (Cambridge, 1988), especially part 1: "The intellectual context" and part 3: "Supplementary material," and chapter 12: "Philosophy and humanistic disciplines" (713–61).

10. Therefore, we can say that Luther fights the Renaissance rather than the Middle Ages. See also below, section 7.

11. In the course of the sixteenth century we see developing many reformational centres of higher academic education. It would be interesting to know whether the form of education and research is scholastic at every stage of the development of these institutions. It seems to be the case that we do not see truly humanistic centers of of higher education on the side of the Reformation. In the sixteenth century every tradition uses humanistically trained authors, but in contrast with the Catholic church, the church of the reformation does not seem to have humanistic institutions. So it is to be asked what be the historical place of reformational scholasticism in general, and what be the historical place of reformed scholasticism in particular. A fruitful approach of this stage of theological development depends on the perspective of the history of the Western universities and all their faculties, including theology and philosophy. There we have also to look for the explanation of the rise of the sciences and humanities—the *wetenschappen/the Wissenschaften* in general.

theology we have to start with the history of our universities and the history of university education and research.

When and where did scholasticism arise?[12] There is no scholasticism in antiquity, but after the Dark Ages *scholastic method* and *scholasticism* already developed in the tenth century:[13]

> Now they got an opportunity to devote themselves to intellectual work. In the beginning of the tenth century there was a such an interest in methodological issues and a methodical approach that one discovered some logical works of Boethius. Only then the scholastic method developed. . . . Since Abbo of Fleury and Gerbert of Aurillac the basis of this critical education enlarged itself more and more during the following centuries, until in the fourteenth and fifteenth centuries there was a complete arsenal of logical techniques, especially the techniques of terminist logic.[14]

What is to be meant by the *scholastic method*? The best description has been given by De Rijk:

> By *scholastic method* I mean: a method applied in philosophy (and in theology) which is characterized, both on the level of *research* and on the level of *teaching*, by the use of an ever and ever recurring system of concepts, distinctions, definitions, propositional analyses, argumentational techniques and disputational methods, which had originaly been derived

---

12. See on the problem of the periodization of medieval history of philosophy and its program L. M. de Rijk, *Middeleeuwse wijsbegeerte. Traditie en vernieuwing* (Assen, 1981), chapters 3 and 4; and Vos, *Scotus,* 1–8. De Rijk's book was translated into French: *La philosophie au moyen âge* (Leiden, 1985), henceforth abbreviated PMA. It summarizes much of De Rijk's splendid teaching on medieval thought that is not to be found in his English works and critical editions. Trained in classical philology and ancient philosophy, De Rijk is very sensitive to the elements of medieval thought that have no counterpart in ancient philosophy. Consult in particular chapters 3 and 4 of PMA. Compare Alan B. Cobban, *The Medieval Universities: Their Development and Organisation* (London, 1975), and Cobban, *The medieval English universities Oxford and Cambridge to c. 1500* (Aldershot, 1988).

13. See *Middeleeuwse wijsbegeerte,* 90–105, 108–38 (PMA, 68–80, 82–105), and Martin Grabmann, *Geschichte der scholastischen Methode,* 2 vols. (Freiburg im Breisgau, 1909–1911; reprint, Graz, 1957).

14. De Rijk, *Middeleeuwse wijsbegeerte,* 114–15 (PMA 87). Regarding terminist logic see *Middeleeuwse wijsbegeerte,* 98–115, and especially 119–20 (PMA 75–87, 91–92), and De Rijk's standardworks, *Logica Modernorum,* 2 vols. (Assen 1962–1967). See also John A. Marenbon, *From the circle of Alcuin to the school of Auxerre* (Cambridge, 1981), and Marenbon, *Early medieval philosophy (480–1150). An introduction* (London, 1983).

from the Aristotelist-Boethian logic, but later on, on a much larger scale, from the indigenous terminist logic.[15]

In the tenth and eleventh centuries the study of elementary grammar of medieval Latin went through such a creative stage that twelfth-century linguistics already saw a mature semantical and syntactical theory of Latin. Then theory of language (*grammatica*) and logic (*dialectica*) met one another. This development of combining logical and grammatical analyses led to a flow of analytical thinking. Scholastic thought is simply to be characterized as critical and precise thinking to be developed in the schools (*scholastic* meaning *wissenschaftlich/wetenschappelijk*) and then maturing as analytical thinking *pur sang*. The confluence of grammar and logic in the eleventh and twelfth centuries created a method of logical and semantical analysis of language. At the same time theology and (canon) law opened their gates to the whole of these powerful tools. Logical analysis of language especially flourished in theology, starting as *sacra pagina*. In this period *theology* was originally an academic endeavour aimed at interpreting the sacred pages of Scripture. The contextual approach of the functions of words in Latin sentences was the cradle of *terminist logic*: the logic of properties of terms and the uses of terms in propositions.[16] The second half of the twelfth century sees the discovery of the recently translated *De sophisticis elenchis* of Aristotle.[17] This systematic confrontation enriches the new style of language analysis. The theory of *fallacies* (*fallacie*) made many original contributions to the *scholastic method*.[18]

This new scholastic logic, or as it was aptly called *logica modernorum*, is the bed of working up traditional, Aristotelist logic. The upshot of this

15. De Rijk, *Middeleeuwse wijsbegeerte*, 111 (PMA 85). Compare E. Dekker, *Rijker dan Midas*, 8–12, and W. J. van Asselt and E. Dekker, eds., *De scholastieke Voetius*, 1–5.

16. See L. M. de Rijk, *Logica Modernorum*, 2:95–130, and de Rijk, "The early origin of the theory of supposition," in Norman Kretzmann, Jan Pinborg and Anthony Kenny, eds., *The Cambridge history of later medieval philosophy* (Cambridge, 1982), 161–73.

17. The *logica nova* comprises the remainder of the *Organon*: the *Analytica Priora* on syllogistic techniques (in Boethius' translation, only rediscovered in the twelfth century) and the *Analytica Posteriora* on theory of science (in the translation of James of Venice [1128]), the *Topica* (probability argumentations) and *De sophisticis elenchis* (fallacies). See L. M. de Rijk, *Petrus Abaelardus. Dialectica*, XIII–XVIII; de Rijk, *Logica Modernorum*, 1:14–15 and *Middeleeuwse wijsbegeerte* 119–20 (PMA 91–92.)

18. See L. M. de Rijk, *Logica Modernorum* 1:13–178, and compare Klaus Jacobi, "Logic (II): the later twelfth century," in Peter Dronke, ed., *A History of Twelfth-Century Philosophy* (Cambridge, 1988), 227–51.

process is that Aristotelist looking logic of the twelfth, thirteenth and fourteenth centuries is quite different from the logic of the Aristotle of ancient history.[19]

IV. Theological (Dis)continuity in the Light of the History of the University

It is not an easy matter to interpret adequately the philosophical and theological texts of the sixteenth, seventeenth and eighteenth centuries. In order to understand properly the thinkers of these centuries, one has to start where these thinkers as young students themselves started. They started with a very demanding training in methodological argumentation and in the sixteenth century this training already had an impressive past of many centuries duration. Originally it was linked up with the *trivium* of the *artes liberales*. The early modern university of the sixteenth century continues the theoretical style of the medieval university. This old tradition of logical analysis is the methodological *Sitz im Leben* of reformed scholasticism. In order to understand the "scientific" output of the "medieval" university in the paradoxically broad sense of this word one has to start with the methodological training which is so characteristic of it.

Here the traditional literature on the subject has failed. Nineteenth-century research was accustomed to making value judgments about what one had to investigate. One acted as a judge instead of exploring the riches of the thought of the past in its own value. Twentieth-century histories of theology often followed the negative attitude of nineteenth-century liberal ideology. We have to free ourselves from these prejudices in order to discover the tradition of Western theology and philosophy and this is especially true of reformational scholasticism and of reformed scholasticism. If reformed scholasticism is cut off from scholasticism in general and if one tries to understand both, without the background of medieval *philosophia christiana*, one prevents oneself from understanding centuries of European and Western thought.

On the basis of the history of learning a different approach for understanding the history of theology can be proposed. The historian is not a *laudator temporis acti*; at any rate he is not a judge or prosecuting attorney of history. Traditional historians of theological scholasticism of

---

19. For details, see the many contributions in Kretzmann, et al, eds., *The Cambridge History of Later Medieval Philosophy*.

the Reformation tended to act as judges and prosecutors. Without appealing to *Tout comprendre c'est tout pardonner* we ought to feel obliged to try to understand. We need to study in detail the three grand centuries of the history of reformational universities in Switzerland and Scotland, the Netherlands and the parts of Germany and France which were reformed during the sixteenth and (or) seventeenth centuries and the history of the oldest universities in the United States. We need to have new knowledge of the academic and theological output during those centuries, e.g., in Basel and Heidelberg, Zurich and Bern, Geneva and Leyden, Franeker and Herborn, Groningen and Utrecht, Harderwijk and Amsterdam, Steinfurt and Bremen, Dordt and Deventer, Aberdeen and Edinburgh, Harvard, Yale and Princeton. There is an abundance of *theologia reformata* and *philosophia reformata* to be investigated with both interest and admiration.

The indicated development gives rise to the question whether there is a specific historical paradox of the history of reformed theology. The two centuries between the last quarter of the sixteenth century and the last quarter of the eighteenth show a remarkable maximum of theoretical intersubjectivity in systematic thought. I do not know a parallel phenomenon of such a strict theoretical continuity of one theological or philosophical tradition during two centuries. It is a consensus shared by members of tens of universities in many countries. Such a consensus cannot be demonstrated during the twelfth and thirteenth centuries. Moreover, the contrast between the two hundred years before and after 1800 is shocking. A maximum of theoretical intersubjectivity is replaced by a minimum of such a consensus. Today, the degree of intersubjectivity in reformed theology is almost zero. The ideas run from strict orthodoxy to a kind of worldview which is almost atheistic. This last fact does not contribute to any academic heroism. In terms of critical intersubjectivity and consensus reformed theology does not exist any more. If we do not have the glorious past, we have nothing.

The traditional view sees a deep gulf between medieval theology before 1500 and reformational theology after 1517. However, this scheme overlooks the degree of continuity in the history of the European university during the three centuries before 1500 and the three centuries after 1500. The medieval university and the "confessional" university of the sixteenth, seventeenth and eighteenth centuries are two types of the same Christian university. Only the nineteenth century saw a new kind of university. The period between about 1775 and about 1825 created a deep gulf. The theoretical continuity of university and learning is broken. The Latin and scholastic university is replaced by the national type of university. The effects are enormous. The thought of the recent past is suppressed and forgotten. Moreover, the nineteenth century is the century of history, but understanding scholasticism requires strong foundations in scholastic expertise. Such conceptual presuppositions for understanding scholasticism were not present any longer in the course of the nineteenth century. The upshot is a distorted picture of the philosophy and theology of our own university tradition. This situation cannot be characterized as a reasonable one. The great nineteenth-century works on systematic theology in the sixteenth and seventeenth centuries sketch a picture which is scarcely recognizable from the purely historical point of view. This disturbing fact makes new research tremendously interesting.[20]

V. A Paradigmatic Change? Two Models of Interpretation

The striking consensus within reformed scholasticism gives rise to the question as to how this theoretical identity developed. It seems that in particular the nineties of the sixteenth century played an important role in this development. The general background is to be sketched as follows: In contrast with the Lutheran tradition, the reformed tradition did not possess academic centers before 1525. The first period (c. 1525 – c. 1550) is almost entirely occupied with practical work and the first cares of the project of reformation. The practical life of the church has to be built. There seems almost no room for a policy for theological learning and university life. During the second quarter of the sixteenth century reformed academic centers are restricted to Switzerland. Martyrs and refugees do not develop a policy for theological research and academic training. Nevertheless, there were plans from the beginning. The two generations after 1550 build the institutional framework of theology and reform the legacy of the Christian university of the Middle Ages. Basel and Lausanne, Geneva and Zurich take the lead in this process, while the oldest medieval university of Germany, the University of Heidelberg, plays a main role after 1560.

---

20. See W. J. van Asselt's critical reflections on the history of historical research of reformed scholasticism: "Herwaardering van de gereformeerde scholastiek," *Kerktijd* 5 (1995): 1–11; van Asselt, "Studie van de gereformeerde scholastiek: verleden en toekomst," *Nederlands Theologisch Tijdschrift* 50 (1996); van Asselt, "De erfenis van de gereformeerde scholastiek," *Kerk en Theologie* 47 (1996): 126–36; A.Vos, "De kern van de klassieke gereformeerde theologie," *Kerk en Theologie* 47 (1996): 106–25.

Let us now pay attention to some aspects of the hypothesis that the identifying paradigm of systematic reformed theology has been shaped gradually during the last third part of the sixteenth century. The theoretical identity of this type of scholastic theology maintains itself magnificently during two centuries and it appears still intact in the monumental series of seven volumes on dogmatics by Bernhardinus de Moor in his *commentary* on à Marck's introduction to systematic theology.[21] The contribution of one concrete figure is to be put in the center. He is one of the most important Dutch theologians, the pivotal figure in the battle around Arminius' theology during the decades before the Synod of Dordt (1618–1619): Franciscus Gomarus (1563–1641).[22]

In spite of his fascinating personality and his impressive academic career his stance in systematic theology is still not well known and he is still a rather neglected figure as a scholar and as a thinker.[23] He was one of the leading professors of divinity in the early years of the theological faculty at the newly founded Leyden University (1594–1611). The new triumvirate (Lucas Trelcatius Sr. (1542–1602), Franciscus Junius Sr. (1545–1602) and the young Gomarus) injected new life into the facuty in this last decade of the sixteenth century. The quantity and quality of the *disputations* increased at a great pace. Let us have a closer look at one of these disputations, that which was defended under Gomarus on 21 January 1595 by Jac. Miggrodius. It was called *Theses theologicae de providentia Dei*. This disputation possesses a programmatic value. Thesis VI introduces God's indefinite foreknowledge:

1. The *indefinite foreknowledge* is in God the most perfect knowledge of universal and individual states of affairs which can obtain.[24]

21. *Commentarius perpetuus in Johannis Marckii Compendium theologiae christianae didactico-elencticum* (Leyden, 1761–1778).

22. Professor of divinity in Leyden (1594–1611), Middelburg (1611–1615), Saumur (1615–1618) and Groningen (1618–1641). See the definite biography by G. P. van Itterzon, *Franciscus Gomarus* (The Hague, 1929/1930); and van Itterzon, "Franciscus Gomarus," in A. de Groot, et al, *Biografisch Lexicon voor de geschiedenis van het Nederlandse protestantisme* (Kampen, 1983), 2:220–25. See also *The Auction Catalogue of the Library of F. Gomarus*, facsimile edition, intr. and indexes by E. Dekker, J. Knoop and C. M. L. Verdegaal, Catalogi Redivivi 10 (Utrecht: 't Goy-Houten, 1996), which contains a short biography in English (vii-x).

23. Isaäc van Dijk (1847–1923) sketched a finely tuned psychological portrait of this easy going man from Bruges in his "Franciscus Gomarus" (1914), *Gezamenlijke Geschriften* II, 2d ed. (Groningen, 1924), 2:439–55.

24. "*Praescientia indefinita* est rerum universarum et singularium, quae fieri possunt, perfectissima in Deo scientia." This thesis recurs, in an elaborate way, in Gomarus'

Thesis VII presents the dual kernel concept of the *prefinition* (*praefinitio*):

> 2. The *prefinition* is *God's act of will* by which He has defined before the creation and gubernation of the world from his foreknowledge of states of affairs.[25]

(1) and (2) constitute the comprehensive concept of *decretum* of thesis V:

> 3. This *decree* comprehends the *indefinite foreknowledge* (which we also call: [*knowledge*] *which is simply insight*) and the *prefinition* or *predestination*, but then understood in its general sense.[26]

In order to have a good grasp of the content of these lapidary theses, we have to ask ourselves in what way the important expressions "all individual states of affairs which can obtain" in (1) and "from his foreknowledge of states of affairs" in (2) have to be interpreted, and in particular which *possibilities* are referred to by the expression "states of affairs which *can* obtain" in (1). Perhaps contrary to our expectation, the "foreknown states of affairs" do not consist of the future of our created world, but they refer to the much larger set of the *a priori* possibilities of our world of creation. Gomarus' concept of *indefinite foreknowledge* refers, in more modern wordings, to all future possibilities or all possible worlds.[27] Such an interpretation stems from the *contingency model* which Gomarus and his old reformed colleagues adhered to.[28]

Conciliatio doctrinae orthodoxae de providentia Dei (1597) and will also recur, in slightly different words, in a disputation on predestination of 1609, a disputation which played its role in the Arminius-conflict which would arise in the meantime. This 1609 disputation on *predestination* has been paid much attention to for the first time in the prize winning Master's thesis of A. J. Kunz (1997).

25. "*Praefinitio* est actio voluntatis Dei, qua ex rebus praescitis, creationem et gubernationem mundi praefinivit."

26. "*Decretum* hoc complectitur *praescientiam indefinitam* (quam *simplicis intelligentiae* vocant) et *praefinitionem* seu *praedestinationem* generaliter sumptam."

27. See also the description and analysis of the conceptual structures of Franciscus Turrettini's theology in A. Vos, "De kern van de klassieke gereformeerde theologie," *Kerk en Theologie* 47 (1996): 115–25.

28. Who is the *auctor intellectualis* or is this paradigm change to be understood as a process to which many theologians have contributed? The work of the young Gomarus was a kind of catalyst, but we have also to take into account the work of the previous generations of Zanchi and Beza, Ursinus and Perkins. In the nineties we observe the culmination of a development prepared for during many years. Gomarus himself refers in 1597 and in 1609 in particular to the *doctor doctorum*, Gregory of Valencia (1549–1603) and his *Commentarii theologici* I–IV (1591–1597) and to Suárez.

The propositions (1) – (3) present a basic structure of the doctrine of God. What is the "contingency model" embodied in this set of propositions and how is this model related to the traditional interpretations of the way of thought of old reformed scholasticism?

In order to identify ways of thought we have to analyze distinctive concepts. We cannot stick to terms because we do not know *a priori* which concepts are meant by which terms. Thus we have to look for definitions and conceptual structures in order to expound what the terms involved mean. The pivotal role of the will in proposition (2) gives us a clue to our model. We have seen that Gomarus worked with the concepts of God's *indefinite (fore)knowledge* and of God's *definite (fore-) knowledge*. This signals the world of God's free knowledge (*scientia libera*) and his *necessary/natural knowledge*, in which the divine will is pivotal indeed.[29]

When we focus on these concepts of God's definite knowledge and of God's free knowledge we have to ask ourselves tradition-historical questions. Where does the origin of these sixteenth and seventeenth century thought forms lie? We find this origin in the discoveries of contingency thought in the line of Augustine and Anselm—the "AA-line." This AA-line is followed by the Victorines and the early Franciscan school of Alexander of Hales in Paris. This way of thought has been enlarged by Bonaventure and Henry of Ghent and many Oxonian theologians during the second half of the thirteenth century, because this AA-line was then exceptionally strong at Oxford University (Robert Grosseteste). Henry of Ghent developed a theoretical framework where God's knowledge of the reality of creation is related to the divine will. In agreement with this innovation, Duns Scotus reconstructed the doctrine of God at the end of the thirteenth century. One of the improvements he made was his answer to the question of what status had to be assigned to the divine knowledge of what is contingent. In the tradition of the theology of the church it was not disputed *that* God knows the

---

29. This way of thought differs in a remarkable way from the model which rests on the distinction between *knowledge which simply is insight* (*scientia simplicis intelligentiae*) and *intuitive knowledge* (*scientia visionis*), without any pivotal function of the divine will while according to this (thomistic) model God's knowledge of factual reality immediately flows from God's essence. Both kinds of God's knowledge (*scientia simplicis intelligentiae* and *scientiae visionis*) function as two necessarily co-ordinated sets of divine knowledge which are, respectively, related to different kinds of not-being, namely what is *never* being and what is *not now* being, but either in the past or in the future. A good example of how complex and misleading the interpretation of texts in terms of models and concepts can be at the textual level, is that Gomarus uses the *term* "knowledge which is simply insight" for the *concept* of "necessary or indefinite knowledge."

contingent, but could one call God's knowledge of the contingent itself contingent? Scotus' answer was affirmative: divine knowledge of the contingent is in the synchronic sense contingent.[30] In later scholasticism this contingent knowledge of God is usually called "free knowledge" (*scientia libera*). Herewith we have in fact met a quite important, non-deterministic conceptual infrastucture. At the same time we have passed by the dilemma of determinism-indeterminism. This basic structure of theological contingency thought conquers the academic scene of the *Ecclesia Reformata* at the beginning of the seventeenth century at a great pace. It will almost completely dominate her theology of reformed scholasticism during the next two centuries.

The theoretical framework defended by Gomarus and many other reformed thinkers of the seventeenth and eighteenth centuries has been interpreted in different ways. An almost completely opposite view has been very influential. This approach may sound rather natural: Because Gomarus is a calvinist, we have to interpret his theoretical foundations in the light of Calvin's doctrine of God. The modern reformed tradition has interpreted Gomarus and Dordt according to the harsh lines of this determinism. God's fatherly face is hidden behind the concept of absolute power, the idol of a mechanically deterministic causality. It would be the dark predestination of a *potentia absoluta* and involves a *decretum absolutum* which does not take into account Jesus Christ.[31] The theology of the *Christian Reformed Church* and the *Reformed Churches* in the Netherlands has defended the banner of the Synod of Dordt and the reformed theology of the seventeenth century from the middle of the nineteenth century onwards. The years between 1955 and 1965 saw a drastic change. G. C. Berkouwer corrected this positive assessment of Dordt in *De verkiezing Gods*.[32] In 1965 A. D. R. Polman severely criticized the old stance. The classic doctrine of election and rejection is always threatened by a causal determinism. Such an abstract and sovereign decree is not biblical, neither pastoral.[33] A kindred description is to be found in the works of S. van der Linde and C. Graafland. I characterize

30. See *Contingency and Freedom*, esp. 150–51, 168–69.

31. See A. D. R. Polman, "De leer der verwerping van eeuwigheid," in R. Schippers, G. E. Meuleman, J. T. Bakker and H. M. Kuitert, eds., *Ex auditu verbi* (Kampen, 1965), 176–93.

32. G. C. Berkouwer, *De verkiezing Gods* (Kampen, 1955); cf. J. Veenhof, "Honderd jaar theologie aan de Vrije Universiteit," *Wetenschap en Rekenschap* 1880–1980 (Kampen, 1980), 83–84 (44–104).

33. See A. D. R. Polman, "De leer der verwerping."

this type of interpretation as "decay ideology." After the golden time of Calvin the flood of orthodox scholasticism came.[34]

I do not wish to dispute the systematic position the aforementioned authors themselves reject in their assessment. I only stress that something has to be brought up for discussion which has been taken for granted, namely just the interpretation of the kind of view defended by Gomarus and many others. The description, interpretation and analysis of the old theories are at stake. Is the old reformed heritage a heritage we are familiar with? Or is it a *terra incognita*, even in the purely historical sense? The traditional assessment rests on the conclusion that the old scholastic type of reformed theology was a philosophical determinism. Surely, the systematic style was philosophical in a grand way, but was it deterministic? Quite the contrary.

VI. Methodical Breaches and Bridges

What is the specific place and function of the Reformed institutions of higher education on the map of university education during the sixteenth, seventeenth, and eighteenth centuries and does the legacy of their (systematic) theology still enjoy a special value in view of the present situation of the Church and her theology?

This vital question presupposes that we are familiar with this legacy of systematic theology. However, this presupposition does not quite hold. At the end of the eighteenth century a sustained opposition to scholastic

---

34. A second type of interpretation, which in a way reinforces the determinist interpretation, has been put forward by historians of philosophy. The greatest historian of the history of Dutch philosophy was Sassen. Sassen characterized the tradition of old reformed thought as a type of christian Aristotelism. It was an unoriginal calvinist Aristotelism. See F. Sassen, *Geschiedenis van de wijsbegeerte in Nederland tot het einde der negentiende eeuw* (Amsterdam/Brussels, 1959), 120–90: "Aristotelisme en Cartesianisme." See 121: "Aanvankelijk werd niets anders gedoceerd dan het gezuiverde en vereenvoudigde Aristotelisme, dat de Laatscholastiek en het Humanisme als vrucht van de onderwijsvernieuwing van de 16de eeuw hadden nagelaten. De Hervorming heeft als zodanig in den inhoud van het wijsgerig onderwijs geen wijziging aangebracht." Cf., 123: "een gereformeerde theologie van Aristotelische signatuur"!

A third type is in fact a variant of the second one. It takes into account that medieval philosophy cannot be a simple Aristotelism, because creation theology cannot be the same as a kind of philosophy which excludes creation, like Aristotle's cosmology and physics do. In 1982 I qualified old reformed thought, incorrectly, as a calvinist thomism. The theoretical background is medieval and christian, but still in a vein similar to the Aristotelist legacy. See A. Vos, "Thomas van Aquino en de gereformeerde theologie. Een theologie-historische impressie," *Jaarboek 1982. Werkgroep Thomas van Aquino* (Utrecht, 1982), 114–19.

theology arose in the bosom of the reformed churches (e.g. in the Netherlands Ypey) and the great works from the nineteenth century on classical reformed doctrine (Gass, Schweizer, Scholten, Sepp, Heppe, Kuyper, Bavinck) suffer from a systematic lack of understanding of the conceptual structures of reformed scholasticism.

So there is a historical urgency to explore the theoretical identity and the contents of classic reformed theology against the background of classic academic theology during the second millennium *post Christum natum*.

An especially clear example of systematic confusion regarding reformed theology is that of Joannes Henricus Scholten (1811–1885). He stirred up a furious debate at Leyden University, about the direction to be taken by theology in the Netherlands Reformed Church. Scholten's deterministic approach and his parallel interpretation of old reformed dogmatics rested on his rejection of what he called "equilibristic freedom." Equilibristic freedom is freedom intrinsically linked up with synchronic contingency. All participants in the debate were still familiar with the central concepts involved, but all except Sytze Hoekstra shared in the basic conceptual and theoretical presuppositions of their opponent Scholten, including orthodox theologians (La Saussaye, Gunning, and later on Kuyper and Bavinck). The old semantical-logical and ontological foundations of classic scholastic theology comprising a tradition of about eight centuries turned out to have been forgotten and the critics did not realize that there was still a historical problem. They were all, unintentionally, conceptual determinists, and did not realize that their ancestors were not.

Is there no determinism at all in Reformed theology? In part, there is. An early deterministic wave is to be discerned during the first phase of sixteenth-century Reformation (Luther, Zwingli, and Calvin). However, this sixteenth-century wave has a church historical context quite different from the flood of determinism in the nineteenth century. Renaissance Christianity tries to reconstruct the reality of the Christian faith and to redefine the concept of what Christian faith is up to. Moreover, this new type of Christianity is supported by the Vatican and modern humanistic theology. The classic theocentric and Christocentric finality of human existence and human destiny is replaced by a *duplex ordo* view: Reality is twofold. It has an absolute foundation in itself, bestowed on it by its Creator. The super-natural reality of faith, church and sacraments is erected upon it. The reality of faith is not part and parcel of the essence of reality as such. Human nature is sufficient in itself; moreover, it is enriched by its relation to God. At this frontier we see Luther thundering. His target was not medieval theology, with which he was not familiar in a historical sense. His target was new Renaissance Christianity.[35] Decay ideology confuses *terms* and *concepts*, *method* and *content*, *cause* and *effect*. Nevertheless, in spite of Luther's spotless intentions, his determinism was not correct either.

If we once again take a look at sixteenth-century theology of the *Ecclesia reformata*, we see that they responded quite differently to the predicament of the early Enlightenment of the sixteenth century than orthodox theology responded to the modern predicament of the nineteenth century. During the second half of the sixteenth century one went to great lengths in order to become familiar with the grand theology of the medieval past. The Iberian thinkers of Spain's and Portugal's Golden Age set an example. In the course of this reorientation Scotus' legacy became a major influence. Even the authoritative handbook of theology—Thomas Aquinas' *Summa theologiae*—was read through Scotistically tinted glasses.[36] In this way the medieval heritage bore reformational fruit. The medieval point of view becomes a key in understanding reformed theology. In order to see the link between Augustinian theology and Scotus' innovations on the one hand and old reformed thought on the other hand we need the historical background of medieval philosophical *and* theological thought in contrast with ancient philosophy:

> No student of medieval speculative thought can help being struck by the peculiar fact that whenever fundamental progress was made, it was theological problems which initiated the development. This applies to St Augustine and Boethius, and to the great medieval masters as well (such as Anselm, Thomas Aquinas, Duns Scotus). Their speculation was, time and again, focused on how the notion of being and the whole range of our linguistic tools can be applied to God's Nature (Being).[37]

35. For a brief description of this important shift toward a duplex-ordo view, see H. Veldhuis, *Ein versiegeltes Buch. Der Naturbegriff in der Theologie J. G. Hamanns (1730–1788)* (Berlin/New York, 1994), ch. 1. This study is based upon more extensive studies by H. de Lubac and J. H. Walgrave. See also A. Vos, "Theologiehistorische dilemma's rond de verzoeningsleer," in E. Dekker, M. C. Batenburg and D. H. J. Steenks, eds., *Solidair en solide* (Kampen, 1997), 144–49 (133–49).

36. See Allan B. Wolter, "Scotism," in Hans Burkhardt and Barry Smith, eds., *Handbook of Metaphysics and Ontology*, (Munich/Philadelphia/Vienna: Philosophia Verlag, 1991), 816–18.

37. L. M. de Rijk, "On Boethius's notion of being. A chapter of Boethian

The originality of medieval philosophy and the creativity of its logic and theory of knowledge make themselves felt in many contributions without any counterpart in ancient philosophy. These novelties possess a tremendous cultural importance in general and a great theoretical interest for modern philosophy and current systematic theology in particular.[38]

VII. Epilogue

Why is our theme of Reformation and Scholasticism so fascinating? The reality and the concept of Reformation refer to the reality of the Church in a humiliating way, because the Church has to be a body which is as such in no need of reform. Therefore, in view of reformation we have to remind ourselves of the words of Paul: "So I must remind you of the Gospel that I preached to you." This initiative of the Gospel of Christ created an ongoing history of salvation and theology belongs to many startling innovations wrought by the Church in the life of the Spirit in the course of this history. On the foundations laid down by the Greek and Latin Fathers the gift of theology as a new way of ideas has been developed through a wealth of new institutions: monastery schools, cathedral schools, universities. The medieval university is the great present of the medieval church and her Christian society to mankind and the world of its learning. This medieval type of university forms the natural background of reformed scholasticism.

The basic structure of the systematic theology of the reformed tradition challenges modern systematic theology. Modern theology itself has become the prisoner of the structures of modern thought. In this light the theme Reformation and Scholasticism implicitly expresses an

---

semantics," in Norman Kretzmann, ed., *Meaning and inference in medieval philosophy* (Dordrecht, 1988), 1 (1–29); E. P. Bos, ed., *L.M. de Rijk. Through Language to Reality* (Northampton: Variorum reprints 1989), 1–29.

38. As alluded to in section 3 above, L.M. de Rijk lists four examples of original contributions that excel the inventions of ancient Greek, Hellenistic and Roman philosophy: (1) terminist logic (which is in fact to be seen as a part of the wider phenomenon of the *logica modernorum*), (2) the metaphysics of Thomas Aquinas (see chapters 6 and 7 of *Middeleeuwse wijsbegeerte* [PMA]), (3) the critical theory of knowledge of the fourteenth and fifteenth centuries, and (4) a way of thought which differs markedly from necessitarian Greek philosophy—to which I connected the term "synchronic contingency." See *Middeleeuwse wijsbegeerte*, 91–93 (PMA 69–71: `Les développements propres à la philosophie médiévale'). Consult also PMA, 3.2 and 3.4.

ecumenical challenge. The great contributions of twentieth-century theology (Troeltsch, Barth, Brunner, Tillich, Rahner) cannot be worked up into the synthesis of one scientific theology. So if we do not dispose of a strong classical theology there is no theology of the Church at all, but in that case there are only individualistic contributions of independent theologians. Therefore, there is a systematic need of exploring the riches of classic theology.

5

Thomism in Zanchi's Doctrine of God

Harm Goris

The title of the symposium from which the present collection of articles resulted was "Reformation and Scholasticism, an Oecumenical Enterprise." This formulation not only suggests that the study of the era of Reformed Scholasticism, which until recently was so often disregarded in academic research, should be a joint enterprise of contemporary Protestant and Catholic scholars. It also suggests that Reformed Scholasticism should itself be looked upon as an ecumenical enterprise: Lutheran, Calvinist and Catholic theologians shared a rich and flexible whole of methods, philosophical tools and technical vocabulary, which served them in developing their own, distinct traditions, and, at the same time, enabled them to engage in interdenominational conversations, however polemical those sometimes might be.[1]

The work of the Italian Girolamo Zanchi (1516–1590), also known by the Latinized name of Hieronymus Zanchius, represents an early but exemplary case of such an ecumenical enterprise. John Patrick Donnelly even coined the expression "Calvinist Thomism" to characterize the efforts of both Zanchi and his teacher, colleague and fellow-countryman Peter Martyr Vermigli (or Petrus Martyr Vermilius, 1499–1562) to put their former Thomistic training to use in formulating, clarifying and defending the Reformed understanding of the Gospel.[2] From the mid-sixties onward scholarly interest in these two Italian reformers has grown and, gradually, their theological views and those of their fellow "Reformed Scholastics" have become more appreciated. Joseph McLelland summarizes nicely the contemporary received view on these thinkers: "In the thesis about Reformed Scholasticism, Calvin himself

1. I want to thank the members of the research group "The theology of Thomas Aquinas" of the Catholic Theological University at Utrecht and the participants in the symposium for their valuable comments and criticisms.

2. J. P. Donnelly, "Calvinist Thomism," *Viator* 7 (1976): 441–55.

must not be separated and exalted so that he represents a pristine Reformed theology over against Beza, Martyr and Zanchi."[3] This article focuses on the way in which Zanchi makes use of the thought of Thomas Aquinas in his doctrine of God. My account will differ from Otto Gründler's on a number of points and it will also become clear that Donnelly's provocative expression "Calvinist Thomism" should be nuanced.[4] I shall limit myself to Zanchi's *De Natura Dei*, his most elaborate systematic account of the divine nature and its attributes. First I shall give some biographical information on Zanchi and a short summary and characterization of *De Natura Dei*. Secondly, I will offer a more detailed account of the Thomistic background of two central parts of Zanchi's doctrine, *viz.* the structure of our God-talk and the content of the doctrine of grace. In the third and final section I shall resume these two issues and I shall indicate how Zanchi's position also differs from Aquinas's.

It will be shown that Zanchi knows Aquinas very well and that he reads him in an intelligent and benevolent way. Occasionally he does not agree with Aquinas's formulations although this does not necessarily imply that their theological views are irreconcilable. However, by assuming a "natural order" among the divine attributes Zanchi seems to introduce a structural element in his theology that is fundamentally foreign to Aquinas.

I. Girolamo Zanchi and *De Natura Dei*

Girolamo Zanchi was born near Bergamo in 1516 and joined the Augustinian canons at the age of fifteen.[5] It is there that he received his

---

3. McLelland J. C., "Introduction," xxxii *in Peter Martyr Vermigli. Philosophical Works.* The Peter Martyr Library vol. 4 (Kirksville MO, 1996). Publications on Martyr outnumber those on Zanchi, but the Thomistic and Scholastic characteristics are more apparent in the latter.

4. In 1965 Otto Gründler published his *Die Gotteslehre Girolami Zanchis und ihre Bedeutung für seine Lehre von der Prädestination* (Neukirchen-Vluyn: Neukirchener Verlag, 1965). This book is largely based on Gründler's (unpublished) doctoral dissertation, *Thomism and Calvinism in the Theology of Girolamo Zanchi* (Princeton, 1961). It is still the only full-length study on Zanchi's theology. Apart from some articles dealing with very specific, theological topics in Zanchi's writings, more general information can be found in: Donnelly, "Calvinist Thomism"; J. P. Donnelly, "Italian Influences in the Development of Calvinist Scholasticism," *Sixteenth Century Journal* 7 (1976): 81–101; and C. J. Burchill, "Girolamo Zanchi: Portrait of A Reformed Theologian and His Work," *Sixteenth Century Journal* 15 (1984): 185–207.

5. The most extensive biography of Zanchi is C. Schmidt, "Girolamo Zanchi,"

training in Aristotle and Aquinas.[6] After completing his studies in 1541 he was sent to the Augustinian house in Lucca where Vermigli was the prior. Vermigli introduced him to the writings of the Reformers and gradually Zanchi converted to Protestantism. In 1552, as the attitude of the Church and the Inquisition in Italy became less tolerant, he left the country and fled to Geneva. After having studied with Calvin for almost a year, Zanchi was called to Strasbourg to become professor of Old Testament. During his residency in Strasbourg the famous controversy with the Lutheran Johann Marbach on the issues of the Lord's Supper and predestination broke out. Weary of all the conflicts, Zanchi finally offered his resignation and left for Chiavenna in 1563 to become a minister. Four years later he succeeded Ursinus as professor of "common-place" theology at the University of Heidelberg. Under the Elector Frederick III (1559–1576) the Palatinate had become Reformed and Zanchi enjoyed the most fruitful period of his life there. However, after Frederick's death his successor resumed a Lutheran policy and Zanchi, with other Reformed scholars, was forced to leave the city. Zanchi was appointed to the chair of New Testament at the newly established academy of Neustadt an der Hardt. He remained there, even when he was asked a few years later to return to Heidelberg after the city had become reformed again. Zanchi died in 1590 while visiting Heidelberg and was buried in the church of the university.

The Heidelberg years were the most prolific of Zanchi's career. He began to write and publish what should have become a Reformed version of Aquinas's *Summa Theologiae,* and which like its example was actually never finished.[7] At the behest of Frederick III, who was annoyed by certain anti-trinitarian groups in the Palatinate, Zanchi began writing the first part of his "summa," entitled *De Tribus Elohim* in which he expounds his theology on the Trinity.[8] The work appeared in 1572 and

---

Theologische Studien und Kritiken 32 (1859): 625–708.

　　6. Cf. Gründler, *Die Gotteslehre Zanchis,* 17. I have found no evidence to corroborate Donnelly's claim that Zanchi was also trained at Padua: Donnelly, "Italian influences," 88.

　　7. Donnelly, "Italian influences," 88; and *id.* "Calvinist Thomism," 444; Burchill, "Girolamo Zanchi: Portrait," 188. Burchill also suggests that Zanchi's initially unpublished treatises which he wrote in Strasbourg to defend his own teaching, served as the blueprint for the systematic works of the Heidelberg period: *ib.* 195. These Strasbourg *Miscellanea* can be found in vol. 7 of Zanchi's *Opera Omnia.*

　　8. It seems, therefore, quite accidental that Zanchi, unlike Aquinas, sets the doctrine of the Trinity prior to the doctrine of divine nature, *pace* Richard Muller, *Christ and the Decree* (Durham N.C.: Labyrinth Press, 1986): 111. Zanchi's remark on the first page of

was later published as volume one of the *Opera Omnia*. In 1577 the publication of *De Natura Dei seu De Divinis Attributis* (the second volume of the *Opera Omnia*) followed. Only after his death Zanchi's sons and heirs took care of the publication of the works on creation (volume three) and on the Fall, sin and the Law (volume four of the *Opera*). The book dealing with Christ and soteriology, which Zanchi had announced at the end of the book on creation, was never completed.

Divided into five books, *De Natura Dei* consists of over 700 folio pages.[9] The first book deals with divine names. The so-called incommunicable divine attributes, like simplicity, eternity and immutability, constitute the topic of book two. God's power, knowledge, truth and will are discussed in the third book. Next, God's goodness and justice are discussed with the related attributes of grace, love, mercy, wrath, hatred and dominion. The fifth and final book covers providence and predestination.

Zanchi's work is usually characterized as "scholastic" and whatever the exact definition of "scholasticism" may be, Zanchi's use of certain methods and techniques justifies this characterization. The organization of the material is ruled by systematic-conceptual considerations and logic plays an important role both in formulating positive teachings and in refuting objections. The care with which strict definitions are sought, technical distinctions and divisions are employed and the extensive use of formal syllogism parallel the procedures followed by the great medieval thinkers. Moreover, Zanchi does not hesitate to appeal to philosophical doctrines, especially Aristotle's, in explicating his theological views. He is well aware of the fact that this is not undisputed and that his readers may take offence. In the letter to the reader which prefaces *De Natura Dei* Zanchi defends the necessity of using philosophy in academic theology: "For there are very many divine attributes that in my opinion cannot be sufficiently explained or even understood unless that which is offered to us by Philosophy is accepted and applied. For we do not immediately leave the School of Christ when we enter the

---

De Natura Dei (henceforward *DND*) that "Methodus itaque veraque docendi ratio postulat: ut quando, quis verus sit Deus, satis cognitum, perspectumque e sacris literis habemus: de huius veri Dei . . . Natura seu attributis, quibus, qualis sit, in S. litteris docetur: disseramus" might be a rationalization afterwards.

9. The edition of 1577 fills 719 pages, followed by a number of indices. The printing in the *Zanchii Opera Omnia Theologica* editions (in 1605, 1613 and 1617–19) is slightly denser. All quotations and page numbers in this article are from the 1577 edition. I shall also adopt the punctuation from this edition.

Lycaeum. Nor do we confuse the sciences when we employ the *artes* in explaining Scripture."[10]

While contemporary studies focus on the Scholastic elements in Zanchi, they tend to take little or no notice of the fact that his work also shows typically humanistic features. I want to point out three characteristics of Zanchi's work that also mark the writings of the humanists: a keen interest in philological and literary matters, consideration of the historical background of doctrines and practices and, finally, a specific concern for the practical effectiveness of theoretical expositions. First, language in its concrete historical manifestations plays a key role in Zanchi's work. He often refers to the literary writers of Antiquity like Euripides, Pindar, Pliny, Virgil and Livy. His Latin is rather elegant and he has a thorough command of Greek and Hebrew. There are long quotations from John of Damascus in their original language and technical philosophical expressions taken from Aristotle appear in Greek. Zanchi also gives detailed etymological and grammatical expositions, especially with regard to Hebrew words and phrases from Scripture. For linguistic reasons he will sometimes criticize existing translations and suggest alternatives.[11] Interest in language is not the only thing Zanchi shares with humanists. Like many of them, Zanchi also has a particular interest in historical explanations of human beliefs and practices. Historical accounts of the origins and motives of specific religious phenomena can even help to alleviate the tensions of doctrinal

10. The whole letter is actually a defense of the use of philosophy in theology. Zanchi states: "Quod cum Theologicis multa hic Philosophica coniunximus, nemo, credo, nobis vitio vertet, qui haec nostra legerit, si diligenter causam cur hoc a nobis factum sit, perpenderit. Plurima enim sunt Attributa Divina, ad quae explicanda, nisi quod a Philosophia nobis porrigitur, acceptum adferatur, non modo non explicari, sed ne intelligi quidem, nostro quidem iudicio, satis recte possint. Neque statim ex Christi Schola egredimur, cum Lycaeum ingredimur: aut scientias confundimus, quando ad scripturam explicationem artes adhibemus . . . Quare licet Christianus esse quis possit, sine Philosophiae, imo etiam sine sacrarum literarum exacta cognitione: ad Theologiae tamen professionem, artes non postremo loco requiruntur." Cf. also 101: "Scriptura quidem sancta aperte tradit Deum vivere et esse Deum viventem et vitam esse aeternam . . . Ceterum, quid sit haec Dei vita et quomodo intelligendum sit Deum vivere, non ita perspicue in eis explicatur . . . Hoc autem discitur ex Philosophia." In a discussion on the transcendentals, Zanchi states: "Haec Physica (sic) doctrina ad intelligendum sacrarum literarum utilissima est." 403.

11. E.g. *DND*, 420 on the Hebrew term "channun": "vertere solent Miseratorem: sed proprie significat Gratificantem, seu (quemadmodum eleganter nostri converterunt) gratiosum;" also 711 where Zanchi corrects the Vulgate on the translation of Ps. 139:16.

oppositions, as is clear from Zanchi's assessment of the Catholic practice to pray for the dead.[12] A third characteristic of Zanchi's work that is distinctly humanistic is the attention he pays to the practical effects of his teachings in the lives of his readers. He is well acquainted with the classical rhetorical tradition of Cicero and Seneca. Furthermore, although one does not find in Zanchi Calvin's or Melanchthon's harsh denunciations of the emptiness and uselessness of Scholasticist *curiositas*, he sides with them in stressing the *utilitas* of all sciences, including theology.[13] The discussion of every particular subject in *De Natura Dei* is concluded by an exposition of the *usus* of the specific doctrine. Zanchi wants every singular doctrine to aim at strengthening the spiritual life of the faithful: a better understanding of Scripture, an increasing trust in God and an enhanced discernment in matters of faith.

In sum, *De Natura Dei* may rightly be called "scholastic," but Zanchi also incorporates specifically humanistic elements in it. To neglect this would result in a distorted, one-sided view on his work. With this *caveat* in mind, we shall now turn to Zanchi's reception of one of the greatest Scholastics, Saint Thomas Aquinas.

II. Thomas Aquinas in *De Natura Dei*

Of all nonscriptural authors referred to in *De Natura Dei* Augustine stands out as the one most frequently mentioned. Over 150 times he is mentioned or quoted, sometimes at great length. Aristotle follows with 35 references, most of which regard technical philosophical expressions and distinctions. Aquinas's name occurs 27 times. Next are Jerome, Cicero, John of Damascus, and Ambrose, with about 20 references each. However, these quantifications are somewhat misleading. Aristotle and others are often mentioned only in passing and without extensive comments while most references to Aquinas have lengthy quotations and elaborate explanations and occur at crucial passages. Moreover, often Aquinas's name is not mentioned but his views are nonetheless clearly adopted.

When Zanchi does mention Aquinas explicitly, he usually indicates

---

12. *DND*, 469–77.

13. Occasionally Zanchi does rebuke the Scholastics for their *curiositas*, but in a rather mild tone: e.g. *DND*, 240: "De scientia Dei ipsa, multae a Scholasticis proponuntur quaestiones: quarum quaedam plus habent curiositatis quam pietatis: et ea re, perniciosae potius sunt quam utiles." In the Middle Ages, Augustine's warning against vicious curiosity in philosophy and theology was often repeated by monastic theologians like Bernard of Clairvaux, but also by Bonaventure and Jean Gerson.

exactly the passage he refers to. This and the accuracy of the quotations give the impression that he has Aquinas's texts at hand to consult. References are made to different works: *Summa Theologiae, Summa contra Gentiles, De Veritate, De Potentia* and to the little-known *reportatio* on the letter to Titus. Aquinas's most voluminous work, his commentary on the *Sentences* of Peter Lombard, is not mentioned. A reason might be that as the *Sentences* had ceased to be the traditional theological textbook in the 16th century, the *Scriptum* was no longer considered to be Aquinas's most important work. References to Aquinas's commentaries on Aristotle are absent from *De Natura Dei* as well. This may be because these works were considered obsolete since the rise of a more humanistic reinterpretation of Aristotle, notably at Padua.[14]

The influence of Aquinas's thought on Zanchi's doctrine of God is already very clear in the first book, the one on divine names. After a general introduction and summary (chapters 1 to 6), Zanchi discusses nine specific questions about the words we use in talking about God (chapters 6 to 10). And although Aquinas's name is mentioned only once, the order and the content of the nine questions follow almost exactly his discussion in the *Summa Theologiae*.[15] Like Aquinas, Zanchi affirms that we can name God, although all our words, both concrete and abstract nouns, verbs and participles, fall short in expressing the divine essence. Using the same arguments, Zanchi refutes the opinion that divine names are never said *substantialiter* but only either negatively or relationally. He also adopts Aquinas's distinctions between proper and metaphorical divine names, between *modus significandi* and *res significata*, between the *impositio a quo* and *ad quem*, between divine names *ex tempore* and *ab aeterno*, and between a real relation and a relation of reason only. Furthermore, he agrees with Aquinas that divine names are not synonyms despite God's simplicity, that names are said primarily of God and that they are predicated of God and creatures neither univocally nor purely equivocally, but analogically: the same word predicated of a creature and of God, does not have in both cases exactly the same

14. Donnelly, "Calvinist Thomism," 448 and *id*. "Italian influences," 84.

15. Aquinas, *Summa Theologiae* 1a, qu. 13 art. 1–7. The only explicit reference to Aquinas is on pages 28–29 in the discussion of the divine names *ex tempore*. Augustine's views are compared with those of Aquinas. Zanchi concludes that their positions agree and that they differ only in literary genre: "Eadem in summa est Thomae explicatio, quae Augustini etiam fuit: sed unus oratorie, eoque magis perspicue: alter scholastice, eoque non omnibus ita dilucide, rem declaravit."

meaning (*ratio*), nor a completely different one.[16] It is noteworthy that in discussing analogy Zanchi does not mention the division into "analogy of attribution" and "analogy of proportionality." This division, introduced by Cardinal Cajetan around 1500, played a key role in the interpretations of Aquinas's doctrine of analogy until the early sixties of this century.[17] One of the major consequences of Cajetan's views on later Thomism was that analogy came to be understood primarily as a metaphysical and not as a logical doctrine. But for Zanchi analogy has to do with the meaning of words, and is therefore in the first place a logical theory, as it was for Aquinas himself.

Like Aquinas, Zanchi bases the analogical meaning of divine names on the real order of causality of the creature to God.[18] For both of them the background is pseudo-Dionysius' threefold way of knowing God, that is, by way of causality, of negation and of eminence. The *via causalitatis* is the reason why words that signify a perfection can be predicated of God.[19] But it is not to be separated from the other two, the *via negationis* and the *via eminentiae*. We know God, Zanchi says, "by way of negation so that all that is said about creatures as perfect and good, is negated of God. Not that the perfections of all things are not in God, but that they are in him more excellent and even in the most perfect way."[20] The three

16. *DND*, 25: "Analogica autem dicuntur, quorum idem quidem est nomen: sed neque eadem omnino, neque prorsus diversa ratio, aut definitio." Cf. Aquinas, *Summa Theologiae* 1a qu. 13 art. 5.

17. Ralph McInerny was one of the first to criticize the appropriateness of Cajetan's division for understanding Aquinas's views. Cf. his *The Logic of Analogy* (The Hague, Nijhoff) 1961. Gründler's discussion of analogy in Aquinas and in Zanchi relies heavily on Cajetan's division: Gründler, *Die Gotteslehre Zanchis*, 71–72.

18. *DND*, 26: "At vero inter Deum et res a Deo creatas, pulcherrimus est ordo. Est enim Deus causa et efficiens et finalis rerum conditarum." The causal order grounds the analogy of our God-talk: 27: "Atque hic proprie est ordo et convenientia, quem habent creaturae ad Deum: cuius ordinis causa, dicuntur nomina analogikw Deo et de creatis rebus praedicari." Cf. Aquinas, *Summa Theologiae* 1a, qu. 13 art. 5: "Et sic, quidquid dicitur de Deo et creaturis, dicitur secundum quod est aliquis ordo creaturae ad Deum, ut ad principium et causam, in qua praeexistunt excellenter omnes rerum perfectiones."

19. *DND*, 7: ". . . hic notanda est causa cur quaecunque etiam de creaturis dicuntur, quae scilicet perfectionem aliquam significant, affirmative de Deo dici, praedicarive possint: nempe ut significetur ipsum esse autorem omnium istarum perfectionum." This does not mean, however, that perfections are only predicated *causaliter* and not *substantialiter* of God: cf. *DND*, 13–15 and 172.

20. *DND*, 7: "Atque hanc Patres optimam, perfectissimamque docent esse regulam, ad cognoscendum Deum: nempe per viam negationis: ut quicquid de rebus creatis dicitur, utut perfectum et bonum, illud de Deo negetur. Non quod omnium

ways form a unity: the ways of negation and of eminence qualify intrinsically what is said affirmatively of God through the way of causality. This will become clearer when we take a closer look at Zanchi's discussion of God's simplicity and perfection in the second book.

The second book of *De Natura Dei* deals with the so-called incommunicable attributes of God: simplicity, eternity (including immutability), infinity, ubiquity and perfection. Also God's life and beatitude, although not strictly incommunicable, are treated in this book. The remaining three books are about the communicable divine attributes.[21] Although the latter cannot be communicated to creatures in the same way as they exist in God, these attributes can be predicated of a creature nominally, but still properly, partially, imperfectly and "by similitude of effects."[22] Again, in the discussion of God's incommunicable attributes, Aquinas's name is often not mentioned, while his views are adopted. The text parallels largely questions 3–11 of the *Summa Theologiae* 1a. There Aquinas discusses what Zanchi calls "God's incommunicable attributes" under the heading of "how God is not" (*quomodo Deus non sit*). As the heading already indicates, Aquinas emphasizes the negative character of this part of his doctrine of God. A similar apophatic tendency is apparent in Zanchi's discussion.

Zanchi bases the doctrine of God's simplicity on the revealed proper name of God, "He who is."[23] Yet, as Zanchi had explained in book one,

---

perfectiones non sint in Deo, sed quod sint in illo excellentiores et perfectissimo etiam modo."

21. Zanchi distinguishes (i) incommunicable from communicable attributes and (ii) non-relational from relational attributes: cf. 6, 73, 197. These two distinctions overlap, but do not completely coincide. However, Zanchi is not always clear about that. Gerrit Immink overlooks this discrepancy in Zanchi: F.G. Immink, *Divine Simplicity* (Kampen: Kok, 1987): 157–58.

22. Cf. *DND*, 22, 61–62 and 73. Like Aquinas, Zanchi uses the Platonic notion of participation to explain this communication: esp. 174–75. He also refers to the Neo-Platonic principle of reception ("all that is received, is received according to the mode of the receiver"). Zanchi elucidates it by quoting from *De Ver.* qu. 5 art. 8 ad 3 and he states that the principle of reception explains the rule that nothing finite is capable of the infinite: 207–8. This rule is a central theme in the work of Calvin, who links it with the notion of "divine accommodation." Zanchi is also familiar with the latter: cf. 11–12, 458.

23. Zanchi's exegesis of the Tetragrammaton in book one of *DND* is rather long: 35–47, followed by the exegesis of "I am who I am" (47–51). Zanchi quotes the three reasons Aquinas adduces in *Summa Theologiae*, 1a qu. 13 art. 11 why "He who is" is the most proper name of God: 50–51. Throughout *DND* Zanchi frequently refers to the Tetragrammaton as stating the identity of esse and *essentia* in God.

like the other divine names, even "He who is" is taken from creatures and cannot express to us perfectly who and how God is (*quis et qualis sit Deus*) and how he is distinguished from creatures.[24] The simplicity that is indicated by the name "He who is", does not so much express something positive about God, but it rather means the negation of all kinds of composition: God is not composed of quantitative material parts, form and matter, subject and accident, act and potency, genus and difference, and, finally, not of *esse* and *essentia*, "the most subtle of all compositions." Although Zanchi blurs the latter composition by identifying it with the composition of form and subject,[25] and although he refers to Aquinas only once in stating that relations and essence differ only *ratione* and not *realiter* in the Trinity,[26] his exposition follows Aquinas's discussion in *Summa Theologiae* 1a qu. 4 very closely and the theological function of the doctrine of divine simplicity is the same: to distinguish God from the non-divine.[27]

Negativity also characterizes Zanchi's discussion of God's perfection. When we attribute a perfection to God, Zanchi says, there are two steps involved. First, we have to remove all defects and imperfections that cling to it as it is found in creatures. Secondly, we have to realize that all perfections are not only infinitely more perfect in God, but they are also in him in the most perfect mode. And that mode "cannot be perfectly explained and even not comprehended by any created intellect."[28] All

24. Cf. *DND*, 10–11.

25. *DND*, 78–79: "Forma enim et subiectum idem esse non possunt in rebus creatis." See also 182. According to Aquinas only material beings have the composition of form and subject, whereas in purely spiritual creatures they are identical. But the latter are still composed of *esse* and *essentia*: cf. *Summa Theologiae 1a,* qu. 3 art. 3–4, qu. 50 art. 2 ad 3 and II ScG c. 54. I do not agree with Gründler's conclusion that, apparently, Zanchi stays more consistently than Aquinas within the natural boundaries of reason (Gründler, *Die Gotteslehre Zanchis*, 81). I think that Zanchi lacks some philosophical acumen. Yet this does not seem to have serious theological consequences.

26. *DND*, 83–84 (cf. 184–86). Aquinas's name occurs once more in the chapter preceding the one on simplicity where Zanchi states that, like Augustine, Aquinas denies that the human soul is of divine substance (66–67).

27. Cf. Immink, *Divine Simplicity*, 85: "Zanchi . . . says that simplicity is the distinguishing mark that sets God apart from everything that is not God" (cf also 30, 158). For Aquinas see Immink, o.c., 29 and my *Free Creatures of an Eternal God. Thomas Aquinas on God's infallible foreknowledge and irresistible will* (Louvain: Peeters Publishers, 1996): 11–12 (incl. references).

28. *DND*, 171–72: "Perfectiones igitur rerum omnium, ita sunt attribuendae Deo: ut prius, quicquid in illis reperitur vitii, defectus et imperfectionis, totum illud cogitatione nostra, inde tollamus; ac tum demum, quod tantum superest bonum, purgatissimum

perfections belong to God in virtue of one, simple form which is his essence. In this way, simplicity and perfection are correlated and together they form the backbone of Zanchi's doctrine of God:

> Because of the highest perfection of God, the perfections of all beings or things are in God; but because of his highest simplicity, they are in him not by way of some composition, but according to the unity of the simple essence.[29]

This brief survey of Zanchi's views on God's simplicity and perfection shows that these two "incommunicable attributes" are closely related to the threefold Pseudo-Dionysian way of knowing and naming God. God's perfection underpins the *via causalitatis*: all perfections we find in creatures are attributed to God. On the other hand, the doctrine of divine simplicity supports the *via negativa*. All perfections are in God not by way of composition, but in an incomprehensible mode. They do not really differ one from another, but are identical with the divine essence. Perfection and simplicity together constitute the *via eminentiae*: all perfections are in God in the most perfect or sublime way, that is, in virtue of the one, simple divine essence.[30] With reference to Pseudo-Dionysius, Zanchi points out that every creaturely perfection preexists in God as its cause. However, because God is not a univocal cause, the perfection does not exist in him according to the same meaning (*secundum eandem rationem*) as it exists in the effect. God is an equivocal cause and the perfection exists in him in a more eminent way (*eminentiori*

---

scilicet, ac defaecatissimum, Deo attribuamus . . . Secundo loco adieci, non solum omnes rerum perfectiones in Deo esse longe, hoc est, infinities, perfectiores, quam sint in ipsis creaturis: verum etiam perfectissimo modo inesse . . . Perfecte enim hic modus explicari non potest: imo ne comprehendi quidem a creato intellectu."

29. *DND*, 172: "Propter summam Dei perfectionem, omnium Entium seu rerum perfectiones sunt in Deo: propter summam vero simplicitatem eiusdem, in eo sunt, non per aliquam compositionem, sed secundum simplicis essentiae unitatem." Also 175: "Imo, argumentum, quo utimur ad ostendendum omnia esse in Deo, ut unam rem, et non multas neque diversas, sumimus ab eius simplicitate. Sicut contra, argumentum sumimus ab eius perfectione ad demonstrandum omnes rerum perfectiones in Deo esse perfectissimas."

30. Cf. *DND*, 174: "Cum itaque Deus prima sit efficiens omnium rerum causa, vidit et concludit Dionysius ille, Deum esse omnia, quia omnia virtute sunt in Deo et eminentiori quidem ac perfectissimo modo, quam in seipsis sint. Denique si perfectiones omnium entium in Deo non sint, nec perfectiores, nec perfectissimo modo, consequeretur, Deum non esse ipsum ens perfectissimum, et suum ipsius Esse."

modo).[31] This is, finally, the reason why words are neither said univocally nor purely equivocally of God and creatures, but analogically. For example, when a concrete term like "just" is said of a human being, it signifies and denotes an inherent, accidental quality that is neither identical with its subject, nor with other perfections the subject may have. However, when said of God, the term does not retain completely the same meaning, for God's justice is identical with the divine essence and does not really differ from his mercy or any other perfection we attribute to him. All divine names have a creaturely mode of signifying.[32] This mode of signifying cannot be rectified or annulled because it is given with the very syntactic and semantic structures of human language.

In sum, Zanchi's apophatic and kataphatic theology constitutes a unity: positive God-talk is intrinsically qualified by negative God-talk. Therefore, it is misleading to suggest as Gründler does that according to Zanchi there are two separate or, at least, distinct ways to come to knowledge of God, one by negation and one by analogy. It follows that Zanchi is more consistent than Gründler thinks in maintaining, like Aquinas, the negative fundamental tone of his theology.[33] Zanchi's view on our knowledge of and our language about God corresponds largely to Aquinas's. I also want to point out that Zanchi is not just interested in speculations about God's essence *in se* by way of impersonal, metaphysical categories as opposed to Calvin's exclusive focus on *Deus*

---

31. *DND*, 174: "Intellexit enim Dionysius iste . . . omnes effectus praeexistere virtute in sua causa efficiente: ac proinde quicquid perfectionis invenitur in effectu, illud prius fuisse et esse in sua causa: vel secundum eandem rationem, qua etiam est in effectu: nempe, si causa sit (ut loquuntur) univoca . . . quia causa univoca generat sibi simile in specie. vel eminentiori modo, nimirum si agens causa sit aequivoca." With the same reference to Dionysius, Aquinas also points out all perfections preexist in God "secundum eminentiorem modum" because God is not an univocal cause: *Summa Theologiae* 1a qu. 4 art. 2 and art. 3.

32. *DND*, 15: "Modum enim habent significandi, qui competit creaturis, non autem Deo: ut nomen iustitiae significat iustitiam, quatenus virtus est finita, et quidem accidens, ab aliis virtutibus realiter distincta."

33. Gründler, *Die Gotteslehre Zanchis*, 66–75. Gründler concludes (p. 75): "Wäre Zanchi in seinen Gedankengangen konsequenter gewesen, hätte er zu dem gleichen Schluß wie Thomas kommen müssen: daß wir nämlich am Ende unserer Aussagen über die Volkommenheiten Gottes doch nicht wissen, was Gott ist." As Donnelly already pointed out, Gründler also misreads two passages from *DND*: Donnelly, "Calvinist Thomism," 445 note 22. Furthermore, on our reading of Zanchi it is not hard to maintain a strong identity between God and his properties, contrary to Immink's view: cf. Immink, *Divine Simplicity*, 158.

erga nos.[34] In discussing God's incommunicable attributes, Zanchi not only settles a number of christological and trinitarian problems, but, more importantly, we have also seen how the doctrines of divine simplicity and perfection support the theory of analogical God-talk. And this theory is our guide in reading Scripture. Near the end of the discussion on analogy Zanchi states:

> For what purpose, you will ask, have all these things about analogical predication been explicated in so much detail? How great the utility and use of this explication are, can only be seen when we come to the praxis, that is, to reading the Holy Writ.[35]

The remaining three books of *De Natura Dei* deal mainly with God's relative attributes, that is, those attributes which imply a relation to creatures, *e.g.* power, knowledge, will, love, mercy, providence etc. Again, even when his name is not mentioned, it is often Aquinas who is in the background of the discussion of a particular subject. Apart from common viewpoints shared by all or most Scholastics, Zanchi adopts a number of typically Thomistic positions. For example, the correspondence-definition of truth and its fourfold relation to God, reality, the human mind and language parallels exactly Aquinas's discussion in *De Veritate*.[36] Also the definition of natural law as a participation in the Eternal Law by rational creatures is derived from Aquinas.[37] And like Aquinas, Zanchi argues that God's will and providence cause not only whatever happens, but also the mode in which it happens, that is, either contingently or necessarily.[38]

However, it is in the discussions on divine grace and on predestination that we find most references to Aquinas. Zanchi makes an effort to point out that Aquinas's position is unlike the one of most later

34. This is where Gründler locates the fundamental oppositon between Calvin's and Zanchi's theological positions: *Die Gotteslehre Zanchis*, 67–68, 82–83.

35. *DND*, 27: "Quorsum vero haec (inquies) tam accurate explicata de praedicatione analogica? Utilitas et usus huius explicationis, quantus sit, videri non potest nisi cum ad praxin, hoc est, ad lectionem sacrarum literarum venitur." Contemporary Thomist scholars have argued that also for Aquinas Scripture is also the core of theological research: see esp. W.G.B.M. Valkenberg, *"Did not our heart burn?": place and function of Holy Scripture in the theology of St. Thomas Aquinas*. Utrecht, 1990.

36. *DND*, 279–81. For Aquinas see *De Ver.* qu. 1 art. 2.

37. *DND*, 368. For Aquinas see *Summa Theologiae* 1a2ae qu. 91 art. 2.

38. *DND*, 335, 553–54. For Aquinas see *De Ver.* qu. 23 art. 5, In *Metaphysicam* VI lc. 3 nr. 1222.

medieval Scholastics. In contrast with *e.g.* Luther and Calvin, who tend to accuse all Scholastics of Pelagianism, Zanchi's assessment is more balanced. He identifies Ockham and Biel by name as Pelagians, but he thinks that others, especially Aquinas, held a different view. Zanchi makes this clear both in his discussion on grace and on predestination. We shall take a closer look at both.

According to Zanchi, the term "grace" has three distinct meanings. The first one is the inherent, non-relational quality of gracefulness (*gratiositas, venustas*). Next, and more commonly, it may mean free favor (*gratuitus favor*). Finally, the term may be used for any gift that is freely given on the basis of that favor. As far as Zanchi is concerned, the point is that the Scholastics usually took the term "grace" exclusively in the third sense, that is, as the gifts and qualities infused in the human soul. Therefore, he says, they erred very seriously in interpreting the biblical texts that state that we are justified and saved by God's grace. For they attributed our justification and salvation to the infused qualities and, consequently, to the fruits thereof, the good works. Zanchi mentions only Aquinas as an exception: "Thomas Aquinas, often convinced by the clear passages in Scripture, understood and interpreted the term "grace" as God's free mercy, which is in God and not in us."[39]

Also in his discussion on predestination, Zanchi favors Aquinas.[40] Three basic positions are distinguished among the Scholastics with regard to questions about the cause of predestination and reprobation.[41] The first one, attributed to Ockham, Biel, and Zanchi's contemporary Albertus Pighius, states that God's foreknowledge of our good or evil works is the cause of both predestination and reprobation. That position,

---

39. *DND*, 421: "quanquam Thomas Aquinas, nonnunquam perspicuis scripturarum locis victus, nomine gratiae intelligit et interpretatur gratuitam Dei misericordiam, quae in Deo est non in nobis." Also 422: "Ac Thomas, qui alioqui purior reliquis esse solet in doctrina de Gratia . . ." Zanchi refers to *De Ver.* qu. 27 art. 1 where Aquinas distinguishes two meanings of the word "grace": grace as a free gift and grace as acceptance (*acceptatio*). For the latter Zanchi prefers the term "favour": "Nos melius Favorem appellamus quam ille, acceptationem." He also refers to *Summa Theologiae* 1a2ae qu. 110 art. 1 where Aquinas adds a third meaning of the word "grace," *viz.* thanks (*DND*, 431) and he quotes a "pium Aquinatis dictum" from Aquinas's not very well-known *reportatio* on the letter to Titus (430). The quotation is from *Ad Titum* c. 2 lc. 3, where Aquinas comments on *Titus* 2:11 "For the grace of God has appeared for the salvation of all men."

40. *DND* esp. 651–54.

41. The identity of the cause of predestination and reprobation, or in other words, the issue of the gratuity of predestination, is the key question: " . . . quia in ea totius salutis, ac huius de praedestinatione disputationis, cardo vertitur." (*DND*, 654)

Zanchi claims, is simply Pelagian. Next he denounces the view of Scotus and his followers who say that predestination is from God's free will only, but reprobation is caused by God's prevision of evil works. The third position is ascribed by Zanchi to Peter Lombard, Thomas Aquinas, Gregory (of Rimini), Durandus (of St.-Pourçain) and "most others among the saner and more learned Scholastics." They follow Augustine's view in stating and arguing that both predestination and reprobation depend solely on God's free will. Zanchi elaborates this view by explaining the gist of Aquinas's position "because it is most suitably written."[42] In doing so, Zanchi refers explicitly only to *Summa contra Gentiles* book III chapter 163, but he also quotes *Summa Theologiae* 1a qu. 23 art. 5 ad 3 without identifying the passage. He may have consulted other passages like *De Ver.* qu. 6 art. 2, and possibly *In I Sent.* ds. 41 as the editor indicated in the margin. Zanchi summarizes Aquinas's view in two points. First, our predestination does not depend on our works both because the latter are effects of the former and because God's will, being the cause of causes, is itself uncaused. Second, although there is a causal order between the effects of the predestination if viewed separately, they have no cause but God's free will if they are taken collectively. The only thing that displeases Zanchi is that Aquinas "calls our good works "merits" in accordance with the custom of the Fathers, also of Augustine himself." But it is added: "Although Aquinas himself explains elsewhere what he means by the word "merit": not properly an undue deed, which demands a reward; but a deed on which a reward follows mercifully and from God's goodness."[43]

From this survey it will be clear that Aquinas plays an important role in Zanchi's doctrine of God. Apart from generically Scholastic elements,

---

42. *DND*, 652: "Summam sententiae Aquinatis, quia appositissime scripta est, placet paulo fusius explicare." See also 675, where again a.o. Peter Lombard, Aquinas, Durandus and Gregory are mentioned as endorsing the same doctrine as Augustine. Zanchi praises especially Aquinas: "Omnia Thomae: quibus quid certius, quid magis pium dici in hoc argumento potuit . . . pie profecto et docte, quia consentanee cum sacris literis." (p. 653f)

43. *DND*, 654: "Hoc tantum displicet in Thoma, quod opera bona vocat merita, iuxta patrum, ipsius etiam Augustini, consuetidinem. Quanquam ipse etiam Aquinas alibi explicat, quid intelligat nomine meriti: non proprie opus indebitum, quod exaequatur praemio; sed opus, quod misericorditer et ex bonitate Dei sequitur praemium." Aquinas does not define the term "merit" in these precise words. He would agree that a merit is not undue (*indebitum*), yet he stresses that within the order of the effects of the predestination the reward has the character of a *debitum* on the basis of God's ordination: cf. *Summa Theologiae* 1a2ae qu. 114 art. 1 and art. 3.

Zanchi also uses specifically Thomistic notions. And he does so at crucial points in his theology: in explaining the deep structure of our God-talk and in discussing the doctrine of predestination, which is "the summary of the whole of Christian wisdom . . . the foundation of our salvation."[44] However, it is also at these two points that Zanchi deviates from Aquinas. In the doctrine of predestination, or more precisely, of grace, he does so explicitly, while in the discussion on divine names, or more precisely, on divine simplicity, he doesn't seem to be aware of it. We shall take a closer look at both in the next paragraph.

III. Divergence between Zanchi and Aquinas

There are only three passages in *De Natura Dei* where Zanchi criticizes Aquinas explicitly. The first one, which I shall not discuss here, concerns Aquinas's interpretation of divine ubiquity *per essentiam*.[45] Next, as we already saw, Zanchi is not happy with the use of the term "merit." Related to this is Zanchi's third and most important criticism, which is directed against Aquinas's view on grace as *gratia gratum faciens*, that is, as a created, supernatural gift, infused in a person by which he becomes worthy of eternal life.[46] If the expression *gratia gratum faciens* is understood in this way, Zanchi says, it has to be rejected unambiguously. As a good Reformed theologian, he stresses the *extra nos* and the "forensic" character of our salvation. On these two conditions, Zanchi leaves some room for *gratia gratum faciens*. If one were to interpret the expression in the sense of God's favor in Christ *extra nos* which makes us pleasing (*grati*) and accepted to God, one would not have to object to it.[47] Also, if this grace were understood as a created gift, but the term "worthy" were taken to mean not that we become properly worthy of eternal life, but that God declares that He has deemed us worthy, it might be acceptable, although it would be an improper use of the term

44. *DND*, 703: "[D]octrina de praedestinatione est compendium totius sapientiae Christianae: et ita ad salutem nostram cognitu necessaria est, ut fundamentum sit salutis nostrae."

45. *DND*, 115.

46. *DND* esp. 423–25.

47. *DND*, 423: "Ac si huius gratiae nomine intelligeret solum Dei favorem, quem ipse vocat acceptationem . . . neque etiam nomen Gratiae gratum facientis reiici. Nam revera, id quod vere nos gratos reddit et acceptos Deo, est ipse gratuitus Dei in Christo favor" and, 424: "Neminem enim servari, ex dignitate sua, vel naturali, vel supernaturali, quae in ipso sit, e sacris literis profitemur: sed tantum ex misericordia Dei, Et propter dignitatem Iesu Christi: quorum utrumque extra nos est."

"worthy."[48]

Zanchi's assessment of Aquinas's doctrine of grace is strikingly balanced. He praises the interpretation of "grace" as God's mercy or acceptance. He also points out Aquinas's statement (*sanctissima propositio* Zanchi calls it) that grace as a supernatural gift does not move God's will to predestine us, but that *vice versa* it is subsumed under the predestination. In this way, the gratuity of the predestination is affirmed.

The main argument, Zanchi says, against Aquinas's view on habitual grace is that it doesn't fit in with the biblical account. Furthermore, God's will to save us and his election are eternal while habitual grace is something in time and, finally, no created gift can make us worthy of something uncreated, that is, of eternal life.[49] It is beyond the scope of this article to answer Zanchi's objections on the basis of Aquinas's texts. I hope to do this elsewhere.

The second major point where his view differs from Aquinas's is not mentioned by Zanchi. It seems that he wasn't even aware of it. We already saw that he adopts Aquinas's account of God's simplicity and its consequences for our God-talk. According to this account, all divine attributes are in reality absolutely identical with the one, perfect, divine essence. This does not turn all divine names into synonyms for the divine attributes differ conceptually (*ratione*). The diversity only inheres in our intellect, and hence in our language, but not in God.[50] However, in the discussions on God's omnipotence, knowledge and will, Zanchi introduces the notion of an "order of nature" (*ordo naturae* or *ordo*

48. *DND*, 424: "Hoc certe dare nullo modo possumus. Nisi forte nomine digni, abutatur pro illo, quem Deus, sicut reputat iustum, sic etiam reputat dignum . . . non quod proprie, ea gratia fiamus digni vita aeterna: sed quod Deus, declaret se, nos dignatum fuisse vita aeterna. Verum talis abusio, in negotio tanti momenti, toleranda non est."

49. *DND*, 423: "Quid ais Thoma? Haec voluntas, qua Deus vult nobis vitam aeternam: aeterna ne est, an temporaria?" and 424: "Nullum enim creatum donum, dignos nos efficere potest, tanto bono, nempe vita aeterna, increato."

50. *DND*, 16: "Proinde dictum a nobis est saepissime: quae in nobis sunt multae virtutes ac perfectiones: eas in Deo esse unam re ipsa: ratione tantum differre, rationeque multas esse. Quid vero est haec ratio, qua differunt? Conceptio, quam intellectus noster de iis perfectionibus per nomina significatis, concipit ex nominibus. Diversam enim rem concipit ex voce misericordiae, quam ex voce iustitiae, mens nostra. Proinde haec ratio, nihil cum simplicitate Dei pugnat: quia in Deo nihil ponit, sed in nostro tantum haeret intellectu . . . Proinde cum diversa ratio, qua inter se apud nos differunt multae Dei virtutes, nihil in Deo sit, sed tantum apud nos locum habeat: efficitur ipsa quoque nomina multa et varia, minime cum ipsa Dei unitate et simplicitate, aliquam habere repugnantiam." Cf. also 301.

naturalis). He uses this notion to establish an order of earlier and later (*prius* and *posterius*) among God's properties and acts. For example, from God's goodness flows His grace and then His love and His mercy;[51] God's knowledge precedes His will, which precedes the realization of the work willed.[52] Also within the divine act of will there is a natural order. First God wills Himself, and next He wills things outside of Him. Again, within the latter act, God wills first the causes and then their effects.[53] Zanchi stresses repeatedly that such a natural order does not deny God's simplicity. All of God's attributes are really identical with each other and with the divine essence and not one of them depends on another or differs from another. The natural order among the divine attributes is established "according to our understanding" and based on Scripture "in which God has adapted Himself to our understanding."[54]

Even if we stipulate that this natural order among God's attributes does not imply a temporal order, but only a structural order, Aquinas would still reject it. The only *ordo naturae* he accepts in God is the order of relations of

---

51. *DND*, 454.

52. *DND*, 273: "Tametsi in Deo non sit, neque prius, neque posterius, quia aeternus est, et simplicissimus: ordine tamen, quem videmus a Deo positum esse in natura: et quem, naturae ordinem appellare solemus: semper cognitio praecedit voluntatem: et voluntas, operis effectionem . . . Scimus, Deum simplicissimam esse essentiam: et tam voluntatem Dei, quam sapientiam Dei, nihil esse ab essentia diversum . . . tamen . . . aliquem inter ipsa attributa ordinem a nobis cogitari, et collocari, aequum est. Quare, si scientiam praeponimus voluntati, nostri captus respectu: nihil divina maiestate indignum facimus." Cf. also 197: "Adde, quod sua natura, aliis anteire videtur omnipotentia . . . ideo cognoscit, quia potuit cognoscere . . ."

53. *DND*, 353: "[T]ametsi in Deo non sit, neque prius neque posterius: ac proinde quanquam uno et eodem actu, tum se tum reliqua omnia intelligat et velit: ordine tamen naturae et pro nostro captu, non possumus aliter cogitare: quam hoc ordine Deum voluisse, et velle: ut nimirum prius se, Deinde quae sunt extra se, voluerit et velit." Zanchi continues by establishing also an order within God's will with regard to the external objects according to the efficient and the final causal relations that hold between them: "Deus primo voluit causas: Deinde effecta." (p. 354)

54. *DND*, 458: "Illud semper est retinendum . . . Deum simplicissimam esse essentiam, in quam nulla cadit compositio: ac proinde in qua non sunt diversae qualitates et virtutes quarum una pendeat ex alia, aut una differat ab alia: sed Deum in Scripturis sese ad nostrum captum accommodasse: et multas sibi ceu qualitates tribuere . . . Ergo, quod quaerimus, undenam in Deo sit misericordia, cum ea nihil aliud re ipsa sit, quam ipsius essentia, quae una est, et qua una sapiens, iustus, misericors est: totum hoc facimus propter nostrum captum: sequuti hac in parte consuetudinem sacrarum literarum . . . atque ita de multis aliis Attributis, quae ordinem aliquem inter se habent naturalem."

origin by which the Divine Persons are really distinguished.[55] God's simplicity excludes any ordering of the essential attributes. There are semantic differences between the divine names, but they inhere only in our language and in our understanding. The doctrine of simplicity functions in Aquinas's theology as a constant reminder of the imperfections of our talking and thinking about God; it regulates and corrects them. For example, we may say that while God knows all He wills, He doesn't will all He knows, but we may not say that God first knows all that is (logically) possible and then wills that which will be actual. It is also true to say that God wills this-because-of-that, but not that God wills this, because He wills that.[56] Likewise, predestination presupposes election and love, but Aquinas would not allow us to say that God first loves a person and then predestines him to eternal life. In this way, certain images of God are ruled out and certain questions are excluded. In Aquinas's view we cannot picture God as contemplating an infinite array of possible scenarios and then choosing one of them to exemplify. Also talking about an order of divine decrees is precluded, so that the question of supra- or infralapsarianism never arises. This is not the case in Zanchi's doctrine of God: he does picture God as choosing from all that is logically possible, and he does raise the question of supra- or infralapsarianism.[57]

Zanchi does not accept the far-reaching consequences of Aquinas's doctrine of divine simplicity. Although he endorses a strong notion of simplicity by stating the absolute identity of all divine attributes, the doctrine becomes in fact theologically idle and inoperative because of the introduction of a natural order among God's attributes "according to our understanding." Simplicity does not supervise anymore our understanding of, and hence our language about God. Our concepts and words are withdrawn from its critical guidance and become immune to its regulations. As a consequence our God-talk tends to become univocal and the specific negativity of theology, which Zanchi stresses elsewhere in his doctrine of God, loses its intensity.[58]

---

55. Cf. *Summa Theologiae* 1a qu. 42 art. 3, I *Sent.* ds. 12 art. 1 and ds. 20 art. 3. The expression is taken from Augustine.

56. Cf. *Summa Theologiae* 1a qu. 19 art. 5.

57. Cf. *DND*, 274: "Ex numero igitur rerum infinitarum, quarum notitia in Deo erat: quasdam . . . per voluntatem divinam, ad executionem fuisse desinatas." It seems to me that this also implies a form of essentialism. On supralapsarianism, cf. especially 689–92. Contrary to Richard Muller, I think that Zanchi defends explicitly a supralapsarian position; cf. Muller *Christ and the Decree,* 111–13.

58. The name of Duns Scotus is not mentioned, nor does his technical expression "*instans naturae*" occur in Zanchi's discussions of the natural order of divine attributes. But the similarity with the view of the *Doctor Subtilis* is striking.

6

An Ecumenical Debate between Reformation and Counter-Reformation? Bellarmine and Ames on *liberum arbitrium*

Eef Dekker

I. Introduction

Sometimes we are so privileged as to be allowed to take a thorough look in someone's private theological library. This is, generally, exciting, for it may tell us a few things about the books which the owner of the library finds important, and give us information which is not in all cases available in a more direct way, by reading the theologian's own writings. In some reformed theologians from the seventeenth century we can look into their libraries since they were auctioned after their death by the family, in which case an auction catalogue was prepared. We have such auction catalogues, for instance, of the libraries of Ames, Arminius, Bogerman, Gomarus, and Voetius.[1]

One of the issues that come to the fore immediately if we look in those catalogues are the vast array of Roman-catholic works in the Reformed libraries. Among these works we find those of Franciscus

---

1. See on Ames's library: *The Auction Catalogue of the Library of W. Ames*. A facsimile edition with an Introduction by K. L. Sprunger, Catalogi redivivi 6 (Utrecht 1988); on Arminius's library: *The Auction Catalogue of the Library of J. Arminius*. A facsimile edition with an Introduction by C. O. Bangs, Catalogi redivivi 4 (Utrecht 1985); on Bogerman's library: *The Auction Catalogue of the Library of J. Bogerman*. A Facsimile Edition with an Introduction and Indexes by C. M. L. Verdegaal and E. Dekker, Catalogi Redivivi 14 ('t Goy-Houten: Utrecht, in preparation); on Gomarus's library: *The Auction Catalogue of the Library of F. Gomarus*. A Facsimile Edition with an Introduction and Indexes by E. Dekker, J. Knoop and C. M. L. Verdegaal, Catalogi Redivivi 10 ('t Goy-Houten: Utrecht, 1996); Voetius's library: *Bibliothecae variorum et insignium librorum theologicorum et miscellaneorum reverendi et celeberrimi Viri D. Gisberti Voetii Pars prior* (Ultrajecti, 1677); *Bibliothecae [. . .] Pars posterior* (Ultrajecti, 1679). See also B. Van Selm, "A list of Dutch book auction sale catalogues printed before 1611," *Quaerendo* 12 (1982): 95–129 for more auction catalogues.

Suárez (1548–1617), the very controversial *Concordia* of Luis de Molina (1535–1600), and those of that important writer against the Protestants, Robertus Bellarminus (1542–1621). This in itself may give us already a first clue to the fact that the Catholic theologians were taken seriously by the Protestants. The monumental *Disputationes de Controversiis Christianae Fidei, adversus hujus temporis Haereticos* ("disputations concerning the controversies of the christian faith, against the heretics of these days") evoked, according to Sommervogel, around two hundred reactions and counterreactions.[2] There was, in other words, a very lively, albeit polemical, discussion among Protestant and Catholic seventeenth-century theologians. If we want to know more about the subjects of discussion, the *Disputationes* of Bellarmine provide an excellent point of departure.[3] They were published in three volumes at Ingolstadt between 1586 and 1593, and a revised edition appeared in 1596, in four volumes. The work was reprinted many times.[4]

Bellarmine treats almost everything that could possibly be treated with respect to the Protestants: the pope, the status of councils, the sacraments, penance, freedom and grace, justification, etc. etc.[5] He also treats his subjects with patience; for example, freedom and grace receives for its treatment 400 densely printed foliopages, and sometimes we are led through arrays of up to 25 arguments concerning why a specific topic is not correct.

In this contribution, my special interest is focused on human freedom. There is no twentieth-century article or book, to my knowledge, in which Bellarmine's doctrine of human freedom is treated in relation to any Protestant, and only a few studies deal with Bellarmine's view of human freedom as such.[6] A factor which may have contributed to this silence is that Bellarmine's scholastic and

2. See C. Sommervogel, *Bibliothèque de la Compagnie de Jésus*, bibliographie (Bruxelles/Paris, 1890), Tome 1, 1165–1180.

3. On the authors which Bellarmine cites, see Robert W. Richgels, "The Pattern of Controversy In a Counter-Reformation Classic: The *Controversies* of Robert Bellarmine," *The Sixteenth Century Journal* 11 no. 2 (1980), 3–15, and Richgels, "Scholasticism meets Humanism in the Counter-Reformation. The Clash of Cultures in Robert Bellarmine's use of Calvin in the 'Controversies.'" *The Sixteenth Century Journal* 6 (april 1975): 53–66.

4. I have used the edition of Ingolstadt, esp. vol. 4, of 1601.

5. Cf. also the contribution of Frits Broeyer, elsewhere in this volume.

6. Cf. the extensive bibliography of A. Mancia, "Bibliografia Bellarminiana nel novecento," in Gustavo Galeota, ed., *Roberto Bellarmino. Arcivescovo di Capua teologo e pastore della riforma cattolica*. Atti del convegno internazionale di studi Capua 28 settembre - 1 ottobre 1988 (Capua, 1990), 809–72, esp. 849–51.

philosophically sounding language is not a popular subject of study for contemporary theologians, while contemporary philosophers are not very eager to study a subject in so clear a theological setting, and, if they do happen to want to study such a subject, they generally focus on medieval predecessors.

According to one voice of the scarce secondary literature, Bellarmine is not original when it comes to free will.[7] This may already sound negative, but in my view, originality is not as such a virtue. If a person succeeds in saying old things in a clear systematic way, and in a language understandable for his or her contemporaries, there is all reason to study that person's thoughts, for they may well have been very influential.

Of the approximately two hundred works that have been published concerning Bellarmine's main work, the majority deals with the first few disputations, and there are relatively few on free choice. This has at least in part to do with the fact that free choice appears only relatively late in the *Disputationes*. Much energy was already spent by the adversaries to refute the first disputations. Some Protestant theologians would have reacted to all disputations if they had only lived long enough (Franciscus Junius [1545–1602], Lambertus Danaeus [c.1530–1595]).[8] However, all seventeenth-century writers of elenctic literature engaged at length with Bellarmine, which makes him one of the most-cited authors in that era.[9]

I have chosen to discuss William Ames or Amesius, who wrote a (late) reaction to Bellarmine, entitled *Bellarminus Enervatus*. It must have been rather popular, for we know of five printings of it during 1625–1633, and Ames wrote a revised edition in 1658. Perhaps some of its popularity can be explained by realizing that it was printed in duodecimo, i.e. a cheap and small pair of booklets.[10] Bellarmine was defended against Ames by a Jesuit author, Vitus Erberman, in a book entitled *Nervi sine*

7. See Gustavo Galeota, in his "Bellarmini," *TRE* 5, 525–31.

8. See Luc Perrottet, "Un exemple de polémique religieuse à la fin du XVIe siècle: La défense de la tradition par Robert Bellarmin (1542–1621) et la république Calviniste," *Revue de Théologie et de Philosophie* 114 (1982), (395–413) 405.

9. See E. P. Meijering, *Reformierte Scholastik und patristische Theologie: Die Bedeutung des Väterbeweises in der Institutio Theologiae Elencticae F. Turrettins unter besonderer Berücksichtigung der Gotteslehre und Christologie,* Bibliotheca Humanistica et Reformatorica 50 (Nieuwkoop: De Graaf publishers, 1991), who calls Bellarmine's doctrines the main point of Turretin's attack (p. 14).

10. I used the second edition of 1658, in which the discussion on free will can be found in tom. IV, pp. 68–82. Hereinafter, I refer to this work simply by "Ames," followed by the page number.

mole sive Controversiae vindicatae. . ., Herbipoli (Würzburg), 1661.[11] Again, a sign that at least some of the Catholics were of the opinion that Ames was worth an attack.

I propose not to treat Bellarmine first and then Ames, but to outline overall characteristics (if such a thing is possible in Bellarmine's case) and then to look at what Ames has to say against him; first on the definition of free choice itself, then on will and intellect, followed by a section on concursus. I may remind the reader that in a contribution of this size, I will necessarily be sketchy and incomplete on the vast issue of free will, and not even touch the question of the powers of the will in matters of faith.

II. Free Choice

The *liberum arbitrium* as Bellarmine defines it, has a set of characteristics which are pretty common in the sixteenth and seventeenth century. One of the polemical issues is, whether or not it is sufficient for freedom of choice to say that the will wills *spontaneously*, i.e. not coerced but following one's own choice. Some claim that indeed this is sufficient, while others do not deny that spontaneity is a necessary condition for free choice, but that *alternatively* should be added, i.e. the possibility to choose an alternative option than that which is chosen. Luther seems to insist upon the former position, whereas others adhere to the second. It is, however, not so simple as this. For one's position depends on the conceptual structure of the complete worldview one adheres to. It is, in effect, even possible that two theologians argue the same position but with almost contradictory terminology. The opposite case is even more tricky: two theologians argue different positions with the same terminology. In the case of the free will discussion, it is very important to have clues as to whether the notion of autonomy is inextricably linked up with freedom.[12] The option of alternativity can be seen in medieval theologians like Duns Scotus,[13] but also with men like Bellarmine, and perhaps, in a way, also

11. Cf. Sommervogel, *Bibliothèque de la Compagnie de Jésus*, Tom. 1, 1178 with William Ames, *The Marrow of Sacred Divinity*, transl. by John Dykstra Eusden (Boston/Philadelpia 1968), vii.

12. See on the matter of autonomy *versus* freedom: Eef Dekker and Henri Veldhuis, "Freedom and Sin. Some Systematic Observations," *European Journal of Theology* 3 (1994): 153–61.

13. See John Duns Scotus, *Contingency and Freedom. Lectura I 39*, Introduction, Translation and Commentary by A. Vos Jaczn. a.o., New Synthese Historical Library 42 (Dordrecht/Boston/London: Kluwer Academic Publishers, 1994).

in the theology of Amesius.

Ames starts with citing the basic definition of free choice which Bellarmine offers after having discussed a few other proposals. Bellarmine says he has gathered it from Aquinas. It is this:

> Free choice is a free power to choose one thing from things which conduce to an end, above another, or to accept or reject one and the same thing, attributed to an intelligent nature to the great glory of God.[14]

Ames's reaction can be taken as paradigmatic for his approach toward Bellarmine. He does not straightforwardly deny or admit the value of the definition, but discusses its possible interpretations, and claims that on one interpretation there would be nothing to discuss, while there is disagreement on the interpretation Bellarmine has.[15]

Ames proposes, therefore, to take another, very brief, definition, in which free choice is the power to act according to counsel (or judgment). He continues to claim that Bellarmine has the same notion in use elsewhere, and quotes it: If we have options, and if the election of one option happens on the ground of a perfect judgment, then we have free choice.[16] We may wonder in which respect these definitions are better, for it seems to me that if one is open to different and diverging interpretations, the other is as well.

Bellarmine treats the threefold distinction of Bernard of Clairvaux, also used by Peter Lombard and for that reason, well known throughout subsequent history. Bernard distinguished between freedom from necessity, freedom from sin and freedom from misery. Only the first type of freedom could be regarded as essential, i.e. as part of the human essence, whether or not man had fallen in sin or is seen as converted.

---

14. Bellarminus, *Disputationes*, vol. 4, Controv. 3, first item: De Gratia et Libero Arbitrio, book iii, chapter iii, (vol. 4, p. 648; below I shall just give the book and chapter number, followed by the page number of the Ingolstadt 1601 edition), also quoted *verbatim* in Ames, 68: Liberum arbitrium est libera potestas, ex his quae ad finem aliquem conducunt, unum prae alio eligendi, aut unum et idem acceptandi, vel pro arbitrio respuendi, intelligenti naturae ad magnam Dei gloriam attributa.

15. Ames, 68: Haec definitio quamvis illum sensum possit habere, ut de ea, non fit contendendi causa, neque tamen est accurata, neque in illo sensu, in quo a Bell. declaratur, potest defendi . . .

16. Ames, 68: Simplex et vera definitio liberi arbitrii est, quod sit: *facultas agendi ex consilio*. Hoc Bell. ipse fatetur cap. 17 [= iii.xvii, 696]: *Satis est ad essentiam liberi arbitrii si quis habeat optionem diversarum verum, et electio fiat cum pleno atque perfecto judicio rationis.*

Freedom from sin is only characteristic of man in so far as he is under grace, and freedom from misery is only the case in heaven. Calvin also discusses this threefold distinction, and to mention just one other theologian: Jacobus Arminius.[17] Ames does not pay attention to the threefold distinction itself. Perhaps he agrees, and only wants to discuss those parts of his adversary's work that need to be argued against.

Bellarmine continues by comparing the notions of freedom from necessity and coaction. Ames cites him thus:

> Bellarmin says: "in order to constitute free choice, we need liberty of necessity, and the liberty of coaction is not sufficient"[18]

At this place Ames replies that Bellarmine is confused here, for

> coaction is necessity, and therefore he should not treat coaction as the opposite of necessity. Moreover, he falsely accuses our theologians, that they only see freedom in the absence of coaction, for of course the people who make use of that phrase, always presuppose the will's freedom from the determination of natural necessity to one point only, just like Bellarmine himself uses it.[19]

Whom Ames particularly has in mind is hard to know, but in general, it is quite important that Ames *sees* his colleague Reformed theologians to have taken precisely the position that even when they only mention freedom from coaction, they as a matter of course also mean freedom from necessity. We may wonder if it applies in all cases. Luther's case, for

---

17. On Calvin and Bernard, see, e.g., Vincent Brümmer, "Calvin, Bernard and the Freedom of the Will," *Religious Studies* 30 (1994), 457–65; On Arminius and Bernard, see Eef Dekker, *Rijker dan Midas. Vrijheid, genade en predestinatie in de theologie van Jacobus Arminius (1559–1609)* (Zoetermeer, The Netherlands, 1993) ch. 6.

18. Ames, 68: Bellarm. *Ad arbitrium liberum constituendum omnino requiritur libertas a necessitate, neque sufficit libertas a coactione. Protest.* [= iii.v, 651]. See also *ibidem*, 650: [. . .] satis constat inter auctores libertatem, a qua dicitur liberum arbitrium, non esse nisi primam [i.e. a necessitate]. Neque enim carent libero arbitrio homines impii, quamvis servi sint peccati et corruptionis, ac per hoc careant secunda et tertia libertate.

19. Ames, 68: Confuse magis proponuntur haec a Bellarm. quam *declarationis* titulus promittebat. Nam. 1. Coactio est necessitas: non debuit igitur necessitati opponi. 2. Per calumniam tribuitur nostris, quod libertatem statuant a coactioni tantum, supponunt enim semper qui illa phrasi utuntur, libertatem voluntatis a necessitate naturalis determinationis ad unum quo fere modo Bell. ipse eandem phrasin interpretatur, quando ex Thoma profertur, cap. 6. prout frequentissime usurpatur, non a Thoma tantum, sed et ab omnibus Scholasticis primis.

146

one, seems to be an example of a denial of freedom from necessity. However it may be, Ames applies an important hermeneutical rule here: try to read not the terminology itself, but what the author may have wanted to say in a consistent way.

In applying this general rule, there is no need for Ames to be concerned with a more specific defense of Calvin's position, which is explicitly attacked at this point by Bellarmine—and not only Calvin's but also Bucer's, and, on the Catholic side, Alphonsus de Castro's.[20] Such a defence would amount to an interpretation along the lines mentioned. Ames is very parsimonious here.

Ames resumes by noting that Bellarmine himself at various points works with a notion of necessity that is compatible with freedom, and, notably, so does Bradwardine.[21] Ames could have quoted any one out of a number of theologians for the same point, but the fourteenth-century theologian Thomas Bradwardine would have been an acceptable authority for Bellarmine.

Then, to make himself most explicit, Ames draws the conclusion regarding his own position, in which there is no room for necessity proper in free choice. He also makes clear that he does not even want to connect necessity to divine ordination or foreknowledge:

> We concede that free choice, in its act, is free from every necessity, so that it cannot properly act necessarily with respect to its exercise, and acts with respect to the divine ordination certainly and infallibly, which certitude is called by many others "necessity"—also by Bellarmine, in book 3, chapters 12 and 13.[22]

---

20. Bellarmine, iii.iv, 650–51.

21. Ames, 68–69: 3. Bell ipse ca. 6. concedit, *necessitatem conditionatam non repugnare libertati, et cap.* 11 dicit, *voluntatem necessario moveri a judicio ultimo rationis et per modum causae naturalis, quae presente objecto non potest non age//re.* 4. Bradwardinus lib. 3 cap. 10 varie distinguit necessitatem ac libertatem: *est* (inquit) *necessitas naturalis, necessitas fatali, necessitas violentiae coactionis, et necessitas Spontaneae stabilitatis permanentiae, seu etiam firmitatis, quae etiam (licet non tam proprie) necessitas immutabilitatis vocatur, libertas dicitur contrariae iisdem modis. Necessitas naturalis fatalis et violente, libertati repugnant.* Idem Bradwardinus lib. 3 cap. 3 docet; *Deum posse necessitare quodammodo omnem voluntatem creatam ad liberum actum suum, ad liberam cessationem et vacationem ab actu.*

22. Ames, 69: Nos tamen concedimus liberum arbitrium, in eo quod agit, liberum esse ab omni necessitate, ut proprie non possit necessario agere quoad exercitium sui actus, quamvis respectu divinae ordinationis certo et infallibiliter agat, quae certitudo sicut a multis aliis necessitas vocatur, sic etiam a Bell. lib. 3 cap.12.13 [= 733–37].

From this quotation it also becomes clear that Ames is acquainted with the distinction between liberty of specification and that of the exercise, or with equivalent terms, liberty of contrarity and contradiction, a distinction which belonged to the standard package of every theologian in those days. Liberty of specification is, for example, the case in willing to walk or to run, while liberty of the exercise is the freedom to will to walk or to abstain from that willing. We can see this claim evidenced in, for instance, Suárez, Molina and Bellarmine in the Catholic camp, and Arminius, Gomarus and others in the Protestant.[23]

III. Will and Intellect

The relationship between will and intellect, and its impact on the will's freedom, was a hotly debated issue in the seventeenth century—and not only in the seventeenth, but in our own time[24] as well as in medieval scholasticism.[25]

Ames discusses an adagium which seems to express Bellarmine's view of the relationship between will and intellect fairly well: "The choice of the will depends necessarily on the ultimate judgment of the practical intellect.[26] Ames has three arguments why this is not a good view:

1. If this is true, then it is false what was said before, "that for free choice it is required that there is freedom from every necessity."
2. This opinion was already publicly condemned among the Catholics

23. Bellarmine, iii.iii, 648–49, in his earlier cited definition. He explains his definition in line with the abovementioned distinction. More references and explanation can be found in, e.g., Eef Dekker, *Rijker dan Midas*, 133–45; Eef Dekker, "The Reception of Scotus' theory of contingency in Molina and Suárez," in Leonardo Sileo, ed., *Via Scoti: Methodologica ad mentem Joannis Duns Scoti. Atti del Congresso Scotistico Internazionale* (Roma, 1995), 445–54.

24. Cf., for instance, the debate between Fischer and Van Inwagen: John Martin Fischer, and Mark Ravizza, "When the Will Is Free," in Timothy O'Connor, ed., *Agents, Causes, and Events. Essays on Indeterminism and Free Will* (New York/Oxford, 1995), 239–69; Peter Van Inwagen, "When is the Will Free?," in *ibidem*, 219–38, and Peter Van Inwagen, "When the Will is not Free," *PS* 75 (1994): 95–113, with further literature.

25. See for example, Michael Sylwanowicz, *Contingent Causality and the Foundations of Duns Scotus' Metaphysics* (Leiden, 1996), 44–56; Dewey J. Hoitenga Jr., *John Calvin and the Will. A Critique and Corrective*, Foreword by Richard A. Muller (Baker Books: Grand Rapids, 1997); Lynne Courter Boughton, "Choice and Action: Willam Ames's Concept of the Mind's Operation in Moral Decisions," *Church History* 56 (1987): 188–203.

26. Ames, 69: Bell. Voluntatis electio pendet necessario ab ultimo judicio practicae rationis.

themselves, see Azorius the Jesuit, book 4 chapter 23: "We have three Parisian articles: Given general and particular knowledge, the will cannot choose its opposite.

Error 1. If the major is factual, and the minor too in a syllogism, the will cannot will the opposite. Error 2. If the action is right, the will is right too. Error 3. If the will exists in the ultimate disposition, a man cannot will its opposite." These articles were condemned by Stephen, bishop of Paris, with consent of the theologians of that academy, in the year 1226.[27] 4. [read: 3.][28] Scotus and the Scotists refuted that assertion with fine arguments, as can be checked in Johannes de Rada . . . who writes on the controversies between Thomas and Scotus. . . .[29] one of which is that after the ultimate judgment, the will remains free.[30]

So, in the first place, Ames discerns a contradiction in Bellarmine's views with respect to free choice. Indeed, it is possible to infer determinism from an intellectualist position. But should we regard Bellarmine as a thoroughgoing intellectualist? In any case, Bellarmine seems to be aware of the problem, and proposes a theory in which the will "acts negatively."[31] I am inclined to believe that Bellarmine is not the

27. Obviously, the year is not 1226, but 1277. In the document of the condemnations, Stephen Tempier refers to the year as 1276, but Paris had a different way of counting then. The text of the condemnations can be found in H. Denifle, A. Chatelain, *Chartularium Universitatis Parisiensis*, I, Paris 1889: 543–58, and was translated in Ernest L. Fortin and Peter D. O'Neill, "The Condemnation of 1277," in Ralph Lerner and Muhsin Mahdi, eds., *Medieval Political Philosophy: A Source Book* (Toronto: Collier-Macmillan, 1963), 335–54.

28. Ames must have been misled by his own frequent use of the number 3 in his second argument.

29. Ames means to refer to Juan de Rada, *Controversiae theologicae inter S. Thomam & Scotum*, 2 vols. (Salamanca: Johannes Ferdinandus, 1586–1599).

30. Ames, 69–70: *Prot.* 1 Si hoc verum est, tum falsum est quod antea dicebatur: *ad liberum arbitrium requiri libertatem ab omni omnino necessitate.* 2. Haec sententia jamdudum fuit inter Pontificos publice damnata; sic Azorius Jesuita, l.4c.23. *Exstant tres articuli Parisienses. 1. Stante scientia in universali et particulari, voluntas non potest oppositum eligere. Error.1. Vel existente majori in actu, et minore in actu, in syllogismo, voluntas non potest oppositum velle. Error 2. Si recta actio est, recta quoque voluntas est. Error 3. Existente voluntate in ultima dispositione, homo non potest oppositum velle.* Isti articuli damnati fuere a Stephano Episcopo Parisiensi, ex consensu Theologorum illius Academiae, an. 1226. 4. Scotus et Scotistae firmis rationibus hanc assertionem refutant, sicut videre apud Joh. // de Rada, Arragonium, Episc. Pactensem in controversiis inter Thomam et Scotum. *par. 2 cont. 15. art. 3 quarum una est, quia post ultimum judicium voluntas libera manet.*

31. See Bellarmine, iii.ix, especially the response to the seventh argument (670). Bellarmine also makes use of this theory in his discussion of divine concursus, which

intellectualist Ames thinks he is.[32]

On the second point, Ames applies a strategy which is always very helpful in such controversial literature: if you can show that the camp of the enemy is divided, you have weakened his overall position. Indeed, the demarcation line is not always to be found exactly between Protestant and Catholic. On many issues, the dividing line runs just through both. Ames substantiates his point by referring to the condemnations of 1277, a major mark in the history of medieval scholasticism. Indeed, in 1270 and again in 1277, an Aristotelian and Averroist, determinist position was condemned by the Church. In a Christian worldview, there is no place for such determinism.

The third point corroborates the second: also in Scotism the freedom of choice was upheld, against intellectualist positions. Ames approves of the Scotist position here, a fact which is not unimportant, given some contemporary voices who claim that Reformed Protestantism is more or less Thomist.[33]

IV. Divine *concursus* and Human Freedom

Bellarmine presents two theories of the relationship between God's government and concurrence on the one hand and human freedom on the other. He opts for the second theory, but gives a very detailed account of the first. He claims that this theory belongs, among others, to Scotus, which is not correct, as we shall see. The theory reads, in Ames's rendering of Bellarmine's words:

> One reason, sufficiently apt to explain that *concursus*, is that of Scotus, Gabriel [Biel] and the like, who say that the *concursus* of God does not impose itself or work *in our will*, but rather, it works immediately *in the*

---

theory is heavily criticized by Ames. Space does not permit me, however, to discuss the theory at length.

32. Bellarmine says, for example, very clearly: "The will is free in choosing, not because it is not necessarily determined by the ultimate practical judgment of reason, but because that ultimate practical judgment itself is in the power of the will." (*ibidem.* Voluntas in eligendo libera est, non quod non determinetur necessario a iudicio ultima et practico rationis, sed quoniam istud ipsum iudicium ultimum et practicum in potestate voluntatis est.) See also the discussion of this point in Rosemary Z. Lauer, "Bellarmine on *Liberum Arbitrium*," *The Modern Schoolman* 33 (1956): 61–89; and in Louis Leahy, "Volition négative, choix positif: Bellarmin et le libre arbitre," *Sciences Ecclésiastiques* 15 (1963): 99–116.

33. Some of these voices are discussed in the contribution of Harm Goris, elsewhere in this volume, with literature.

effect [of our will]. An example: two carry a heavy stone, which cannot be carried by either of the persons alone. God and the will work at exactly the same moment. God works, however, since his will does not act contrarily. God has in a way obliged himself to it, in creating a free human will.[34]

Very important is the exact way in which the simultaneous activity of God and human being is conceived. Scotus distinguishes between so-called essentially and accidentally ordered causes. The latter type of cause applies to Bellarmine's example of two persons carrying a heavy stone, for the distinctive characteristic of an accidental ordering of causes is that if one of the causes were powerful enough, that cause could have brought the effect about just by itself. In the case of an essentially ordered pair of causes, one cause cannot replace the influence of the other. An example of it would be the coming together of man and wife in bringing forth offspring. In that case, each cause by its own cannot produce the effect, but each needs the other.[35]

The last clause of the above quotation suggests that Bellarmine adds a crucial detail to the theory (to remind the reader: which he does not hold), namely, that the creature can give the act its specific character. This in turn means that the *concursus* meant here is general, rather than specific. Such a general *concursus* functions for example in the theory of Bellarmine's contemporaries, Suárez and Molina. Also, on the Protestant side, Arminius works with the concept of general *concursus*.[36]

Ames does not have much patience with this position, and indeed in

---

34. Italics mine. Ames, 70: Bell. 1. *una ratio satis accommodata ad istam concordiam explicandam est Scoti, Gabr. etc. concursum Dei nihil imprimere, aut operari in voluntatem nostram, sed immediate influere in effectum. Simile est, cum duo ferunt ingentem lapidem, quem unus ferre non posset. Simul operantur Deus et voluntas, in eodem prorsus momento temporis. Deus tamen operatur, quia voluntas operatur non contra, quia ad hoc se libere quodammodo obligavit, quando liberam voluntatem creavit.* Here Ames seems to give an exact quotation, but this text is in fact collected from several pieces. See Bellarmine iv.xv, 742.

35. For more explanation on this topic, cf. William A. Frank, "Duns Scotus on Autonomous Freedom and Divine Co-Causality," *Medieval Philosophy and Theology* 2 (1992): 142–64, with Eef Dekker, "Does Duns Scotus Need Molina? On Divine Foreknowledge and Co-causality," in E. P. Bos, ed., *John Duns Scot (1265/6–1308). Renewal of Philosophy* (Amsterdam: Rodopi, forthcoming). See for a discussion of the simultaneity of the two causes and the concept of a cause directly working on the effect of another cause, Freddoso's introduction in Luis de Molina, *On Divine Foreknowledge* (Part IV of the *Concordia*), Translated with an Introduction and Notes by A. J. Freddoso (Ithaca/London, 1988), 18–19.

36. See Eef Dekker, *Rijker dan Midas*, 128–31.

the way it is taken here, his arguments against it are mostly to the point. He gives seven counterarguments, of which I quote five:

> This reasoning is falsely called "apt," for (1) it detracts the dominion of God's efficacious providence and guidance to all operations of the human will, or the will insofar as its operation is concerned. (2) It removes the subordination of first and second causes in their operation. (3) It makes man not subordinate to God but his comrade. (4) The guidance or direction of human acts and that which flows from them, depends firstly and primarily on man's choice. . . . (7) It is not only against Aristotle, Augustine, Thomas and the Thomists (as Alvarez explains in disputation 18), but even against the Tridentine Catechism, which says in number 22 on the first article of the Creed: "God impells with an intimate power, by his providence, whatever moves and does something, to move and act."[37]

I take the main point of Ames's opposition to consist in the fact that man can determine God's providence, as it were, and is no longer dependent upon God. As I have explained, however, it is quite possible to give a picture which at first sight is very close to the one under critique here. In that alternative, human and divine will are not regarded as being on the same level in the sense of it being possible that if the human will were stronger, it would adduce more to its acts.[38]

Alvarez is quite often adduced as an ally to the Reformed. Also Ames' contemporary Gisbertus Voetius often cites him. It shows once more that the dividing line is not to be drawn between Reformed or Protestant and Catholic, but between different positions, which can be found in both Protestant and Catholic theologians. Moreover, Ames applies the same strategy which he had applied earlier on, namely to show that the other party is divided in itself, thereby weakening its position.

The second position Bellarmine wants to defend is a Thomist position. It is telling, however, that he does not straightforwardly head

---

37. Ames, 70–71: *Prot.* Haec ratio falso dicitur accommodata: Nam. 1. Subtrahit dominio providentiae et gubernationi Dei efficaci operationis omnes voluntatis humanae, vel voluntatem quoad suam operationem. 2. Subordinationem primae, et secundarum causarum, in suis operationibus tollit. 3. Hominem non subditum, sed socium Dei facit. . . . // Adversatur (ut Alvarez *disputatione*, 18 ostendit) non tantum Aristoteli, Augustino, Thomae, et Thomistis, sed ipsi catechismo Tridentino Romano; in quo ad *prim. art. symbo. num* 22. haec verba habentur: *Deus providentia sua, quae moventur, et agunt aliquid, intima virtute ad motum atque actionem impellit.*

38. Cf. the literature mentioned in note 35 above.

toward that preferred position and goes a long way to examine the alternative position which we have discussed.[39] It means, so it seems to me, at least that Bellarmine is a nuanced and careful theologian, who does not put forward a position without trying to see some truth in an alternative position. It may also mean that Bellarmine is to some degree sympathetic to the alternative position, and chooses the Thomist position only because such a position is more in line with what Bellarmine is expected to say.[40]

Ames quotes this second position thus:

> The other reasoning which aims at reconciling human freedom with divine cooperation, and which is maybe even more probable, is that which is in accord with the opinion of Thomas: God moves the operative powers of free causes and applies them to their jobs.[41]

It is quite important to realize that there are different ways of constructing a picture in which God moves the powers of free, human causes. In one interpretation, the free causes lose their freedom by being led to wherever the leading power leads it. Yet, in another interpretation, freedom can really be maintained.[42] However this may be, the first focus of Ames' critique lies elsewhere:

> Bellarmine shows here that he behaves like a skeptical Sophist in such grave matters: "maybe even more probable." This in truth is the opinion which Bellarmine started to refute in chapter 14, but in this way it is deformed by a sophistical, obscure and absurd interpretation.[43]

Ames corroborates my observation that Bellarmine may have extrinsic reasons to choose the Thomist position, while his intrinsic arguments in

---

39. Running throughout iv.xv (742–47). The preferred position takes iv.xvi (747–51).

40. Perhaps the same could be said with regard to Bellarmine's "intellectualism," which is far closer to voluntarism than it might seem at first glance.

41. Bellarm. Altera ratio conciliandi libertatem humanam, cum cooperatione divina, et fortasse etiam probabilior est juxta sententiam Thomae, Deum virtutes operatrices causarum liberarum movere et applicare ad opus.

42. Cf. what was said above, in connection to note 35.

43. *Protest.* 1. Bellarm. hic satis ostendit, quod scepticum Sophistam agat in gravissima quaestione: *fortasse probabilior*. 2. Haec vera est sententia, quam Bellarm. antea cap. 14. conatus est refutare, sed sophistica, obscura, et absurda interpretatione a Bellarm. hunc in modum depravatur.

fact point at another position. I take Ames to have correctly seen that Bellarmine's arguments seem to refute rather than underpin a Thomist position.

The phrase "maybe even more probable" may refer to a subtle mechanism of qualifications internal to the Roman-Catholic debate if, and to which degree, a position would be tenable for, or rather, preferred by, the Church. If this is true, it may have escaped Ames' attention.[44]

V. Conclusion

In this preliminary sketch of Ames' examination of Bellarmine's doctrine of free will, we have seen that the dividing lines do not run exactly along the Protestant-Catholic divide. Ames is quite capable of pointing at problems in Bellarmine's text, and in this way he contributes to the search for truth, wherever it may lie. One of the main problematic points is, perhaps surprisingly, the way in which Bellarmine wrestles with his arguments for and against Thomism and Scotism, respectively. Ames seems to be—as far as this short contribution allows for such a far reaching verdict—in sympathy with a Scotist position.

---

44. Owe this information to dr. T. H. M. Akerboom and prof. C. Augustijn, for which I am in their debt.

7

Traces of the Rise of Reformed Scholasticism in the Polemical Theologian William Whitaker (1548–1595)

Frits G. M. Broeyer

By the second half of the sixteenth century the chasm separating the Reformation from Rome had grown so wide that bridging it had become practically impossible. The Tridentine Council (1545–1563) closed the door to any possibility of compromise such as had still been hoped for during the reunion conference of Ratisbon in 1541. The subsequent theological developments also failed to provide any grounds for hope. In the meanwhile there had been so many attempts at resolving the situation in a violent manner that only the occasional solitary individual still dared to hope for a compromise. Those few irenic souls were quite out of step with their contemporaries. Yet disputations between Reformational and Catholic theologians still occasionally took place in the second half of the sixteenth century, even if they were primarily intended by the participants as a means of demonstrating publicly that they were in the right. Primarily for this reason theologians from the two camps attacked one another in writing. The result was that the populations of the various countries found themselves at the receiving end of a veritable avalanche of polemical literature.

How did the polemicists approach their task? Quotations from the Bible, references to the Church Fathers, historical facts, prophecies, intellectual arguments: everything was employed in demonstrating the rightness of one's own position. For strategic reasons, polemicists had recourse to the methods of their opponents too. Catholics sought to achieve success by producing as many Biblical quotations as possible. Protestants for their part made use of that very scholasticism that had been so vehemently rejected during the first phase of the Reformation. Since logic as a discipline was in any case a fixed part of the curriculum of Protestant universities, they had little difficulty in holding their own in a scholastically colored debate. Moreover, scholasticism came to be re-evaluated in a more nuanced fashion in Protestant circles. Even if it might seem wise not to use Lombard's *Sententiarum Libri Quattuor* as a textbook anymore, not everything that scholasticism had achieved had to be regarded as evil. Some good things were even to be found in Lombard himself. This shift towards a more nuanced view of scholasticism also occurred in England. In the English confession of faith in the *39 Articles*, the rejection of the *scholastic* teaching in article 22 of the original draft was replaced, in the final version, with the declaration that the *Roman* teaching was being rejected. It seems reasonable to surmise that what lay behind this adaptation was the idea that scholasticism could not simply be equated with Roman Catholicism, that is to say, the scholastics had produced not only objectionable results.[1]

One of the most prominent polemicists of the sixteenth century was William Whitaker (1548–1595) of Lancashire.[2] He had already developed an interest in the Protestant-Catholic debate during his school years in London, due to the influence of an uncle of his, Alexander Nowell, with whom he had stayed at the time, and who had stimulated him in that direction. Nowell, who was the Dean of St. Paul's Cathedral, had had to flee from England at the time of Mary Tudor, and so, as a former exile, thought that it was supremely important to combat the Roman Catholic Church with the pen. Moreover, Whitaker was also influenced by his Calvinist approach to theological doctrines.

William Whitaker is remembered especially for two outstanding achievements: his polemic against the most important Catholic polemicist of his day, Robert Bellarmine (1542–1621); and the major part he played in a dispute at Cambridge in 1595 concerning predestination, which eventually led to the formulation of a dogmatic declaration, the *Lambeth*

---

1. For the present judgement of protestant scholasticism, see R. A. Muller, "Calvin and the Calvinists: Assessing continuities and discontinuities between the Reformation and Orthodoxy," parts 1 and 2, *CTJ* 30 (1995): 345–75; 31 (1996): 125–60; Muller, *Post-Reformation Reformed Dogmatics*, 2 vols. to date (Grand Rapids 1987–). For the older view, see B. Hall, "Calvin and the Calvinists," in G. E. Duffield, ed., *John Calvin*, Courtenay Studies in Reformation Theology 1 (Appleford, 1966), 12–37; B. G. Armstrong, *Calvinism and the Amyraut Heresy. Protestant Scholasticism in seventeenth-century France* (Madison, London, 1969).

2. For William Whitaker, see H. C. Porter, *Reformation and Reaction in Tudor Cambridge*, (Cambridge, 1958); F. G. M. Broeyer, *William Whitaker (1548–1595). Leven en werk van een anglocalvinistisch Theoloog* (Utrecht, 1982) (as to an English summary of this book about the "life and work of an Anglo-Calvinist Theologian," see 349–52); P.(G.) Lake, *Moderate Puritans and the Elizabethan Church* (Cambridge, 1982); Broeyer, "William Whitaker 1548–1595. A Cambridge Professor on the doctrine of the Church," in J. M. Fletcher, H. de Ridder-Simoens, eds., *Lines of Contact*, Studia Historica Gandensia 279 (Gent, 1994), 5–20.

Articles. Whitaker was the compiler of these articles, the content of which was decisive for his reputation as a Calvinist. His Catholic opponent, the Louvainian professor Thomas Stapleton, always labeled him an Anglo-Calvinist.[3] By that, Stapleton simply meant that Whitaker was an Englishman like himself, but then an Englishman with Calvinist views. This characterization is in fact quite accurate, not least because it conjures up the term Anglo-Catholic, which was to become popular at a later stage. Moreover, the prefix "Anglo" suggests a further specification of the concept "Calvinist." Whitaker certainly held some views that are not normally associated directly with the Calvinism of that period and later ages. His ideas regarding the relation between state and Church in particular were rather different from those of Calvinists elsewhere. He welcomed the English idea of a State Church with its positive appreciation of the influence of government on the Church. He did not object to the Episcopal system either. Whitaker had very cordial relations with John Whitgift, the Archbishop of Canterbury.

Robert Bellarmine must surely count as Whitaker's most important Catholic opponent, for it is primarily his defense of the Church of Rome in the *Disputationes de Controversiis Christanae Fidei* with which he was engaged. He was the first Protestant theologian to engage with this work. The phrase "especially against Bellarmine" in the complete title of his first book against the latter, the *Disputatio de Sacra Scriptura* of 1588, became a standard expression.[4] Many Protestant polemical theologians against the Catholic Church adopted this formulation as a subtitle to their own books.[5] That Whitaker took the initiative against this Jesuit of the *Collegium Romanum* had much to do with the unique situation obtaining in England at the time. In 1570, Pope Pius V had excommunicated Queen Elizabeth as a Calvinist heretic, in the bull *Regnans in excelsis*—a characterization with which she can not have been particularly happy.[6] Since then, the English had been feeling seriously

3. Cf. the title of Thomas Stapletonus, *Authoritatis Ecclesiasticae circa S. Scripturarum Approbationem . . . Defensio libris III digesta contra Disputationem de Scriptura Sacra Guilielmi Whitakeri Anglocalvinistae* (Antverpiae, 1592). Anglo-Catholicism was rooted in Anti-Calvinism (see N. Tyacke, *Anti-Calvinists. The Rise of English Arminianism 1590–1646* [Oxford, 1987]).

4. Cf. the title of Guilielmus Whitakerus, *Disputatio de Sacra Scriptura, contra huius temporis Papistas, imprimis Robertum Bellarminum* (Cantabrigiae, 1588).

5. See Jacobus Gretserus, *Controversiarum Roberti Bellarmini S.R.E. Cardinalis Amplissimi Defensio*, vol. 1 (Ingolstadii, 1607), p. C3 ro.; R. Brodrick, *The Life and work of Blessed Robert Cardinal Bellarmine*, 2 vols. (London, 1928), 2:140.

6. For the ascendancy of Calvinism during the reign of Elizabeth I and James II,

threatened—a feeling that was further strengthened when priests who had been trained on the Continent began doing mission work in England. The English judiciary hunted down these priests. Many of them were executed on the charge of high treason because, from the English authorities' point of view, they were seeking to lure people away from their duty to remain loyal to queen and country. The attack by the Spanish Armada in 1588 was interpreted as confirmation of the suspicion that the Catholic nations were conspiring to destroy England.[7] In the light of this situation, it is not surprising that English spies were operating in those countries. Probably, some of those spies were responsible for the fact that, already in 1586, Whitaker had access to transcripts of Bellarmine's lectures in Rome. Not a single volume of the latter's *Disputationes de Controversiis Christanae Fidei* had been published at the time. Government institutions in London had sent the transcripts to Oxford and Cambridge so that their contents could be refuted there. Thanks to this governmental intervention Whitaker was in a position to publish a work against Bellarmine before any other European scholar could do so. He also brought great skill to this task of refutation. According to an anecdote, Bellarmine had a portrait of Whitaker in his study. When an Englishman once inquired about it, he replied that Whitaker was the most erudite heretic he had ever read.

When Whitaker added the word *Disputatio* to the title of his lectures on Holy Scripture, he was not just following Bellarmine's example. The later volumes of his lectures against Bellarmine, published by his pupils, were also collected under the title *Disputatio*. It was, furthermore, with good reason that he gave the name *Quaestiones* to the subsections of his *Disputationes*. Whitaker associated this manner of division with the educational methods of the Middle Ages, which had by no means been discarded in the sixteenth century. The Protestant scholars of his age had distanced themselves from the content of medieval theology, but that was not necessarily the case with respect to their way of approaching

---

see N. Tyacke, "Puritanism, Arminianism and Counter-Revolution," in C. Russell, ed., *The origins of the English Civil War* (London, 1978): 119–43; P. Collinson, *The Religion of Protestants. The Church in English Society 1559–1625* (Oxford, 1982), 81, 82; W. J. Sheils, Reformed Religion in England. 1520–1640, in S. Gilley, W. J. Sheils, *A History of Religion in Britain. Practice and Belief from Pre-Roman Times to the Present* (Oxford, Cambridge, Mass., 1994), 162–67.

7. For the fear of Roman Catholic conspirations and the chauvinistic feelings, see L. B. Smith, *Treason in Tudor England. Politics and Paranoia* (London, 1986): 178–91; P. Collinson, *The Birthpangs of Protestant England. Religious and Cultural Change in the sixteenth and seventeenth centuries* (Basingstoke, 1988), 1–27.

their subjects. In fact, even much of the traditional content had been retained, in spite of the diffusion of Reformational principles. For example, why should one have to discard the ramification of the carefully thought-out concepts for the doctrine of God?

This connection with the medieval past can easily be traced in the career of William Whitaker. He spent the greatest part of his life in Cambridge. In 1564 he enrolled there as a student in Trinity College, where he was subsequently appointed as a Fellow in 1569. As a Fellow he gained the necessary teaching experience for an academic career. In the seventies he also published his first writings. Thanks to these achievements, and to the necessary support from above, which was indispensable in those days, Whitaker became Regius professor of theology in 1579. Apart from his responsibilities as Master of St John's College since 1587, he continued to teach until his death in 1595. Both Trinity College and St John's College, the two colleges with which he was associated, had been founded only in the sixteenth century, and thus provided an education in which the humanist ideals had been incorporated. Yet even there, much of the old academic curriculum of the seven *Artes* subjects was retained. Disputation was still one of the regular exercises engaged in on a weekly basis by students, Fellows and professors alike, as had always been the case.

Precisely because of this rather traditional curriculum, Whitaker became thoroughly acquainted with the work of the medieval scholastics. In a contemporary biographical sketch Abdias Ashton related how, subsequent to obtaining his Masters degree, Whitaker began to immerse himself in patristic literature, and then turned his attention to medieval and contemporary theologians.[8] It goes without saying that during those days he already read the scholastics, whom he would later quote in his lectures and writings, and Thomas Aquinas in particular.

Whitaker had a very high regard for Thomas, even though he could obviously not avoid denouncing part of his views. He called Thomas "the great leader of the scholastics" and the "most sharp-witted representative of scholasticism." As such these were not very high accolades. Whitaker's proximity to the reformers meant that he could make such statements only with some hesitancy. Thus he qualified statements of Thomas by sometimes specifying them as coming from "your teacher" (*magister*

---

8. Abdias Ashton, "Vitae et Mortis Guilielmi Whitakeri ... Descriptio," in Guilielmus Whitakerus, *Opera Theologica*, 2 vols. (Genevae, 1610) 1:699a, b.

tuus).[9] It is even conceivable, given that Whitaker in his writings assigned Thomas to the category of the "wiser" scholastics, that his reference to those scholars in general masked an understatement.[10] In his view Thomas had formulated his thoughts "skillfully, learnedly and piously," "not badly," "quite appropriately."[11] Thus even though Whitaker regarded Thomas first of all as belonging to the opposition, he did so with great reluctance. During that eclectic age, it was of course customary to use the enemy's weapons to serve one's own cause. Whitaker therefore occasionally stated that Thomas had in fact vindicated the truth of the Protestant faith. It always gave him great satisfaction when he succeeded in showing that contemporary Catholic opponents were propounding views that were in conflict with Thomas Aquinas.

Already in his first polemical writings Whitaker, striving to engage his opponents effectively, gratefully made use of the knowledge he had gained of scholastic theology. He knew what literature his opponents were drawing from. He was well versed in that literature—up to and including the scholastic literature of the second half of the sixteenth century. Some of the important contemporary Catholic authors, whom Whitaker had read, were Thomas Caietanus, Melchior Cano, Alfonso de Castro, Ambrosius Catharinus, Domingo de Soto, and Domingo Bañez. What strikes one about this list of names is that they were all Thomists. That prominent Catholic theologians of the second half of the sixteenth century belonged to the school of Thomas Aquinas is not so surprising. It was precisely in the sixteenth century that Thomism underwent a revival, which may rightly be called a Thomas renaissance. The nominalists of the late Middle Ages had caused much uncertainty with regard to questions of truth. Thomism offered a harmonious theological system, which could even be adapted in response to new questions. Over against the Reformation, Thomism provided Catholic theologians with attractive possibilities for logical argumentation. It was, after all, based on the idea that one could speak of revelation in a way that was also convincing in the eyes of outsiders. The Thomas renaissance subsequently reached the post-Reformational theologians who, for their part, liked to show that, precisely within that systematic whole of Thomistic concepts, they could prove that Luther and Calvin had been right.

Naturally, the outlook of those Protestants who had recourse to

---

9. Cf. Whitaker, *Opera*, 1:113b; 1:177b.
10. Whitaker, *Opera*, 1:651b.
11. Whitaker, *Opera*, 1:561b; 1:665a; 2:720b; 2:272b.

scholasticism differed from that of the Catholics. Catholic scholars wrote commentaries on Thomas. Their Reformational contemporaries did not. They could not accept Thomas's system as it stood. They read Thomas Aquinas, or his followers, only for the sake of finding arguments and views that they could use for their own purposes. The same applies to Whitaker. He regularly quoted Thomas in order to show what the teaching of the Catholic Church was with respect to a particular question regarding the faith. But he much preferred to invoke Thomas when he thought that, by doing so, he could give further support to one of his own views. During the heated controversy over predestination in 1595 in Cambridge, Whitaker was the leader of the party that defended a number of central tenets derived from Calvin's teaching. He saw Thomas as a valuable witness in support of Calvin's views on that very occasion too.[12]

As a matter of course, the question arises what level of Whitaker's knowledge of scholasticism had. Due to his eclectic approach, it is difficult to determine what exactly Whitaker had read. After all, he only mentioned what he had found useful. In the case of Thomas, however, he quoted passages from so many works that he must have gone through countless pages anyhow. For the extent of his reading in general Whitaker was praised even by extremely critical figures, like Joseph Scaliger and Isaac Casaubonus.[13] As to Thomas Aquinas he was, in any case, well acquainted with the *Summa Theologiae* and *the Summa contra Gentiles*. He often quoted from Thomas's commentary on Lombard, the *Scriptum super Sententiis,* as well as the *Quaestiones Disputatae* and the *Quaestiones Quodlibetales.* Furthermore, judging from his citations, he was familiar with works like the *Reportatio in Symbolum Apostolorum* and the *Opusculum contra Errores Graecorum.* Remarkably, Whitaker was also well versed in Thomas's commentaries on the books of Holy Scripture. Usually these commentaries did not get much attention. He consulted them, once again because in them he could find the material necessary and useful for the refutation of his opponents. From among the commentaries, he made use, first of all, of those on the Pauline epistles. Thus he quoted Thomas's commentaries on Romans, 1 Corinthians, Galatians, Ephesians, Colossians, 1 and 2 Timothy, and Titus.

Whitaker also referred to Thomas's commentaries on the general

---

12. I shall consider this point in more detail below.

13. *Casauboniana,* ed. J.C. Wolf (Hamburg, 1710), 28; *Scaligeriana,* ed. J. J. P. P., 2d ed. (Hagae Comitum, 1669), 3452.

epistles and Revelation. He was unaware of the fact that these commentaries had been mistakenly attributed to Thomas Aquinas. Yet such a mistake is to a certain extent irrelevant. The main point remains valid, namely that Thomas was being cited as an authority by a Calvinist. This is not at all meant to suggest that the authenticity of writings was unimportant in the polemical debates of that period. For example, an appeal to a work by Augustine lost much of its weight if an opponent could point out that Augustine had not been the author of the text under discussion, so that the latter was inauthentic. With reference to a certain quotation, which Bellarmine had attributed to Cyril of Alexandria, Whitaker was quick to point out that the passage did not appear in the work cited as its source. Thomas had been the first to make this mistake. Other authors had followed him, so that, finally, Bellarmine had also fallen into the trap.[14] It is worth noting in this regard that it was quite customary at the time to use secondary or imprecise quotations. With this kind of remark aimed at Bellarmine, Whitaker could show that he was well acquainted with the primary sources.

However, Whitaker himself was not really concerned with doing justice to authors from the past. He was mainly interested in seeking support for his own views in the theological literature of the early Church and the Middle Ages. Research for the sake of constructing a maximally accurate portrayal of the past would require an attitude quite different from that of a sixteenth century polemical theologian.

I. Revelation and Reason

The medieval scholastics saw the relation between revelation and reason as one of the most fundamental issues to be dealt with. Whitaker also concerned himself with this subject. He had to address it, so as to arrive at a principled position on the question, because he was engaged in discussions with his opponents about the authority of Scripture. The Biblical revelation naturally raised the question of what human reason could accomplish apart from it. In 1592 Stapleton, in a lengthy work on the authority of the Church with respect to Scripture: *Authoritatis*

---

14. Whitaker, *Opera*, 2:616a. Whitaker was right in his criticism, see O. Bardenhewer, *Geschichte der Altkirchlichen Literatur*, 5 vols. (reprint, Darmstadt, 1962), 4:45 and the reference there to F.H. Reusch, *Die Fälschungen in dem Traktat des Thomas von Aquin gegen die Griechen* (München, 1889). Whitaker referred to a place in Thomas Aquinatis, *Opusculum contra Errores Graecorum*, cap. 35–38 (see Thomas, *Opera Omnia*, R. Busa, ed., 7 vols. [Stuttgart, Bad Cannstatt 1980], 3:508b,c. Throughout this essay I quote from Busa's edition of Thomas's *Opera*.).

Ecclesiasticae circa S. Scripturarum Approbationem Defensio, responded to Whitaker's lectures on Holy Scripture that had been published in 1588. Stapleton declared that the Church was needed for the sake of determining what could legitimately be derived from Scripture as truth. Whitaker in turn responded to Stapleton's refutation of his *Disputatio de Sacra Scriptura*. In 1594 he published his *Adversus Thomae Stapletoni . . . Defensionem Ecclesiasticae Authoritatis Duplicatio*. In it, he insisted that absolute authority was due to Scripture alone. In this debate, the fundamental question of whether there were any truths of faith that were evident to reason, was brought to the fore. Whitaker answered it in the affirmative. In his view it was possible purely by rational argumentation to arrive at the conclusion that God existed, that God had created everything, that God was the highest good, as well as just, almighty, merciful and true. The contemplation of that which was present on earth led one to infer God's existence, and God's action in the world. Put differently: The acts of God were the proofs of God's existence. In support of this view he appealed to Thomas.[15] Here he had undeniably taken over a whole package of scholastic theology, and appropriated it for his own use.

Belief in God was for Whitaker a fundamental issue. In his opinion such belief necessarily implied that unassailable truth had to be attainable. Stapleton had argued that the Apostolic Creed contained not a single article declaring faith in Holy Scripture. Whitaker replied that this entailed a misguided approach to the Creed. After all, belief in God implied belief in the Biblical revelation. Whoever confessed belief in God thereby confessed that God was true in his Word, and thus accepted Holy Scripture as witness to the truth.[16] Interesting in this regard is Whitaker's quotation from the *Summa Theologiae*, II–II, q. 2, art. 2, on "belief in God," "belief in the existence of God" and "trust in God" ("credere in Deum," "credere Deum," "credere Deo").[17] Here Whitaker pointed out that in Thomas's view, as in his own, these were not three distinct acts of faith. There was only one act of faith. In this single act of faith three different ways of the relationship with God were brought to expression. In the statements of the Apostolic Creed pertaining to the

15. Whitaker, *Adversus Stapletoni Defensionem Duplicatio*, in *Opera*, 2:171b, cf. 413a, cf. Thomas, *Opera*, 2:1-152.

16. Whitaker, *Adversus Stapletoni*, in *Opera*, 2:172a, cf. *Disputatio de Sacra Scriptura*, in *Opera*, 1:320a; cf. Thomas, *Summa Theologiae*, II–II, *q*.1, art. 6, 7 (*Opera*, 2:525).

17. Whitaker, *Adversus Stapletoni*, in *Opera*, 2:173a; cf. Thomas, *Summa Theologiae*, II–II, qu.2, art. 2 (*Opera*, 2:527a).

relation with God, faith in all its fullness was already being unfolded.

The central issue in the debate between Whitaker and his opponents about Holy Scripture was whether belief in the truths of revelation required the authority of the Church in order to acknowledge them obediently. Referring to Thomas, he stated that no one ever believed on the authority of the Church, since belief was only possible by virtue of God's own testimony. After all, belief rested on no revelation other than the one that God had given to the prophets and apostles, and which had been written down in the canonical books of the Bible.[18] God was an eternal God, in contrast to the Church, which had appeared in time. Therefore the declarations of the Church on the truths of faith could never be more important than what had been written in Holy Scripture about those truths. Here, once again, he appealed to Thomas in support of his argument. The highest truth was to be found in Scripture, since the highest truth could not be found anywhere but with God Himself.[19] The Church had no more than a serving function with respect to the truth. Certainly, Jesus had provided the Church with a *magisterium*, but did not do so because the Gospel was in need of confirmation. He adopted this term because the Church had received the Gospel from Christ.[20] The *magisterium* involved a serving function, for the function of the Church could be compared to that of an instrument. The Church functioned as God's instrument on earth.[21] In Holy Scripture, however, the voice of God sounded immediately. In this regard Whitaker recalled the Creed, once again with a reference to a statement by Thomas. Following Thomas, he declared that the Church did not confirm the Apostolic Creed with its authority. Rather, the Creed contained truths of faith that were believed on their own terms.[22] In this regard, the fact that the Creed had only gradually acquired its familiar shape was irrelevant. For during the history of the development of the Creed, the Church had not validated the newly added articles by buttressing them with its authority. In fact, the Creed had not undergone any essential changes.

18. Whitaker, *Adversus Stapletoni*, in *Opera*, 2:272a; cf. Thomas, *Summa Theologiae*, I, q.1, art. 8 (*Opera*, 2:186).

19. Whitaker, *Adversus Stapletoni*, in *Opera*, 2:165b; cf. Thomas, *Summa Theologiae*, II–II, q.1, art. 1 (*Opera*, 2:523c, 524a).

20. *Duplicatio*, in *Opera*, 2:152b.

21. Whitaker, *Adversus Stapletoni*, in *Opera*, 2:154a; cf. Thomas, *Summa Theologiae*, I, q.19, art. 4 (*Opera*, 2:216a,b).

22. Whitaker, *Adversus Stapletoni*, in *Opera*, 2:168a; cf. Thomas, *Summa Theologiae*, II–II, q.1, art. 7 (*Opera*, 2:525b).

The changes pertained mainly to its form.[23]

Whitaker obviously liked to appeal to *Summa Theologiae*, I, q. 1, art. 8, for in his opinion the Protestant view, that Scripture owed its credibility not to the witness of the Church, but to itself, had been very clearly formulated there.[24] It is said there, namely, that only those arguments that derive from Scripture ought to be accorded unassailable authority (*ex necessitate*). The arguments deriving from the Church fathers and the teachers of the Church attained no more than a certain degree of probability (*probabiliter*) in asserting their claim to acceptance.[25] According to Thomas, explained Whitaker, nothing ought to be added to the truths pronounced by Scripture; neither may anything be removed.[26] Whitaker had encountered this last statement by Thomas in both his *Summa Theologiae* and his commentary on 1 Timothy.[27] He derived another, closely related, idea from Thomas's commentary on Ephesians, namely that what the prophets had foretold as future events, had been proclaimed as completed history by the apostles.[28] Whitaker took this as proof that the Reformers were right in their view of the relation between Scripture and tradition. Whatever had to be regarded as necessary for salvation had already been made known by the apostles.

Once more taking his point of departure in Thomas's commentary on 1 Timothy, Whitaker argued that the teaching of the prophets and apostles could be called canonical because they provided the clue with which reason, basing itself on Biblical data, operated.[29] He strongly

23. Whitaker, *Adversus Stapletoni*, in *Opera*, 2:168a; cf. Thomas, *Summa Theologiae*, II–II, q.1, art. 7 (*Opera*, 2:525b).

24. Whitaker, *Adversus Stapletoni*, in *Opera*, 2:130a, cf. *Opera*, 2:272a,b; cf. Thomas, *Summa Theologiae*, I, q.1, art. 8 (*Opera*, 2:186b). Thomas's words are: "Innititur enim fides nostra revelationi apostolis et prophetis facta, qui canonicos libros scripserunt, non autem revelationi, si qua fuit aliis doctoribus facta."

25. Whitaker, *Responsionis ad Decem Rationes Defensio*, in *Opera*, 1:129b; *Adversus Stapletoni*, in *Opera*, 2:337a; cf. Thomas, *Summa Theologiae*, I, q.1, art. 8 (*Opera*, 2:186b). Thomas's words are: "Sacra doctrina...auctoritatibus autem canonicae scripturae utitur proprie, ex necessitate argumentando, auctoritatibus autem aliorum doctorum ecclesiae, quasi arguendo ex propriis, sed probabiliter."

26. Whitaker, *Sacra Scriptura*, in *Opera*, 1:397a; cf. Thomas, *Summa Theologiae*, III, q.60, art. 8 (*Opera*, 2:863b).

27. Whitaker, *Sacra Scriptura*, in *Opera*, 1:407a; cf. Thomas, *Reportatio super ad Timotheum I*, cap. 6, lc. 1 (*Opera*, 6:498c).

28. Whitaker, *Sacra Scriptura*, in *Opera*, 1:404b; cf. Thomas, *Reportatio super ad Ephesios*, cap. 2, lc. 6 (*Opera*, 6:452c).

29. Whitaker, *Sacra Scriptura*, in *Opera*, 1:260b; cf. Thomas, *Reportatio super ad Timotheum I*, cap. 6, lc. 1 (*Opera*, 6:498c).

opposed the view, put forward by his Catholic opponents, that obscure texts stood in need of an authoritative exegesis from the side of the Church. For Thomas had said that what is expressed figuratively in certain parts of Scripture, is expressed clearly and distinctly elsewhere in the same Scripture.[30] Perhaps the scholastic method does not seem so apparent in this example of Whitaker's use of the works of Thomas. At first sight his concern seems to be simply to point out that the difficult passages in Scripture can be clarified in the light of other passages. However, logical reasoning played a major role in the exegesis of his time: solutions to all kinds of problems were expected to come from the logical method that was being taught in the universities. In his exegetical lectures he managed to arrive at all kinds of applications, that were often also relevant to several central dogmatic, institutional and ethical issues, simply by means of the analysis of short textual fragments and words. His elaborations went much further than those of Calvin, who was always more to the point, and stuck more consistently to the context.[31] During these lectures Whitaker made extensive use of syllogisms.

This tendency can be illustrated strikingly by recalling Christopher Marlowe's caricature (the *Che sarà, sarà* passage) of this kind of exegesis. In his *Doctor Faustus*, Faust argues as follows, by means of a syllogism, from Biblical texts: 1. The reward of sin is death (Rom. 6: 23a); 2. If we say we have no sin, we deceive ourselves (1 John 1:8). The conclusion that follows is 3. that eternal death awaits us.[32] Remarkably enough, a variant of this argument is also found in Whitaker, so that it seems very probable that Marlowe, who had studied at Cambridge at the time of Whitaker, had got the idea from him. Whitaker used one of Marlowe's premises in his lectures on the Song of Songs as well: The reward of sin is death (Rom. 6: 23a). The other premise was nearly identical: the going astray like sheep of all alike (Is. 53: 6), and Paul's confession that, despite his wish to the contrary, he still sinned (Rom. 7: 15–19). However, Whitaker's conclusion, unlike that of Faust, was not aimed against being

30. Whitaker, *Sacra Scriptura*, in *Opera*, 1:340a; cf. Thomas, *Summa Theologiae*, I, q.1, art. 9 (*Opera*, 2:186c).

31. For the continuity between medieval exegesis and Calvin's way of interpreting the Bible, see D.C. Steinmetz, *Calvin in Context* (Oxford, 1995).

32. Christopher Marlowe, *Doctor Faustus*, J. D. Jump, ed., 8, 9. Marlowe wrote: "The reward of sin is death: that's hard. *Si peccasse negamus, fallimur, et nulla est in nobis veritas.* If we say that we have no sin, we deceive ourselves, and there's no truth in us. Why, then, belike we must sin, and so consequently die. Ay, we must die an everlasting death. What doctrine call you this; *Che sarà, sarà*: What will be, shall be! Divinity, adieu!"

saved as such, but against the importance of works in Catholic teaching. Whitaker argued as follows: 1. No one is without sin; 2. The reward of sin is death. The conclusion following in 3. is then: the eternal life cannot be earned.[33] Rom. 6:23 was even a favorite text of Whitaker, but of course because of its second part, the pronouncement that God's gift of grace is eternal life in Christ Jesus.[34]

Whitaker, in line with Reformational theologians in general, rejected the exegesis based on the scheme of Scripture's fourfold meaning. Like them, he felt that the application of the fourfold meaning of Scripture gave rise to arbitrariness. For in the search for an allegorical meaning, fantasy had free reign. In principle the literal meaning alone was valid. However, in Whitaker's opinion logical consequences could be drawn from the literal meaning of a text. His only qualification in this regard was the rule that an inferred meaning ought not to be so far removed from the text that it became a totally different meaning in addition to the text.[35] He would thus have rejected out of hand the syllogism that Marlowe had come up with in his famous *Che sarà, sarà* passage. Those who interpreted the Bible, explained Whitaker, spoke with authority. If a preacher succeeded in persuading his audience, it was not due to the power of his personality, but to the power of his interpretation, which had succeeded in making clear what was meant in a particular text.[36]

Whitaker's denial that the authority of Scripture depended on that of the Church was closely related to his Reformational distinction between the visible and invisible Church. Protestant theologians tended to emphasize very strongly the limitations of the Church on earth, which naturally detracted from its authority. Over against this emphasis on the invisible Church, Bellarmine coined what has become perhaps his most famous definition. He declared that the Church is just as visible as the kingdom of France and the republic of Venice. He adopted this position in order to stress the true Church-hood of the hierarchically ordered

---

33. Oxford, Bodleian Library, Ms. Bodley 59, Whitaker, Praelectiones in Cantica Canticorum, 4: 6, 7. The text reads: "Quod tamen Papistae contendunt, et non sibi tantum meritis suis, sed et aliis se vitam aeternam promereri posse affirmant. Verum nullus homo est qui non habeat peccatum. Si vero habeat peccatum dignum est peccati mercede, morte scilicet sempiterna, tum non poterit vitam mereri aliis et sibi, utrumque enim non potest et mortem et vitam, quae maxime contraria sunt, mereri, nam stipendium peccati mors est. Absurdissima ergo haec Papistarum sententia."

34. Cf. Whitaker, *Ad Sanderi Demonstrationes Responsio*, in *Opera*, 2:744b.

35. Whitaker, *Sacra Scriptura*, in *Opera*, 1:347a,b; *Adversus Stapletoni*, in *Opera,* 2:175b.

36. Whitaker, *Adversus Stapletoni*, in *Opera*, 2:391b.

Church of Rome.[37] Whitaker defended the Reformational view, that that Church of which believers confess that it is "holy" and "catholic" could not be identified with any visible assembly of people. The Church of the confession consisted of the elect. Here too, Whitaker could exploit his familiarity with the corpus of Thomas Aquinas's writings. Thomas, he explained, had compared the Church with the body and soul of a human being. The Church was like a body animated by the soul, the Holy Spirit.[38] In connection with this idea, Whitaker quoted *inter alia* Thomas's commentary on Romans, in which it had been said that the Church was a *corpus mysticum* (at Rom. 12). The unity of this mystical body was of a spiritual nature, for the members were bound to one another and to God by faith and love. For Whitaker, this idea of Thomas meant that those who were without faith and love could not belong to the Catholic Church of the confession.[39] Therefore, Bellarmine and his other Catholic opponents could not possibly be right in holding a view of the Church, which made room for people without faith, and without the love that issued from faith. As far as ecclesiology was concerned, Whitaker naturally distanced himself from Thomas's recognition and approval of the monarchic papal supremacy with its center in Rome.

II. Sin and Grace

William Whitaker very often appealed to Thomas when formulating his views on the fall and the attainment of salvation. His point of departure was the Augustinian anthropology according to which sinful humanity was incapable of anything but vice unless assisted by God in Christ. After the fall humans had lost the possibility of ever pleasing God through their own achievements. He rejected the scholastic theory, put forward by his opponents, that humanity had lost a supernatural gift due to the fall, so that it was only since the fall that one could speak of natural humanity. Whitaker held that Adam, in his pre-fall state of original righteousness, had been natural. Because of the fall, the natural had been spoiled by total corruption. In support of the view that original

37. Robertus Bellarminus, *De Ecclesia Militante*, cap. 2, in *Disputationes de Controversiis Fidei adversus Haereticos huius temporis*, I, 2, (Ingolstadii, 1588), 148.

38. Whitaker, *Responsionis*, in *Opera*, 1:113b; cf. Thomas, *Reportatio in Symbolum Apostolorum*, art. 9 (*Opera*, 6:20b).

39. Whitaker, *Praelectiones de Ecclesia*, in *Opera*, 1:454a,b; cf. Thomas, *Commentarium super ad Romanos*, cap. 12, lc. 2 (*Opera*, V, 484c). See for Whitaker's thinking about the Church also Broeyer, "William Whitaker 1548–1595. A Cambridge Professor on the doctrine of the Church," in Fletcher, De Ridder-Simoens, eds., *Lines of Contact*, 10–20.

righteousness had been natural, rather than supernatural, he referred to Thomas.[40] According to the latter, explained Whitaker, original righteousness was a righteousness (*rectitudo*) involving the subordination of human reason to God, and the subordination of the lower faculties to reason. Moreover, this state of righteousness did not only contain the possibility of the good, but a perfect practicing of the good. Adam had possessed original righteousness as a *habitus*. Righteousness belonged to his nature.[41]

From the preceding it will be clear that Whitaker had difficulties with that theory of original sin which stated that the latter involved no more than the absence of the possibility of consistently doing good. Adam's loss of original righteousness had had much more radical consequences. He heard his own opinions echoed in Thomas, who had spoken of a corrupted *habitus*.[42] Yet, in his view, Thomas's account of the sinfulness of humanity was only partly satisfactory. For Thomas had taught that, despite the fall, the ability to do at least some good had not been entirely lost. However, Whitaker thought that he had identified an internal contradiction in Thomas's account, which counted in his favor and brought the medieval theologian on his side. For Thomas had also said that the good had been completely wiped out by evil. Whitaker was in full agreement with this last statement.[43]

Whitaker greatly appreciated the fact that Peter Lombard had disapproved of the conception that original sin was no more than the culpability for the first sin committed by Adam. From that point of view Adam's descendants would have had to undergo both the temporal and the eternal punishment for that sin. Lombard had identified this mistaken definition in some earlier theologians. Whitaker himself encountered this conception once again in later theologians like Duns Scotus and Gabriel Biel, and as to his own century in Albertus Pighius.[44]

---

40. Whitaker, *Tractatus de Peccato Originali*, in *Opera*, 1:637b; cf. Thomas, *Summa Theologiae*, II–I, q. 38 (= 83), art. 2 (*Opera*, 2:456b,c). See also, Whitaker, *Opera,* 1:664a, cf. Thomas, *Summa Theologiae*, II–I, q.85, art. 1 (*Opera*, 2:467a,b).

41. Whitaker, *Tractatus*, in *Opera*, 1:638a; cf. Thomas, *Summa Theologiae*, II–I, q.85, art. 1, 2 (*Opera*, 2:467). See also, Whitaker, *Opera,* 652a,b; cf. Thomas, *Summa Theologiae*, I, q. 95, art. 3 (*Opera*, 2:325a,b).

42. Whitaker, *Responsionis*, in *Opera*, 1:175a; cf. Thomas, *Summa Theologiae*, II–I, q. 82, art. 1–2 (*Opera*, 2:464). See also, Whitaker, *Tractatus*, in *Opera*, 652b, cf. Thomas, *Summa Theologiae*, I, q. 100; q. 101, art. 1,2 (*Opera*, 2:329c,330).

43. Whitaker, *Tractatus*, in *Opera*, 1:664b; cf. Thomas, *Summa Theologiae*, I, q. 48, art. 4 (*Opera*, 2:258a).

44. Whitaker, *Tractatus*, in *Opera*, 1:633a.

Original sin was a total corruption and a habitual tendency towards evil. Thomas, he explained, had rightly spoken of a disease. Of the first man it could be said that he had contaminated nature with his sin, and subsequently all people on earth were contaminated with this spoilt nature. All the human faculties were corrupted.[45] As far as the relation of concupiscence (*concupiscentia*) to sin is concerned, Whitaker rejected the interpretation that focussed too much on the fleshly aspect. Once again appealing to Thomas, he stated that concupiscence expressed itself in all kinds of sin, and affected also the higher faculties of the soul. Concupiscence had entered into, and perverted, human nature. From concupiscence sprung all the different sins committed by people. Whitaker also went along with Thomas's exegesis of Rom. 5:12, "in Adam all have sinned."[46] Human nature had been contaminated due to Adam's failure. Just as the body parts together belonged to one body, all human beings shared, as it were, a single human nature. In this sense, everybody had sinned in Adam.[47]

As mentioned already, Whitaker was well aware that, according to Thomas, humanity had not completely lost the ability to do good. He preferred, however, to quote him in connection with the insight that humanity had been wholly overcome by sin. Whitaker described sin a number of times by means of a definition taken from Thomas. Sin could be described as a "deviation from a rule or goal," for human actions ought to be in accordance with the rule of God's will.[48] Sin was contravention of the divine law.[49] Fallen humanity had a corrupted habitus; mankind suffered, as it were, from a disease, which resulted in an abnormal vulnerability to various other kinds of illness. If anybody liked to speak of a continuing possibility of doing something good, that could only pertain, in Whitaker's view, to certain social skills enabling people to govern society and function in it in an appropriate way. Thus

45. Whitaker, *Tractatus*, in *Opera*, 1:641b, 642a; cf. Thomas, *Summa Theologiae*, II–I, q. 83, art. 1 (*Opera*, 2:465a,b). Cf. Whitaker, *Opera*, 656b; 661b, cf. Thomas, *Summa Theologiae*, II–I, q. 82, art. 1–3 (*Opera*, 2:464) and Whitaker, *Opera*, 663a, cf. Thomas, *Summa Theologiae*, II–I, q. 85, art. 3 (*Opera*, 2:467c, 468a).

46. Whitaker, *Tractatus*, in *Opera*, 1:640b; cf. Thomas, *Commentarium super ad Romanos*, cap. 7, lc. 3 (*Opera*, V, 465).

47. Whitaker, *Tractatus*, in *Opera*, 1:647a,b; cf. Thomas, *Commentarium super ad Romanos*, cap. 5, lc. 2 (*Opera*, V, 459, 460a).

48. Whitaker, *Tractatus*, in *Opera*, 1:635a; cf. Thomas, *Summa Theologiae*, II–I, q. 71, art. 6 (*Opera*, 2:447a,b).

49. Whitaker, *Praelectiones de Romano Pontifice*, in *Opera*, 2:731b; cf. Thomas, *Summa Theologiae*, II–I, q. 71 (*Opera*, 2:446a–47b).

human beings could build houses that were, technically speaking, perfectly constructed, and they could lay out vineyards that would yield excellent grapes. Certainly such activities could rightly be called good, but in relation to God a different activity was involved: In that relationship, sinful humanity's willing and doing always went wrong.[50]

The Protestant polemicists, who emphasised so strongly the doctrine of justification by faith alone (*sola fide*), liked to accuse their Catholic opponents of seeking righteousness through works. Already in his first polemical works Whitaker touched upon this issue. The Scotsman John Durie had written a book entitled *Confutatio Responsionis ad Rationes Decem* against Whitaker's *Ad Rationes Decem Responsio*, which in turn had been a response to Edmund Campion's *Decem Rationes*. Whitaker then devoted an entire work, his *Responsionis ad Decem Rationes Defensio*, to a defense against Durie's book.[51] Durie had criticised Whitaker for distinguishing between justification and sanctification. According to Durie, Paul himself had made no such distinction. Whitaker denied this, claiming that the distinction between justification and sanctification was especially clear in Paul. In this regard he referred to Rom. 8: 30 "those He called, He justified; and those He justified, He glorified." Appealing to Thomas's commentary on Romans he argued that this text spoke of a renewal of life, which would later, in the hereafter, be brought to completion.[52] It is of course obvious that Thomas's soteriological views were unacceptable to Whitaker at several points. Thus he could not quote Thomas's utterances on those matters as proof-texts in support of his own views. Here it is again abundantly evident that Whitaker dealt very eclectically with the works of Thomas Aquinas, just as, for similar reasons, he attached more importance to Thomas than to Duns Scotus or other important figures of the scholastic period. The reason why he tried to find as many suitable quotations as possible in Thomas is precisely because Thomas had so much authority among his opponents. Where this was not possible, he simply ignored him. For instance, Whitaker thought quite differently about grace. That he was very much aware of

---

50. Whitaker, *Tractatus*, in *Opera*, 1:667a; cf. Thomas, *Summa Theologiae*, I, q. 109, art. 2 (*Opera*, 2:512a,b). Cf. Whitaker, *Opera*, 1:675a; cf. Thomas, *Summa Theologiae*, II–II, q. 10, art. 4 (*Opera*, 2:537b), and also Whitaker, *Opera*, 1:664b; cf. Thomas, *Summa Theologiae*, I, q. 48, art. 4 (*Opera*, 2:258a).

51. The works mentioned were published in respectively 1581, 1581, 1582, and 1583.

52. Whitaker, *Responsionis ad Decem Rationes Defensio*, in *Opera*, 1:177b; cf. Thomas, *Commentarium super ad Romanos*, cap. 8, lc. 6 (*Opera*, V, 472b).

the differences with regard to the doctrine of grace is shown by a reference to the *Summa Theologiae*, in his book against Durie, where Thomas had not, as in most cases, approached grace as an infused gift. In that particular passage Thomas had defined grace as the love of God. Whitaker quoted this characterization of grace as God's benevolence, commenting that Thomas had here been "conquered by the power of unmistakable truth."[53] With much relish, he dug up a similar quote from Thomas's commentary on the epistle to Titus. Thomas had there defined grace as "the mercy of God."[54] All this makes clear how Thomas had to meet certain requirements before he could be quoted approvingly by Whitaker.

It is noteworthy, as has been mentioned, that Whitaker appealed to Thomas when, in 1595, he publicly expressed concern about certain predestinatory views that deviated from the standard Calvinist account. During that controversy he strongly emphasized that, with respect to several fundamental points, Thomas's ideas were in agreement with both those of Augustine and, later on, Calvin. He maintained that Thomas could be regarded as a representative of the position he himself held. In a public lecture to some eminent guests from London, delivered in February 1595, he already touched upon the problem of predestination. Two months later the controversy about this doctrine, which would eventually lead to the *Lambeth Articles*, erupted in Cambridge. In his public lecture Whitaker explained what he held to be the correct understanding of the doctrine of predestination. He argued that, apart from the will of God, no other cause of predestination could be admitted. God did not elect or reject on the basis of his foreknowledge regarding the course of people's lives, but because in one way or another He willed it thus. "And Thomas did not deviate one hairbreadth from Augustine," declared Whitaker. Predestination had no cause but God. The only cause was God's simple and absolute will. God's honor was at stake.[55] The lecture dealt with the question of how to interpret of 1 Tim. 2:4, where Paul states that God wills "that everyone should be saved." Whitaker disapproved of John of Damascus's theory that one could speak of an "antecedent will" (*voluntas antecedens*) and a "consequent will" (*voluntas consequens*) in God. Thus it was not the case that, on the one hand, God

---

53. Whitaker, *Responsionis*, in *Opera*, 1:176b; cf. Thomas, *Summa Theologiae*, II–I, q. 110, art. 1 (*Opera*, 2:514b,c).

54. Whitaker, *Responsionis*, in *Opera*, 1:176b; cf. Thomas, *Reportatio super ad Titum*, cap. 2, lc. 3 (*Opera*, 6:551a).

55. Whitaker, "Praelectio habita Februarii 27," in *Opera*, 1:629b.

had willed that everyone should be saved (according to the *voluntas antecedens*), and that this subsequently did not occur unless people availed themselves of the means of salvation provided by God (according to the *voluntas consequens*).[56] Whitaker said that he preferred to this another distinction, namely the one made by Thomas, among others, between "God's will of the sign" (*voluntas signi*) and the "will of [his good] pleasure" (*voluntas beneplaciti*). The *voluntas beneplaciti* belonged to the divine attributes. Of this will could be said that it was always necessarily fulfilled. The same did not apply to the *voluntas signi*, for that will ought not be associated with the attributes of God. The *voluntas signi* involved, namely, an act of God, by which He confronted mankind with the conditions for salvation and the promises of the Gospel. In that case the will of God was not being spoken of in the real sense of the word.[57] It is interesting that here, in a conflict among Protestants, Whitaker made use of scholastic terms and distinctions without any perceptible hesitation. A Calvinist scholar, who for the sake of polemics had familiarized himself with scholasticism, reached here for the tools provided by the knowledge he had gained in his dispute with Rome, in order to settle a dangerous dispute that had arisen on the homefront. Purely Biblical arguments would not have been sufficient. Thus he had recourse to the drawing of logical conclusions from Biblical passages. In doing so he saw no insuperable objections to side-step the material that scholasticism offered him.

In the early eighties Whitaker, in his lectures on 1 Timothy, had pointed out, with reference to this same text 1 Tim. 2: 4, that Thomas Aquinas had rejected the conditional interpretation of teh wording.[58] Thus salvation could not depend on a human decision to accept or reject God's offer of salvation. Around the same time, Whitaker had responded to Durie that it was completely inaccurate to attribute the salvation of those who were saved to the fact that God had foreseen their merit. The saved owed their salvation wholly and exclusively to the will of God operative in their election. According to Whitaker, no fiercer opponent

56. Whitaker, "Praelectio habita Februarii 27," in *Opera*, 1:627b. As to the reference to John of Damascus, see Johannes Damascenus, *De Fide Orthodoxa*, II, 29 (PG, tom. 94, 908, 909).

57. Whitaker, "Praelectio habita Februarii 27," in *Opera*, 1:628a. Whitaker referred also with this distinction to Thomas Aquinas, cf. *Summa Theologiae*, I, q. 19, art. 11 (*Opera*, 2:218a, b).

58. Oxford, Bodleian Library, MS. Bodley 156, Whitaker, In priorem Epistolam ad Timotheum 2:3, 4.

than Thomas could be found to Durie's theory of predestination, based as it was on the idea of God's foreknowledge of merit.[59] In his public lecture of February 1595 he put forward a similar account of 1 Timothy 2:4. Thomas, so he claimed, had identified himself unqualifiedly with Augustine's view that there were a fixed number of elect.[60] There were no grounds for calling God unjust simply because He did not act the way humans thought He should. In judging thus, he appealed once more to Thomas who had written in the same vein in his commentary on Romans with reference to the ninth chapter on election and rejection.[61] The apparent injustice of God, in a doctrine of predestination according to which everything had already been determined in advance, was of course a bone of contention in the controversy, which erupted in Cambridge shortly thereafter. There Whitaker recalled Rom. 11:33 "O the depth of the riches and wisdom and knowledge of God! How unsearchable are his judgements and how inscrutable his ways!" According to him, this text acquired its profound significance only if some were rejected regardless of their sinfulness, while others, who were no more deserving of God's love in any respect whatsoever, were predestined to eternal salvation. On this occasion, Whitaker said that he had encountered this view *inter alia* in Lombard and Thomas. However, he emphasised, it was also found in some modern Catholic theologians like Bañez.[62]

Roman Catholics regularly raised serious objections to the doctrine of predestination as it was put forward by Calvin and his followers. The Catholic denunciation of this doctrine was possibly the most significant cause of the fierce controversy about it inside the Calvinist camp, both in England in 1595, and subsequently in the Republic of the United Netherlands in 1604 and 1619. Those who adhered to the strict Calvinist view of double predestination were, of the opinion that criticisms against this doctrine of election and rejection would finally result in a return to Rome. As soon as the emphasis was laid on God's foreknowledge of human behavior, instead of his decision regardless of that behavior, the notion of righteousness through works would creep in by a backdoor once

---

59. Whitaker, *Responsionis*, in *Opera*, 1:181b; cf. Thomas, *De Veritate*, q. 28, art. 1 (*Opera*, 3:173).

60. Whitaker, "Praelectio habita Februarii 27," in *Opera*, 1:629a; cf. Thomas, *Summa Theologiae*, I, q. 23, art. 7 (*Opera*, 2:223c, 224a,b).

61. Whitaker, "Praelectio habita Februarii 27," in *Opera*, 1:629a; cf. Thomas, *Commentarium super ad Romanos*, cap. 9 (*Opera*, V, 473b–77c). Whitaker appealed also to Thomas, *Summa contra Gentiles*, III, cap. 161 (*Opera*, 2:113b).

62. Whitaker, "Cygnea Cantio," in *Opera*, 1:693b.

again. After all, salvation and damnation would then depend too much on the good works of believers. Someone like Whitaker was therefore greatly concerned about the critical voices being raised inside Cambridge itself. One of the basic arguments, from the Catholic side, against the Calvinist doctrine of predestination, was the consequences that could be drawn from it. If, as the Calvinists maintained, nothing happened without God's will, then that also meant that God willed sin—that He was, in other words, the author of sin. Already in 1581, in his booklet against Campion, Whitaker had rejected this conclusion. He had done so, to be exact, with an appeal to Thomas. The latter had made a distinction, with regard to sin, between the deed itself and the sinfulness of the deed. When it came to an assessment of the sinful events in the world, the events as such were the result of God's will. Their sinfulness, however, was to be counted the exclusive responsibility of humans.[63] In 1595 Whitaker again argued in favour of this approach. The fact that God allowed sin was not to be regarded as the cause of sin in the world. Rather, the fact that He so permitted it was the result of the divine rejection.[64]

Just as noteworthy is the fact that Whitaker thought he could defend justification through faith alone (*sola fide*) with the help of Thomas Aquinas. First, he maintained with an appeal to Thomas's commentary on Paul's epistle to the Galatians, that it was impossible to obey the law perfectly. To this statement he added the remark that Calvin had later taught precisely this doctrine.[65] According to the same commentary, the works of the believers did not cause their justification. Rather, explained Whitaker, they were "manifestations of righteousness." "Neither Luther, nor we teach anything else."[66] Elsewhere he invoked the quotation from Thomas in order to prove that righteousness resulted not from merit, but from the remission of sins. Whitaker there joined to the quotation the triumphant words: "Let me add to this, for your consideration, a short statement by your own Thomas."[67]

63. Whitaker, *Ad Rationes Decem Responsio*, in *Opera*, 1:33b; cf. Thomas, *Quaestio disputata de Potentia Dei*, q. 1, art. 6 (*Opera*, 3:190).

64. Whitaker, "Cygnea Cantio," in *Opera*, 1:693b; cf. Thomas, *Summa theologiae*, I, q. 19, art. 9 (*Opera*, 2:217c–18a). For the whole issue of the doctrine of the predestination in Reformed theology, see Muller, *Christ and the Decree. Christology and Predestination in Reformed Theology from Calvin to Perkins* (Grand Rapids: Baker, 1988).

65. Whitaker, *Responsionis*, in *Opera*, 1:202a,b; cf. Thomas, *Reportatio super ad Galatos*, cap. 3. lc. 4 (*Opera*, 6:432c).

66. Whitaker, *Responsionis*, in *Opera*, 1:203b; cf. Thomas, *Reportatio super ad Galatos*, cap. 3. lc. 3, 4 (*Opera*, 6:432b,c).

67. Whitaker, *Responsionis*, in *Opera*, 1:183b.

III. The Sacraments

We have already seen that Whitaker did not always succeed in quoting Thomas as a chief witness in defense of his own views. Thus he failed to produce a contra-argument from the works of Thomas Aquinas when Durie described how Thomas had seen the connection of grace with the sacraments. In fact, Whitaker revealingly kept silent on this very essential difference from the Protestant approach.[68] In his *Praelectiones de Sacramentis*, published in 1624, long after his death, Whitaker criticised Thomas's theory about the connection of grace with the sacraments.[69] Also with respect to other facets of sacramental doctrine, he was well aware that Thomas and he were not of one mind. For instance, in 1583, in his *Ad N. Sanderi Demonstrationes quadraginta*, a work written against Nicholas Sanders, he explicitly rejected Thomas's view that a sacrifice took place on the Church altar, reproducing the sacrifice of Jesus's body on the cross.[70] Yet even in the doctrine of the sacraments he occasionally found ways of interpreting Thomas in his own favor. This is characteristically illustrated by one of his objections against the doctrine of transubstantiation. Whitaker resisted the dogma of the change of substance in the bread and wine to the body and blood of Jesus Christ, by arguing that the teaching of this dogma was contrary to reason, because one body could not be in more than one place at the same time. Thomas had taught, explained Whitaker, that reason and revelation could never contradict one another. Since the doctrine of transubstantiation was contrary to reason, it had to be judged mistaken on the basis of what Thomas had written on the relation between reason and revelation.[71] As such, this citation is another typical example of Whitaker's eclectic approach to writings that were in some way useful to

68. Whitaker, *Responsionis*, in *Opera*, 1:192a.

69. Whitaker, *Praelectiones de Sacramentis in genere, et in specie de S.S. Baptismo et Eucharistia*, J. Allenson, S. Ward, ed., (Francofurti, 1624). The book could not be inserted in the two volumes of the collected works because of their much earlier publication (1610). As to Whitaker's criticism of Aquinas, see *Praelectiones de Sacramentis in genere*, 663a,b with reference to Thomas, *Summa Theologiae*, III, q. 79 (*Opera*, 2:901c–903c).

70. Whitaker, *Ad Sanderi Demonstrationes*, in *Opera*, 1:767b. Whitaker referred here to a spurious work of Thomas Aquinas. In the edition of Thomas's works by Busa it is inserted with the entry: "Ignoti Auctoris." As to this reference, see *De Venerabili Sacramento* (*Opera*, 7:668a). Whitaker's *Ad Sanderi* was published in 1583 in London.

71. Whitaker, *Praelectiones de Ecclesia*, in *Opera*, 1:524a; cf. Thomas, *Summa contra Gentiles*, I, cap. 7 (*Opera*, 2:2b,c).

him. For in Thomas himself, this criticism of transubstantiation on the basis of the relation between reason and revelation is nowhere to be found. Thus Whitaker drew conclusions from the definition that had formed the foundation of Thomas's system, which Thomas himself would never have drawn given his position on the sacraments. However, Whitaker himself here applied a form of scholastic argumentation.

Whitaker had made a thorough study of medieval sacramental theology in behalf of his lectures on this doctrine against Bellarmine and other Catholic theologians, the *Praelectiones de Sacramentis*. For instance, in dealing with the question of what a sacrament actually implied, he gave extensive consideration to the medieval theologies in which this subject had been addressed. With regard to that subject he presented his listeners with various definitions deriving from medieval theologians, among them Hugh of St Victor and Peter Lombard, even without passing over the contemporary definition of the *Catechismus Romanus*. He mentioned of course that Lombard had been the first to teach that there were seven sacraments. He also gave an extensive exposition of the mark (*character*) which according to Catholic theologians the sacraments were said to effect. He himself rejected the doctrine of the mark. Thomas, he explained, had understood the mark as a capacity (*potentia*). Whitaker pointed out that the scholastic theologians had differed among themselves about the question of whether this mark, this *potentia* in the intellect, was to be located in the will, or somewhere else. Over against Duns Scotus, who had located the mark in the will, Thomas maintained that it was situated in the intellect.[72] Many such expositions, in which Whitaker incorporated the ideas of Thomas and other scholastics into his own view, could be mentioned. After all, in polemical discussions, it was convenient with respect to various dogmatic conceptions to have recourse to scholasticism in order to develop one's own view more effectively.

As far as baptism was concerned, he also regarded certain assumptions as non-negotiable, such as the conviction that baptism did not involve any infusion of grace. In line with Calvin, Whitaker understood baptism as a sign and seal of God's grace. But certain details were in need of further clarification. So it was an arguable topic of discussion whether baptism could be effective in cases where unbelieving parents presented a child for baptism. On this *casus*, Whitaker quoted

---

72. Whitaker, *Praelectiones de Sacramentis in genere*, 160a,b; cf. Thomas, *Summa Theologiae*, III, q. 63, art. 2, 4–5 (*Opera*, 2:866a–68a).

Thomas. Thomas had stated, namely, that the belief or unbelief of the parents was quite irrelevant, since the community of believers, rather than the parents, were the ones who presented the child for baptism.[73]

Occasionally, Whitaker felt compelled to express fierce criticism of Thomas Aquinas. This happened especially where the name of Thomas was associated with doctrines or customs in the Catholic Church that were particularly repugnant to Reformational theologians. This was of course the case with respect to his views on the pope, and as already mentioned, the connection between sacrament and grace. In his argument against Catholics' use of images in the church, Whitaker acknowledged that Catholic doctrine distinguished between veneration and worship, and explicitly taught that worship was due to God alone. In practice, however, images were worshipped. In this regard he laid much of the blame on Thomas Aquinas.[74]

IV. Conclusion

In studying Whitaker, one soon notices that, of all the medieval authors, he quoted Thomas most often in his argumentation. His interest in Thomas far exceeded the interest in other authors from the same period. Whitaker often spoke admiringly of him. His interest must have been fuelled especially by the Thomas renaissance among the Catholic theologians of his day. Before entering into debate with them, one had to study their most important spokesman, Thomas. However, Thomas Aquinas surely attracted him purely as a scholar as well—not only through his main works, but also through his Bible commentaries.

Whitaker approached Thomas eclectically. He appealed to him as and when he found it useful during the course of his arguments. This eclecticism resulted in a certain one-sidedness, since Whitaker's aim was to defend views, which he had for the greatest part already assumed beforehand. One may speak, therefore, of a consistently Calvinist reception of Thomas. He sought to outdo his opponents by showing that Thomas's thought differed from theirs. A great number of quotations were mainly intended to show that the Protestant teachings were in many respects closer to the theology of his opponents' beloved Thomas, than were the Catholic. Thus on the one hand he showed a great

73. Whitaker, *Praelectiones de Sacramentis in genere,* 290a–91b; cf. Thomas, *Summa Theologiae,* III, q. 68, art. 9 (*Opera,* 2:879c, 880a).
74. Whitaker, *Responsionis,* in *Opera* 1:263a and *Praelectiones de Ecclesia,* in *Opera,* 1:518a, 565b; cf. Thomas, *Summa Theologiae,* III, q. 25, art. 3, 4 (*Opera,* 2:808a,b).

appreciation of Thomas, while on the other, he clearly regarded him as a representative of the opposing camp.

It would go too far to claim that Whitaker was deeply influenced by medieval theology. Whitaker also had an impressive knowledge of the patristic writings. In this regard he resembled countless later theologians of the Church of England. Of the *patres*, none was more often quoted than Augustine. His approach to Augustine may also be called typically Calvinist. Of course he referred to Augustine even much more than to Thomas. Yet to speak of a strong Augustinian influence would be just as unfounded as to claim a strong Thomistic influence. In the final analysis, it is clear that above all Calvin had influenced Whitaker, and that Whitaker read other theologians through Calvinist spectacles. Those points, at which Whitaker differed from Calvin, for instance in his views regarding the relationship of Church and state, and on the Episcopal system, can be explained in the light of the situation of the Church of England.

Despite this Calvinist conditioning of his thought, one may state qualifiedly that the medieval scholastics, and Thomas in particular, had made some impact on Whitaker. He had digested Thomas so thoroughly that he could not wholly escape the effects which familiarity with a theological system of that kind must inevitably have. The manner of theologizing in particular gave a strong impulse to his thought. In the conflict with Catholic theology it was of course unnecessary to polemicise about each and every subject. There was a broad consensus on certain *theologoumena*. With respect to the doctrine of God and Christology, as the first four councils had defined these, no need for discussion was felt. It is true that, with respect to the dogmas of the early Church, polemical theologians occasionally tried to show by means of logical reasoning that the opposition had succumbed to heretical ideas. But then they were playing with each other. Logical reasoning, however, was certainly necessary with regard to those subjects about which there were major differences of opinion, like the relation between Scripture and Church, the doctrine of sin and grace, or the meaning of the sacraments. Of course, Whitaker sought first of all to prove his case from Scripture, and secondly—witness the *patres*—that the Church of England was in agreement with the early Church. But he also regarded reason as a valuable instrument with which to achieve victory in the battle for the truth. For the latter purpose, scholasticism offered a powerful apparatus. In their polemic against Rome, supporters of the Reformational cause, like Whitaker, found that scholasticism provided a seasoned and refined method, which could be applied effectively in the debate. Therefore Whitaker may be regarded as a transitional figure in the rise of Reformed scholasticism. With him, the spontaneity of a direct appeal to Holy Scripture, so characteristic of the thought of the first generation of Reformers, made room for a consistent systematization of a doctrinal corpus, which had to be faithfully preserved.

8

John Owen: A Reformed Scholastic at Oxford

Sebastian Rehnman

I. Owen's Training

In this paper I intend to talk about three things: John Owen's academic training, his literary sources, and conclude with some modern reflections.[1]

John Owen was born to a Reformed minister in 1616 in Stadham, outside Oxford, a village which was noted for its Puritan and Reformed sympathies.[2] After preparatory studies at a grammar school, John Owen

---

1. The material in this essay is taken from my thesis *"Theologia Tradita:* A Study in the Prolegomenous Discourse of John Owen (1616–1683)."

2. For the biographical information on Owen I depend in particular on the anonymous *Life,* Asty's "Memoirs," William Orme's *Memoirs of the Life, Writings, and Religious Connexions of John Owen, D.D.* (London: printed for T. Hamilton, 1820), and Peter Toon's *God's Statesman: the Life and Work of John Owen, Pastor, Educator, Theologian* (Exeter: Paternoster Press, 1971). "Stadham" was later changed into present-day "Stadhampton." On Stadham see R. B. Pugh, ed., *The Victoria History of the Counties of England:A History of the County of Oxford* (London, 1962), 7:81–92. John Owen describes his father as "a Non-conformist all his days, and a painful labourer in the vineyard of the Lord." John Owen *A Review of the True Nature of Schism: with a Vindication of the Congregational Churches in England from the Imputation thereof* (1657), 13:224. On this strain of English Protestantism the following works have been of service: Patrick Collinson, *The Elizabethan Puritan Movement* (London: Jonathan Cape, 1971); M. M. Knappen *Tudor Puritanism: A Chapter in the History of Idealism* (Chicago, 1939); A. G. Dickens, *The English Reformation,* 2d ed. (London, 1989); Everett H. Emerson, *English Puritanism from John Hooper to John Milton* (Durham, 1968); William Haller, *The Rise of Puritanism* (New York, 1938); Perry Miller, *The New England Mind* (Cambridge, Mass, 1953). On education see: Rose-Mary O'Day *Education and Society 1500–1800: The Social Foundations of Education in Early Modern Britain* (Burnt Mill, 1982); Christopher Hill "Puritanism and the Family in 17th-century England", and Edmund S. Morgan *The Puritan Family: Essays on Religion and Domestic Relations in Seventeenth-Century New England* (Boston, Mass., 1944). For a good recent discussion of the concept of "Puritanism" and related issues, see Schaefer "The Spiritual Brotherhood on the Habits of the Heart," 1–33. For a short summary of the importance of family instruction see "Epistle to the Christian Reader, Especially Heads of Families" and "The Directory for Family-

entered the University of Oxford in 1628.[3]

Humanism and the Reformation made their demands upon Oxford University, but most of the mediaeval curriculum was retained. New currents of thought were rather assimilated into the traditional curriculum. The faculty of arts at Oxford remained almost unchanged and thus Owen studied at probably the most conservative arts faculty in Europe. In theology the university remained firmly Reformed until the first quarter of the seventeenth century.[4] So at the time of Owen's entrance at Oxford two of the dominant figures were the Reformed theologians John Prideaux (1578–1650)[5] and Thomas Barlow (1607–91).[6] Moreover, the colleges of Oxford had increased in importance and enjoyed a place of prestige and function in society, having a liberal arts programme which was highly esteemed by the Protestants. Queen's College—which once had nurtured John Wycliffe (c. 1330–1384) and was together with Brasenose and Exeter one of the prime "nurseries for godly preachers" in Elizabethan times[7]—was the place chosen for William and John Owen. By that time Queen's flourished and from the

---

Worship" in *The Westminster Confession of Faith* (1646; reprint, Glasgow, 1976).

3. A good deal of information has been obtained for Owen's university studies from the following works: William T. Costello, *The Scholastic Curriculum at Early Seventeenth-Century Cambridge* (Cambridge, 1958); Mark H. Curtis, *Oxford and Cambridge in Transition* (Oxford, 1959); John Griffiths, ed., *Statutes of the University of Oxford Codified in the year 1636* (Oxford, 1888); Strickland Gibson, ed., *Statuta antiqua universitatis oxoniensis* (Oxford, 1931); R. H. Hodgkin, *Six Centuries of an Oxford College: A History of Queen's College 1340–1946* (Oxford, 1949); Hugh Kearney, *Scholars and Gentlemen* (London: Faber, 1970); John R. Magrath, *The Queen's College*, 2 vols. (Oxford, 1921); Charles Edward Mallet, *A History of the University of Oxford*, 3 vols. (London, 1924–27); James McConica, ed.,*The Collegiate University* (Oxford: Clarendon Press, 1986).

4. On Reformed theology at Oxford see especially C. M. Dent *Protestant Reformers in Elizabethan Oxford* (Oxford, 1983); cf. S. L. Greenslade "The Theology Faculty," in McConica, ed. *The Collegiate University*, 330–32; Nicholas Tyacke, *Anti-Calvinists* (Oxford, 1987), 1–8, 58–86, 248–65. Dent, *Protestant Reformers*, 154: "Oxford had no Emmanuel but preachers and godly tutors were constantly encouraging their undergraduates to exercise a painful and zealous ministry of pastoral care and self-sacrifice." On the heresy statute of 1579 and required Reformed textbooks see Gibson, ed., *Statuta antiqua universitatis Oxoniensis*, 413–15, 521–27; S.L. Greenslade "The Faculty of Theology," 326–27; Dent, *Protestant Reformers*, 87–93, 185–88.

5. On Prideaux and Exeter College at this time see John E. Platt, "Sixtinus Amama (1593–1629): Franeker Professor and Citizen of the Republic of Letters," in G. Th. Jensma, F. R. H. Smit, and F. Westra, eds., *Universiteit te Franeker 1585–1811: Bijdragen tot de geschiedenis van de Friese hogeschool* (Leeuwarden, 1985), 241–43; *DNB*, 16:354–56.

6. On Barlow see *DNB*, 1:1144–49.

7. Dent, *Protestant Reformers*, 167.

diary of one of the Fellows, Thomas Crosfield (1602–1663), we catch a glimpse of its life.[8] A succession of capable Provosts had established it not only in a tradition of scholarship and learning, but in the Reformed faith.

The responsibility for the education of the students or scholars fell increasingly upon the colleges and the work of the college tutors was "definitely . . . the most important influence on a scholar's education."[9] Owen was to have his studies superintended by Thomas Barlow. In the words of William Orme, "Barlow was a Calvinist in theology, an Aristotelian in philosophy, and an Episcopalian in church government."[10] Another important figure for Owen's academic formation was John Prideaux, whom Owen thought had a "great name among the world of learned men".[11] Owen studied the seven years' course of liberal arts and completed the B.A. and the M.A. He then became a candidate for the Bachelor of Divinity degree in 1635, but it would seem that due to his opposition to the Laudian ceremonial and theological policy, Owen only completed two of the seven years for the B.D. degree.[12]

II. Owen's Sources

Since Owen did not write an autobiography two aspects in particular will

8. F. S. Boas, ed., *The Diary of Thomas Crosfield* (Oxford, 1935). McConica "Elizabethan Oxford: The Collegiate Society," in McConica, *The Collegiate University,* 645–732, also describes university life at this time.

9. Mark H. Curtis, *Oxford and Cambridge in Transition* (Oxford: Clarendon, 1959), 107. Cf. Anonymous notebook "Analecta sacra magistri Barlow, novitiiss theologiae candidatis aliguantillum fortasse profutura," in the Bodleian Library MS Rawlinson C 945, 443ff. In the beginning the year 1661 is written. Later John Locke took notes on the same lecture. His notebook is better organized; see Bodleian MS Locke 17, 23–71. Posthumous editions of the introductory lectures are found in Thomas Barlow *Autocediavsmata, De studio Theologiae: or, Directions for the Choice of Books in the Study of Divinity* (Oxford, 1699); idem *The Genuine Remains* . . . (London, 1693),1–71. Another important text: John Rainolds, *A Letter of Dr. Reinolds to his friend, concerning his aduice for the studie of Divinitie* , *4 July, 1577* (London, 1613); John Wilkins, *Ecclesiastes, or A Discourse Concerning the Gift of Preaching as it Fals under the Rules of Art* (London, 1646); Curtis, *Oxford and Cambridge in Transition*; Boas, ed., *The Diary of Thomas Crosfield*.

10. Orme, *Memoirs,* 12; cf. Barlow *The Genuine Remains*, 122–30; Bodleian MS Locke 17 contains a long list of Barlow's library, 42–71.

11. Owen, *The Doctrine of the Saints' Perseverance* (1654), 11:497; cf. 11:623; 618; Owen, *Vindiciae Evangelicae: or The Mystery of the Gospel Vindicated* (1655), 12:27; Owen, *Of The Divine Original . . . of the Scriptures* (1659), 16:288.

12. On the Bachelor of Divinity course and academic theology in general see Greenslade, "The Faculty of Theology," 295–334. On Arminianism at the university at this time see Nicholas Tyacke, *Anti-Calvinists*, 58–86.

receive attention in locating his intellectual background and formation: (1) the intellectual context with its currents of thought and (2) the auction catalogue of his library from 1684.[13]

The *first* and most obvious influence is that of *the Reformed tradition*. Oxford libraries were well stocked with continental Reformed authors from the last quarter of the sixteenth century onwards[14] and Owen's writings refer to the numerous Reformed thinkers his private library possessed. He owned such works as the *opera omnia* of Calvin, Musculus, Vermigli, Junius, and other prominent Reformed theologians.[15] Judging from his own remarks it becomes clear that Bucer, Calvin, Martyr, and Beza are the "principal" and "eminent" authors.[16] In another instance the same men are mentioned with the exchange of Musculus for Beza.[17]

---

13. Edward Millington, ed., *Bibliotheca Oweniana, sive Catalogus librorum . . . Rev. Doct. Vir. D. Joan. Oweni . . .* (London, 1684). What Owen called "my own small library" (Owen *The Death of Christ* (1649), 10:471) contained almost three thousand books. It included the major authors of patristic, mediaeval, and contemporary theology. Classics appear to have been one of Owen's great interests and there are fine collections on philosophy, history, geography, and travel. The library certainly confirms the wide reading attested to in Owen's writings. The library catalogue is divided into two parts with separate pagination and is henceforth referred to as "*BO*." The parts are referred to with Roman numerals and page reference with Arabic numerals.

14. Cf. Dent, *Protestant Reformers*, 93–99.

15. Calvin, *Opera omnia* (Amsterdam, 1671); Musculus, *Opera omnia* (Basel, 1610); Martyr, *Opera omnia* (Zürich, 1567); Davenant, *Opera omnia* (Cambridge, 1631); Junius, *Opera omnia theologica* (Geneva, 1608); Gomarus, *Opera omnia theologica* (Amsterdam, 1644); Cameron, *Opera omnia theologica* (Geneva, 1642) (in *BO*, I.2); Zanchius, *Opera omnia theologica* (Geneva, 1619); Cloppenburg, *Syntagma* (Franeker, 1655); Cloppenburg, *Exercitationes super locos communes thelogicos* (Franeker, 1653) (*BO*, I.5); Maccovius, *Loci communes theologici* (Franeker, 1650)(*BO*, I.6); Maccovius, *Distinctiones et regulae theologicae et philosophicae* (Oxford, 1656) (*BO*, I.15); Scharpius, *Cursus theologicus* (Geneva 1622) (*BO*, I.7); Ursinus, *Corpus doctrinae Christianae sive catechismus* (Hanover, 1639); Keckermann, *Systema theologiae* (Hanover, 1605) (*BO*, I.12); Trelcatius, *Loci communes* (Geneva, 1611) (*BO*, I.13); Ames, *Medulla theologica* (Amsterdam, 1641) (*BO*, I.16); Downame, *Sum of Christian Divinity* (London, 1678) (*BO*, II.8); Usher, *Principles of the Christian Religion* (London, 1647) (*BO*, II.20), and several writings of Coccejus (*BO*, I.2,5,15,17). Note in particular the entire second (English) part of *BO* for the amount of Puritan literature.

16. Owen, *Causes, Ways, and Means*, 4:229.

17. Owen, *The Doctrine of the Saints' Perseverance*, 11:489; cf. 487; Owen, *A Dissertation on Divine Justice: or, The Claims of Vindicatory Justice Vindicated*, translation Hamilton and Goold (1653), 10:488. According to Wallace, the writings of Bullinger and Calvin were most influential in England at this time and, according to Collinson, Bullinger and Vemigli. Wallace, "Life and Thought of John Owen," 37; Patrick Collinson, "England

Owen reflects the reception of influences from a plurality of Reformed thinkers and centres.[18] However, actual quotations are very sparse. A partial explanation of this state of affairs comes from the habit of seventeenth century authors of refraining from referring to contemporary authors because those of greater antiquity were more fashionable.[19] Reformed writers certainly exercised considerable influence on him but were, according to the fashion of the day, too modern to refer to.

There were, of course, also other influences on Owen's thought. The tutorial instruction Owen received from Barlow reflects the several currents of thought and complex intellectual environment of Western society from the fourteenth to the early seventeenth century.[20] Kristeller's work on Renaissance culture provides an apt tool to account for his intellectual locale. Owen's thought fits in well with Kristeller's view of Renaissance culture as a broad cultural and literary movement, with a primary concern for eloquence through devotion to the *studia humanitatis* and classical scholarship, and with only a secondary concern for a particular theology, philosophy or political ideology.[21] This plurality

---

and International Calvinism 1558–1640," in Prestwich, ed., *International Calvinism,* 214–15; cf. John von Rohr, *The Covenant of Grace in Puritan Thought* (Atlanta, 1986), 2, 31.

18. Cf. Dent, *Protestant Reformers*; David A. Weir, *The Origins of the Federal Theology in Sixteenth-Century Reformation Thought* (Oxford, 1990), vii–viii; Richard A. Muller, "Calvin and the 'Calvinists': Assessing Continuities and Discontinuities Between the Reformation and Orthodoxy: Part II," in *CTJ* 31 (1996): 134–38; Muller, *Christ and the Decree,* 13, 90, 176–82; contra Hall, "Calvin against the Calvinists," 19–37; Clifford, *Atonement and Justification,* 214; Kendall, *Calvin and English Calvinism.* Note the statements of Pierre du Moulin (quoted in Armstrong *Calvinism and the Amyraut Heresy,* 87, 159) and Joseph Scaliger (quoted in Benjamin B. Warfield *Calvin and Augustine,* ed. Samuel G. Craig (Philadelphia, 1956), 481) which presuppose a plurality of influences from early Reformed theologians on later orthodoxy.

19. G. Mattingly "International Diplomacy and International Law," in R.B. Wernham, ed., *The Counter Reformation and the Price Revolution, 1558–1610,* New Cambridge Modern History 3 (Cambridge, 1968), 168–69; Muller, *Thought of Arminius,* 37–38.

20. Cf. Barlow, *De studio theologiae.* For an overview of the intellectual turbulence from the fourteenth to the seventeenth century see for example H. Oberman, *Masters of the Reformation*; Oberman, "Fourteenth-Century Religious Thought: A Premature Profile"; and the first chapters in Alister McGrath, *Intellectual Origins of the European Reformation* (Oxford: Blackwell, 1987), and Jaroslav Pelikan, *The Christian Tradition* (Chicago, 1971–1983), vol. IV.

21. Kristeller, *Renaissance Thought,* 10, 32, 95; Kristeller, "The Role of Religion in Renaissance Humanism," Trinkhaus and Oberman, eds., *The Pursuit of Holiness,* 367–70. Other scholars also argue for a general definition, e.g. William J. Bouwsma, "Two

and variation corresponds to the several influences present in Owen's corpus. Moreover, this affinity becomes the more clear when we consider that this culture had a broad recognition of Christianity.[22] The plurality of influences present in Owen's thought firmly establishes him as a typical Renaissance man.

The most influential contemporary currents of thought were Augustinianism, Aristotelianism, scholasticism and humanism.[23] These all grew out of the cultural programme which we call the Renaissance and by no means excluded each other. Moreover, the Christian history of ideas reveals an eclectic tendency and Owen with his Reformation heritage ought to be considered in connection with this tradition. We should expect continuity with the Christian tradition and similarities with surrounding society, especially since recent historians have shown that several strains of thought could and did serve in the sixteenth and seventeenth centuries as instruments for a renewed and refined synthesis of Christianity, in both its patristic and mediaeval versions, and classical thought. As was noted already by Nordström, concerning the Renaissance: "It is simply a blossoming branch on the grandiose trunk of mediaeval culture."[24]

Secondly, humanism had a formative impact on Protestantism.[25] Its

---

Faces of Humanism: Stoicism and Augustinianism in Renaissance Thought," in Heiko A. Oberman and Thomas A. Brady, Jr., eds., *Itinerarium Italicum: The Profile of the Italian Renaissance in the Mirror of Its European Transformation* (Leiden, 1975), 3–4, 52; Gerrish, *Grace and Reason*, 153; Steven Ozment, "Humanism, Scholasticism and the Intellectual Origins of the Reformation," in *Continuity and Discontinuity in Church History* (Leiden: Brill, 1979) 137ff.; Charles B. Schmitt, "Andreas Camutius on the Concord of Plato and Aristotle with Scripture," in *Neoplatonism and Christian Thought* (Albany, 1982), 180.

22. Cf. Kristeller: "we should remember that most, if not all, humanists were Christian believers, although they may not have touched on religious subjects in their work as scholars or writers." Paul Oskar Kristeller, "Humanism" in Schmitt, et al., eds., *The Cambridge History of Renaissance Philosophy*, 133; Kristeller, *Renaissance Thought*, 3–23. On the contribution of monasteries see the interesting article "The Contribution of Religious Orders to Renaissance Thought and Learning," by Paul Oskar Kristeller in *Medieval Aspects of Renaissance Learning*, 95–114.

23. For these currents of thought and the character of the Renaissance see Schmitt, *Aristotle and the Renaissance*; Schmitt, *John Case;* Schmitt, et al., eds., *The Cambridge History of Renaissance Philosophy*; Kristeller, *Renaissance Thought*; Pelikan, *The Christian Tradition*, 4:16–17.

24. Johan Nordström "Medeltid och renässans: en utvecklingshistorisk överblick," in Sven Tunborg and S. E. Bring, eds., *Nordstedts världshistoria* 6 vols. (Stockholm, 1929), 6:346: "Den är själv blott en blommande gren på den medeltida odlingens mäktiga stam."

25. E.g. Ozment, "Humanism, Scholasticism, and the Intellectual Origins of the

influence on Owen is clear already from the curricular emphasis on the study of Scripture and Aristotle.[26] McConica regards the "blend of humanism and protestantism" as "utterly characteristic of the teaching of arts" in late sixteenth century Oxford.[27] Later Owen bought many of the finest editions of the age and also manuscripts.[28] Furthermore, Protestantism benefited from the stress of the Renaissance on eloquence, culture and education. In *Theologoumena* Owen plays the role of educator. His writings reveal his wide reading in the literary sources of Western society. In accordance with the best humanist spirit, classical, patristic and medieval literature is a resource for him in defending and establishing his Reformed theology. Writers much appreciated by Owen were Aristotle, Homer, Horace, Juvenal, Plato, Plautus, Plutarch, Seneca, Terence, and Virgil.[29] Classical writers are most often used for erudite illustration and exemplarism for which their literature served as a frame of reference and ideal.[30] There are, however, several instances where

---

Reformation"; Alister McGrath, *Intellectual Origins,* 32–68; Bouwsma, *John Calvin,* 113–27; Ganoczy, *The Young Calvin,* 178–81; Battenhouse, "The Doctrine of Man in Calvin and in Renaissance Platonism," 447–71; W. Stanford Reid, "Calvin and the Founding of the Academy of Geneva," *WTJ* 18 (1955), 4.

26. E.g. Fletcher, "The Faculty of Arts," 196; Greenslade, "The Faculty of Theology," 316–18; McConica, "Elizabethan Oxford: The Collegiate Society," 702, 708; Schmitt, *Aristotle and the Renaissance.*

27. McConica, "Elizabethan Oxford: The Collegiate Society," 699.

28. In the library catalogue there are, for example, many versions of the Bible (*BO,* I.1); the *opera omnia* of Augustine, Jerome, Ambrose, Tertullian, Cyprian, Anselm, Philo, Basil, Gregory of Nyssa, Epiphanius, Justin Martyr, Clement of Alexandria, Origen, Chrysostom (*BO,* I.1–4), Seneca (ibid., I.21), Lactantius, and Irenaeus (ibid., I.12); the *opera omnia graeco-latina* of Plutarch, Plato, Plotinus; *opera omnia* of Cicero, Horace, Virgil, and the *opera omnia graece* of Plato (*BO,* I.19–22) and Aristotle (*BO,* I.23). There is a small collection of manuscripts (ibid., I.32). There are the *opera omnia* (*BO,* I.21) and separate works (ibid., I.24) of the Dutch humanist Justus Lipsius, and writings by Joseph Scaliger (ibid., I.29,31). Owen's library contained lexicon and dictionaries for the close study of texts in many languages (*BO,* I.20–21).

29. There are the following number of references: Aristotle 57 (of which 16 are in *Theologoumena*), Homer 33, Horace 59, Juvenal 31, Plato 42 (of which 26 are in *Theologoumena*), Plautus 25, Plutarch 44 (of which 27 are in *Theologoumena*), Seneca 38 (of which 17 are in *Theologoumena*), Terence 16, and Virgil 71 (of which 16 are in *Theologoumena*). The overwhelming majority is affirmative.

30. E.g. references to Aristotle, Pliny (Owen, *Ebenezer; A Memorial of the Deliverance of Essex County* [1648], 8:111); Horace, Plautus, Virgil, Aristophanes, Aelian, Varro, Xenophon, Plato, Plutarch, and the discussion of the literary genre of dialogues (Owen, *Truth and Innocence Vindicated* [1669], 13:358–63); Sophocles, Seutonius, Ennius, Horace, and Demosthenes (Owen, *Of the Death of Christ and of Justification* [1655], 12:591–94), Menander (Owen, 12:603; idem *A Vindication of the Animadversions on Fiat*

pagan authors are used by Owen for a more doctrinal purpose. Throughout *Theologoumena* classical philosophers witness to the universal access to and degeneration of the natural knowledge of God, in *The Death of Death* references to classical literature abound on the subject of the origin of human sacrifices,[31] and in *A Dissertation on Divine Justice* classical literature proves the universal consent of mankind for the vindicatory justice of God.[32] Owen could likewise undergird his doctrine of God from the testimony of pagan authors.[33] In political theory Plato's *Republic* and Cicero's *Laws* are regarded as the authorities.[34] Moreover, classical literature was used by Owen for ascertaining the meaning of words.[35]

A frequent use of patristic literature is also prominent in Owen. Although *Bibliotheca Patrum* was used by Owen,[36] I have already referred to the many *opera omnia* he had in his library and it is clear from his writings that he was well acquainted with the church fathers.[37] Also in

---

Lux [1664], 14:238), Lucretius (Owen, *The Doctrine of Justification by Faith* [1677], 5:373), Martial (Owen, *Vindiciae Evangelicae*, 12:471), Ovid (Owen, *A Display of Arminianism* [1643], 10:18; idem *The Duty of Pastors and People Distinguished* [1643], 13:5), Sophocles and Sallust (Owen, *Vindiciae Evangelicae*, 12:82, 587), and Thucydides (Owen, *The True Nature of a Gospel Church and its Government* [1689], 16:62). It is believed that these are of first hand acquaintance, for only in a few instances does Owen refer to a collection such as that of, for example, Diogenes Laertius (Owen, *The Death of Death*, 10:153; *A Dissertation on Divine Justice*, 10:497). Other examples are when he quotes Euripides and Hesiod from Aristotle's *Nicomachean Ethics* (Owen, *Of Communion with God the Father, Son, and Holy Ghost* [1657], 2:28; *Vindication of Animadversions*, 14:186).

31. Owen, *The Death of Death*, esp. ch. 4.

32. E.g. Owen: *A Dissertation on Divine Justice*, 10:517–24, 541; cf. *Ebenezer*, 8:109; *An Humble Testimony unto the Goodness and Severity of God in his Dealing with Sinful Churches and Nations* (1681), 8:603; *Vindiciae Evagelicae*, 12:97, 107, 434–35, and the appendix to *A Brief Declaration and Vindication of the Doctrine of the Trinity* (1669), 2:446–51; *Communion with God*, 2:94, 167n.1. This apparent wide use of natural theology is conditioned by the "testimony of Scripture" and "every sinner's conscience," ibid. Owen holds to this view in opposition (cf. *A Dissertation on Divine Justice*, 10:522–23) to Samuel Rutherford *Disputatio scholastica de divina providentia* (Edinburgh, 1650), 354–56, who denies the use of the natural conscience for this purpose.

33. Owen: *Vindiciae Evangelicae,*12.:97–98, 106–07, 350; *A Display of Arminianism*, 10:22; *The Death of Death*, 10:153.

34. Owen, *Theologoumena*, 17:6:iv.8.

35. E.g. Thucydides, Aristophanes, Herodotus, Sallust, Ulpian, Aristotle, and Isocrates (Owen: *Vindiciae Evangelicae*, 12:291–92, 420, 434, 438; *The Death of Death*, 10:262; *Truth and Innocence Vindicated*, 13:412); Suetonius (Owen, *The Death of Death*, 10:334), Pliny, and Seneca (Owen, *The Doctrine of Justification*, 5:166).

36. Owen, *A Discourse Concerning Liturgies*, (1662), 15:20

37. The following numbers of references are found: Ambrose 36, Augustine 206 (references in Owen *Pneumatologia*, 3:337–66 are excluded since this part is a summary

this respect there is evidence of the influence of his education at Oxford, where there was a strong tradition of fine patristic studies.[38] Bypassing the many references to councils and synods, we find that patristic literature is useful for Owen's argument and is interspersed in all his writings. We may note a few examples. In an appendix to *The Death of Death* Owen listed patristic testimonies which allegedly prove that the Reformed doctrine of limited atonement was taught throughout the Christian tradition.[39] In *The Reason of Faith* he argues in a similar way for the catholicity of his doctrine.[40] Moreover, Church Fathers were used for a defence of Congregationalism.[41]

It is obvious from Owen's writings that he mastered Hebrew and Greek, and it is his habit to quote and comment on Scripture in the original languages. The best examples of Owen's familiarity with these languages and the exegetical resources of his time are perhaps *The Divine Original* and *Of the Integrity and Purity of the Hebrew and Greek Text of the Scripture* (1659).[42] He had some of the finest works in textual criticism in his time.[43] In addition to the emphasis on the original Hebrew and Greek

of *Confessiones*), Chrysostom 57, Clement of Alexandria 50, Clement of Rome 33 (excluding the references in the analysis of the epistle of Clement to Corinth, in Owen, *An Inquiry Concerning the Original, Nature . . . and Communion of Evangelical Churches* [1681], 15:282–89), Epiphanius 36, Eusebius 94, Gregory of Nazianus 16, Gregory of Nyssa 2, Hilary 12, Ignatius 25, Irenaeus 30, (cf., Owen, *Inquiry Concerning Evangelical Churches,* 15:293–96), Lactantius 32, Origen 55, and Tertullian 122. References to numerous minor patristic writers are also found.

38. Cf. Greenslade "The Faculty of Theology," 321–24.

39. Owen, *The Death of Death,* 10:422–24.

40. Owen, *The Reason of Faith,* 4:111–15.

41. Owen, *Inquiry Concerning Evangelical Churches,* 15:289–96.

42. Owen has received criticism for the text critical position taken in these works by later generations, criticism which seems to be an example of judging an earlier age with later scholarly canons. E.g. Orme, *Memoir,* 271–73; Thomson, "Life," I.lxxiv–vi; F.F. Bruce, *Tradition: Old and New* (Exeter, 1970), 156–62; cf. Theodore Letis, "Edward Freer Hills' Contribution to the Revival of the Ecclesiastical Text," in *Journal of Christian Reconstruction* 12.2, 40–60; Letis, "John Owen Versus Brian Walton: A Reformed Response to the Birth of Text Criticism," in Theodore Letis, ed., *The Majority Text: Essays and Reviews in the Continuing Debate* (Grand Rapids, 1987), 145–90; Richard A. Muller, "The Debate over the Vowel Points and the Crisis in Orthodox Hermeneutics," *Journal of Medieval and Renaissance Studies* 10/1 (1980): 53–72. On the canon and integrity of Scripture in seventeenth century Reformed theology see Muller *PRRD,* 2:389–463.

43. Johannes Buxtorf, *Tiberias sive commentarius Masorethicus triplex,* 2 vol. (Basel, 1620), R.D. Owen, *Novum Testamentum notis et aliquibus manuscr.observat.* 6 vol. (1515?), Louis Capel, *Critica Sacra, sive de variis quae in Vetus Testamentum lectionibus occurunt* (Paris, 1650); Matthew Poole, *Synopsis criticorum et aliorum commentaria in Biblia* 8 vols.

Testaments, rabbinical learning flourished in the Renaissance.[44] In passing we note also his use of Josephus (c. 37–c. 100), Philo (c. 20 B.C.– c. A.D. 50), and Maimonides (1135–1204).[45]

A *third* strain of thought that influenced Owen was the *scholasticism* which was renovated and revitalised by humanism in the Baroque Age.[46]

(London, 1669), and Brian Walton, *Polyglotta cum apparatu* 8 vol. (London, 1660), in *BO* I.1, 3.

44. Rabbis of "greatest note" are listed in Owen *Vindiciae Evangelicae*, 12:457. *BO* has a section called "Rabbini" (I.19). Beyond this there are, for example, Bombard, *Talmud Babylonicum cum amplissimis Rabbinorum lectionibus,* 12 vols.(Venice, n.d.), Rabbi Kimchi, *Commentaria in Cant. Eccles. Lamentat. Ruth. Ester. Psalm. Prov. Job. Esra. Chronio.* (?), Isaac Abarbaniel, *In Prophetas omnes posteriores commentaria hebraice* (?) (*BO*, I.3), Rabbi Juda, *Liber cosri hebraice* (?), L'Empereur *codex Middoth sive de mensuris Templis* (Lyons, 1630), and *Liber Jesirah Abraham. Patriarchae commentariis Rabbi Abraham* (Amsterdam, 1642) (*BO*, I.8). Note, for example, the use of rabbinical works in Owen, *Vindiciae Evangelicae*, 12:455–85.

45. References to Josephus are 42, Maimonides 29, and Philo 21.

46. On Protestant scholasticism see John W. Beardslee, ed., *Reformed Dogmatics* (1965; Grand Rapids, 1975), "Introduction"; Christopher J. Burchill "Girolamo Zanchi: Portrait of A Reformed Theologian and His Work," *SCJ* 15 (1984), 185–207; Frederick Copleston, S. J., *A History of Philosophy*, 9 vols. (London, 1946–75), vol. III; Paul L. Dibon *L'Ensignement philosophique dans les Universités néerlandaises `a l'époque précartesiénne (1575–1650)* (Paris, 1954); Donnelly, *Calvinism and Scholasticism*; Donnelly, "Italian Influences on the Development of Calvinist Scholasticism," *SCJ* 7 (april 1976); Donnelly, "Calvinist Thomism," in *Viator,* Medieval and Renaissance Studies 7 (1976); Fatio, *Méthode et théologie;* Hägglund, *Teologins historia*, 274–302; Bengt Hägglund, *Die heilige Schrift und ihre Deutung in der Theologie Johann Gerhards: Eine Untursuchung über das altlutherische Schriftverständnis* (Lund, 1951); Hägglund, "Johannes Rudbeckius som teolog: en introduktion till hans föreläsningar i dogmatik 1611–13," *Svensk Teologisk Kvartalskrift* 68 (1992); Paul Oskar Kristeller, *Renaissance Thought: The Classic, Scholastic, and Humanist Strains* (New York, 1961), esp. ch. 5; Leroy E. Loemker, *Struggle for Synthesis: The Seventeenth Century Background of Leibniz's Synthesis of Order and Freedom* (Cambridge, Mass., 1972); Léon Mahieu "L'ecleticisme Suarézien," *Revue Thomiste* 8 (1925), 250–85; Muller, *PRRD*; Muller, *The Thought of Arminius*; Muller, "Scholasticism Protestant and Catholic," *Church History* 55/2 (1986): 193–205; Muller, "*Vera Philosophia,*" *SCJ* 15/3 (1984): 341–65; Platt, *Reformed Thought and Scholasticism;* Preus, *The Theology of Post-Reformation Lutheranism* (St. Louis: Concordia, 1970–1972); Scharlemann, *Aquinas and Gerard;* Charles B. Schmitt, et al., eds., *The Cambridge History of Renaissance Philosophy* (Cambridge, 1988); Schmitt, *Aristotle and the Renaissance;* John A. Trentman, "Scholasticism in the Seventeenth Century" in Norman Kretzman, Anthony Kenny, Jan Pinborg, eds., *The Cambridge History of Later Medieval Philosophy* (Cambridge, 1982), 818–37; Johannes Wallmann, *Der Theologiebegriff bei Johann Gerhard und Georg Calixt* (Tübingen, 1961); Weber, *Foundations of Dogmatics,* I.120–27. The older works include those of Paul Althaus, *Die Prinzipien der deutschen reformierten Dogmatik im Zeitalter der aristotelischen Scholastik* (Leipzig, 1914); J.A. Dorner, *History of Protestant Theology Particularly in Germany,* 2 vols., translation George Robson and Sophia Taylor

The merging of humanism and scholasticism was present from the very beginning in Musculus and Vermigli. In Calvin it is, for example, manifested in the academy he established in Geneva,[47] thereby making Reformed orthodoxy receptive to the increasing revival of scholasticism. Thomas Barlow and John Prideaux provided Owen with an excellent training in scholasticism.[48] It has been shown that Oxford masters of the Elizabethan period in general held to Aquinas', Scotus', and Zabarella's commentaries on Aristotle.[49]

Owen was receptive to this teaching and was acquainted with the writings of Albert the Great (c. 1200–1280), Petrus Galatinus (1460–1540), and Rupert of Deutz (c. 1075–1129).[50] The *opera omnia* of Anselm were on the shelves of his library and he is quoted in defence of the doctrine of the atonement.[51] He associates Abelard (1079–1142) with Pelagianism and Socinianism and therefore dismisses him as "a sophistical scholar."[52] The references to Peter Lombard (c. 1100–1160)

(Edinburgh, 1871); Ernst Lewalter, *Spanish-jesuitish und deutsch-lutherische Metaphysik des 17. Jahrhunderts* (Hamburg, 1935; Darmstadt, 1968); Peter Petersen, *Geschichte der aristotelischen Philosophie im protestantischen Deutschland* (Leipzig, 1921); Hans Emil Weber, *Der Einfluss der protestantischen Schulphilosophie auf die orthodox-lutherische Dogmatik* (Leipzig, 1908); Weber, *Die philosophische Scholastik des deutschen Protestantismus im Zeitalter der Orthodoxie* (Lepzig, 1907), and Max Wundt *Die deutsche Schulmetaphysik des 17. jahrhunderts* (Tübungen, 1939).

On the humanist exaggeration of the opposition of scholasticism: Kristeller, *Renaissance Thought*, 100, 113; Ozment, "Humanism, Scholasticism, and the Intellectual Origins of the Reformation," 137; Grane, "Luther and Scholasticism,", 52–68.

Such a fusion was not without precedence in the mediaeval period. See Beryl Smalley, *English Friars and Antiquity in the Early Fourteenth Century* (Oxford, 1960); Denys Hay, "England and the Humanities in the Fifteenth Century," Oberman and Brady, eds., *Itinerarium Italicum,* 305–67.

47. Reid "Calvin and the Founding of the academy of Geneva;" cf. Theodore Beza, *Theses theologicae in schola Genevensi ab aliquot sacrarum literarum studiosis sub D.D. Th. Beza & Anton. Fayo.*, 2d. enl. ed. (Geneva, 1591); Beza, *Propositions and Principles of Divinitie Propounded and Disputed in the University of Geneva under M. Theod. Beza and M. Anthonie Faius* (Edinburgh, 1595).

48. E.g. Barlow, *De studio theologiae*, 35–37; Prideaux, *Fasciculus controversiarum ad juniorum aut occupatorum captum sic colligatus* (3rd. enl. ed. Oxford, 1664); Prideaux, *Manuductio ad theologiam polemicam* (Oxford, 1657); Prideaux, *Viginti-duae lectiones de totidem religionis capitibus* (Oxford, 1648); cf. Marvin W. Anderson, "Thomas Cajetan's *Scientia Christi*" *Theologische Zeitschrift* 26 (1970), 99–108.

49. Fletcher, "The Faculty of Arts," 178–79.

50. E.g. Owen: *A Dissertation on Divine Justice*, 10:498,501; *Christologia: or, A Declaration of the Glorious Mystery of the Person of Christ* (1679), 1:23.

51. Owen, *Of the Death of Christ*, 10:466. Anselm *Opera omnia* (Paris, 1549) in *BO* I.1.

52. Owen: *The Doctrine of the Trinity*, 2:375; *Vindiciae Evangelicae*, 12:28, 402.

can likewise be negative,[53] but he is also quoted in the affirmative.[54] There is some preference for John of Damascus (c. 675–c. 749), "a learned Christian," whom Owen quotes in the original Greek.[55] Bernard of Clairvaux (1090–1153) is similarly held in high regard.[56] When Duns Scotus is referred to in *A Dissertation on Divine Justice* the references are all negative since Owen is here restating the Thomist argument of the absolute necessity of satisfaction, strengthened by Suárez.[57] Durandus is also an opponent in this work,[58] but was relied upon in other instances to strengthen Owen's argument,[59] which is also the case with Scotus in different contexts.[60] The negative references and citations should probably be viewed in the perspective of the semi-Pelagian doctrine of late mediaeval Nominalism, which is explicitly the cause of Owen's strictures on Ockham and Biel.[61] Henry of Ghent (d. 1293), Alexander of Hales (c. 1186–1245) and Bonaventure (c. 1217–74) are referred to in the affirmative.[62]

However, the most important of the mediaeval scholastics for Owen was Thomas Aquinas.[63] He is a typical English Protestant of the seventeenth century in his high estimation of Thomism and thorough knowledge of Thomas' *Summa* and commentary on *Sententiae*.[64] Thomas was regarded "without question" as "the best and most sober of all your [Roman] school doctors."[65] In Owen's early years the dependence upon

---

53. Owen, *Christologia*, I.224.

54. Owen: *The Doctrine of the Saints' Perseverance*, 11:37; *Vindiciae Evangelicae*, 11:130.

55. There are 11 references and quotations to Damascenus, most of which are affirmative.

56. There are 16 references to and quotations from Bernard, most of which are affirmative.

57. Owen, *A Dissertation on Divine Justice*, 10:501,587–89; cf. Herman Witsius, *Oeconomia*, II.viii.; Francis Turretin, *Institutio theologicae elencticae*, 3 vols. (Geneva, 1679–85), 14:x.

58. Owen, *A Dissertation on Divine Justice*, 10:501,550.

59. Owen: *A Display of Arminianism*, 10:46; *The Doctrine of the Saints' Perseverance*, 11:22; *Vindiciae Evangelicae*, 12:130.

60. Owen: *Theologoumena*, 17: I.vii.25; *Vindiciae Evangelicae*, 12:130.

61. Owen, *Pneumatologia*, 3:309.

62. Owen: *Of Schism*, 13:130; *Christologia*, 1:22,23; *Commnion with God*, 2:18; *The Reason of Faith*, 4:101

63. 55 mostly positive references; cf. Trueman, "John Owen's *Dissertation on Divine Justice*."

64. Cf. Ryan, "The Reputation of Thomas Aquinas Among English Protestant Thinkers."

65. Owen, *Vindication of Animadversions*, 14:261.

Thomas is unmistakable in *A Vision of Unchangeable, Free Mercy* and especially in *A Display of Arminianism*. In the latter work Owen is notably fond of adhering to Thomas' definitions. A decade passes and Thomas is associated with "horrid terms and expressions,"[66] but is still a fine ally in the defence of the Reformed faith.[67] Ryan has argued for a general decline in the knowledge and use of Aquinas in the later part of the seventeenth century.[68] Owen's library possessed a copy of Aquinas' *Summa theologiae* and his writings show how well versed he was in it.[69] Manifesting a preference for Thomas' *Summa* would appear to align him with the traditional and dominant Thomism, which followed the mature Thomas of the *Summa* and not the young Thomas of the *Sententiae*, something which may have been facilitated in the case of Owen and other Protestants by the unambiguous Augustinian doctrine of justification *sola gratia* found in the mature Thomas.[70]

Moreover, Owen's Thomist orientation is obvious from his wide reading and use of leading Jesuit and Dominican philosophers and theologians which were the most gifted, influential, and leading representatives of and pioneers in Thomist and scholastic studies at this time.[71] Owen specifically relies on this revived Thomism in metaphysics.[72]

---

66. Owen, *The Doctrine of the Saints' Perseverance*, 11:70.

67. Owen: *The Doctrine of the Saints' Perseverance*, 11:71,72; *Vindiciae Evangelicae*, 12:71,111,130,131; *Of Schism: The True Nature of it Discovered and Considered with reference to the Present Differences in Religion* (1657). 13:127.

68. John K. Ryan, "The Reputation of St. Thomas Aquinas Among English Protestant Thinkers of the Seventeenth Century," *The New Scholasticism* 22 (1948): 1–33, 126–208.

69. E.g. *BO*, I.2; Owen: *Christologia*, 1:22; *Communion with God*, 2:18, 24, 28, 158, 161; *A Vision of Unchangeable, Free Mercy*, 8:8, 10, 23; *Ebenezer*, 8:105; *Of Toleration; and The Duty of the Magistrate about Religion* (1648), 8:166, 67; *A Display of Arminianism*, 10:23–24, 28, 31, 44, 45, 73, 110; *The Death of Death*, 10:275; *The Death of Christ*, 10:451, 467; *A Dissertation on Divine Justice*, 10:498, 501, 544; *Vindiciae Evangelicae*, 12:111, 130–31; *Of Schism*, 13:126, 27; *Vindication of Animadversions*, 14:439. Thomas Aquinas, *Summa contra gentiles* is quoted in Owen: *The Doctrine of the Saints' Perseverance*, 11:22,72, and *Vindiciae Evangelicae*, 12:71

70. Cf. Oberman, "Fourteenth-Century Religious Thought," 5.

71. References and quotations are found to the following works: Diego Alvarez, *Disputationes theologicae in primam secundae Sancti Thomae* (Trani, 1617) (Owen: *A Display of Arminianism*, 10:52,73,86107]); *De auxiliis divinae gratiae* (Cologne, 1621; *The Doctrine of the Saints' Perseverance*, 11:21–22, 71, 72; *Vindiciae Evangelicae*, 11:130); Rodrigo de Arriaga, *Disputationes theologicae in primam partem d. Thomae*, 8 vols. (Antwerp, 1643–55) (Owen, *Vindiciae Evangelicae*, 12:140); Juan Azor, *Institutiones morales* (Cologne, 1602) (Owen, *Vindication of Animadversions*, 14:235, 416, 439); Domingo Bañez, *Scholastica*

There are certainly rhetorical rejections of "Jesuits and Dominicans"[73] which may obscure the dominant philosophical influence they had on him, whilst in other instances he just defends his view with a reference to "Sic scholastici omnes"[74] or "Scholasticos passim."[75] In suitable contexts Alvarez can, for example, be ascribed the epithet one of "the more learned schoolmen".[76] As compared to the number of schoolmen he quotes, Owen himself possessed at the end of his life a small number of them.[77]

---

commentaria in primam (secundam secundae) partem . . . S. Thomae (Douai, 1614, 1615) (Owen, *Of Schism*, 13:126); Cajetan (possibly) *In prima partem secunde partis sume theologie Thomas Aquinitatis commentaria* (Paris, 1510) (Owen, *A Dissertation on Divine Justice*, 10:501, 505); Cajetan, *De ente et essentia* (?) (Owen, *Vindiciae Evangelicae,*12:71); Cajetan, *Commentaria illistres . . . in quinque Mosaicos libros* (Paris, 1539) (Owen, *The Divine Original*, 16:285); Ferrariensis (possibly), commentary on the *Sententiae* (Owen *A Dissertation on Divine Justice,*10:501); Gregory of Valencia (possibly), *Commentariorum theologicorum tomi quatuor* (Ingolstadt, 1591–97; rev. 1603) (Owen: *The Reason of Faith*, 4:115; *The Divine Original*, 16:285); Gregory of Valencia, *De idol.* (?) (Owen: *Of Toleration*, 8:165; *Vindication of Animadversions*, 14:216); Juan Martines de Ripalda, *Brevis expositio magistri Sentent. cum quaestionibus* (Lyons, 1636) (Owen, *Vindiciae Evangelicae*, 12:130); Alphonso de Mendoza, *Controversiae theologicae* (Cologne, 1603) (Owen, *Vindiciae Evangelicae*, 12:139); Petrus de Palude, . . . *Quartus sententiam* . . . (Paris, 1514) (Owen, *A Dissertation on Divine Justice*, 10:501); Pesantius *Commentaria brevia ac disputationes in universam theologiam d. Thomae* (Venice, 1606) (Owen, *A Dissertation on Divine Justice*, 10:467, 498, 501); Dominic Soto, *De natura et gratia* (Paris, 1549) (Owen, *A Dissertation on Divine Justice*, 10:501); one of Antonio Ruvio's commentaries on Aristotle (Owen, *Vindiciae Evangelicae*, 12:139); Francesco Suárez, *Varia opuscula theologica* (Lyons, 1600) (Owen: *A Vision of Unchangeable, Free Mercy*, 8:22; *The Death of Christ,*10:464; *A Dissertation on Divine Justice*, 10:498, 501–02, 541,542); Suárez, *De legibus priv.* (?) (Owen, *A Dissertation on Divine Justice*, 10:614), Suárez, *De perpetuitat. vel Amis. Grat.* (?) (Owen, *The Doctrine of the Saints' Perseverance,*11:73), Suárez, *Disputationes metaphysicae* (Owen, *Vindiciae Evangelicae*, 12:71), Suárez, a commentary on Thomas (Owen, *Vindication of Animadversions*, 14:201), and Vasquez, *Commentariorum ac disputationum in primam partem Summa theologiae Sancti Thomae Aquinitatis* (Venice, 1600) (Owen: *The Doctrine of Justification*, 5:11, 60, 151, 166, 227, 373; *The Death of Christ*, 10:464; *Vindiciae Evangelicae*, 12:139). It has not been possible to trace all references.

72. E.g. Owen: *A Display of Arminianism*, 10:86; *Vindiciae Evangelicae*, 11:71, 130, 132, 139, 140; *Vindication of Animadversions*, 14:201–02.

73. E.g. Owen, *Of Schism*, 13:115.

74. Owen, *A Display of Arminianism*, 10:23n.1.

75. Owen, *Vindiciae Evangelicae*, 12:104.

76. Owen, *A Display of Arminianism*, 10:107.

77. Thomas Aquinas, *Summa theologica* (Paris, 1632) Diego Alvarez, *De auxiliis divinae gratiae & human. arbit. virib. & libert.* (Lyons, 1620); Petrus Galatinus *De arcanis catholicae veritatis cum Reuchlino de Cabala* (Frankfurt, 1612); Pesantius *Disputationes et brevia commentaria in universam theologiam* (Cologne, 1613) (*BO*, I.2); Anselm, *Opera omnia*

Closely and implicitly associated, though not identical, with scholasticism and Thomism was the *philosophical eclecticism* of the Christian tradition, which will be the next current under consideration. Quoting Clement of Alexandria, Francis Turretin (1623–1687) argues that true philosophy is the gathering of various strains of pagan thought into one whole.[78] The union of the philosophical current during the seventeenth century was to the advantage of Aristotelianism over Platonism.[79] References to Ramus seems to be absent from the pages of Owen.[80] Toon thinks that Owen may never have been introduced to the Ramist critique of Aristotelianism.[81] Instead we find the Aristotelian scholasticism of Owen's tutors.[82] The impact of this Aristotelianism on Owen's college is reflected in Cotton Mather: "I am sure they [at Harvard] do not show such a veneration for Aristotle as is express'd at Queen's Colledge in Oxford; where they read Aristotle on their *knees,* and those who take degrees are *sworn* to defend his philosophy."[83]

Turning to the influence of philosophy, Owen did, of course, dismiss

---

(Paris, 1549) in (*BO* I.1); Peter Lombard, *In quatuor libros Sententiarum* (Paris, 1528) (*BO,* I.17); Suárez, *Metaphysicarum disputationum* (Cologne, 1608); Suarez, *Mori enchiridion metaphysicum* (London, 1671); Suarez, *Tractatus de legibus* (Mog. 1619) (*BO,* I.20); Christoph Scheibler, *Metaphysica duabus libris cum proemio de usu philosophia* (Geneva 1636) (*BO,* I.25).

78. Turretin, *Institutio,* I.xiii.6.

79. Shedd, *History,* I.92 n.2: "In Baxter and Owen, both of whom were also diligent students of the schoolmen, we perceive more of the influence of the Aristotelian system."

80. A copy of Ramus, *Commentaria de fide Christiana* (Frankfurt 1576); and *Schola mathematica* (Frankfurt, 1627) are found in his library (*BO* I.13).

81. Toon, *Correspondence,* 6.

82. Cf. Barlow, *De studio theologiae,* 35–38. Owen had the following works in his library: Prideaux, *Fasciculus* (Oxford, 1652) (*BO* I.9); Prideaux, *Lectiones viginti duae de totidem religionis capitibus* (Oxford, 1648) (*BO* I.2); *Marmora Oxoniensia sive Arundeliana* (Oxford, 1676) (*BO,* I.21.). Thomas Barlow, *Exercitationes aliquot metaphysicae, de Deo: Quod sit objectum metaphysicae, quod sit naturaliter cognoscibilis, quouque, & quibus mediis. Quod aeternus, & immanentus (contra verstium) & quomodo, & c.,* 2d. ed. (Oxford, 1658) (*BO,* I.24); Christoph Scheibler, *Metaphysica duabus libris cum proemio de usu philosophia* (Geneva 1636) (*BO,* I.25); Suárez, *Metaphysicarum disputationum libri duo cum 5 indicibus* (Cologne, 1608) (*BO,* I.20); Suárez, *Mori enchiridion metaphysicum* (London, 1671). On Barlow see *DNB,* 5:2–3. On Aristotelianism at Oxford see James McConica "Humanism and Aristotle in Tudor Oxford," *English Historical Review* 94 (1979), 291–317; Sarah Hutton, "Thomas Jackson, Oxford Platonist, and William Twisse, Aristotelian," *JHI* 39 (1978): 635–52.

83. Mather, *Magnalia Christi Americana,* 2:21. Kearney *Scholars and Gentlemen,* 83: "It was most clearly marked at Oxford at Queen's, then the largest college."

Greek philosophers as opposed to Scripture,[84] but in reality this relationship was more complex and he, for short, adhered to the traditional Christian assimilation of classical philosophy. He regards Aristotle, like his mediaeval predecessors, as the philosopher *par excellence*.[85] He was even acquainted with translations of Aristotle in Hebrew.[86] Such negative references to Aristotle as do occur are unspecific, without references or citations and are made in connection with the scholastics' allegedly pertinacious adherence to his philosophy and/or the proliferation of technical terms.[87] In all instances in which Owen quotes him he does so positively. Just after his academic period in the 1650s, references and citations are perhaps more cautious.[88]

Another important authority is "magnus Plato,"[89] "divinus philosophus."[90] Although the dominant interest in the Oxonian curriculum lay in Aristotle, Plato was absorbed, as McConica points out, less directly but more indirectly through patristic sources and early commentators.[91] Owen no doubt studied Platonism. Plato is in nearly every instance quoted in the affirmative, only in passing does Owen direct negative statements to "Platonics," "Platonists," and "sectarians of Platonic philosophy,"[92] who then are associated with speculations.[93] He considered the church fathers too steeped in Platonism.[94]

Furthermore, it was undoubtedly Owen's wish that ethics should be based upon the canonical Scriptures rather than the writings of pagan

84. Owen, *Theologoumena*, 17:VI.ix.20.

85. Owen: *A Display of Arminianism*, 10:5,49; *Communion with God*, 2:8; *A Vindication of Some Passages in a Discourse Concerning Communion with God* (1674), 2:343; *Vindiciae Evangelicae*, 12:64,113.

86. Owen, *Truth and Innocence Vindicated*, 13:412.

87. Owen: *The Doctrine of Justification*, 5:12, 56; *Truth and Innocence Vindicated*, 13:412; idem *Vindication of Animadversions*, 14:315, 329; *Theologoumena*, 17:I.ii.1; I.vii.15–16, 19, 23.

88. E.g. Owen: *Vindication of Animadversions*, 14:186, 195, 216, 220; *Theologoumena*, 17:I.i.2; I.v.6, 11; I.vii.2; I.viii.5; III.ix.7; II.i.2; 362.

89. Owen, *Theologoumena*, 17:Iviii.6,57; cf. Parker, *Of the Preexistence of the Souls, and his Platonic Philosophy* (Oxford, 1666), *BO* , II.9.

90. Owen, *Theologoumena*, 17:III.vi.8.

91. McConica, "Elizabethan Oxford: The Collegiate Society," 706. 712–13.

92. Owen: *A Review of the Annotations of Hugo Grotius* (1656), 12:634–35; *A Dissertation on Divine Justice*, 10:519; *Theologoumena*, 17:III.v.7; *Pro sacris scripturis*, 16:429, 431, 432.

93. Owen, *Theologoumena*, 17:III.vi.6; 283.

94. Owen, *Pro sacris scripturis*, 16, exercitatio 1.

philosophers.[95] However, Plotinus, "philosophus praestantissimus,"[96] is one of "those contemplative philosophers" who "endeavoured to refine and advance heathenism into a compliance with" the gospel.[97] Owen has a marked preference for Plotinus' *Enneades* and he regards him together with Amelius, Eumenius, Proclus, Hierocles, and Celsus as more sober philosophers[98] who sometimes fell into allegorising of idolatrous prose and poetry.[99] Owen is able to rely on Neoplatonism in ontology, epistemology, and the doctrine of God.[100] Philo in particular is followed on the immutability, incorporality, and impassibility of God,[101] although reproached for his subordinationism of the Logos,[102] while Seneca "the best of the philosophers"[103] who belongs to "the more refined Paganism,"[104] is referred to in particular for the natural knowledge of God.[105] Also of interest is Owen's familiarity with the commentaries of Simplicius, Themistius, Theophrastus, Porphyry's *Isagoge*, Julius Petronellus, and Keslerus.[106] However, as regards Marsilio Ficino, there

95. Owen, *Theologoumena,* 17:VI.ix.20.

96. Owen, *Theologoumena,* 17:I.iii.2.

97. Owen: *The Work of the Holy Spirit in Prayer,* 4:329; *Theologoumena,* 17:III.v.7; III.vi.6. Plotinus, together with Theophrastus and Seneca is likewise associated with "refined Paganism" in Owen, *A Display of Arminianism,* 10:30. Owen recognises that Plotinian influence is found in the doctrine of prayer in certain Christian traditions (*The Work of the Holy Spirit in Prayer,* 4:329).

98. Owen, *Theologoumena,* 17:I.ix.24.

99. Owen, *Theologoumena,* 17:III.vi.4.

100. E.g. Owen: *Theologoumena,* 17:I.i.1; I.iii.2; I.v.6; *Vindiciae Evangelicae,* 12:103, 107, 125; *Communion,* 2:80; *A Vision of Unchangable, Free Mercy,* 8:10; *A Display of Arminianism,* 10:30, where he quotes Galen *De methodo medendi*, Plotinus *Enneades,* Posidonius, Alcinous *Introductio in Platonis platonicam philosophiam* (Oxford, 1667), Maximus of Tyre *Dissert*[?], Theophrastus *Ad Picum* (*BO,* I.31).

101. Owen: *A Display of Arminianism,* 10:14; *Vindiciae Evangelicae,* 12:97, 106, 110. References are to Philo: "lib. quod sit Deus immutabilis"; *Alleg. Leg.,*; *De opificio mundi.* Cf. Lloyd "The Life and Work of Owen," 144. Cf. Pannenberg, "The Appropriation of the Philosophical Concept of God as a Dogmatic Problem of Early Christian Theology," 2:119–83; cf. Watson *Greek Philosophy and the Christian Notion of God.*

102. Owen, *A Review of Grotius,* 12:632,634, with references to *De agric.* and *De mund. opific.*

103. Owen, *The Doctrine of Justification By Faith,* 5:23, although the only negative reference or quotation is found here to Seneca.

104. Owen, *A Display of Arminianism,* 10:22, 30.

105. E.g. Owen: *Communion with God,* 2:87, 94; *Pneumatologia,* 3:36; *Display of Arminianism,* 10:30; *Dissertation on Divine Justice,* 10:496, 497, 541; *Vindiciae Evangelicae,* 12:97, 107, 128, 438; *Theologoumena,* 17.

106. Owen: *Theologoumena,* 17:284, 85; III.viii.9,11; *The Nature of Apostasy from the*

is only a negative reference to the work *De vita coelesti comparanda.*[107] Goold has pointed out Owen's use of the psychology of Epicurus.[108]

No doubt Owen found this philosophical approach in agreement with the writings of Augustine, Boëthius, Dionysius the Areopagite, Damascenus, Thomas, and Suárez.[109] The traditional philosophical approach of eclecticism by Christians was probably stimulated by three further things. The view of Scripture as the sole authority in all things, the variety of philosophical preference found among the early Reformed theologians, and the view that no single mediaeval model was sufficient and complete. From these concerns a plurality of elements was incorporated in the Reformed theological systems. However, the eclectic philosophical paradigm of pre-Enlightenment Reformed thought always remained clearly hedged by the doctrines of Scripture and man.[110] Only with a paradigm-shift did philosophy attain a domineering role: "Rationalist philosophy was ultimately incapable of becoming a suitable *ancilla* and, instead, demanded that it and not theology be considered

---

Profession of the Gospel (1676), 7:191; *Toleration,* 8:186; *A Vision of Unhangable, Free Mercy,* 8:10; *A Display of Arminianism,* 10:30; *Communion with God,* 2:49; *Vindiciae Evangelicae,* 12:51, 125.

107. Owen, *Theologoumena,* 17:III.vii.10.

108. Goold's editorial comments on Owen's *A Dissertation on Divine Justice,* 10:517n.2.

109. For Augustine and Thomas see above. Owen quotes Boëthius (*Vindiciae Evangelicae,* 12:125), pseudo-Dionysius *De div. nom.* (*Theologoumena,* 17:I.i.4), and John of Damascus, *De orthodoxa fide* (*Christologia,* 1:23; *Vindiciae Evangelicae,* 12:76; *Review of Grotius,* 12:634). The eclectic character of Suárez is noted in J. Dalmau "Francisco Suárez," *NCE*; Mahieu "L'eclecticisme Suarézien."

110. E.g. Junius, *De vera theologia,* cols. 1763–64 ; Polanus, *Syntagma,* cols. 3–5; Owen: *Theologoumena,* 17:458, 459; *Animadversions on a Treatise Entitled Fiat Lux* (1662), 14:76,74; *Vindication of Animadversions,* 14:357–58; Turretin, *Institutio,* I.viii.2,7; I.ix.1; I.x12; I.xii.14–15, 25, 33; I.xiii.1; Coccejus, *Aphorismi breviores,* § 20: "Ratio subservit Theologiae non imperat." Cf. §21; Braunius, *Doctrina foederum,* I.i.19, 22; I.ii.1; Prideaux, *De usu logices in theologicis* in *Viginti-duae lectiones de totidem religionis capitibus* . A more popular treatment of this subject in the face of Socinianism is found in Herman Witsius, *An Essay on the Use and Abuse of Reason in matters of Religion,* translation John Carter (Norwich, 1795). For fine discussions of reason in Reformed scholasticism see Martin I. Klauber, "The Use of Philosophy in the Theology of Johannes Maccovius (1578–1644)," *CTJ* 30 (1995), 376–91; Muller, *PRRD,* 1:231–49; Muller, *"Vera Philosophia,"* 341–65; Evans, *Problems of Authority,* 86–112. A less successful overview is John Morgan, *Godly Learning: Puritan Attitudes Towards Reason, Learning, and Education* (Cambridge, 1986), 41–59. See also my forthcoming "Alleged Rationalism: Francis Turretin on Reason."

the queen of the sciences."[111]

Finally, we shall add another current of thought. I mention *Augustinianism* lastly, but certainly not because it had the least influence on Reformed thought; rather it may be said to have been predominant.[112] We have already seen that references to Augustine outnumber any other author in Owen and that his library possessed Augustine's *Omnia opera*. There are primarily two Augustinianisms that are influential on Owen: the anti-Pelagian and the mystical. First, from the beginning Reformed theology revealed continuity with leading features of the anti-Pelagian *schola Augustiniana moderna* and several of the distinctive features of Reformed thought can be partially explained by the influence of this school of thought.[113] The outstanding feature of Oxford life in the 1620s was the controversies about the doctrine of grace and they must have pressed themselves on Owen's mind.[114] His writings reveal that he read widely in the Augustinian corpus, but there is a preponderance of the treatises defending grace.[115] Moreover, he

---

111. Muller, *PRRD,* 1:39.

112. Cf. Harnack, *History of Dogma,* 7:17; Pelikan, *The Christian Tradition,* 4:22; Kristeller, *Renaissance Thought* , 55; Oberman, *Masters,* 64–110; Oberman, *Forerunners,* 123–40; Miller, *The New England Mind,* 4.

113. See William J. Courtenay "Late Medieval Nominalism Revisited: 1977–1982," *JHI* 44 (1983), 159–64; Alister McGrath, "John Calvin and Late Medieval Thought: a Study in Late Medieval Influences upon Calvin's Theological Development," 58; McGrath, *Intellectual Origins,* 86–121; Pelikan, *The Christian Tradition,* 4:17ff.; Kristeller, *Renaissance Thought,* 55ff; 82ff.; Frank A. James III, *"Praedestinatio Dei:* The Intellectual Origins of Peter Martyr Vermigli's Doctrine of Double Predestination" (D.Phil. thesis University of Oxford, 1993); Frank A. James III, "A Late Medieval Parallel in Reformation Thought: *Gemina Praedestinatio* in Gregory of Rimini and Peter Martyr Vermigli," in Frank A. James and Heiko A. Oberman, eds.,*Via Augustini: Augustine in the Later Middle Ages, the Renaissance, and the Reformation* (Leiden, 1991), 157–188; James argues that Vermigli was particularly indebted to the academic Augustinianism of *schola Augustiniana moderna* and Gregory of Rimini for his doctrine of predestination, although Aquinas was an important intellectual contributor in other ways, influences which in turn exercised a considerable influence on the doctrinal development of Reformed theology. The explicit references to Augustine in Calvin's *Institutio* (1559) are six times as many as any other extra-biblical author. "Augustine is easily Martyr's favorite author. References to Augustine out number those to any other non-scriptural source several times over." Donnelly *Calvinism and Scholasticism,* 34.

114. Cf. Tyacke, *Anti-Calvinists,* 58–86; Mallet, *History of the University of Oxford,* 2:237; Wood, *History and Antiquities,* 2:354–55.

115. E.g. Owen: *The Doctrine of the Saints' Perseverance,* 11:60–61, 66–67; *A Display of Arminianism,*10:115.

considered Thomas Bradwardine a "profoundly learned doctor"[116] "who with singular diligence and scholastick ability opposed the spreading of Pelagianisme in and over the Roman Church."[117] Owen also quotes John Major's (c. 1469–1550) commentary on the *Sententiae*,[118] which connects him with anti-Pelagian and Scotist thought. Not surprisingly we find an interest in Jansenism in Owen[119] and in 1669 he wrote the foreword to Theophilus Gale's *The True Idea of Jansenism: Both Historick and Dogmatick*.

Secondly, in Puritanism and Owen we find a late mediaeval brand or usage of Augustine which Pelikan calls "Augustinian subjectivism."[120] This current viewed the Christian life as a life of interior knowledge in detachment from sensible things and had developed as an attempt to relate doctrine to experience. Of particular interest is that "personal religious experience" was identified "as an epistemological principle in theology"[121] and that Augustine's *Confessionum*, was made it into "a paradigm for the inner life".[122] Following this mystical tradition, Owen uses Augustine's autobiographical account as an outline of conversion,[123]

116. Owen, *The Doctrine of the Saints' Perseverance*, 11:69.

117. Owen, "Preface" to Theophilus Gale *The True Idea of Jansenisme: Both Historick and Dogmatick* (London, 1669) 27 (my pagination). Note his personal copy of Thomas Bradwardine, *De causa Dei contra Pelagium* ed. Savilius (London, 1618) (*BO* I.2).

118. Owen, *Vindiciae Evangelicae*, 12:130.

119. References to Jansen are: Owen *Vindication of Animadversions*, 14:315; *Theologoumena*,17:V.xv.17; 6:viii.10,16; to Pascal, Owen: *Theologoumena*, 17:III.vi.9; *Of Schism*, 13:115; *Vindiciae Evangelicae*, 12:560. In his library Jansen, *Harmonia in suam concordiam ac totam historiam Evangelic.* (Mog. 1624); Jansen, *Augustinus* (Rotherdam, 1652) (I.3), and Jansen, *Iprensis suspectus* (Paris, 1650) are found (*BO*, I.17). Moreover, there is the volume *Logica sive ars cogitanda per Jansenistas* (Lud. 1674) (*BO*, I.29).

120. Pelikan, *The Christian Tradition*, 4:21; 3:304–06; cf. Mary T. Clark, "A Neoplatonic Commentary on the Christian Trinity: Marius Victorinus," in O'Meara, ed., *Neoplatonism and Christian Thought*, 26, 31; Miller, *The New England Mind.*, esp. chs. 1–2; Knappen, *Tudor Puritanism*, 387; Jerald C. Brauer, "Puritan Mysticism and the Development of Liberalism," *CH* 19 (1950), 151–70; Brauer, "Types of Puritan Piety," *CH* 56 (1987), 39–58, esp. 50–58; Geoffrey Nuttall, "Puritan and Quaker Mysticism," *Theology* 78 (1975), 518–31; B.R. White, "Echoes of Medieval Christendom in Puritan Spirituality," *One in Christ* 16 (1980), 78–90; Bernard McGinn, "Love, Knowledge, and Mystical Union in Western Christianity: Twelfth to Sixteenth Centuries," *CH* 56 (1987), 7–24; King, "The Affective Spirituality of John Owen," 223–33. On Puritan spirituality in general see Geoffrey F. Nuttall, *The Holy Spirit in Puritan Faith and Experience* (Oxford, 1946); Schaefer, "The Spiritual Brotherhood on the Habits of the Heart."

121. Pelikan, *The Christian Tradition*, 2:259.

122. Pelikan, *The Christian Tradition*, 4:21

123. Owen: *Pneumatologia*, 3:337–366; *The Grace and Duty of Being Spiritually Minded* (1681), 7:344–45, 385, 444, 453. In Owen's library we find Hugh of St. Victor, *Augustini*

which concept is Plotinian in the sense that conversion and the vision of God are regarded as purifying the human senses.[124] The book is regarded as a unique history of the soul given in providence and through Augustine's experience the way to the knowledge of God and self is found, a pilgrimage from the abyss of the soul to the vision of God. Owen's continuity with mediaeval mysticism is also seen in his comments on the Song of Solomon,[125] on which it has been noted that "the interpretation is controlled by Owen's own thought on spiritual experience, to the point that this becomes the exegetical principle itself."[126]

III. Conclusion: Owen in Historical Perspective

Let me conclude by way of summary and a word of application for Reformed theology today. From what has gone before it is clear that the academic formation and the sources used by Owen connects him to the entire Christian tradition and to the contemporary intellectual currents. He has absorbed the best currents of the Western tradition and Renaissance culture into his Reformed theology. McConica's characterisation of the Oxford schools under Elizabeth I is equally applicable on Owen:

> catholic and eclectic, sensitive to the whole of the tradition of learning in the past including the medieval achievement, widely read in contemporary continental thought, yet staunchly protestant and if anything Calvinist.[127]

All these strains of thought are found in Owen's library and writings. He

---

Regula (Dilling., 1571) (*BO*, I.9); *Regulae penitentiae Franciscanorum* (n.p., n.d.) (*BO*, I.14), separate prints of Augustine's *Confessiones* (Cologne, 1629) and *Soliloquia sive Meditationes* (Cologne, 1629) (*BO* I.14), the *opera omnia* of Francis Assisi and Anthony of Padua (Paris, 1641) (*BO*, I.1) and *Theologica Germanica, or Mystical Divinity* (London, 1648) (*BO*, II.21).

124. J. J. O'Meara, "The Neoplatonism of Saint Augustine," in O'Meara, ed., *Neoplatonism and Christian Thought*, 37–38; cf. Augustine, *De Trinitate*, in *PL* 42, VIII.iii.4, trans. A. W. Haddan, *On the Trinity*, in *NPNF*1 vol. III.

125. Cf. Owen, *Communion with God*, with E. A. Matter, *The Song of My Beloved: The Songs of Songs in Western Medieval Christianity* (Philadelphia, 1990); White, "Echoes of Medieval Christendom in Puritan Spirituality," 86–87; McGinn, "Love, Knowledge, and Mystical Union in Western Christianity: Twelfth to Sixteenth Centuries."

126. Sinclair Ferguson, *John Owen on the Christian Life* (Edinburgh, 1987), 79.

127. McConica, "Elizabethan Oxford: The Collegiate Society," 713.

deliberately employs the models and patterns of the Christian tradition, paradigms which provided a most suitable framework for the execution and defence of Reformed theology. Moreover, referring to the title of the symposium from which this collection of articles resulted, Owen's theology was truly an "ecumenical enterprise." It belongs to the whole world or the whole intellectual tradition. More narrowly, Owen shows himself to belong to the whole Christian world or the universal church. His theology is ecumenical in the sense that he is seeking to transcend the differences of the traditon.

What shall we think of this ecumenical enterprise of Owen if we are Reformed theologians today? People affiliated to the Reformed tradition have taken interest in Owen and reveal different reponses to his intellectual locale and wideranging use of various sources. The "Calvin vs. the Calvinists" thesis has had its representative, claiming distortion by means of this "ecumenicity."[128] The Pietist interpretation of Owen resolutely disregards the relationship to his contemporary context.[129] Time does not allow me to go into these interpretations, but it is sufficient to say that both fail miserably in understanding Owen and, as I think, my own research and that of others prove them scholarly inadequate.[130] I therefore suggest that we take a different approach.

What attitude are we then to take towards Owen's ecumenical theology? First, we cannot deny that he has absorbed and uses the entire Western canon. Secondly, all sound and credible theology participates in its sorrounding culture. This "enhypostatic" relation of theology to culture is necessary since the Christian message makes claims upon people in their culture and, from a Reformed point of view, Christ does not redeem a person in isolation from, but with his or her entire culture.[131] The church is therefore constantly called to present a message relevant to its setting and Christian doctrine must talk in terms that partake of the very fabric of our lives and our historical setting—

---

128. Alan C. Clifford, *Atonement and Justification: English Evangelical Theology, 1640–1790: An Evaluation* (Oxford: Clarendon Press, 1990).

129. See, for example, the early biographers; Ferguson, *John Owen,* 187–88,192; articles in *British Reformed Journal* 16 (1996), 17 (1997), and 18 (1997).

130. Much has been written here, but see especially the work of Richard Muller, John Platt, and Carl Trueman.

131. E.g. Guenther Haas, "The Effects of the Fall on Creational Social Structures: A Comparison of Anabaptist and Reformed Perspectives," *CTJ* 30 (1995), 108–129; John Bolt, "The Relation Between Creation and Redemption in Romans 8:18–27," *CTJ* 30 (1995), 34–51; Niebuhr, *Christ and Culture,* 156ff.

entailing the constant risk of becoming unduly influenced by the context in the work of reformulation. On the other hand, if this contextualization is successful, the message will be appropriated by the believer and enable him or her to understand and transform his or her culture in a Christian way. I think therefore we should regard Owen's theology as being adapted to the linguistic and cultural life-situation of the seventeenth century by drawing upon all its sources. It was thus in general an effective—to use a modern term—contextualization of the Christian message.

There are things to be learnt here for modern theologians. Not only Owen's theology—which has not been dealt with here—but his ecumenical praxis is worth our consideration. I am not calling for a "repristination theology"; that is not a live option. There are certainly elements, aspects, and areas in Owen's thought which we would not like follow. However, my view is that we should take inspiration from his precise reasoning, his explorations in the tradition and the contemporary society. In this paper I have devoted our attention to his ecumenical praxis. In our time Reformed theologians should likewise explore the resources of not only their own tradition but the entire ecumenical tradition as the surrounding society in order to construct a credible theology in the next century.

9

Gisbertus Voetius (1589–1676): Basic Features of His Doctrine of God

Andreas J. Beck

I. Introduction

While the new Dutch republic became an important center of cultural and scientific developments in the mid-seventeenth century, the city of Utrecht became a center of religious renewal.[1] Next to the cathedral lived the famous Anna Maria van Schurman and her brother Johan Godschalk; their house was regularly visited by a group of ministers inspired by English puritanism and committed to the progress of the Reformation inside and outside Utrecht (*Nadere Reformatie*). To this circle belonged, among others, not only the passionate preacher Jodocus van Lodensteyn, but also Andreas Essenius and Johannes Hoornbeeck who were professors in theology.[2] The *primus inter pares*, however, was their former teacher and present colleague, Gisbertus Voetius. This experienced minister and former delegate of the Synod of Dort (1618/19) has left his mark on Utrecht University ever since its foundation (1634: Illustrious School; 1636: University). He was especially concerned with the connection between piety and the academic enterprise, a concern already expressed in his inaugural address, which can be seen as a manifesto for his entire work: *Pietas cum scientia coniugenda*. Until his death in 1676 he was dedicated to this goal with reformed zeal, both as a professor and as a minister. Theologians from abroad visiting the influential "Papa Ultrajectinus" sometimes had to wait as Voetius was enthusiastically teaching young orphans from the

---

1. The investigations that resulted in this article were supported by the Foundation for Research in the Field of Philosophy and Theology, which is subsidized by the Netherlands Organization for Scientific Research (NWO).
2. This was the situation between 1651 and early 1653, when Essenius became professor. After that the Van Schurman's stayed in Cologne for one and a half year, and Hoornbeeck left for Leiden in 1664.

catechism.[3]
According to Wilhelm Goeters and Karl Reuter, Voetius's significance
has mainly been practical-theological.[4] We might state, however, that he
has been as important for dogmatic theology. Although he did not write
a dogmatic textbook, he did write works which seem to be of major
importance to the development of dogmatic theology. These works—
extensive disputations on selected subjects—by far surpass that which is
offered in popular textbooks like the *Synopsis purioris theologiae* from
Leiden (1625) and the *Collegium theologicum* of Maresius (1645), both in

3. The standard biography of Voetius is the work of A.C. Duker, *Gisbertus Voetius*, 4
vol. (Leiden 1897–1914; repr. Leiden: Groen, 1989). Additional bibliographic materials
can be found esp. in J. A. Cramer, *De Theologische Faculteit te Utrecht ten tijde van Voetius*,
(Utrecht: Kemink en Zoon N.V.,1932); D. Nauta, "Voetius, Gisbertus," in *Biografisch
lexicon voor de geschiedenis van het nederlandse Protestantisme*, vol. 2, (Kampen: Kok, 1983),
443–49; J. van Oort, ed., *De onbekende Voetius: Voordrachten wetenschappelijk symposium
Utrecht 3 maart 1989* (Kampen: Kok, 1989). The latter study contains two short surveys
of Voetius's theology by C. Graafland ("Voetius als gereformeerde theoloog," 12–31)
and W. van't Spijker ("Voetius practicus," 242–56). For additional surveys, see W. Gass,
Geschichte der Protestantischen Dogmatik in ihrem Zusammenhange mit der Theologie überhaupt,
vol. 1 (Berlin: Georg Reimer, 1854), 454–81; A. de Groot, "Gijsbert Voetius," in Martin
Greschat, ed., *Gestalten der Kirchengeschichte*, 61, vol. 6 (Stuttgart: Kohlhammer), 1982,
149–62; W. van't Spijker, "Gisbertus Voetius (1589–1676)," in T. Brienen a.o., ed., *De
Nadere Reformatie en het Gereformeerd Piëtisme* ('s-Gravenhage: Boekencentrum, 1989),
49–84. Cf. also H. A. van Andel, *De zendingsleer van Voetius* (Kampen: Kok, 1912); M.
Bouwman, *Voetius over het gezag der synoden* (Amsterdam: Bakker, 1937); C. Steenblok,
Voetius en de Sabbat (Hoorn: Edecea, 1941); Jan A. B. Jongeneel, "The Missiology of
Gisbertus Voetius: The First Comprehensive Protestant Theology of Missions," *CTJ* 26
(1991): 47–79; J. A. van Ruler, "New Philosophy to Old Standards: Voetius' Vindication
of Divine Concurrence and Secondary Causality," *NAKG/DRCH* 71 (1991): 58–91;
Johannes van den Berg, "Die Frömmigkeitsbestrebungen in den Niederlanden," in
Martin Brecht, ed., *Der Pietismus vom siebzehnten bis zum frühen achtzehnten Jahrhundert*.
Geschichte des Pietismus 1 (Göttingen: Vandenhoeck & Ruprecht, 1993), 57–112 (esp.
78–88). The most important recent studies on Voetius's theology are: Gisbertus
Voetius, *De praktijk der godzaligheid (TA AΣKHTIKA sive Exercitia pietatis—1664)*, 2 vols.,
ed. C. A. de Niet, Monografieën van Gereformeerd Piëtisme 2 (Utrecht: De Banier,
1995); Johan A. van Ruler, *The Crisis of Causality: Voetius and Descartes on God, Nature and
Change*, Brill's Studies in Intellectual History 66 (Leiden: E. J. Brill, 1995); W. J. van
Asselt and E. Dekker, ed., *De scholastieke Voetius: Een luisteroefening aan de hand van
Voetius's "Disputationes Selectae"* (Zoetermeer: Boekencentrum, 1995).

4. Wilhelm Goeters, *Die Vorbereitung des Pietismus in der reformierten Kirche der
Niederlande bis zur labadistischen Krisis 1670* (Leipzig/Utrecht: J. C. Hinrichs'sche
Buchhandlung, 1911), 61; Karl Reuter, *Wilhelm Amesius, der führende Theologe des
erwachenden reformierten Pietismus*, Beiträge zur Geschichte und Lehre der Reformierten
Kirche 4 (Neukirchen: Neukirchener Verlag, 1940), 10.

scope and depth. Voetius's disputations are not only a model of theology-in-context, but also of ecumenical relevance. J. H. A. Ebrard was right in his remark that Alexander Schweizer could not have maintained his pantheistic-deterministic interpretation of reformed orthodoxy if he had studied the voluminous systematic-theological *oeuvre* of, especially, Voetius.[5] This is a striking remark indeed considering the fact that the supralapsarian theology of Voetius in particular has been branded as Aristotelian and scholastic.

Until the middle of this century most scholars endorsed the view that the inveterate inflexibility of Voetius's Aristotelianism and scholasticism was responsible for his fame as a fervent adversary of the renewing and liberating thought of Descartes. Recent theological and philosophical investigations point in a different direction, however.[6] First of all, it has

5. Cf. Johannes Heinrich August Ebrard, *Christliche Dogmatik*, vol. 1 (Königsberg: August Wilhelm Unzer, 1851), XI–XII, 53, 72–74; 74: "Namentlich die Prädestinationslehre ist gerade bei Gisb. [Voetius] so haarscharf bestimmt, daß jener ganze *Determinismus*, welchen Schweizer als reformirte Lehre darstellen möchte, hier in allen seinen nur möglichen Formen ausdrücklich verworfen wird, (wenn schon die *absolute Prädestination selbst* gelehrt wird.)"; Alexander Schweizer, *Die Glaubenslehre der evangelisch-reformierten Kirche dargestellt und aus den Quellen belegt*, 2 vols. (Zürich: Orell, Füssli und Comp., 1844/1847).

6. For the older research, cf. A. C. Duker, *School-gezag en eigen-onderzoek: Historisch-kritische studie van den strijd tusschen Voetius en Descartes* (Leiden: D. Noothoven van Goor, 1861); Josef Bohatec, *Die cartesianische Scholastik in der Philosophie und reformierten Dogmatik des 17. Jahrhunderts. Teil 1 [alles]: Entstehung, Eigenart, Geschichte und philosophische Ausprägung der cartesianischen Scholastik* (Leipzig 1912; repr., Hildesheim: Olms, 1966); Ernst Bizer, "Die reformierte Orthodoxie und der Cartesianismus," *Zeitschrift für Theologie und Kirche* 55 (1958), 306–72 (English transl. in *Journal for Theology and the Church* 2 (1965), 20–82). The new research was inaugurated by Paul Dibon, *L'Enseignement philosophique dans les universités néerlandaises à l'époque pré-cartésienne (1575–1650)* (Amsterdam: Institut Français d'Amsterdam, 1954); Louise Thijssen-Schoute, *Nederlands cartesianisme*. Avec sommaire et table des matières en français. Verzorgd en van aanvullende bibliografie voorzien door Th. Verbeek (repr. Utrecht: Hes Uitgevers, 1989 (Amsterdam 1954)); Hans-Martin Barth, *Atheismus und Orthodoxie: Analysen und Modelle christlicher Apologetik im 17. Jahrhundert*. Forschungen zur systematischen und ökumenischen Theologie, 26 (Göttingen: Vandenhoeck & Ruprecht, 1971). Decisive for the new interpretation are: Thomas A. McGahagan, "Cartesianism in the Netherlands, 1639–1667; The New Science and the Calvinist Counter-Reformation," Ph.D. Dissertation, University of Pennsylvania, 1976; René Descartes and Martin Schoock, *La Querelle d'Utrecht*. Textes établis, traduits et annotés par Theo Verbeek; préface de Jean-Luc Marion (Paris: Les impressions nouvelles, 1988); Antonie Vos, "Voetius als reformatorisch wijsgeer," in Van Oort, *De onbekende Voetius*, 220–41; Theo Verbeek, "Descartes and the Problem of Atheism: The Utrecht

been shown that the qualification "scholastic" primarily refers to the application of a specific method. This method was developed in the Middle Ages as a sophisticated way of solving problems by "using a system of concepts, distinctions, proposition analyses, argumentation techniques and disputation methods."[7] As such this method is not linked up, materially, with a theological or philosophical position (like Aristotelianism). There are scholastic Cartesians like Abraham Heidanus, Johannes De Raey, Johannes Clauberg and Frans Burman.[8] Secondly, to Voetius and most of his contemporaries Aristotelianism signifies "no more than the articulation of common sense."[9] For Voetius this means, above all, that human knowledge can proceed from empirical reality and the principle of non-contradiction, as both are "guaranteed" by the essential faithfulness of God. He basically objects to Descartes for disrupting the relation between faith and knowledge by his subjective foundation of all knowledge by means of hyperbolical doubt. In this way not only the reliability of God's revelation is undermined, but also the intersubjective academic dialogue and the construction of a "unified science" is fundamentally endangered.

An influential hermeneutic flaw of the older research was that protestant scholastic theology was interpreted against the background of ancient philosophy. In addition to that, the Reformation was interpreted by means of neo-Kantian, neo-orthodox and existentialist anti-metaphysical ideas. In this framework of interpretation the continuity between the Reformation and protestant scholastic theology is practically lost. Continuity only appears if both are seen as emerging from their immediate background which in fact is the theology and *philosophia*

Crisis," *NAKG/DRCH* 71 (1991), 211–23; Verbeek, *Descartes and the Dutch* (Carbondale, Ill.: Southern Illinois University Press, 1992); Verbeek, "From 'Learned Ignorance' to Scepticism: Descartes and Calvinist Orthodoxy," in Richard H. Popkin and Arjo Vanderjagt, eds., *Scepticism and Irreligion in the Seventeenth and Eighteenth Centuries*, Brill's Studies in Intellectual History 37 (Leiden/New York/Köln: E. J. Brill), 1993, 31–45; Van Ruler, *The Crisis of Causality*. Cf. also Aza Goudriaan, "Die Rezeption des cartesianischen Gottesgedanken bei Abraham Heidanus," *Neue Zeitschrift für systematische Theologie und Religionsphilosophie* 38 (1996): 166–97.

7. L. M. de Rijk, *Middeleeuwse wijsbegeerte: Traditie en vernieuwing*, 2nd ed. (Assen: Van Gorcum, 1981), 111 (French translation: *la Philosophie au moyen âge*, Leiden 1985, 85). For the entire theme, cf. Richard A. Muller, "Calvin and the 'Calvinists': Assessing Continuities and Discontinuities between the Reformation and Orthodoxy," *CTJ* 30 (1995), 345–75, and 31 (1996), 125–60; for Voetius in particular, see Van Asselt and Dekker, *DSV*, "Inleiding," 10–25.

8. Cf. Verbeek, *Descartes and the Dutch*, 70–77.

9. Verbeek, *Descartes and the Dutch*, 7.

christiana of the Middle Ages. Recent research has shown that medieval philosophy and theology can be seen as a Christian emancipation of ancient Greek thought. This development can be detected in Thomas Aquinas, but even more clearly in the Augustinian-Franciscan tradition of Alexander of Hales, Bonaventure and Duns Scotus, especially after the condemnation of radical Aristotelianism (Latin Averroism) in 1270 and 1277 (Paris and Oxford). In more recent research the work of Scotus is even considered to be "the second beginning of metaphysics."[10] As a hermeneutic consequence, the study of the Reformation and protestant scholastic theology is presented with three options if one asks to which main stream of late medieval thought a particular author is linked: Thomism, Scotism or nominalism.

Since 1950 various investigators have pointed to the fact that the theology of Calvin resembles the theology of Duns Scotus in essential respects, especially in their emphasis on the divine will.[11] To my mind,

10. Cf. the results of this new research in Norman Kretzmann, Anthony Kenny, and Jan Pinborg, eds., *The Cambridge History of Later Medieval Philosophy: From the Rediscovery of Aristotle to the Disintegration of Scholasticism, 1100–1600* (Cambridge: Cambridge University Press, 1982). For "the second beginning of metaphysics" (Wolfgang Kluxen; Ludger Honnefelder), see E. P. Bos, ed., *John Duns Scotus (1265/6–1308): Renewal of Philosophy*. Elementa, 72 (Amsterdam/Atlanta: Rodopi, forthcoming). Cf. also Antonie Vos Jaczn., *Johannes Duns Scotus*, Kerkhistorische monografieën 2 (Leiden: Groen, 1994); John Duns Scotus, *Contingency and Freedom: Lectura I.39*, with introduction, translation, and commentary by A. Vos Jaczn. a.o. (Dordrecht: Kluwer Academic Publishers, 1994).

11. Cf. François Wendel, *Calvin: Ursprünge und Entwicklung seiner Theologie* (Neukirchen-Vluyn: Neukirchener Verlag 1968), 105–8 (translation of *Calvin, Sources et évolution de sa pensée religieuse* [Paris: Presses Universitaires France, 1950]); Karl Reuter, *Das Grundverständnis der Theologie Calvins: Unter Einbeziehung ihrer geschichtlichen Abhängigkeiten*, Beiträge zur Geschichte und Lehre der Reformierten Kirche 15/1 (Neukirchen-Vluyn: Neukirchener Verlag, 1963), 20–28, 142–54 (via John Major); Alister E. McGrath, "John Calvin and Late Medieval Thought: A Study in Late Medieval Influences upon Calvin's Theological Development," *Archiv für Reformationsgeschichte* 77 (1986): 58–78; Thomas F. Torrance, *The Hermeneutics of John Calvin* (Edinburgh: Scottish Academic Press, 1988), 80–95 (John Major!); David C. Steinmetz, "Calvin and the Absolute Power of God," *The Journal of Medieval and Renaissance Studies* 18 (1988), 65–79, esp. 77–79 (repr. in Steinmetz, *Calvin in Context* [New York/Oxford: Oxford University Press, 1995], 40–52, esp. 49–50); Heiko A. Oberman, *Initia Calvini: The Matrix of Calvin's Reformation*, Mededelingen van de Afdeling Letterkunde, nieuwe reeks, 54/4 (Amsterdam: Koninklijke Nederlandse Academie van Wetenschappen, 1991), 10–19. Alexandre Ganoczy, *Le jeune Calvin: Genèse et évolution de sa vocation réformatrice*, Institut für Europäische Geschichte Mainz 40 (Wiesbaden: Steiner, 1966), denies the influence of John Major on Calvin. But even

the theology of a reformed scholastic like Voetius is faithful to Calvin in this respect. Despite many references to Thomas, the cast of Voetius's doctrine of God is unmistakably more Scotist than Thomistic (while Thomistic thought, in turn, is more Aristotelian than Scotist thought is).[12] This can partly be concluded from this article, which presents a brief reconstruction of Voetius's doctrine of God in its basic structure. The next paragraph (§ 2) will sketch its framework as presented by Voetius. I intend to show, subsequently, that this doctrine is characterized by a modal-ontological model (§ 3) which underlies the basic distinctions of the divine attributes and thus allows for the *contingent* relationship of God's necessary being to his contingent creation (§ 4). This exposition is concluded by some evaluative remarks (§ 5).

II. The Framework of the Doctrine of God

As I have already said, Voetius did not compose a dogmatic system. His doctrine of God can be reconstructed from various texts, most of which can be found in the first and final part of the five extensive volumes of his *Selectae Disputationes*.[13] However, he did compose a survey covering the entire field of dogmatic theology in his *Syllabus problematum*.[14] In conformity with reformed orthodox theology

---

if Ganoczy is correct—the contrary is asserted by McGrath and Torrance—this would not affect the thesis that there is some continuity between Scotus and Calvin.

12. Antonie Vos Jaczn., "De kern van de klassieke gereformeerde theologie: Een traditiehistorisch gesprek," *Kerk en Theologie* 47 (1996): 106–25, has come to the same conclusion for Francis Turretin. For Voetius in relation to the Reformation, see W. J. op 't Hof, "Gisbertus Voetius's evaluatie van de Reformatie," *Theologia Reformata* 32 (1989): 211–42.

13. Gisbertus Voetius, *Selectae disputationes [theologicae]*, 5 vols. (Utrecht [vol. 4: Amsterdam]: Joh. à Waesberge [vol. 5: Ant. Smytegelt], 1648–1669); cited as *Sel. Disp.*

14. Gisbertus Voetius, *Syllabus problematum theologicorum: Quae pro re nata proponi aut perstrinigi solent in privatis publicisque Disputationum, examinum, collationum, consultationum exercitiis. Pars prior* (Utrecht: Aegidius Roman, 1643). This work is a collection of thousands of questions together with their briefly formulated answers. It is meant as an aid for students, to enable them to check to what extent they have mastered the subject. Cf. Van Asselt and Dekker, *DSV*, "Inleiding,"19–20. Additional important sources for Voetius's doctrine of God are his following works: *Thersites Heautontimorumenos: hoc est Remonstrantium Hyperaspistes, catechesi, et liturgiae Germanicae, Gallicae, et Belgicae denuo insultans, retusus* (Utrecht: Abr. ab Herwick and Herm. Ribbius, 1635); *Dissertatio epistolica de termino vitae ad Joh. Beverovicium*, (Utrecht: Esdras Wilhelmus, 1641) (also reprinted as an appendix in *Sel. Disp.* V with own pagenumbers; I cite from this edition as *DTV*); *Disputatio theologica de concursu Dei determinante, an determinabili?* Resp. Matthias Nethenus (Utrecht: Joh. à

Voetius's doctrine of God is preceded by prolegomena and the doctrine of Scripture. It is remarkable, however, that between these two parts a chapter on "The Highest Good or Blessedness" (*"De Summo Bono seu Beatitudine"*) is inserted.[15] Since this theme is discussed immediately before discussing Scripture as principle of knowledge (*principium cognoscendi*) and God as principle of being (*principium essendi*), the enjoyment of the perfect community with God—who Himself is the *summum bonum*—obviously is to Voetius's mind the gate to the entire field of dogmatic theology. So the governing subject of theology is eternal beatitude, and not the divine decrees. This is in accordance with the fact that according to Voetius—who is Scotist in this respect—the nature of the theology of the "viatores" as a whole is practical, which means that it is not a goal in itself, but directed to faith, hope and love.[16]

The doctrine of God itself is divided along lines derived from a scholastic *quaestio*. Voetius poses a number of questions in a specific order. The first main question reads:

1. *An sit Deus?*

The question "whether God exists" is a preliminary one, since there is no point in discussing something which does not exist. For this reason a confirmative answer to this question is a precondition for discussing the next main question:

Waesberge, 1645); *Disputatio Philosophico-Theologica, continens Quaestiones duas, de Distinctione Attributorum divinorum, & Libertate Voluntatis.* Resp. Engelbertus Beeckman (Utrecht: Joh. à Waesberge, 1652); *Disp[utatio] Theol[ogica] de eo quod Deus est.* Resp. Joh. Scriba Moersensis (Utrecht: Meinardus à Dreunen, 1665); *Catechisatie over den Heidelbergschen Catechismus,* 4th. ed. by C. Poudroyen (Dordrecht: Abr. Andriessz, 1662); edited anew by A. Kuyper (Rotterdam: Gebroeders Huge, 1891), esp. 275–312.

15. *Syllabus,* A2r-A4r. Cf. also *Sel. Disp.* II, 1193–228.

16. Cf. *Sel. Disp.* III, 1–3. Voetius's disputations *De theologia practica* are translated in John W. Beardslee III, "Introduction," in John W. Beardslee III, ed., *Reformed Dogmatics: J. Wollebius, G. Voetius, F. Turretin.* A Library of Protestant Thought (New York: Oxford University Press, 1965), 265–334. Cf. also *Catechisatie* 53: Theology is a discipline of living well and blessed here and in eternity. Note the similarity with the definitions of Ramus and Ames. See also the discussion in Richard A. Muller, *Post-Reformation Reformed Dogmatics,* vol. 1: *Prolegomena to Theology* (Grand Rapids: Baker), 215–26.

2. *Quid sit Deus?*

Asking "what God is"—asking for God's "whatness" (*quidditas*) or essence—
we are dependent on the names and attributes by which God has revealed
himself. The proper name *par excellence* is the tetragrammaton *yhwh* (Ex.
3:14) signifying, for Voetius, "the primary, eternal and immutable essence
of God" in an exclusive way.[17] After these questions the doctrine of the
Trinity is discussed. This doctrine is the answer to the question:

3. *Quis sit Deus?*

Voetius emphasizes that only the dogma of the Trinity expresses "who
God is." For this reason this doctrine belongs to the articles of faith.
These three questions and their answers are followed by discussing the

4. *Decreta Dei* [*i.e.*, the divine decisions, his immanent or
intramental and thus eternal acts of volition].[18]

Here Voetius draws on a classic model. The first two questions posed in this
context have their origin, formally, in the Aristotelian theory of science.
Together with the third question they build a scheme which can already be
found in John of Damascus.[19] Next, Voetius discusses God's decrees, and
here he follows the Augustinian-Franciscan tradition emphasizing the key
role of God's acts of will. We shall see, moreover, that the divine acts of
volition already play an important part in Voetius's discussion of the divine
attributes, which pertains to the second question (see § 4 of this article).

---

17. For *yhwh* see *Sel. Disp.* V, 51–57, esp. 52: "Est nomen subjectivum, et non epitheticon
seu per modum epitheti: proprium, non appellativum, nec metaphoricum. Significat non
tantum officium et dignitatem, sed etiam essentiam Dei primam, aeternam, immutabilem:
quia ipse in se et per se est, independenter scil. a quocunque alio [ ], et omnium entium ac
existentium causa est; quia essentia et existentia omnium rerum, accidentium, actionum ab
illo dependet." Cf. also I, 228. Following Zanchi Voetius analyzes the biblical proper name
yhwh much more extensively than e.g. Aquinas in his *Summa theologiae* I q. 13 a. 11.

18. Cf. *Syllabus* D1r-K1v; *Sel. Disp.* I, 478. It should be noted that the doctrine of
providence and predestination *proper* are not treated until later, when the *extramental*
divine acts are discussed. The doctrine of providence follows the doctrine of creation,
whereas the doctrine of predestination and covenant are not treated until the
soteriological second part of the *Syllabus* (cf. *Syllabus* T4v-Z2r; Hh1r-Ii1v).

19. Cf. E. P. Meijering, *Reformierte Scholastik und patristische Theologie: Die Bedeutung
des Väterbeweises in der Institutio Theologiae Elencticae F. Turrettins unter besonderer
Berücksichtigung der Gotteslehre und Christologie* (Nieuwkoop: De Graaf, 1991), 101, 174.

We should not draw the wrong conclusions from this framework. One might think, for instance, that the *proofs* for God's existence discussed in the context of the first question lay the foundation of the doctrine of God in order to construe a "natural theology" in a rationalistic way. It is remarkable in this regard, however, that Voetius stresses the fact that the believer does not need any proof of God.[20] Yet this does not take away the fact that the non-believer who denies—or hyperbolically doubts—the truth of the proposition *Deus est* violates his own epistemological capacity which is a gift of God *(cognitio Dei insita)*. Moreover, it follows from the principle of non-contradiction that the proposition *Deus est* is either true or false. Departing from the traditional concept of God as the most perfect necessary being, the truth or falsity of the proposition *Deus est* is necessary itself. This means that the non-believer would have to maintain that the concept of God is inconsistent, which is an absurdity for anyone whose thinking follows faith in search of understanding *(fides quaerens intellectum)*.[21]

Another premature conclusion from the order in which Voetius presents the doctrine of God would be, that the doctrine of the Trinity is supposed to be overshadowed by the doctrine of divine attributes. It should be noticed, however, that both doctrines are inextricably connected, for the principle of division simply is that the properties common to the three persons are discussed before their personal properties. Thus from the very beginning the triune God is in fact envisaged. Like Turrettini, à Marck and Van Rijssen in a later period, Voetius considers the doctrine of the Trinity to be of great importance; he extensively argues against the Socinians that it is necessary for salvation and therefore one of the fundamental articles of faith.[22] Besides, Voetius claims that this doctrine too cannot be inconsistent, since God is one and three *in different respects*. In spite of the fact, however, that the consistency of the Trinitarian dogma can be shown, the mystery remains. For one thing the "how" of the Trinitarian relations

20. *Sel. Disp.* I, 167; V, 48–49.

21. Voetius, *Disp[utatio]. Theol[ogica]. de eo quod Deus est*, A2r-A3r, A4v; *Sel. Disp.* I, 141; V, 459–60.

22. Cf. *Sel. Disp.* I, 466–519 ("De Necessitate et Utilitate Dogmatis de S.S. Trinitate"); esp. 478: "Cognitio et fides, quis sit unus ille verus Deus, habet usum et praxin verae religionis (Christianae scil.) immo magnam ejus partem facit; nec omnis ejus praxis haberi aut absolvi potest cognitione *tou* quod et quid sit verus Deus. Iam vero solum dogma de Trinitate tradit, quis sit verus Deus." (*Tou* is greek—in transliteration—signifying that the subsequent phrase is to be read as a genitive).

exceeds our understanding.[23]

From the structure of the doctrine of God as presented by Voetius we can conclude that the Trinitarian God is presupposed by the doctrine of divine decrees. This means, among other things, that in those respects in which Christ is characterized as *logos asarkos,* God's decisions must also have a christological—and *mutatis mutandis* a pneumatological—foundation. Moreover, God's essential attributes, like his goodness, justice and veracity also precede his decrees. This twofold precedence is sufficient to rule out the (still influential) thesis of Schleiermacher's pupil Alexander Schweizer, that the eternal predestinarian decree is considered to be the "Centraldogma" and axiomatic governing principle of orthodox reformed theology, in virtue of which it is supposed to have build a synthethic, deductive and inviolable system.[24] Even apart from the remarkable anachronism, this interpretation is characterized by some categorical mistakes. Even if the decree were ontologically basic in all respects—and of course it is not, regarding, for one thing, God's essential attributes—this would not entail that it is fundamental in the epistemological sense and hence as self-evident as for instance the principle of non-contradiction is.[25] For this reason reformed scholastics will say that we can only know God's decision to the extent that he has revealed it. Thus, there is no other basis for salutary theology than divine revelation. Consequently, Scripture is the primary *principium cognoscendi,* God the *principium essendi.*[26]

---

23. Like Calvin and most reformed theologians Voetius is very reluctant with respect to the medieval theories concerning psychological analogies of the *processiones.* He tends to favour the sophisticated and nuanced opinion of Scotus, however; cf. *Sel. Disp.* V, 136–47.

24. Cf. Richard A. Muller, *Christ and the Decree: Christology and Predestination in Reformed Theology from Calvin to Perkins,* Studies in Historical Theology 2 (1986; Repr., Grand Rapids: Baker, 1988), 1–9.

25. Cf. the similar observations of Paul Helm, "Calvin (and Zwingli) on Divine Providence," *CTJ* 29 (1994): 388–405 (esp. 388–90).

26. See *Sel. Disp.* II, 533 (note the *Errata* at the end of the volume). The secondary principle of knowing is the *lumen rectae rationis* which is, roughly, our capacity for argumentation, cf. *Thersites,* 174; *Sel. Disp.* III, 846; V, 512; I, 7; cf. also the discussion by Muller, *PRRD,* 1:295–311. By the way, Richard Muller has intensely searched for a specimen of such a "decree-theology" and has finally found one in Pierre Poiret's *L'Oeconomie divine, ou système universel* (1678). Ironically, this is a Cartesian work dominated by the idea that everything is caused by divine decision, and will end in universal atonement. Cf. Richard A. Muller, "Found (No Thanks To Theodore Beza): One 'Decretal' Theology," *CTJ* 32 (1997): 145–53, and cf. also Muller, "The Myth of

The main thesis of my article is that for Voetius the doctrine of decrees does not entail a deductive, necessitarian theological system, but on the contrary, is meant to avoid the conclusion that created reality and the history of salvation emanates from God's being. The decretal acts of the divine will are expression of the decisive aspect of freedom in the divine being and as such involve a distinction between a necessary and a contingent dimension within the divine attributes. In the history of the doctrine of God the Voetian doctrine of decrees avoids both essentialism (Thomism) and extreme voluntarism (nominalism). In order to clarify this thesis we need to pay attention to Voetius's modal-ontological model first.

III. The Key Concept of "Synchronic Contingency"

In the *Syllabus problematum* the following question is used, for students, as a means of testing whether they are able to argue for the right answer:

> Is it possible for God to do that which he does not do, or to leave that which he does?

Voetius replies: "We affirm with a distinction."[27] This means, first of all, that he affirms that God *can* do things which he does not do. Voetius adds that this statement needs further explication ("with a distinction"). This explication is not given in the *Syllabus* itself; but in the fifth part of the *Selectae Disputationes,* defending his confirmative answer against objections of Maresius, Voetius refers to it. The explication runs as follows. The answer is positive if the question is read "in the divided sense," and negative if read "in the composite sense."[28] Here Voetius uses a syntactical "instrument" from the scholastic method. Elsewhere he remarks that this instrument is an excellent aid for theology; by referring to the Hispanic Roman Catholic theologian Diego Alvarez (d. 1635) he indicates how exactly this distinction should be understood.[29] Against the

---

'Decretal Theology,'" *CTJ* 30 (1995): 159–67.

27. Voetius, *Syllabus,* G1v: "An Deus possit facere quae non facit vel praetermittere quae facit? A[ffirmatur] cum D[istinctione]."

28. Voetius, *Sel. Disp.* V, 115: "*Resp[ondetur].* In sensu composito. *Neg[atur].* In sensu diviso, *Aff[irmatur].*"

29. Voetius, *Sel. Disp.* II, 369. Voetius refers to Didacus Alvarez, *De auxiliis divinae gratiae, et humani arbitrii viribus, et libertate, ac legitima eius cum efficaci eorundum auxiliorum concordia* (Köln: Petrus Henningius, 1621), lib. 2, cap. 11, n. 1–6, p. 234–41. See esp. n. 4, p. 238–39: "Sicut enim dicimus: *Album potest esse nigrum*; in sensu composito non significamus, quod *albedo* sit aut esse

background of these remarks Voetius's answer can be reconstructed:
Read in "the composite sense" a positive answer to the question would lead to the statement that

1. God has the possibility of (simultaneously doing p and not-doing p).

This reading cannot possibly be true since the sentence between brackets in fact is a contradiction. There can be a different reading, however. Taken in "the divided sense" the statement says that

2. God does p, and he has simultaneously the possibility of not-doing p.

In this sense the statement is true. Applying this distinction, Voetius in fact follows Scotus's innovative concept of synchronic contingency showing that a contingent state of affairs (for instance, "God's doing p") does not exclude the synchronic *possibility* of the opposite state of affairs ("God's not-doing p").[30] Voetius, moreover, frequently uses the Scotist

---

possit seorsum in aliquo subiecto; vel *nigredo* sit aut esse possit in aliquo subiecto; sed sensus est, quod *albedo* et *nigredo* simul sint compossibiles in eodem subiecto: et propterea propositio illa in sensu composito est falsa, quia impossibile est, quod aliquid simul sit *album* et *nigrum*.." Cf also n. 6, p. 240–41: "Ex quo apparet, Concilium Tridentinum esse intelligendum in sensu diviso, cum definit, liberum hominis arbitrium a Deo motum, et excitatum posse dissentire, si velit: nam sensus compositus illius propositionis est, haec duo simul esse compossibilia: *Motio Dei efficax ad consentiendum est in libero hominis arbitrio, et nihil[ominus] dissentiri*; qui sensus est falsus. Unde non potuit esse a Concilio intentus: sensus autem divisus illius definitionis est, quod liberum arbitrium, *etiam pro instanti, quo movetur* a Deo efficaciter ad consensum, retinet veram facultatem et potentiam, qua potest dissentire si velit, quod sufficit ad libertatem, quam adversus Lutheranos intendebat statuere Concilium; nam libertas consistit in facultate ad utrumlibet oppositorum, nimirum ad velle, et nolle divisive, non autem ad velle, et nolle simul habenda; nam id est impossibile." Note especially "etiam pro instanti, quo movetur" (= synchronically), my emphasis; for the Council of Trent cf. *DS* 1554 (= can. 4). Note the oecumenical relevance of Voetius's acceptance of that distinction. For Alvarez see Jean-François Genest, *Prédétermination et liberté créée à Oxford au XIVe siècle: Buckingham contre Bradwardine*, Études de philosophie médiévale 70 (Paris: Libraire philosophique J. Vrin, 1992), 160–61, 168–70. Genest, though not referring to the place in Alvarez, shows by referring to other places that Alvarez, like Thomas Bradwardine, uses the Scotist concept of synchronic contingency.

30. See *Contingency and Freedom*, 23–36; 112–41; cf. Andreas J. Beck, "Divine Psychology and Modalities: Scotus's Theory of the Neutral Proposition," in Bos, ed., *John Duns Scotus* (forthcoming). The distinction between *in sensu diviso* and *in sensu composito* stems from Aristotle, but is not taken in the synchronic sense until Scotus. Cf. also Tilman Ramelow, *Gott, Freiheit, Weltenwahl: Der Ursprung des Begriffes der besten aller möglichen Welten in der Metaphysik der Willensfreiheit zwischen Antonio Perez S. J. (1599–1649) und G. W. Leibniz (1646–1716)*, Brill's Studies in Intellectual History 72 (Leiden

idea of distinct structural moments *(instantia naturae* or *signa rationis)* within isolated temporal moments or the one indivisible "moment of eternity" *(nunc aeternitatis).*[31] Thus the diverse categories of time and modality, which were merged in Aristotle's ontological model, are properly disconnected. It is not unimportant to observe that historically, the difference between (1) and (2) is rejected by William of Ockham and Gabriel Biel, whereas Gregory of Rimini and in particular Thomas Bradwardine elaborate on it. These last two theologians, in turn, seem to have influenced Calvin. There is also a clear link between Gregory and Peter Martyr Vermigli, and, more importantly, it was no less than William Twisse who was responsible for the first printed edition of Bradwardine's *De causa Dei* in 1618.[32]

If time and modality are "unlocked" or "unchained," it follows not only that God's decision can be shown to be eternal yet contingent, but also that a state of affairs is not supposed to (diachronically) change its modal status any more. By this nuanced view Voetius is enabled to refute the Remonstrants who claim that the divine decree would suspend the difference between what is possible and what is impossible, and would destroy the contingency in things. According to Voetius God's decision does not break the synchronically contingent structure of reality. In other words, if something has been decided and is contingent, then its not-being or being-differently is simultaneously possible. For example, at this moment you, as a reader, are factually reading this article; yet you could have been walking in the woods at this very same moment. The act by which God decides does not determine what is possible, for if something is possible, then it is consistent and therefore necessarily possible, and if something is impossible, then it is necessarily inconsistent (see also the denial of (1)). God's decree does determine what is actual, yet without removing the possibility of its opposite and the free causality of the human will.[33]

---

etc.: Brill, 1997); this study, valuable as it is, suffers from an incorrect reading of the Scotist explanation of the divided and composite sense (p. 11–12, 50).

31. Cf. *Sel. Disp.* I, 246, 249, and A. J. Beck and E. Dekker, "Gods kennis en wil," in Van Asselt and Dekker, *De scholastieke Voetius*, 48.

32. Cf. Genest, *Prédétermination*, esp. 147–50 (Bradwardine, Ockham, Gregory); 157–63 (Twisse). Not only Twisse, but also many Roman-catholic theologians welcomed *De causa Dei*. P. Gonzalez e.g. ironically remarks that in this work both the errors of the Pelagians and those of the Lutherans and the Calvinists are avoided (163). For Calvin and Vermigli, see McGrath, "John Calvin," 58–78.

33. Cf. *DTV* 38, 77, 101–9 (modal-ontological questions) and *DTV* 109–16 (freedom of will). Cf. also *Quaestiones duae,* A43-B1v; *De concursu Dei,* D1r-D3r; *Sel. Disp.* V, 229–30.

IV. The Unfolding: *Theologia Necessaria* and *Theologia Contingens*

The modal-ontological model of synchronic contingency and necessity, synchronic possibility and impossibility enables Voetius to do justice both to the necessity of God's being and the contingency of his acts. In Voetius's doctrine of God a necessary dimension—that is, God in his essential being—is distinct yet inseparable from a contingent dimension—that is, God in relation to created reality. Using Scotist terminology we might say that Voetius's doctrine of God is structured by the distinction between *theologia necessaria* (the divine essence) and *theologia contingens* (the divine acts).[34]

One of the major reasons for Voetius to adopt this dichotomy of a necessary and contingent dimension is his intention to acknowledge the biblical data concerning God and created reality. Adhering to the classical tradition Voetius maintains the view that God's existence and essential attributes are necessary and immutable. Yet, important theological concepts like sin, guilt and responsibility as well as grace, incarnation, forgiveness and love would lose their meaning if created reality necessarily emanated from God's being and could not have been different from what it is. Necessitarianism must therefore be rejected and the doctrine of God cannot imply determinism.

We shall see that the distinction between *theologia necessaria* and *theologia contingens* underlies both the division of the divine attributes and, more clearly, other basic distinctions on which Voetius insists. Concerning the first point, Voetius clearly admits of different divisions.[35] There is one condition, however: Attributes which are not related to created reality must be fundamentally distinguished from attributes which are somehow related to creation and thus are principles of divine acts *(operationes)*.[36] The

---

34. For this distinction in Scotus, see his *Ordinatio*, prologus pars 3 q. 1–3 n. 169–71, esp. n. 171 (ed. Vat. I, 112–14); cf. pars 4 q. 1–2 n. 210–13 (ed. Vat. I, 144–46); pars 5 q. 1–2 n. 350 (ed. Vat. I, 226–27); *Lectura*, prologus pars 3 q. 1 n. 111–18 (ed. Vat. XVI, 40–43); pars 4 q. 1–2 n. 172 (ed. Vat. XVI, 57). Cf. also Johannes Duns Scotus, *Teksten over God en werkelijkheid*, tr., intr., and comm. by A. Vos Jaczn. a.o., 18–28 (English translation is in progress).

35. *Sel. Disp.* V, 63; the division presented below is also borrowed from this passage. In his *Syllabus*, D2r-G3r; *Catechisatie*, 291–309; *Sel. Disp.* I, 226; cf. 246, 403 somewhat different divisions are used by Voetius.

36. Cf. *Sel. Disp.* I, 246. The non-related attributes, roughly, coincide with what Voetius calls "negative predicates" *(via negationis)* elsewhere, and the "somehow" related attributes comprise both the positive attributes *(via eminentiae)* and the relative attributes proper *(via causalitatis)* of the two other Pseudo-Dionysian ways, cf. *Sel. Disp.* V, 60–61;

attributes of the first class are derived from God's unity *(unitas)*, infinity *(infinitas)* and immutability *(immutabilitas)*. They belong to the divine essence and are regulative with respect to the acts pertaining to the attributes of the second class which belong to the divine life.[37] This second class includes, among other attributes, God's knowledge *(scientia)*, God's will *(voluntas)*, God's righteousness and justice *(ius et iustitia)* and God's power *(potentia)* (the list is not complete). By means of his word God, the *summum bonum*,[38] has revealed himself to human beings as having these and other properties. In a very brief way Voetius can say what God essentially is (referring to Joh. 4:24): a Spirit or an infinite spiritual being.[39]

It can be shown that the basic distinction between necessity and contingency indeed underlies in a way Voetius's interpretation of all these properties. This is already the case in the first class of attributes, for in Voetius's interpretation this class not only represents to a large extent the necessary dimension, but also supplies the *conditions* of the possibility of the contingent dimension which, in turn, mainly emerges in the second class.[40] In some cases, moreover, even in the first class the contingent dimension is present.[41]

1. According to Voetius's division the first attribute of the first class is

---

I, 277, 243, 435. The positive attributes appear to be related to the aspect of the possibility of creation whereas the relative attributes are related to the aspect of the actuality of the same creation.

37. Cf. *Sel. Disp.* I, 403 with 380. This distinction between the divine essence and the divine life goes back at least to Aquinas (cf. *Summa theologiae*. I q. 18) and was further elaborated by Scotus and adopted by Suárez and Arminius, cf. the substantial discussion in Richard A. Muller, *God, Creation, and Providence in the Thought of Jacob Arminius: Sources and Directions of Scholastic Protestantism in the Era of Early Orthodoxy* (Grand Rapids: Baker, 1991), 114–27. According to Muller, "the Reformed writers of the seventeenth century—with notable exceptions, like the semi-Cartesian federalist, Heidanus—tended away from the classification of attributes into those of essence and those of life" (123). Voetius, then, is another "notable exception" in this respect. Besides, Voetius not only defended (against Maresius) the expression of Ames that there are divine attributes *quasi in esse secundo*, but he also used the language of two "moments" *(momenta)* of the divine nature, as Arminius did. Cf. *Sel. Disp.* V, 61, 583–84; I, 403.

38. Cf. *Syllabus* G2r; *Sel. Disp.* I, 576; III, 81.

39. *Catechisatie* 281; cf. 292. Cf. *Sel. Disp.* V, 62. A similar "definition" is given by Polanus. According to reformed scholastics God cannot be defined in the proper sense, since for a proper definition a genus and a specifying difference must be pointed out. God in his transcendence, however, cannot have such predicaments. Keckermann, Polanus and Voetius found a "solution" to this problem by speaking of a *quasi genus* and a *quasi differentia*, *Sel. Disp.* V, 61–62.

40. Cf. below, (1) and (3).

41. Cf. below, (2).

unity. One of the aspects of unity, however, is simplicity. *Simplicitas* only excludes what must be excluded when we speak about God. This means that simplicity excludes every distinction of extremes which are different in such a way that their coexistence in God would introduce a composition and hence, would entail that he would have to be composed by a cause outside himself.[42] However, the distinction of the divine attributes which are inseparable both from one another and from God's one being does *not* have to be excluded. Voetius speaks of a conceptual distinction rooted in God himself, especially in his relation to created reality. With this distinction Voetius, like Francisco Suárez whose terminology he has borrowed in this case, comes close to the Scotist formal distinction (*distinctio formalis ex natura rei*).[43] If the notion of simplicity were to exclude even this kind of distinction, there would be no room for the distinction of contingency and necessity either.

2. Let us turn to a second attribute pertaining to the first class of divine attributes: infinity. Although infinity is not a property which entails some action, it clearly shows a necessary as well as a contingent dimension. Infinity proper is a non-relational attribute (*absoluta*). However, in relation to space it is called immensity (*immensitas* or *immensurabilitas*) and in relation to time it is called eternity (*aeternitas*). Now it is possible that God would not have created the actual world and its space or would have created a different world with different space. So there are not only different possible worlds, but also possible spaces. Divine immensity and eternity, then, must be related to all possible spaces. Here we encounter the necessary dimension of these properties.[44]

---

42. Voetius, *Sel. Disp.* I, 229: "*Quarta,* [simplicitatem Deo competere probamus] quia dato in Deo esse extrema tam distincta ut compositionem ingredi possunt, tamen non possent inter se uniri et coalescere, nisi per actionem alicuius causae efficientis. Atqui ubi et quae est illa causa prior et superior Deo, quae Dei substantiam componeret?" So a composition of corporeal parts, of subject and accidens, of genus and difference and of essence and existence are excluded. Cf. *Sel. Disp.* I, 227, 229–30.

43. Cf. Voetius, *Sel. Disp.* I, 232–41; V, 59–63; *Quaestiones duae*, A2r-A3v. Voetius speaks of a *distinctio rationis ratiocinatae* cq. *ex natura rei virtualis*, "[quae] coincide[t] fere cum Scoti dicta distinctione *Ex natura rei formali.*" (V, 60). Cf. Suárez, *Disputationes metaphysicae*, VII.i.iv–viii (ed. Vivès, tom. 25, 231a–32b).

44. Although Voetius' doctrine can be transposed into a modern modal-ontological model, he does not use the concept of "possible world" in the sense of modern possible worlds semantics. For Voetius a possible world is not a maximal and consistent set of states of affairs—however cf. *Sel. Disp.* I, 293–95—but a Ptolemaic cosmic system. Voetius argues (against Maresius) that there can be two or more such systems actual at the same time. Extrapolating this conception to possible worlds semantics and leaving

In relation to actual space, however, not immensity, but ubiquity or omnipresence *(ubiquitas, omnipraesentia)* is ascribed to God. Here we find their contingent dimension.[45]

3. Turning to the third attribute of the first class of divine attributes, immutability, we observe that Voetius breaks the Aristotelean connection of necessity and immutability. If this connection were to be maintained, a contingent dimension of being could not be acknowledged for God. For this would entail that God can change through time, which would imply an imperfection. Obviously, Voetius intends to say that God's will is not only free and contingent, but also unchangeable. For this reason he disconnects necessity and immutability, which in itself is an implication of his—and Scotus's—model of synchronic contingency. This disconnection offers another example which runs against Aristotelian logic and physics; yet it is in accordance with both medieval and contemporary modal logic.[46]

For the second class of attributes—consisting of God's knowledge, will, justice and power—the distinction between necessity and contingency appears to be even more vital. As has been said above, turning to these properties we turn to God as a being who acts. Before taking them separately we should pay attention to Voetius's discussion of a major preliminary issue. The divine acts, he says, must be distinguished in acts *ad intra,* directed to God himself (like "knowing himself") and acts *ad extra,* directed to his creation (like "knowing creatures"). In both cases these acts are *in mente divina;* as such they take place in eternity *(actiones immanentes seu internae)*. They are distinct from God's extramental, external acts performed in time *(actiones emanantes seu externae)*, like "creating the world."[47] Now the important thing is that the distinction between necessity and contingency does not coincide with that of the intramental and extramental dimension of God's acts, but with that of

---

out the incorrectness of Ptolemaic cosmology, we might say that every consistent set of several Voetian cosmic systems would constitute a proper possible world. For this aspect in Scotus cf. Vos a.o., *Contingency and Freedom*, 28–33 and Beck, "Divine Psychology," 127–37.

45. Cf. Voetius, *Sel. Disp.* V, 66–85 (esp. 66); cf. 119–31 ("An per absolutam Dei potentiam, plures mundi produci possint") and 132–36 ("De praesentia seu ubietate Dei ante mundi creationem"). It may be surprising that Voetius distinguishes between God's relation to possible and actual spaces, and not between God's relation to possible and actual times (which would be analogous).

46. Cf. Voetius, *Syllabus,* E3v, F1v-F2v; cf. *DTV* 105–9.

47. Voetius, *Sel. Disp.* I, 403; V, 115; cf. I, 240 and 246.

their *ad intra* and *ad extra* dimension. The extramental dimension is contingent, but the intramental *ad extra* dimension is contingent as well; only the intramental *ad intra* dimension of God's being and attributes is necessary.[48] Again we see that logical modalities are disconnected from succession in time. A clear distinction between intramental and *ad intra* acts is needed to avoid serious complications, like Vorstius and some Remonstrants and Socinians have experienced.[49]

We now turn to the attributes of divine knowledge, will, justice and power separately in order to see how they can be elucidated against the background of the distinction between necessity and contingency.

1. A being having perfect knowledge must be omniscient. In his doctrine of God's omniscience Voetius breaks with the Aristotelian correspondence or even equivalence of thinking and being. In God's case this equivalence would imply that everything that God *can* think of, must actually exist. To Voetius' mind, however, this would contradict the idea of a creator, who creates in a contingent way. Voetius in fact distinguishes two aspects of divine knowing by recurring to a classical medieval distinction. Terminologically, Voetius adopts this distinction from Aquinas, but materially he takes it in a Scotist sense: God has *knowledge of unqualified intelligence* (*scientia simplicis intelligentiae*) and *visionary knowledge* (*scientia visionis*).[50] The first kind of divine knowledge is knowledge of all possibilities; the second, of the entire actual reality. So the rationale of the two dimensions of divine knowledge is the difference between possible and actual states of affairs. Again a distinction in a divine property (here the property of knowing perfectly) is ultimately

48. The structure of acts which pertain to the three divine persons in common (*actiones communes*) corresponds to the structure of acts which—either *proprie* or *per appropriationem*—pertain to a specific divine person (*actiones notionales seu personales*), cf. *Sel. Disp.* I, 403; V, 115. In this respect the doctrine of God is, as a whole, a doctrine of the Trinity.

49. Cf. Voetius, *Sel. Disp.* V, 113–15; I, 249–41. They attempt to harmonize God's *necessitas essendi* with God's *libertas agendi* by introducing a *distinctio realis* in God. Notably Voetius seems to share their basic intention on this point; he "only" rejects their solutions.

50. There is no uniform translation of these technical terms available, let alone a translation which would clearly convey its systematic content. Aquinas confines the *scientia simplicis intelligentiae* to possible things which will never become actual, see *Summa Theologiae*, I q. 14 a. 9. Unlike most orthodox reformed theologians Aquinas does not define these two kinds of knowledge in terms of the will choosing from all possibilities (known in the *scientia simplicis intelligentiae*) those possibilities that become factual (known in the *scientia visionis*).

derived from that between the necessary and the contingent. This can be illuminated by Voetius's claim that God knows more states of affairs than the actual ones since there are more possibilities than the ones that are actualized. Now how does a possible state of affairs become actual? Voetius answers: by the will of God. From the infinite number of possible states of affairs the actual ones are chosen by God. So the two aspects of divine knowledge are in fact interlocked by God's will.[51]

In virtue of this distinction God can be seen as a maximally omniscient being without the implication that actual reality necessarily emanates from this omniscience. God remains the free creator of reality. His act of will is contingent, and in his act of knowing a necessary dimension must be distinguished from a contingent dimension. God's necessary knowledge not only of his own being, but also of the range of all possibilities is the necessary dimension of divine knowing, for in Voetius's modal-ontological model modalities are iterative, which means that the possible necessarily is possible. God, therefore, necessarily knows the necessary, and contingently knows the contingent. Voetius sometimes even speaks of "necessary knowledge" *(scientia necessaria)* and "free knowledge" *(scientia libera).*[52] Since Voetius considers these two categories of knowing to be exhaustive, there is no need of supposing a third category, as was proposed by Molina in his concept of middle knowledge *(scientia media)*, a concept which was adopted, among others, by Arminius.[53] In a comprehensive disputation Voetius tries to show that in a sense God's contingent act of will is also constitutive for his knowledge of conditional future contingents, because there is a counterfactual divine decree which is an alternative to his actual decision.[54] According to Voetius, moreover, the theory of middle knowledge implies a restriction to God's freedom which introduces the "stoic fate" and eliminates human freedom.[55]

---

51. Cf. Voetius, *Sel. Disp.* I, 246–54, and esp. V, 85–91 with the translation and commentary in Beck and Dekker, "Gods kennis en wil," 34–54.

52. Voetius, *Sel. Disp.* I, 247–48. Voetius also uses another conceptual pair: *scientia indefinita—definita*, which can be related to the Scotist "theory of the neutral proposition." Cf. Beck, "Divine Psychology," 123–37.

53. For this concept, cf. Eef Dekker, "Was Arminius a Molinist?," *Sixteenth Century Journal* 27 (1996): 337–52.

54. Voetius, *Sel. Disp.* I, 285–339 ("De conditionata seu media in Deo scientia," in 4 sections; the original (co)-author is Matthias Nethenus), esp. 293–95. The explanation given by Gass, *Geschichte der protestantischen Dogmatik*, 467–71, is confusing.

55. Cf. Voetius, *Sel. Disp.* I, 331–38 ; *DTV* 47–48, 50 –51, 66, 101, 105–8, 133.

2. As in God's knowledge, in God's will there is a distinction derived from two kinds of objects. On the one hand God necessarily wills himself and all that is necessary by means of a voluntary affirmation; on the other hand he contingently wills all that is contingent.[56]

3. In divine righteousness *(ius)* and justice *(iustitia)* a similar structure can be discerned. God necessarily is a just or righteous God. Yet, justice *(iustitia)* is a relational concept. As such, however, it is rooted in "what is right" *(ius)*. Divine justice means, therefore, that God's willing and acting are in accordance with what is right, like it is in accordance with what is good, holy and pure.[57] Voetius extensively argues for the idea that divine righteousness is not only immutable, but also necessary. This means that God cannot *de potentia absoluta* will to command or do something which contradicts this righteousness. As a consequence God cannot even will to be capable of doing such a thing, for if God could will that, it would inevitably entail a contradiction, which simply is impossible.[58] For example, it contradicts divine natural righteousness *(ius divinum naturale)* that God would invite to sin, or that he would inflict the torments of hell upon an innocent human being. Another example: because of his natural righteousness God cannot simply forgive a sinner without *satisfactio;* however, he can punish our sins in someone who is innocent and freely consents to that. This idea is a corner stone of Voetius's christological doctrine of vicarious atonement *(satisfactio vicaria).*[59]

Remarkably, Voetius's emphasis on the divine will does not entail extreme voluntarism. God's acts of will are navigated by his natural righteousness which is necessarily anchored in his nature. Whatever springs from this righteousness is not just or right because God wants it, but God wants it because it is right or just. However, there is also a contingent righteousness or law *(ius divinum positivum)*. In this respect Voetius's view differs from the Thomistic doctrine of divine eternal law *(lex aeterna)*; in fact, here Voetius explicitly follows Scotus and explains that *this* righteousness does depend on God's will.[60] Anything that is derived from this righteousness is therefore right because God wills it. An example of this law is the fourth commandment demanding that every seventh day should be sanctified. Anyone denying the contingency

---

56. Cf. Voetius, *Syllabus*, F1v-F2v.
57. Cf. Voetius, *Sel. Disp.* I, 357–69.
58. Cf. Voetius, *Sel. Disp.* I, 365–72; V, 92–98.
59. Cf. Voetius, *Sel. Disp.* I, 351–53.
60. Cf. Voetius, *Sel. Disp.* I, 345–51.

of this commandment, as Maresius is supposed to have done according to Voetius, is obliged to prove that sanctifying every sixth or eighth day is contradictory and hence impossible. Being a sabbath, however, is not an essential feature of any day, but a feature that can contingently be assigned to a specific day.[61]

4. Finally, if we turn to divine power or omnipotence, we find another illustration of a property in which a necessary and contingent dimension are distinguished. Voetius resumes the view that with respect to God's power we must distinguish between God's absolute power *(potentia absoluta)* and his ordained power *(potentia ordinata)*. In virtue of his absolute power God can do everything that does not entail a contradiction and does not contradict his nature. For instance, God cannot die, he cannot change or lie (Voetius is convinced, like Ambrose, Augustine and Aquinas, that these possibilities do not reflect a power, but a weakness). The *potentia absoluta* has nothing to do with capriciousness or arbitrariness, for his essential attributes, like goodness, belong to the same necessary dimension of God's being as his disposal over illimited possibilities belongs. For this reason God can never act *inordinate*. Although he can act in a way different from the actual and contingent order, every alternative order of divine acting can only be in accordance with his essential goodness, righteousness, veracity etc. Here too the decisive mediation between absolute and ordained power is the divine will. For Voetius, as for Scotus, the range of the *potentia absoluta* is everything that *can* be willed by God, whereas the range of the *potentia ordinata* is the actually willed, synchronic contingent order in which God has organized his acts.[62]

---

61. *Sel. Disp.* V, 94–113 (for the example see esp. 97–100); 98: "Sunt enim illa [quae 4. 5. 6. 8 praeceptis decalogi praescribuntur] et manent juris moralis ac perpetui, et consequenter naturalis, quamvis proxime ac immediate libero Dei beneplacito, et non ex necessitate naturae Divinae praescripta sint, et ideo juste sint, quia Deo voluit; qui tamen absque implicatione oppositum velle et alicui mandare posset." The resemblance with Scotus is striking, see Allan B. Wolter (transl. and selection), *Duns Scotus on the Will and Morality* (Washington D.C.: The Catholic University of America Press, 1986), 1–29, 47–75, 239–318.

62. Cf. *Sel. Disp.* V, 113–23; I, 402–34; and esp. 402–9. This text is discussed by Gijsbert van den Brink, "Gods almacht," in Van Asselt and Dekker, *De scholastieke Voetius*, 55–85.

V. Concluding Considerations

Contrary to what could be expected from the older tradition of research, the doctrine exposed by Voetius as a representative reformed scholastic theologian is neither necessitarian nor voluntaristic (in the strong sense). Considering the structuring principle of *theologia necessaria* and *theologia contingens*, which in turn presupposes Voetius's modal-ontological model of synchronic contingency, a better historical predicate would be "Scotistic." God's contingent willing, knowing and acting are completely in accordance with all that belongs to the *theologia necessaria*, yet they do not follow from it. If they did, everything that God *can* will, know and do, would be actually willed, known and done by God. Thus, the world would necessarily emanate from God's being—as is the case both in ancient Greek thought and in Spinoza. All things would fundamentally coincide with God's essence. The actual world would be the only one possible. This is what Voetius calls "stoic fate."

Viewed from the perspective of the *theologia necessaria,* this "stoic fate" depriving both God and creatures of freedom and thus also destroying the *theologia contingens*, is in fact absurd. In terms of possible worlds semantics, one can say by extrapolation that for Voetius, considering God's (infinite) possibilities, there necessarily is more than one possible world. Yet, only one possible world can be the actual world; for if not, the actual world would consist of a contradictory set of actual states of affairs. Voetius rightly insists on the fact that contradictions are necessarily false. The only way out of the problems involved in the relation between the possible and the actual is offered by the contingent, or free, dimension inherent in the divine decision. The living God himself is the only possible "candidate" capable of determining which possible world is the actual world. In this way the world we live in, including its freedom and dependence, is sustained by God's free and essentially good hands.[63]

63. I thank Dr. N. den Bok (who has also prepared the translation into English in the genuine sense of the verb "trans-ferre"), Dr. E. Dekker, Dr. H. Goris, Dr. A. Vos and the participants in the symposium for their valuable comments.

10

Cocceius Anti-Scholasticus?

W. J. van Asselt

I. Introduction

In 1859 at the University of Utrecht the prospective Reformed minister A. van der Flier[1] defended under the presidency of professor H. E. Vinke a doctoral thesis entitled *Specimen historico-theologicum de Johanne Coccejo antischolastico*. Like his colleague G. van Gorkom[2] three years before, he portrayed Johannes Cocceius as an important seventeenth-century theologian, who cleared the way for an *organica et historica expositio Scripturae*. According to Van der Flier, Cocceius' theology was a *specimen* of the *odium theologiae scholasticae*, although with the reservation that Cocceius had not yet succeeded in developing a pure *theologia biblica*. Van der Flier's thesis was adopted by Christiaan Sepp in his major work on Reformed theology in the Netherlands during the sixteenth and seventeenth centuries. He added, however, that it was not altogether correct to typify Cocceius as a mere *antischolasticus*, because of the fact that Cocceius, like his orthodox opponents such as Gisbertus Voetius and Samuel Maresius, freely used scholastic definitions and distinctions in his dogmatic works.[3] In their biographical dictionary of Protestant theologians in the Netherlands, De Bie and Loosjes agreed with Sepp's proviso; at the same time they underscored the fact that it had been the merit of Cocceius "to assure exegetical science a prominent place in the study of theology."[4] Cocceius' starting point was not, as with Voetius, the

---

1. A. van der Flier (1835–1902) was successively a Reformed minister at the villages of Bunschoten (1860), Broek op Langendijk (1863), Zwartsluis (1865), Harlingen (1874), Lienden (1887) and 's-Hertogenbosch (1902) in the Netherlands.

2. G. van Gorkom, *Specimen theologicum inaugurale de Joanne Coccejo, Sacri codicis interprete* (diss., Rhen. Traj., 1856).

3. C. Sepp, *Het godgeleerd onderwijs in Nederland gedurende de 16e en 17 eeuw* (Leiden, 1874), 2:62–63; Cf. J. H. Maronier, *Geschiedenis van het Protestantisme van den Munsterschen vrede tot de Fransche revolutie* (Leiden, 1897), 2:9.

4. J. P. de Bie en J. Loosjes, *Biographisch woordenboek van Protestantsche Godgeleerden*

doctrine of the Reformed church, but the teachings of the Bible.

Notwithstanding the nuances in the judgements of these nineteenth-century authors, the trajectory for later scholarship was settled. Heinrich Heppe,[5] Gottlob Schrenk[6] and Otto Ritschl[7] presented Cocceius' theology as a renaissance of ancient biblical truth. More recent authors like Charles McCoy[8] and Heiner Faulenbach[9] depicted Cocceius as an exegetical expert with a great distaste for metaphysics and scholasticism. Cocceius developed his entire theological system exclusively on the basis of Holy Scripture. Both McCoy and Faulenbach grounded this assertion on the contents of Cocceius' monograph on the Covenant, the *Summa doctrinae de foedere et testamento Dei* (1648), without examining his theology in its entirety. The following remark of Faulenbach may serve as an illustration of this one-sided view of Cocceius' theology and its relationship to Reformed scholasticism:

> Damit verwirft er im Gegensatz zu vielen seiner theologischen Zeitgenossen alle Elemente philosophischer und naturwissenschaftlicher Art in der Theologie, weil sie in der Schrift keinen Grund haben ... Gegenüber der in dogmatischen Lehrformeln erstarrten und mit logischen Mitteln operierenden orthodoxen Dogmatik war dies jedoch in Wirklichkeit eine grosse Neuerung. Coccejus will kein dogmatisches System, für das die Schrift nur Beweisstellen liefert, das die Schrift in eine zweitrangige Position verweist, sondern die Schrift selbst ist für ihn das Lehrgebäude, das mit den in ihr angebotenen Mitteln zu erklären ist.[10]

---

in Nederland (The Hague: M. Nijhoff, 1949), 2:140.

5. H. Heppe, *Geschichte des Pietismus und der Mystik* (Leiden, 1879), 226.

6. G. Schrenk, *Gottesreich und Bund im älteren Protestantismus, vornehmlich bei Johannes Coccejus* (Gütersloh, 1923), 14–17.

7. O. Ritschl, *Dogmengeschichte des Protestantismus. Die Reformierte Theologie des 16. und 17. Jahrhunderts in ihrer Entstehung und Entwicklung* (Göttingen, 1926), 3:435: "Die epochemachende Bedeutung von Coccejus liegt nicht allein in seiner Lehre von Gottes Bund und Testament, sondern zugleich in der von ihm begründeten Richtung eines prinzipiell biblizistisch bestimmten Betriebes der Theologie ... Coccejus ist in seiner ganzen theologischen Haltung nicht mehr durch die scholastischen Methoden belastet gewesen, denen seit mehr als einem halben Jahrhundert alle reformierten Theologen mehr oder weniger Tribut entrichtet oder wenigstens unwillkürliche Zugeständnisse gemacht hatten."

8. C. S. McCoy, *The Covenant Theology of Johannes Cocceius* (Ph.D. dissertation, Yale University, 1956), 90, 236. McCoy, 89: "His theology is drawn from Scripture and represents a rejection of Scholasticism as the source and guide of doctrine ... Cocceius interpreted the Scriptures without presupposition."

9. H. Faulenbach, *Weg und Ziel der Erkenntnis Christi. Eine Untersuchung zur Theologie des Johannes Coccejus* (Neukirchen-Vluyn, 1973).

10. Faulenbach, *Weg und Ziel*, 46, 47.

To me, however, it seems that scholastic elements are definitely present in Cocceius' writings, especially in his doctrine of God as explained in his main systematic work, the *Summa theologiae ex Scripturis repetita* (1662) and in some parts of his doctrine of covenant.[11] From another perspective, Stephen Strehle[12] and Richard Muller[13] have also pointed out that the description of Cocceius as unique for his time as a representative of a antischolastic and biblical theology is a product of a set of historical and systematic inaccuracies and misunderstandings. Strehle is especially critical of the anti-scholastic interpretation of the federal method of Cocceius. A comparison between the medieval (nominalistic) conceptions of covenant and those of sixteenth- and seventeenth-century Reformed theologians suggests far more continuity between medieval scholasticism, Calvinism and federal theology than was assumed by earlier scholarship. In the doctrine of covenant both the medieval and Reformed traditions emphasized the freedom of God's will and operated with a voluntaristic covenant concept (*pactum*), which no doubt influenced Cocceius' conceptualization of this theme.

Muller, in particular, criticizes the anachronistic use of the term "biblical theology" by earlier scholarship. If by this terminology a distinction is made between dogmatics and "biblical exegesis," and this distinction is applied to the theology of Cocceius, then, according to Muller, we are introducing an anachronism. It was not until the eighteenth century that such a distinction was made. The German theologian Johann Philipp Gabler (1753–1826), professor at Altdorf, was the first one to make a distinction between contemporary dogmatics and a historical conceived biblical theology in his inaugural address of 1787. The juxtaposition of "biblical theology" with "scholastic or dogmatic theology that appears in many of the discussions of Cocceius' thought can only be viewed as an anachronistic application of Gabler's distinction. Like his orthodox contemporaries and opponents Cocceius intended to

---

11. See W. J. van Asselt, *Amicitia Dei. Een onderzoek naar de structuur van de theologie van Johannes Coccejus (1603–1669)*, Ede 1988, 42–44; 74–75. My main thesis, based on the old scholarship on scholasticism, was that the anti-scholastic element was not dominant in Cocceius' theology.

12. S. Strehle, *Calvinism, Federalism and Scholasticism. A Study of the Reformed Doctrine of Covenant* (Bern-Frankfurt am Main-New York-Paris, 1988), 243–46.

13. R. A. Muller, *Post-Reformation Reformed Dogmatics*, 2 vols. to date (Grand Rapids, 1987–), 1:264–67, 2:117–22; *ibid.*, 2:121: "'Cocceius' federalism and biblicism did not produce a 'biblical theology' in the usual sense of the term."

present a biblically grounded contemporary dogmatics. Therefore, the expression "biblical theology" is not an appropriate way for indicating Cocceian thought.

To this a third point of criticism should be added, which concerns both the use and the evaluation of the term "scholasticism." Almost without exception most of the earlier scholarship is operating with a somewhat diffuse and even negative conception of the historical phenomenon called "scholasticism." It is not always clear what the critics have in mind when they criticize scholasticism: a literary genre or a historical period. In most cases it concerns both phenomena. The negative and even pejorative use of the term also colors opinion on Cocceius' relationship to scholasticism. Therefore, the way in which this relationship is conceived largely depends on the definition of the term scholasticism that is used. In this connection the question could be raised whether Cocceius in his protest against scholasticism had the same phenomenon in mind as the modern opponents of scholasticism, or whether it is possible that the current definition of scholasticism needs revision in order to understand the nature of Cocceius' attack on the scholasticism of his adversaries.

Indeed, when we, like Faulenbach, think of scholasticism in terms of a "rigid," "dry," and "excessively formalized" theology, then it is very easy to have a negative impression of Cocceius' relationship to scholasticism. On the other hand, if we take into account the results of recent research on scholasticism in general, and Reformed scholasticism in particular, then our opinion on Cocceius' relationship to scholasticism needs radical revision. In this article we propose to test the correctness of the traditional view that sees a contrast between scholastic theology of the Reformed orthodox in the seventeenth century and the so-called "biblical theology" of Cocceius. At the same time, this article is intended to be a contribution to the ongoing debate over Reformed scholasticism.

II. Previous Research

It is not my intention to give a complete and chronological survey of all the discussions on Protestant scholasticism that have taken place during the last decades.[14] It suffices to indicate the two major alternatives in

---

14. For a synopsis of the history of scholarship on Reformed Orthodoxy, see the introduction to this collection of essays.

dealing with this problem. One school, epitomized by Brian Armstrong, argued that Reformed scholasticism was a form of speculative thought, which was characterized by a strong emphasis on God's eternal decrees at the cost of biblical preaching of the Gospel. According to Armstrong the Reformed scholastics were primarily rationalists who exchanged Calvin's Christological focus for one based on the divine decrees. The most important feature of Reformed scholasticism was its use of two sources for theological knowledge: faith *and* reason. The extensive use of Aristotelian categories in logical, rationally defensible systems resulted in the fact that reason "assumed at least equal standing with faith." Therefore, Reformed scholasticism was a fatal deviation from the central concerns of the exegetical and theological insights of the Reformers, especially Calvin's. Because Reformed scholastics interpreted the Bible as "a body of propositions" that were once and for all revealed by God, their theology ceased to be a theology of revelation and was characterized by an ahistoric and timeless methodology.[15]

In recent years this approach of Armstrong et al. has come under increasing criticism. Richard Muller has pointed out that Protestant scholasticism was an institutional theology, confessionally in continuity with the insights of the Reformers and doctrinally in continuity with the Christian tradition as a whole. This double continuity must be understood as one example of the way in which Christian intellectual tradition maintained useful forms, methods and doctrinal ideas while at the same time incorporating the advances of exegetical and theological investigation. Muller defines scholasticism as an organizational structure, viz. "the technical and logical approach to theology as a discipline characteristic of theological system from the late twelfth through the seventeenth century."[16] In a recent article entitled "Calvin and the

---

introduction to this collection of essays.

15. B. G. Armstrong, *Calvinism and the Amyraut Heresy: Protestant Scholasticism and Humanism in Seventeenth-Century France* (Madison-Milwaukee-London, 1969), 32. Armstrong identifies "four more-or-less identifiable tendencies" in Protestant scholasticism (1) A theological approach which asserts religious truth on the basis of deductive ratiocination from given assumptions or principles, thus producing a logically coherent and defensible system of belief, invariably based upon Aristotelian philosophical commitment; (2) In this system reason assumes at least equal standing with faith; (3) The sentiment that the scriptural record contains a unified, rationally comprehensible account; (4) Interest in metaphysical matters, in abstract, speculative thought, particulary with reference to the doctrine of God.

16. Muller, *PRRD*, 1:18, 21–39, 2:3–11 Although Muller's work has fundamentally altered the landscape of scholarship on Protestant scholasticism, he is not the first one

Calvinists," Muller sums up ten points, indicating the principal premises of reappraisal which point to where the standard definition of Reformed scholasticism needs to be modified. At the same time these points summarize Muller's criticism on earlier research.[17] For our purpose, the most important four points that he proposes are as follows:

1. Previous research has failed to set the question of continuity and discontinuity between Reformation and later orthodoxy against the background of an examination of continuities and discontinuities running through the history of thought from the Middle Ages into the sixteenth and seventeenth centuries.
2. Previous research has failed to examine the meaning of the term "scholasticism" as found both in scholary studies of the Christian tradition prior to the Reformation and in the writings of sixteenth- and seventeenth-century Protestant theologians.
3. The way in which the "old school" identified the terms "rationalism" and "scholasticism" must be rejected on historical, philosophical and theological grounds. It is incorrect to confuse the usage of rational argumentation in theology with "rationalism."
4. Previous research did not notice the continuities and discontinuities in the interpretative or exegetical traditions. They must be given equal weight with developments in scholastic method and philosophical usage.

Muller's conclusion is that the hermeneutics of the old school's view on Reformed scholasticism was primarily determined by nineteenth- and twentieth-century theological agendas. In sound historical investigation, these modern agendas cannot be allowed to play a decisive role. All too often it has happened that one's own theological positions are projected onto the writings of the Reformers, at the same time making their ideas a

---

to emphasize the continuity between Reformation and Orthodoxy. For an analysis of Muller's thesis, see Martin I. Klauber, "Continuity and Discontinuity in Post-Reformation Reformed Theology: An Evaluation of the Muller Thesis," in *Journal of the Evangelical Theological Society* 33–34 (1990): 467–75. For new developments in Roman Catholic scholarship on scholasticism, see U. G. Leinsle, *Einführung in die scholastische Theologie* (Paderborn-München-Wien-Zürich, 1995).

17. R. A. Muller, "Calvin and the Calvinists: Assessing Continuities and Discontinuities between Reformation and Orthodoxy," parts 1 and 2, *CTJ* 30 (1995): 345–75; 31 (1996): 125-60.

standard for judging the Reformed character of individual orthodox thinkers and treatises. Such "historical" studies only reflect and justify (modern) theological insights.

In this article we propose to test these four points of Muller by examining the way in which Cocceius conceived his relationship to scholasticism. The argument will proceed as follows. First, I will discuss Cocceius' own judgement on scholasticism. Second, I will outline some features of his view on the use of reason in theology, and, third, I will attempt to address the issue of exegetical continuity. The last section of this article deals with the question of methodological continuity between medieval, Reformation and post-Reformed thought, especially in the doctrine of God.

III. Cocceius' Judgment on Scholasticism

It is very easy to select from Cocceius' writings numerous passages that reflect a negative judgment on scholasticism. These passages principally express his concern to be a theologian who wants to discover in Scripture the thought-forms and correct language for considering and speaking of the faith of the Church. It is, however, an equally easy matter to compose a fine anthology from his works which reflects his use and mastery of the scholastic method and its tools, such as linguistic, philosophical, and logical analysis.

Therefore, the first thing to do is to explain clearly the content and significance of Cocceius' declamations against "scholastic theology." How should these declamations against the scholastics be explained? Were they directed against the dogmatic content of the scholastic treatises of his contemporaries or did they refer only to the method used by these scholastics? On the basis of Muller's second point—the meaning of the term "scholasticism" as found in the writings of sixteenth- and seventeenth-century Protestant theologians themselves—we will now examine the way in which Cocceius defined scholasticism and compare his criticism of this phenomenon with that of his most scholastic opponent, Gisbert Voetius.

In Cocceius' utterances on scholasticism we can distinguish a formal and a material aspect. As far as concerns the material aspect, Cocceius can wield a sharp pen. In his commentary on Revelation 16:2, he compared scholasticism with "foul and evil sores" that had brought so much unwholesome division of opinion in the Church.[18] He accused the scholastic theologians of inventing and solving "stupid questions" (*quaestiones stultae*); their disputations can be compared with "the itching eruption of the skin of a sick Church." Referring to 1 Tim. 6:20, a passage in which Timothy is admonished to "avoid the godless chatter and contradiction of what is falsely called knowledge," he wrote that academic disputations, during which all sorts of problems were discussed without there being a single reference to Holy Scripture, were completely reprehensible:

> Calvin calls them [disputations] subtleties (*argutias*) with which mankind hunts for idle glory for itself. Danaeus calls them useless disputations. In the same way we entitle those disputations that prevent piety. Such disputations have no spiritual significance and demonstrative force, because they use arguments not supported by the Holy Spirit, even when they seem to defend the truth. Our theologians have very properly observed that this is the case with the scholastic theology of the papists.[19]

From this quotation it appears that Cocceius' declamations against scholasticism were primarily directed against certain extreme forms of scholasticism as found in the writings of medieval schoolmen and Counter-Reformation theologians. Furthermore, it is obvious that it is the content of this scholasticism that is condemned by Cocceius. His main objection to it lies in his presumption that the heresy of semi-pelagianism has ensconced itself in this theology. Even when one finds something good in it, it is always "a tiny nucleus hidden under many layers" or "one corn under much chaff."[20] Cocceius seems to combat only the outgrowths of a specific form of scholasticism characterized by ingenious speculations and impious *quaestiones*. The real purpose of theology is to direct man to Him who is the Way, the Truth, and the Life:

---

18. J. Cocceius, *Cogitationes de Apocalypsi S. Johannes Theologi,* cap. 16 § 2, *Opera Omnia* V (Amsterdam, 1673),: "Adde innumerabilem multitudinem quaestionum ineptarum, & scholasticarum disputationum vitiliginem: non sine familiarum q. haereditaria dissensione, ut Scotistarum et Thomistarum, aliarumque. Fecit hoc ulcus etiam scabiem & rupturam ad tempus quidem in schismate."
19. J. Cocceius, *Commentarius in Epistulam I ad Timotheum,* cap. 6 § 96, *Opera Omnia,* V (Amsterdam, 1673).
20. J. Cocceius, *Commentarius in Epistulam I ad Timotheum,* cap. 6 § 96.

The whole teaching of the Church is in truth nothing else than an exhortation to seek God and his Word (. . .). Therefore, those who teach are those who strive to bring their hearers and the readers of their books to the hearing and reading of the Word of God, and to aid in an understanding of God, each one according to his own method.[21]

The real measure of theology, he writes, is the extent to which it leads men to an understanding and love of God, and persuades them to seek God. For Cocceius, there was nothing wholesome in a "non-existential" theology.

Two remarks are here in order. A question to be answered is whether Cocceius' objection to the contents of Roman Catholic scholasticism also implied a complete rejection of the scholastic method in itself as a useful tool for theological analysis. Second, if this question is answered in the negative then the conclusion can be drawn that it is incorrect to maintain that Cocceius is an enemy of all forms of scholasticism. We shall approach both aspects of the problem in the light of Cocceius' treatment of this subject in the correspondence he conducted with one of his colleagues.

In letter to Antonius Perizonius,[22] professor in oriental languages at the *gymnasium illustre* in Deventer, he wrote that he had no objection whatsoever to organizing public disputations for students according to the long established academic rules, with a student as *respondens* and the *quaestio* as basic unit of discussion. Perizonius, then, asked for Cocceius' opinion on the use of non-biblical scholastic terminology during such a public disputation. Was it allowed? Cocceius wrote in reply:

> . . . I tolerate many [scholastic] terms which I myself do not use. The terms I accept I explain willingly. I prefer to use the language of Holy Scripture and compare Scripture with Scripture until it appears that what the Church believes to be true or not to be true is in conformity with Holy Scripture.[23]

As is clear from the quotations given, Cocceius did not object to academic disputations and the traditional procedures and techniques that

21. Preface to the *Summa theologiae ex Scripturis repetita*, 1662, *Opera Omnia* VII (Amsterdam, 1673).

22. For Antonius Perizonius (1626–1672), see *Biografisch Lexicon voor de Geschiedenis van het Nederlandse Protestantisme* (Kampen, 1983), 2:358–59.

23. Epistola nr. 122, *Opera Omnia* VI (Amsterdam, 1673), 58.

accompanied these disputations. These procedures were characterized by the medieval technique of a *quaestio disputata* for theological discourse.[24] It indicates a particular method in teaching and writing which concentrates on identifying the order and pattern of argument suitable to technical academic discourse. On the day of the actual dispute an issue was presented in the form of a thesis or a question. The official task of the *respondens* (a student) was to respond to objections that came from the audience, in the order in which they were presented on the point proposed by the professor under whose presidency the disputation took place. The student's task was also to provide arguments contra the objections made by the audience. During the following week, after considering each argument pro and con the professor gave his *determinatio*, or resolution, to the entire question. He offered a formulation of an answer or an elaboration of the thesis with due respect to all known sources of information and to the rules of rational discourse, followed by a full response to all objections. This *quaestio*-technique, or outlines of it, can be easily orbserved, not only in Cocceius' systematic works such as his *Aphorismi per universam theologiam* and his *Disputationes selectae*, but also in his exegetical works, for example in the diagrams he attached to the publications of his commentaries on Romans and Hebrews.[25]

To be sure, Cocceius did level some criticism against his orthodox colleagues who used the scholastic method in their teaching and writing. With some of them he noticed that their use of scholastic terminology created an artificial language overgrowing and obscuring the language of Scripture. A firm rootage in the language and text of Scripture remained crucial for Cocceius' labors in theology. In a letter from Duisburg, dated 16 August 1656, his cousin Martin Hundius wrote to Cocceius:

You are right in writing that today the words of St. Paul are rather

---

24. For a full description of the technique of the *quaestio disputata*, see W. J. van Asselt and E. Dekker, eds., *De scholastieke Voetius. Een luisteroefening aan de hand van Voetius' Disputationes Selectae* (Zoetermeer, 1995), 14–25. Cf. also R. A. Muller, *Scholasticism and Orthodoxy in the Reformed Tradition: An Attempt at Definition.* Inaugural Address, delivered in the Calvin Seminary Chapel, 7 September, 1995, 4.

25. J. Cocceius, "Diagrammata rerum dicendarum in Pauli Epistolam ad Romanos," *Opera Anekdota, Tomus Alter* (Amsterdam, 1706), 27–196; Cocceius, "Diagrammata quibus summam rerum in Epistolam ad Hebraeos dicendarum," *Opera Anekdota*, Tomus Alter, 315–431. For the *Aphorismi per universam theologiam (breviores et prolixiores)* and the *Disputationes selectae*, see Cocceius, *Opera Omnia* VI (Amsterdam, 1673).

enigmatic to us, because we are so used to scholastic terminology and have such a delight in it that we turn up our nose at investigating the meaning of the words used by the Holy Spirit in Scripture; that is the reason why we no longer understand so well those who use them.[26]

IV. Voetius' Judgment on Scholasticism

In a disputation on scholastic theology (1644), the second of the disputations published in the first volume of his *Disputationes selectae* (1648), Gisbertus Voetius gave a detailed exposition of his view on the scholastic approach to theology by the medieval doctors and their Protestant and Roman Catholic successors in the seventeenth century.[27] In the first part (*pars critica*) of this disputation he made a distinction between a formal or methodological and a material or substantial appreciation of scholasticism. From his remarks in this context the conclusion can be drawn that he accepted scholasticism as a method for theology, but that he rejected it when considered in respect of some of its contents. He argued, that there are many things that can be approved in scholastic method, especially that of Thomas Aquinas. In the course of time the scholastics had developed an arsenal of concepts that enabled them to clarify matters that otherwise would have been incomprehensible. They discussed theological problems *to the point*, without the traditional finery of rhetorical and poetical digressions which obscured more theological discourse than they clarified. However, the roads of Voetius and the scholastics part when it comes to the content of their scholastic theology. For example, their conception of grace and free will is unacceptable to Voetius. In this respect, Voetius like Cocceius had no good word to say for the medieval and more recent Roman Catholic scholastics. He had no hesitation in saying that scholasticism conceived in

---

26. Epistola nr. 193, *Opera Anekdota*,Tomus Alter (Amsterdam, 1706), 699.

27. G. Voetius, "De theologia scholastica," *Disputationes Selectae* I (Utrecht, 1658), 12–19. He distinguishes between scholasticism in a most broad (*latissime*), a broad (*late*), and a strict sense (*stricte*). The reasoned refutation of heretics in the Gospels and the letters of St. Paul, for example, he considered as a form of scholasticism in the most broad sense. Scholasticism in a broad sense was in Voetius' view "everything that took place in the medieval schools," and in this sense, he argues, almost all theology can be called scholastic. Scholasticism in a strict sense refers to "the method of theology that will be found primarily and succinctly in the four books of the *Sententiae,* exposed in more detail by Thomas Aquinas in the three parts of his *Summa theologiae*." According to Voetius, scholasticism in the strict sense included also "later commentators on Lombard and recent authors who wrote commentaries on Thomas Aquinas."

this way was a corrupt theology that led many true believers in the Church astray.

V. The Use of Reason in Theology

In order to relativize somewhat more the idea of previous research that Cocceius presented a "biblical theology" as opposed to the "scholastic theology" of Voetius, it is instructive to examine the discussions of both theologians on the function of reason and logic in theology. With this issue we touch upon the third point of Muller's criticism of previous research, viz. the identification of scholasticism with "rationalism." As we saw above, one of Muller's criticisms was that the definition of rationalism used by previous scholarship suggested that, for Protestant scholastics, reason and faith, philosophy and revelation, were in fact two equivalent quantities or two separate sources for theological knowledge. Voetius' use of logic had, according to the critics of Reformed scholasticism, a narrowing effect upon the content of Christian theology. In this section, we will attempt to show that this view is not historically credible.

Voetius discussed the problem of faith and reason in a disputation *De ratione humana in rebus fidei* (on human reason in matters of faith),[28] the first of the disputations published in the first volume of his *Disputationes selectae*. Here, he drew a distinction between the use of the term reason (*ratio*) in a proper and improper sense. In its proper sense reason is a natural faculty; it is the human ability to understand things, to formulate propositions and to pass judgments on matters. Used in its improper sense, "reason" indicates "the light of natural knowledge" that Voetius identifies as a common sense (*communis sensus*), given to humankind by God, and therefore a rationality innate in man. In its turn this innate reason must be distinguished from "acquired reason" which is a *habitus* or disposition by which God enables man to cultivate science (*scientia*). This disposition or habitus, Voetius explains, consists in the intellectual ability to collect actual knowledge, to frame concepts and to draw conclusions (*consequentiae*) from principles (*principia*).

Furthermore, reason used in its proper sense can be viewed both in an objective or abstract way and in a concrete or subjective manner. In this last instance one must take into account the status of mankind in salvation history: reason in its natural state before the fall must not only be distinguished from reason in its fallen state but also from reason

---

28. G. Voetius, "De ratione humana in rebus fidei," *Disputationes selectae* I, 1–12.

restored by grace in redemption. In its fallen state reason is corrupted, but the effect of redemption for man's corrupted reason is a restoration of the ability of reason once again to attain "spiritual insight," although still in an imperfect way. Only in the state of eternal bliss will reason "perfectly shine in the light of God's glory." In academic theology, Voetius continues, reason is always used in a subjective or concrete sense, viz. "reason totally corrupted by the fall but restored by grace, albeit in an imperfect way."[29]

Subsequently, Voetius enumerates nine arguments indicating that human reason can never be a principle or a cognitive foundation of theology and Christian faith.[30] Against the Socinians, he argues that reason cannot be the ultimate norm for religion. Against the Roman Catholics, he argues that reason is, nevertheless, an important instrument for ordering, analysing, and applying the doctrines revealed in Holy Scripture. Anyone who rejects the use of reason in theology is very soon a victim of inconsistencies and absurdities, and tongue-tied in confrontation with heretical opinions. Voetius concludes his disputation by defending an organic use of reason in theology. He compares this organic use of reason in theology with the way in which we use our eyes, our ears and tongue in doing theology. In a *corollarium* in addition to this

29. Voetius, "De ratione humana in rebus fidei," 2: "Nos hic plurimum eam accipimus subjective, ut per lapsum totaliter corrupta est, aut per gratiam liberata est, sed non perfecte."

30. Voetius, "De ratione humana in rebus fidei," 3: "His praemissis dicimus nullam rationem humanam esse principium *quo* seu *per quod*, aut *ex quo* seu *cur* credamus, aut fundamentum aut legem, aut normam credendorum ex cujus praescripto judicemus: atque adeo salsum non esse habendum illud in rebus fidei e.g. *trinitatem, peccatum originale, Christum theanthropon ejusque satisfactionem*, quidquid lumen naturale aut ratio humana ex prioribus & notioribus non capiat, vel quod ad accuratam definitionem, vel quod ad demonstrationem, vel quod ad utrumque." His nine arguments run as follows: (1) the blindness of reason in every unregenerated man; (2) the mysteries of the Christian faith which remain incomprehensible for even regenerate Christians too; (3) knowledge of God's essence and attributes is always inadequate and can only be grasped by way of negation, causality or by the way of eminence; (4) the knowledge of the regenerate is always partial and imperfect; (5) Scripture is the cognitive principle of all religious knowledge; (6) human reason does not precede faith; it does not add new knowledge to faith, and does not give more certainty than faith; (7) in their exposition of the Christian faith, Christ, his prophets and apostles exclusively referred to God's Word; (8) the priority of reason induces absurd conclusions and blurs out the wide difference between nature and grace, philosophy and theology; (9) the theology of the Socinians with its absurd conclusions shows what happens when reason is used as a principle of theology.

disputation, he wrote:

> It is lack of love when our theology is ranked with the opinions of the
> Socinians, as if we had made reason a standard and principle of
> theology. When we consider reason and logic to be a requirement [for
> theology] then logic and reason are in no way the foundation, principle
> and rule of our faith any more than our eyes, ears and tongues are:
> without them we cannot teach religion, nor defend it against opponents.
> Therefore, they are means and requisites without which there is no faith
> or theological knowledge possible. But in no way do we consider them
> as principles, standards and foundations of theology.[31]

As for Cocceius, he dealt with the problem of faith and reason in his
Aphorismi per universam theologiam (ca.1650) and in his principal systematic
writing *Summa theologiae ex Scripturis repetita* (1662). His account of the
role of reason in theology hardly differs from Voetius' explanation of this
topic. In his *Aphorismi* he too distinguished a fourfold status for
considering reason, the modi of which were determined by salvation
history and informed by the ideas of creation, fall, redemption and
eternal bliss.[32] Furthermore, Cocceius asserts that after the fall human
reason was not totally destroyed. Sin did not affect human reason in such
a way that it was unable to apply the rules of logic. Human reason also
played a part in careful reflection on items revealed in Scripture, which,
for the reader, were not connected in an obvious way. To be sure, reason
is subordinate to faith, but this subordination does not imply that faith
destroys reason: it perfects and often surpasses reason.

Here, Cocceius suggests that the use of logic and reason in theology is
not a *metabasis eis allo genos*, for no theology can do without some logical
thinking. If, however, we assume that reason is the guiding principle of
theology, there is a great danger for theologians in using such concepts.[33]

In the *Summa theologiae* we come across similar remarks. In addition,
Cocceius distinguishes between "corrupted" reason and "reason
illuminated by the Holy Spirit." Corrupted reason Cocceius describes as
a form of pointless logic-chopping without any connection with the Word
of God. Cocceius wants to stick to the rule of St. Paul, formulated in 2

---

31. Voetius, *De ratione humana*, 12. Voetius refers to three Lutheran theologians
(Eckhardus, Stechmannus en Meisnerus), who accused Reformed theology of having
Socinian opinions.

32. J. Cocceius, *Aphorismi prolixiores*, disp. 1, § 4.

33. J. Cocceius, *Aphorismi breviores*, disp. 1, § 20, 21 and 24.

Cor. 10:5, "to take every thought captive to obey Christ." Here Cocceius seems to be led by the intensity of his concern for the knowledge of piety and to reject as "logic-chopping" everything in theology that results in "disinterested" or speculative questions about the nature of God:

> Therefore, faith conquers all fruitless reasoning and takes every thought captive to obey Christ. Yet faith does not abolish the sobriety of the intellect and the light of truth known by nature; faith does not exclude reason but gains credit by reason (. . .) For God does not contradict himself (. . .) Faith is a reasonable service, a *logikè latreia*, and not an unreasonable one. Therefore, faith does not destroy reason but stimulates it; faith does not confuse reason but gives guidance to reason; it does not infatuate the mind but enlightens it. Faith does not suppress reason but frees it from (. . .) desire, error, ignorance, superficial judgments, opinions and objections to God's truth, prompted by Satan's devices in which it got entangled, to do the will of God.[34]

In these sentences Cocceius defines reason not primarily in terms of its propositional content (although clearly that is present), but in terms of the religious and moral response that must accompany it. Compared to Voetius' observations on this subject, however, it would be a mistake sharply to contrast Cocceius' approach to the problem of faith and reason with that of Voetius. Both theologians claim that reason and logic in no way determine the content of theology. They are only instrumental tools in theology.

VI. The Doctrine of Legitimate Conclusions

Before turning to the most interesting issue in the debate between Muller and the "old school," we should take a brief look at another point of Muller's criticism. It relates to the issue of exegetical continuity. It has been suggested that Reformed scholastics used scriptural proofs without

---

34. J. Cocceius, *Summa Theologiae*, cap. 46 § 6: "Igitur fides vincit sane ratiocinationes et omnem rationem captivat in obedientiam Christi, sed tamen mentis sobrietatem et lucem et notam naturaliter veritatem non tollit vel excludit, sed per eam vincit. Nam Deus sibi non est contrarius . . . Fides est . . . rationalis cultus, non . . . ratione carens. Non igitur fides interimit rationem, sed excitat; non intricat, sed dirigit, non excaecat mentem, sed illustrat; non premit, sed liberat: nimirum a cupiditatibus, erroribus, ignorantiis, temariis judiciis et opinionibus et obmurmurationibus contra veritatem Dei, tanquam laqueis satanae, quibus innodata erat ad faciendum voluntatem eius, 2 Tim. 2:25, 26."

exposition within the scholastic systems. They used this technique of citation, it is claimed, in order to vindicate their dogmatic standards. Scripture was considered by them only as a harness-room for their system. Thus it is claimed, the Reformed scholastics frequently indulged in proof-texting (*dicta probantia*), citing Bible texts apart from their context and apart from any consideration of the results of exegesis. All this is supposed to be in contradistinction to Cocceius who is assumed to pay attention exclusively to biblical exegesis. This idea is an embarrasing example of misrepresentation and can be removed when we realize that there was a longstanding hermeneutical tradition in which both Cocceius and Voetius participated and which originated in the medieval schools, viz. the doctrine of legitimate consequences, i.e. the use of logic to draw doctrinal consequences in matters of faith.

In their arguments to prove legitimate the use of logical conclusions from the text of the Bible both Voetius and Cocceius leveled criticisms on two fronts. In the first place they opposed the claims of the Socinians[35] and the Remonstrants whose ideas were continuous with the opinions of the Socinians. Secondly, they disputed the view of the Roman Catholic Church, particularly the claims of some Counter-Reformation theologians.[36] As we noted earlier, the Bible was for Voetius as well as for

---

35. See Voetius, *Disputationes selectae* I, 1: "De usu rationis humanae in rebus fidei duplex est controversia: Una cum Socinianis eorumque asseclis; alterum neotericis quibusdam Pontificiis." Cf. Cocceius, *Summa theologiae*, cap. 6 § 58: "Altera est fallacia Socinianorum, qui non quidem in docendo & refutando consequentias rejiciunt, sed dicunt, necessaria esse in iis, quae nullam habent controversiam & contradictionem."

36. Voetius fought against the claims of the Jesuits Gunterus and Verronus in Germany and France. See *Disputationes selectae* I, 5/6: "Accedamus nunc ad novum *heurèma* pontificiorum, qui contendunt a nostris Papismum refutari debere tantum ex expressis scripturae verbis, absque ulla ratiocinatione, discursu, consequentiarum nexu & probatione, atque adeo rejiciunt & removent a collationibus & disputationibus nobiscum omnem Logicam naturalem, & artificialem, docentem & utentem. Quod inventum primus videtur prodidisse Iesuita Gunterus in colloquio Durlacensi, Anno 1612 non tam habito, quam tentato: perfecerunt Pandoram illam tandem Iesuitae in Gallia inter quos emicuit Verronus, qui nescio quae epinicia editis libris non cecinerit, quae miracula illi non tribuerit." Cocceius combatted the views of two Roman Catholic priests in Westphalia, the Walenburg brothers, Adriaan and Pieter. See Cocceius, *Summa theologiae*, cap. 6 § 75: "Neque pluris est Walenburgiana *methodeia*, quae hoc satagit, ne ea, quae ex scriptis per necessariam consequentiam conficiuntur, videantur esse revelata ad fidem. Quasi non, quae necessario consequuntur ex scriptis & immediate revelatis, aequipolleant revelatis, & Dei testimonium sint, atque ita fidem obligent & ea accipiantur." Like Voetius he called these Roman Catholic opponents "novi methodistae."

Cocceius in a direct sense the normative Word of God. From this they concluded that the Bible also had to furnish clear proofs for the Church doctrines which were formulated in later times. Roman Catholics and Socinians both agreed on the point that this was an impossible claim, although the conclusions they drew from this impossibility were very different. Both claimed that Church doctrines were not included in the Bible as well as that it was impossible to deduct these doctrines from the Bible. According to the Roman Catholic theologians, however, the doctrines of the Church did not need to be included in Holy Scripture, because the Church had received from God the unique authority to explain Holy Scripture. According to the Socinians, the Church doctrines could in no way be traced in Holy Scripture and, therefore, must be rejected completely.

With an appeal to the Church Fathers and the medieval doctrine of legitimate consequences in matters of faith,[37] Voetius as well as Cocceius defended the claim that the drawing of logical conclusions from the text of the Bible (*sacra pagina*) had been at all times an integral part of exegetical method. Like the medieval doctors they intented to draw *sacra doctrina* and *sacra theologia* out of the *sacra pagina*.[38] The procedure is as follows: on the basis of a syllogism, logical conclusions can indeed be drawn from a scriptural text, only on the condition that the predicate of the first premise or the major, as well as the subject of the second premise or the minor, include *expressis verbis* scriptural terms. The middle term should also contain words borrowed from Scripture or, at any rate, words that referred to scriptural texts. Voetius offers a series of nine arguments to prove legitimate the use of such syllogisms to draw doctrinal consequences. Cocceius has only two arguments, but these arguments are verbally identical with those in Voetius' disputation. The first argument they have in common notes that Scripture itself uses all kinds of words and terms that express a drawing of conclusions in matters of faith. For example, New Testament verbs like *logizesthai, krinein, sunkrinein, dokimazein, dialogesthai* etc. all suppose some sort of

---

37. For the origins and the development of this doctrine, see F. Schupp, *Wilhelm von Osma. De consequentiis. Ueber die Folgerungen. Textkritisch herausgegeben, übersetzt, eingeleitet und kommentiert* (Hamburg 1991).

38. See Muller, *PRRD*, 2:522. Muller considers the drawing of logical conclusions as "the final hermeneutical step in the method [of the Protestant exegetes], closely related to the application of the *analogia Scripturae* and the *analogia fidei*."

discursive thinking by means of which conclusions are drawn.[39]

Furthermore, both Voetius and Cocceius comment, it is the nature of God's wisdom that He fully understands the consequences of all that He says and that He wishes people to understand his word to include all that can be gathered from his pronouncements. The best proof of the legitimacy of this practice, however, is given by Christ himself and the apostles, especially St. Paul. While the apostles argued Jesus to be the Messiah by drawing conclusions from the Old Testament, Christ himself refuted the Sadducees by proving the doctrine of the resurrection of the dead as a consequence of the doctrine of the covenant. In his letters to the Romans and Galatians, Paul proved the doctrine of justification and in the first letter to the Corinthians he did the same with the doctrine of the resurrection of the dead. Furthermore, he did not refute the philosophers on Mars Hill in Athens without using conclusions drawn from Scripture. To this Voetius added the argument that doctrines are indeed conclusions drawn from Scripture, but in such a way that these doctrines are elicited by Scripture itself, because the *principia* of the doctrines are potentially and virtually present in Scripture itself. Denying the legitimacy of drawing logical conclusions from Scripture, Voetius concludes, would imply that there is no way to test and refute contradictions and inconsistencies erroneously drawn from the scriptural text by pagans, atheists, heretics and papists.[40]

Voetius spent more than one page in his disputation on enumerating several passages from the writings of the Church Fathers to prove that all of them applied in their works the rules of some sort of logical argumentation. Beside Gregory of Nazianze, Basil the Great and Athanasius he most frequently quoted Augustine. In this context Voetius referred to Augustine's sentences in Book II, chapter 34, of the *De doctrina christiana,* to emphasize the difference between the truth of a conclusion and the validity of a conclusion.[41] Logical analysis, he concludes, never shows the truth of statements involved. It never

---

39. Voetius, *De ratione humana*, 7, 8. Cf. Cocceius, *Summa theologiae,* cap. 6 § 35.

40. Voetius, *De ratione humana*, 8, 9. Cf. Cocceius, *Summa theologiae,* cap. 6 § 76–80.

41. Voetius, *Disputationes selectae* I, 9: "Accedunt testimonia patrum, quibus usum principiorum rationibus commendant Nazianz. *oratio 6. de Spir. S.* . . . Vide eundem in *Orat. funebr.* in laudem Basilii Magni. Augustin. *de doctr. Christ.* lib. 2. c. 34. Aliud est nosse regulas connexionum, aliud sententiarum veritatem: in illis discitur quod sit consequens, quid repugnans. Consequens, si orator est, homo est. Repugnans, si homo est, quadrupes non est, hic ergo de ipsa connexione judicatur."

restricts the content of the statements of an argument. The only thing logic can do is to show whether the combination of certain statements is logically consistent.

Voetius' appeal to Augustine is also present in Cocceius. In exactly the same way as Voetius did and using exactly the same examples, Cocceius indicates that the validity of a statement is something other than its truth. For a valid conclusion is one thing, but a true conclusion is still another.[42]

From this it can be concluded, that both Cocceius and Voetius were in fundamental agreement on the point that it was impossible to cultivate and to teach theology as a science without the help of the doctrine of legitimate consequences. Referring to Psalm 32:9, Voetius declares that every theologian, who would deny this, looks like a snorting horse trotting through Scripture.[43]

VII. God's Omnipotence

If there is one characteristic, common to all scholastic theologians from the eleventh century up to and including the seventeenth century and, if there is any recognizable continuity in the history of scholastic theology despite all the lines of fracture, then this one characteristic concerns the methodological exposition of the doctrine of God. Therefore, we now turn to the question whether Cocceius used the scholastic framework and, if so, to what degree he disassociated himself from the content of Reformed scholastic theology. Here we touch upon the first point of Muller, concerning the issue of the continuity between the theology of the Reformers and the medieval schools on the one hand, and the

---

42. Cocceius, *De Potentia sacrae scripturae,* cap. XXII § 27: "Condonent nobis Fratres, quod dubitamus, an satis perciperint, quod Augustinus citatus num. 54 ex 2. de doctr. Christ. cap. 34 intelligat per Regulas connexionum. Neque enim intelligit tantum regulas formandi Syllogismum, quamquam & illas intelligit. Sed intelligit maxime propinquitatem sententiarum & certa principia, ex quibus perspici potest, sententias inter se, sive veras sive falsas, vere esse connexas . . . Haec consequentia sive veritas connexionis non pendet sane a forma ulla syllogistica, sed a rerum propinquitate & necessitudine, &, ut candissimus doctor [Augustinus] loquit, ratione perpetua & divinitus instituta."

43. Voetius, *Disputationes selectae* I, 10: "Ex absurdis consequentiis *primo*, quia sequeretur homines *alogoos* se habere circa res divinas absque ratiocinatione: breviter esse tanquam equos & mulos contra Psalm. 32:9. *Secundo*, non posse non alios erudire, reprehendere, convincere, atque adeo finem illum scripturarum (de quo 2 Timoth. 3:16) obtinere."

continuity between the theology of the Reformation and the post-Reformation period, on the other hand.

In order to make a link I start with the observation that in the seventeenth century all Protestant scholastics, in their composition of the doctrine of God, made an extensive use of the definitions and distinctions developed by the medieval schoolmen. For the purpose of this essay it suffices to concentrate on the doctrine of God's communicable attributes as this enables us to think and speak about the most important aspects of the present issue.

The first thing to note is the fact that Cocceius, at least in his *Summa theologiae,* composes his doctrine of God analogous to the classical scheme that was used by the medieval schools from the time of Aquinas and onwards. First the question is discussed whether God exists (*quod sit*); secondly, the question what God is (*quid sit*) and, thirdly the question who God is (*quis sit*). The first question is answered by an exposition of the proofs for God's existence. The second question concerning the nature of God's essence is discussed by an exposition of God's attributes and, finally, the third question is dealt with by an exposition of the doctrine of Trinity.[44]

The central question for our purpose here concerns the way in which Cocceius deals with the doctrine of the divine attributes. It appears that his discussion of these attributes corresponds substantially to that of his Reformed orthodox contemporaries, for example, the division of the divine attributes in *communicabilia* and *incommunicabilia.* Like Voetius, Cocceius considers God's knowledge, will, and power as the most important *communicabilia* to be discussed and he deals with all the current distinctions in this *locus.* It is striking, however, how he criticizes each distinction he borrows from the medieval and Reformed tradition by commenting on it with the stereotypical sentence:

> I am not sure if this term is sufficiently appropriate for teaching. The words taught by the Holy Spirit are much more suited to inform us. Human terminology is nearly always liable to contest.

Having made this observation Cocceius proceeds to examine the

---

44. Cocceius, *Summa theologiae,* cap.8 § 1: "Ut doctrina de foedere et testamento Dei (ex quo spes est vitae aeternae, & amor ejus, qui eam spem facit & dat; in quo totius Theologiae apex, consummatio & finis est) tradi possit, necesse est, animum auditoris firmari in ea cogitatione, *quod Deus sit.*"

contents of the terms relating to the matter in question. Strong criticism is leveled against the medieval concept of the *potentia Dei* or the power of God. Like Calvin, Cocceius refuses to explore the concept of God's *potentia absoluta*, but in his treatment of this concept he nevertheless elaborates Calvin's theory on this point.[45] With reference to Christ's prayer in Gethsemane, he writes:

> Christ, in his agony in the garden of Gethsemane, intimated that something which is possible in itself, is impossible in respect of certain other grounds and causes: "All things are possible to thee," Mk. 14: 36 and Lk. 22: 42 (. . .) All things our mind can draft are possible to God. But it is impossible that God's will is not done, nor is his will unwise and unjust. Here we can use the distinction used by the scholastics, that something, which is possible to God in an absolute way, is at the same time impossible when considered and measured by another causal order. However, we must be on our guard against the practice of misusing such expressions as God's absolute and ordained power in order to assert that God by his absolute power can do everything people can think of; as if God's ordained power only depends on his decree and not on his wisdom and on what is becoming to him (. . .). It is impossible for God, however, to will his glory to be suppressed and obscured (. . .). Therefore, we reject the idea of an absolute power which disconnects the essence of possible things and their purposefulness.[46]

45. For Calvin's position on this point, see D. Steinmetz, *Calvin in Context* (Oxford, 1995), 40–52 (Calvin and the Absolute Power of God). Steinmetz ascertains: "Calvin is unwilling to entertain even a hypothetical separation of God's power from his justice (. . .). What the scholastics regard as useful experiment in thought, Calvin regards as shocking blasphemy" (49). The difference between the medieval scholastics and Calvin, according to Steinmetz, was that Calvin not only warned against the misuse of the distinction, but that he rejected the distinction in itself. The question arises wether this is a correct interpretation of Calvin. In my view, Calvin only rejected a certain (late) medieval interpretation of the distinction. Calvin never assailed the authentic meaning of the *potentia absoluta*.

46. Cocceius, *Summa theologiae*, cap. 14 § 6, 7: "Ita Christus in agoniai sua in horte innuit, esse aliquid possibile in se, quod non sit possibile ex certa ratione & causa. Ita enim ad Deum dixit: Omnia tibi possibilia sunt, Marc. 14:36, Luc. 22:42 (. . .). Omnia, quae mente concipi possunt, Deo sunt possibilia. Sed non est possibile, neque ut voluntas Dei non fit; neque ut voluntas Dei non sit sapiens & justa. Possumus hic uti vocabulo Scholasticis usitato, ut aliquid absolute possibile, idemque secundum ordinem & propter causam impossibile dicamus. Cavendum est tamen, ne nomine Potentia absoluta & ordinata abutamur: ut dicamus, omnia Deum facere posse potentia absoluta, quae ab hominibus cogitari possunt: quasi ordinatio potentiae, ut loquuntur, sit a solo decreto, & non pendeat a decentia & sapientia." Cf. cap 10 § 75: "Neque enim

This is just one of the many instances in which Cocceius confirms his own teaching by quoting from the very heritage of scholastic theology which later interpreters believe he undermined. Although Cocceius admits that God can do more than He actually does, he does assert that God can do nothing that contradicts his honor and wisdom. In using the word "purposefulness" (*finis*) he intends to warn against a power theory that isolates God's power from his wisdom. That is to say, God's absolute power may never be used in such a way that God is supposed to do every possible thing people could conceive of. Like his ordained power, i.e. God's power determined by his decree, God's absolute power must always be related to God's righteousness and wisdom, i.e. the other properties which make up his character. In no way, Cocceius avers, must one allow God's omnipotence to undermine his goodness, righteousness and faithfulness and to relativize the covenant. In his opinion, it were the late medieval, radical nominalistic schoolmen who used the distinction between God's absolute and ordained power to claim that it is factually possible that God can change the established order. They over-emphasized divine power, creating an image of God as a capricious agent who cannot be relied upon. Like his orthodox and scholastic Reformed contemporaries Cocceius tried to overcome these serious shortcomings by emphasizing that God's power coincides with his will and that God's will in turn coincides with his goodness, wisdom and righteousness.[47]

When we take only a brief look at Voetius' discussion of the *potentia*-distinction,[48] Cocceius' disquisition fails to impress the reader. Voetius' conceptual apparatus appears to be rather advanced and delicate. That does not alter the fact that both theologians are in complete agreement in their protest against the late medieval *potentia*-distinction. The surprising part of it is that both defend the same points concerning God's absolute power. In the first place, Voetius like Cocceius refutes the

---

agnoscimus potentiam absolutam, quae separet a rerum possibilium essentia eorum respectum ad finem. Propter hanc potentiam omnia possibilia sunt, quae Deum & gloriam ejus narrare possunt."

47. Cocceius, *Summa theologiae*, cap. 14 § 8: "Ceterum, ut a possibilitate fiat transitus ad rem extantem, necesse est etiam intercedere voluntatem Dei. Quemadmodum dicit Apocalyps. 4. vers. 11 . . .: propter voluntatem tuam sunt, & condita sunt. Ex quo etiam intelligitur, id, quod propter voluntatem Dei est, esse Deo *thelèton*. Deus autem non potest velle, ut gloria sua opprimatur, aut extinguatur."

48. Voetius, *Disputationes selectae* I, 402–9. For a thorough analysis of Voetius' idea of omnipotence, see G. van den Brink, "Gods almacht," in Van Asselt & Dekker, *De scholastieke Voetius*, 69–82.

late nominalistic interpretation of God's omnipotence. Even if God could actualize his power in other possible worlds, he does not have the power to act beyond his essential righeousness.[49] Secondly, Voetius like Cocceius emphasizes God's will as the point differentiating the absolute power from his ordained power. Thirdly, both Voetius and Cocceius defend the same position which Calvin took on the *potentia*-distinction. As we noted earlier, Calvin's refusal to speak of divine power apart from divine willing did not imply a rejection of God's omnipotence in its authentic meaning.[50] According to Voetius, Calvin's protest against the distinction was on line with Erasmus' remonstrance against the blasphemous disputations of the late medievals in which "they examined endlessly and immoderately what God could do and what He could not do.[51]

Cocceius as well as Voetius, then, kept aloof from the late nominalistic speculations about the *potentia*-distinction and linked up with the stand taken earlier by Thomas Aquinas and by Scotus.[52] These medieval theologians used the distinction between *potentia absoluta* and *ordinata* to emphasize God's freedom, on the one hand, and his faithfulness, on the other hand. God's absolute power indicates that the created order does

49. Voetius, *Disputationes selectae* I, 407: "Probl. 1. Quid sentiendum de distinctione illa Lombardi & quorundam antiquorum scholasticorum: *Deus quaedam potest de Potentia, quae non potest de justitia?* Resp. si justitia juris divini positivi & revelati intelligitur, utique admittenda est: sin vero de justitia juris divini naturalis, negamus illum praeter, aut supra, aut contra illam quid posse; quia implicat contradictionem."

50. Calvin, *Institutio*, III, 23, 2: "Neque tamen commentum ingerimus absolutae potentiae: quod sicuti profanum est, ita merito detestabilis nobis esse debet. Non fingimus Deum exlegem, qui sibi ipsi lex est."

51. Voetius, *Disputationes selectae* I, 411: "Sed merae sunt calumniae. Si quis enim autores inspiciat, videbit illos rationibus, instantiis, et autoritatibus, quas adducant, nihil aliud velle, quam quod Erasmus, qui in notis ad 1 Timoth. 1 (ubi vide) reprehendit periculosas, ineptas, absurdas, temerarias, immo et blasphemas nonnumquam disputationes scholasticorum, quibus sine fine sine modo disquirunt, An Deus hoc vel illud possit."

52. Van den Brink, "Gods almacht." in *De scholastieke Voetius*, 72, 80 and 82. Cf. Thomas, *Summa theologiae*, I, q. 25 art. 5. Hotly debated is the interpretation of W. Courtenay, that Scotus shifted the points and prepared the way for the *potentia*-distinction of later nominalists, who considered the *potentia absoluta* and *ordinata* as two independent power reservoirs or power dispensations. To this view it can be objected that Scotus' emphasis on the *potentia absoluta* does not need to be problematic when it is related to his doctrine of synchronic contingency. In addition, Scotus underlined that the *potentia absoluta* is not allowed to contrast with God's essential attributes. See A. Vos Jaczn., *Johannes Duns Scotus* (Leiden, 1994), 242–45.

not coincide with God's possibilities, while God's ordained power indicates that the created order is grounded in the free action of God's will as found in his eternal decree. According to Aquinas it is impossible that God by his absolute power breaks through the order in the work of Creation and through the order in the work of Salvation, once they are established by God's eternal decree. To be sure, the rejection of the late medieval speculations by the Reformers and their successors explains why later Reformed tradition emphasized so much the covenant idea. The roots of covenant theology can already be found in the early medieval schools. In this connection, it seems to me that it is not incorrect to claim a strong continuity between medieval, reformation and post-reformation theology concerning a key concept in the doctrine of divine attributes.

VIII. Conclusion

Measured by the four Muller points, and considering our review of Cocceius' declarations on scholastic method, it appears to be a misconception to construe a radical difference between the theological method of Cocceius and the scholastic method of his Reformed orthodox contemporaries. The comparison with Voetius, as the most important representative of seventeenth-century Reformed orthodoxy, goes a long way towards disproving the claim that "there are differences between Cocceius and the scholastics on most issues in theology" or that "he regarded scholasticism as a method essentially alien to Reformed thought."[53] Furthermore, a close examination of his doctrine of divine attributes in the *Summa theologiae ex scripturis repetita* does not permit us to agree with those interpreters who label his theology as a specimen pre-eminently of a "biblical" and, therefore, "antischolastic theology."

Therefore, the conclusion seems to be justified that Cocceius' declamations against the scholastic theology use the term in a very strict and narrow sense. It rather concerned certain contents of late medieval scholasticism such as semi-pelagianism and certain forms of seventeenth-century Reformed scholasticism such as prolix and disputative elaborations of theological points which left no room for the development of novel exegetical methods. Cocceius did not attack his scholastic opponents on account of their logically argued theology; rather he contested its function as a standard for judging his orthodoxy.

---

53. McCoy, *The Covenant Theology of Johannes Cocceius*, 236.

If, however, by "scholasticism" one indicates "the more general phenomenon of a logically argued theology, resting on traditional distinctions and definitions,"[54] then there is little difference between Cocceius' theology and the theology of his Reformed opponents.

At any rate, Cocceius deserves to be celebrated today primarily for developing new exegetical insights which he attempted to incorporate into the orthodox system of Reformed theology without being hindered by fixed and standardized positions. Only when scholastic method degenerated into some sort of "drilling" and "teaching tricks" in stead of being used as a form of logical analysis, scholasticism was the object of his protest. Scriptural language and biblical concepts, he insisted, should not be allowed to lose their original splendor and color. Scripture should tell its own story without being overgrown by a blanket of words and concepts invented by men. In short, Cocceius' conflict with Reformed orthodoxy did not so much concern the interpretation of the classical loci of Reformed dogmatics, but rather his dynamic interpretation of salvation history and his perception of the relationship between Old and New Testament, together with the implications of his view on this relationship for Christian ethics. The question, however, whether Cocceius indeed succeeded in applying his historical-covenantal model to the orthodox Reformed system, is still hotly debated in current Cocceius-research.[55]

---

54. Muller, *PRRD*, 2:121.

55. For this debate, see Schrenk, *Gottesreich*, 83 (Anm. 2); McCoy, *The Covenant Theology*, 152, 160; Faulenbach, *Erkenntnis Christi*, 145ff; Van Asselt, *Amicitia Dei*, 26–27.

11

Puritan Theology as Historical Event:
A Linguistic Approach to the Ecumenical Context

Carl R. Trueman

I. Introduction

In 1662, with the passing of the Act of Uniformity, those within the Church of England who wished for a more thorough reformation of its practices, and who found themselves unable to accept what they regarded as the popish aspects of the Book of Common Prayer, were forced to make a difficult choice: either they should conform and give up their deeply-held beliefs about the church; or they should leave the church in protest. Nearly two-thousand chose the latter option and thus Puritanism made the transition to non-conformity.

This event had more than just immediate ecclesiastical significance. It effectively excluded the Puritans from the English establishment, political, educational, and ecclesiastical, and thus guaranteed that the Reformed theology for which most of them stood would no longer be a significant force in any of these three realms. The thinking that had undergirded much of the Parliamentary cause in the Civil War, which had exerted such an influence on several generations of Cambridge students, and which had formulated the Westminster Confession of Faith, would henceforth play no direct role at the centers of power.

One of the long-term effects of this displacement of Puritanism was the image it came to possess in the secondary scholarship which grew up around the events of the seventeenth century. For many, Puritanism was a mere embarrassment, a rather crude aberration whose only real contribution to English society was the restriction of personal freedom and the wanton destruction of much beautiful ecclesiastical art.[1] Only outside of the Oxbridge and Anglican establishment could anything approaching a more positive appraisal be found: for example, in the

---

1. For a discussion of this, see Carl R. Trueman, *The Claims of Truth: John Owen's Trinitarian Theology* (Carlisle Paternoster, forthcoming), ch. 1.

massive scholarly work of S. R. Gardiner whose adherence to Irvingism ironically excluded him from holding an academic position at either Oxford or Cambridge.[2]

The situation has been somewhat different over recent decades. In America, Perry Miller almost single-handedly started a scholarly industry examining Puritanism, particularly in terms of its New England context.[3] William Haller and M. M. Knappen also produced significant studies in the field which have become standard resources for later studies.[4] Then, with the passing of the Anglican monopoly of higher education in England, and the rise of historical schools interested in understanding the events of the seventeenth century with reference to the wider changes which that period experienced in terms of social and economic relations, Puritanism has once again re-entered the historical narrative and is being taken seriously by historians. For example, the work of Patrick Collinson has brilliantly demonstrated the impact of the various Puritan controversies on the shape of English society and politics in the late sixteenth century.[5] Then, the monumental work of Christopher Hill, written from a predominantly Marxist perspective, has examined Puritanism in terms of the rising bourgeoisie and the development of the mercantile economy. To Hill, therefore, the Civil War became the first of the modern bourgeois revolutions, and Puritanism an inherently early modern movement.[6] The work of such as Collinson and Hill has sparked a significant amount of subsequent interest in the social and political dimensions of Puritanism. Much of the focus has in consequence been predominantly on the social and political context: Puritan thought in itself features in these various narratives mainly as the ideological superstructure for the underlying social and economic changes, or as a subsidiary part of larger discussions of church and court politics.

Nevertheless, despite the overwhelming dominance of the social and economic historians in this field, a small tradition of scholarship has been developing which looks more seriously at the thought of Puritans and

2. For example, see his *History of the Great Civil War*, 4 vols. (Adlestrop: Windrush Press, 1987).

3. For example, see Miller's *The New England Mind: The Seventeenth Century* (Cambridge: Harvard University Press, 1939).

4. W. Haller, *The Rise of Puritanism* (New York: Columbia, 1955); M. M. Knappen, *Tudor Puritanism* (Chicago: University of Chicago Press, 1939).

5. For example, see Collinson, *The Elizabethan Puritan Movement* (Oxford: Clarendon Press, 1967).

6. For example, see Hill, *Society and Puritanism in Pre-Revolutionary England* (London: Secker and Warburg, 1967).

which regards this as important in its own right as part of the intellectual history of the Christian church. Pre-eminent among such scholars is Geoffrey Nuttall, whose work on the Holy Spirit in the theology and the experience of Puritans remains a classic of its kind.[7] Then, in addition to Nuttall, a second strain of studies of Puritan theology has developed which focuses even more closely upon the doctrinal content of Puritan thought. This tradition is the result not simply of changes in the interests of academics in the United Kingdom but rather more of the rise to prominence of neo-Calvinism particularly within English non-conformist circles from the 1950s onwards. The establishment of the Puritan Studies Conference (now the Westminster Conference) and the Banner of Truth Trust in the 1950s bears witness to this revival, and, in this context, the personal influence of the great preacher, D. Martyn Lloyd-Jones (1899–1981) and of the popular evangelical churchman and scholar James I. Packer (1926–) was highly significant.[8]

The tradition of Puritan studies which developed in the wake of Lloyd-Jones and Packer was far more interested in the theological and doctrinal aspects of Puritanism than the more mainstream academic tradition had been, but was driven to a large extent by contemporary dogmatic interests. This tradition in many ways culminated in the monograph of R. T. Kendall, *Calvin and English Calvinism to 1649*, which was a revision of the author's Oxford D.Phil. thesis and which contributed to a debate within English neo-Calvinist circles concerning the extent of the atonement and the nature of assurance.[9] Kendall made no secret of his sympathy for the Amyraldian reading of Calvin, and regarded the Puritans as "experimental predestinarians" whose theology, as it related to Christian experience, was little different from those of the Arminians whom they opposed. Kendall's thesis has met vigorous opposition from within the academic and theological community but the tradition of "Calvin against the Calvinists" scholarship within which it must be located has continued to find some support despite the obvious

---

7. Nuttall, *The Holy Spirit in Puritan Faith and Experience* (Chicago: University of Chicago Press, 1992).

8. For an account of this movement, see Iain H. Murray, *D. Martyn Lloyd-Jones: The Fight of Faith 1939–1981* (Edinburgh: Banner of Truth, 1990). For good collections of essays in this tradition, see D. Martyn Lloyd-Jones, *The Puritans: Their Origins and Successors* (Edinburgh: Banner of Truth, 1987); J. I. Packer, *Among God's Giants: The Puritan Vision of the Christian Life* (Eastbourne: Kingsway, 1991).

9. Kendall, *Calvin and English Calvinism to 1649*, 2d ed., (Carlisle: Paternoster, 1997).

flaws in the traditions methodology and approach to sources.[10] Nevertheless, these flaws are themselves so crucial that it is unlikely that this tradition will last much longer.

In the context of the above—the emphasis of social historians on broader issues of social and economic change, and the anachronistic dogmatic focus of recent theological studies of Puritan theology—the time would seem ripe for a new agenda. Sixteenth century studies, as epitomised by the work of Heiko Oberman and the exegetical investigations of David Steinmetz and his students, is a growing field in which the ideas of the age have been taken with tremendous seriousness and where history has been rescued from both the systematic theologians and the radical materialists alike.[11] Recently, this approach has been applied to the Reformed Orthodoxy of the late sixteenth and early seventeenth centuries by Richard Muller in a way that has transcended the terms of debate as pursued by the older scholarship and pointed to the fundamental continuity between Reformed Orthodoxy and the ongoing Western theological tradition.[12] Muller, however, has focused primarily, though not exclusively, on continental thinkers, and it is the argument of this paper that the time is now ripe for a more extensive study of British Puritan theology in terms of the wider scholarly debates currently being pursued by Muller and others, and that developments within the field of the history of ideas currently taking place within English scholarship offer an ideal way for this to take place. What is needed is an approach which allows due attention to be given to the continuities between Puritanism and the wider intellectual context—both synchronic and diachronic—in order to see where, if at all, Puritan theology makes a distinctive contribution. Too much scholarship on Puritanism has started by stressing the discontinuities—whether social, ecclesiastical, or theological—for its location within the wider theological trajectories to be mapped with any degree of accuracy.

II. Puritan Texts as Linguistic Events

The history of ideas is a much reviled field—in the English-speaking

10. One of the earliest, and most devastating, critiques of the Kendall thesis is that by Paul Helm, *Calvin and the Calvinists* (Edinburgh: Banner of Truth, 1981).

11. For example, see Heiko A. Oberman, *The Harvest of Medieval Theology* (Durham: Labyrinth, 1983); David C. Steinmetz, *Calvin in Context* (New York: Oxford University Press, 1995).

12. For example, see his *Post-Reformation Reformed Dogmatics* (Grand Rapids: Baker, 1987–).

world, Sir Lewis Namier spoke for many when he argued that ideas were simply *a posteriori* justifications of actions which had already been taken or decided upon. This attitude, combined with a strong philosophical tendency towards materialism, has served to marginalise the subject within mainstream history faculties and drive it into exile, where, for example, it serves as the handmaid of other disciplines, such as philosophy or science. The result is that the history of theology has become simply part and parcel of the theological discipline, and is now regarded by "mainstream" historians as confessional dogmatics in disguise or simply as a form of academic antiquarianism which makes no real scholarly contribution to historical debates as now pursued.

There is, as always, some truth in these claims: the work of R. T. Kendall, for example, is driven, quite openly, by a dogmatic agenda. Indeed, the "Calvin against the Calvinists" debate is, to a large extent, a discussion about the systematic content and importance of sixteenth and seventeenth century Reformed thinking in relation to its present day usefulness rather than an attempt to produce historically informed analyses of the relevant documents. Such an agenda finds little sympathy among mainstream historians and merely confirm their suspicions about the history of ideas. Nevertheless, the history of ideas does not have to be a thinly-disguised attempt to establish one's own present day identity, as the work of the Regius Professor of Modern History at the University of Cambridge, Quentin Skinner, has sought to demonstrate.

Skinner's work is not without its critics—"a disturbing number of them," as he himself says[13]—and there is not space here to debate the strengths and weaknesses of his position. For the record, I myself consider his approach to be a sound one, and will therefore confine myself to describing it and pointing to its usefulness for the field of Puritan studies.

Skinner's major methodological statement is his 1969 article, "Meaning and Understanding in the History of Ideas,"[14] and his later work is essentially an application and development of the agenda he there describes. The argument of the paper is summed up near the end:

> The essential question which we therefore confront, in studying any given text, is what its author, in writing at the time he did write for the

13. Q. Skinner, *Liberty Before Liberalism* (Cambridge: Cambridge University Press, 1997), 106.

14. Skinner, "Meaning and Understanding in the History of Ideas," *History and Theory* 8 (1969): 3–53.

audience he intended to address, could in practice have been intending to communicate by the utterance of this given utterance. It follows that the essential aim, in any attempt to understand the utterances themselves, must be to recover this complex intention on the part of the author. And it follows from this that the appropriate methodology for the history of ideas must be concerned, first of all, to delineate the whole range of communications which could have been conventionally performed on the given occasion by the utterance of the given utterance, and, next, to trace the relations between the given utterance and the wider *linguistic* context as a means of decoding the actual intention of the given writer.[15]

What Skinner is proposing is a history of ideas that is fundamentally a linguistic enterprise, one which focuses on establishing authorial intention by analysing the range of plausible intentions which underlie any given text. Basic to this is the idea that sentences are not simply grammatical and syntactical constructions which can be understood purely by judicious use of a dictionary and a grammar, but that they are in fact *historical acts* which both partake of the forms of their age and are intended to fulfil a particular purpose. As historical acts, such texts must be set, like any other historical act or event, in context before they can be properly understood, a move which involves placing them both in the broader contemporary scene and against the background of the tradition/culture/history from which they emerge. Only when both dimensions of the context are understood will the true meaning of the words or text emerge. That is the task of the history of ideas. Within this task, of course, the social context has its role—but not as that which ultimately *determines* what is said; rather, it is that which provides the final court of appeal, to use Skinner's own phrase, of what it might have been possible or plausible for someone within a given society to intend to communicate.

The Skinner approach to history offers a methodological approach to studying Puritanism which is at once both contextualised, in that it takes seriously the historical situation in which Puritan works were written, and yet which also takes with absolute seriousness the intellectual content of the various texts studied. Puritan works are no longer to be viewed as abstract dogmatic treatises, written in isolation from the historical context. Instead, they must be firmly set within the time frame in which they were written—the time frame that determined the range of possible

15. Skinner, "Meaning and Understanding," 48–49.

language used and fields of meanings and intentions which it was possible to express. By looking at Puritan texts as *linguistic* phenomenon and therefore as *historical* acts in and of themselves, Skinner's suggestion provides a way of avoiding the kind of dogmatically driven confessionalism evident in certain studies while yet not succumbing to the kind of materialist ideology which underpins the analyses offered by, for example, Marxist historians. This ideology underplays the ultimate significance of the text's linguistic meaning in favour of the social and economic concerns hidden beneath the surface.

In addition, such a linguistic approach inevitably highlights the need to move Puritan texts from the narrow English or British context in which they are so often studied, particularly by the social historians, into the European context of whose intellectual and theological culture they were an integral part and in relation to which they must be studied. The prevalent tendency to view Puritanism as a distinctively Anglo-Saxon phenomenon is due, in part, to the problems associated with the name: Puritanism as a phenomenon emerged in the context of ecclesiastical and liturgical debates surrounding the Protestant settlement under Edward VI and Elizabeth I, and as such does represent something of a peculiarly English phenomenon; but the theological content of most Puritan thought is not so easily defined in terms of its national context, with all leading Reformed and, later, Puritan intellectuals from the reign of Henry VIII onwards, being involved in studying, reading and dialoguing with their continental counterparts. A glance at any Puritan library catalogue, or at the marginalia or citations index of any major Puritan theological tome will bear witness to the fact that the intellectual world occupied by these men was no respecter of national boundaries but was, in fact, an international zone, occupied to a large extent by continental authors, Reformed, Luthern, and Catholic, as well as by the great thinkers of the past, classical, patristic, and medieval.[16]

Theology as an intellectual discipline was pursued by these men primarily in an international context, and while books still appear bearing names such as *Scottish Theology*, such titles are at best misleading, privileging as they do the categories of nationhood and geography in a subject where these are of secondary importance when compared with

16. For good examples of Puritan library catalogues, see G. F. Nuttall, "A Transcript of Richard Baxter's Library Catalogue: A Bibliographical Note," *Journal of Ecclesiastical History* 2 (1951): 207–21; Nuttall, "A Transcript of Richard Baxter's Library Catalogue (Concluded)," *Journal of Ecclesiastical History* 3 (1952): 74–100; John Owen, *Bibliotheca Oweniana* (London, 1684).

the international intellectual context.[17] It was this, and not the national ecclesiastical or political situation which provided the intellectual framework for their work and which determined the possible range of ideas which they were able to articulate and the various means of expression which they were able to choose, issues which, as Skinner, highlights, lie at the very heart of a credible history of ideas. A careful distinction must therefore be made between the shape of national church politics and the shape and content of the theology held by individuals within particular ecclesiastical contexts: the former can be regarded as, to a large extent, dependent upon the context of national politics; the latter is shaped by the wider intellectual context, something which is emphatically international in nature. Theology in England or Scotland, whether in the seventeenth or the twentieth century and regardless of national peculiarities, is first and foremost an integral part of the wider international picture, and this international picture must provide the primary categories for analysis of its intellectual content. The theologies of Knox and Rutherford, Perkins and Owen are first and foremost European events in terms of their sources, content, dialogue partners and means of expression, as well as their authors' self-understanding as being part of a Europe-wide movement for the reformation of the church. It is not surprising that works which place primary emphasis on national categories when dealing with intellectual history are in the main considered to be of only marginal interest by serious intellectual historians.

What emerges from the study of the way in which the Puritans use the language of their day is the importance of setting Puritanism within what might be termed the wider ecumenical scene: Puritan theology partakes of the same intellectual and linguistic culture of other contemporary "theologies," continental Reformed Orthodox, Remonstrant, and Roman Catholic. A case for its national identity can therefore only be made when its *distinctive* use of this *common* culture and tradition is examined in detail. When this is done, however, Puritan theology, and its Scottish counterpart in the work of, for example, Samuel Rutherford, emerges not as an idiosyncratic national movement which relates only to the developments within the context of British Reformation and post-Reformation life and thought, but as part of a wider phenomenon which can only be understood when related to the Western theological tradition as a whole.

17. T. F. Torrance, *Scottish Theology* (Edinburgh: T. and T. Clark, 1996).

III. The Language of Causality in John Owen's Theology

A good example of the way in which the application of Skinner's thinking can enlighten Puritan studies can be given by using his approach to analyse John Owen's 1647 text, *The Death of Death in the Death of Christ*.[18] This work is, without doubt, the most controversial of Owen's writings, dealing as it does with the doctrine which has come to enjoy notoriety as "limited atonement" but which is perhaps better described as "particular redemption"—the idea that Christ only died in intention to save a particular number of people, the elect.

The text can be analyzed on a number of different levels. For example, we can start by looking at Owen's use of Aristotelian language. Given Brian Armstrong's emphasis on the importance of Aristotle as a factor which leads post-Reformation Reformed thought to deviate from that of the earlier Reformers, it might be tempting to understand this linguistic distinctive as that which decisively shapes the content of the treatise and which causes Owen's theology to take the direction which it does.[19] Such an interpretation is entirely plausible, and would seem, at first glance, to be adopting the kind of linguistic approach to Owen which has been recommended above. Nevertheless, this kind of linguistic approach falls down because of its naive failure to take sufficient account of both the diachronic and synchronic linguistic contexts. At its most blatantly banal, such argumentation involves the apparent assumption that there is a direct and necessary link between a certain kind of theology or theological conclusion and the use of Aristotelian language.[20] Theological "distinctives," such as limited atonement, are then interpreted as a result of this commitment to Aristotelian language.[21] Given these basic suppositions within the argument, the existence of any other theological system which used Aristotelian language and structure

---

18. The edition of Owen's writings which I have used is *The Works of John Owen*, 24 vols. (London: Johnstone and Hunter, 1850–55), hereafter *Works. The Death of Death* is found in volume 10.

19. For Brian Armstrong's influential discussion of Protestant Scholasticism, see his *Calvinism and the Amyraut Heresy* (Madison: University of Wisconsin Press, 1969), 30–31.

20. On occasion, such a naive approach has even assumed that direct comparison can be made between Aristotle's use of language and that by the seventeenth-century Puritans without taking any account of semantic developments in the intervening two-thousand years. For a particularly clear example of such argumentation, see the claims of Alan C. Clifford, *Atonement and Justification: English Evangelical Theology, 1640–1790—An Evaluation* (Oxford: Clarendon Press, 1990), 96.

21. Clifford, *Atonement and Justification*, 96.

and yet expressed at an opposite, or even merely substantially different, conclusions, would be enough to invalidate the basic thesis.

In applying a linguistic approach at this point, the first thing to examine in addressing the question of Owen's use of Aristotle is the possibility or likelihood of choosing an alternative conceptual vocabulary for the task he has undertaken: is his choice of Aristotelian language one that has peculiar significance or can it be explained on the basis of the lack of alternatives? This question can be answered in two parts: first, by looking at whether one particular pedagogical vocabulary and apparatus was dominant at this time; and, secondly, by seeing if, given the existence of a dominant tradition, there were good grounds for someone like Owen to reject this in favour of an alternative.

The first issue, that of the existence of a dominant pedagogical vocabulary can be easily answered: yes there was, and it was that which had developed in European universities during the Middle Ages, undergoing modification during the Renaissance. This issue has been dealt with at great length by Charles B. Schmitt who has demonstrated conclusively that the tradition of vocabulary and scholarly apparatus developed during the Middle Ages and Renaissance was dominant within European intellectual life until the end of the seventeenth-century.[22] Central to this apparatus was a variety of terms drawn from Aristotelian philosophical traditions: the language of causality, for example, and of being, act and potency. The accepted language of university discourse cannot be reduced to that of Aristotle—there had, after all, been over 2000 years of pedagogical development between Aristotle and the seventeenth century—but it is undeniable that many elements of Aristotelian terminology enjoyed widespread acceptance as part of the everyday vocabulary of intellectual life. Furthermore, the existence of a broadly accepted vocabulary is not to argue that European thought was monolithic at this time—it is self-evident that this was not the case—but it is to make the point that the language of learned discourse reflected the broad commitment of European intellectual culture at this time to what might be characterized as a means of expression which drew upon the language of the Medieval and Renaissance university tradition, an important part of which involved terms such as the language of causality, act, etc. The arguments have been well-rehearsed elsewhere, and so need

22. See Charles B. Schmitt, *Studies in Renaissance Philosophy and Science* (London: Variorum Reprints, 1981).

not take up space here.[23] What is important to grasp is that the almost all of the world-views which found acceptance in the intellectual culture of the seventeenth-century expressed themselves using similar language. Indeed, even when these pre-modern world-views began to break down under the pressures of the Galilean and Newtonian attacks, such was the nature of educated discourse that the very agents of the modern onslaught were forced to use the language of the despised tradition in order to bring about its destruction.[24]

Given this situation, the question regarding Owen's use of the language of Aristotelian causality becomes not, "Why does he use such language?," but rather, "If not even radical thinkers such as Galileo and Newton were able to free themselves from the linguistic grasp of prior traditions, is it at all surprising that a relatively traditional thinker such as Owen should utilize them?" The answer, self-evidently, is "No." Furthermore, it should also be noted that the universality of the language of causality in seventeenth-century theology actually meant that all theologies, from the Arminian to the Reformed to the Roman Catholic, used this vocabulary—and this should indicate immediately that no necessary link between language and content can be established at any very profound level.[25]

As to the second issue mentioned earlier, whether Owen might realistically have opted for an alternative language of discourse, two things must be borne in mind. First, the use of a particular language does not, as noted above, commit one to a particular philosophical or religious viewpoint. Thus, the use of Aristotelian language of causality, or of act and potency, or of substance and accidents, does not indicate the presence of or a commitment to Aristotle's own understanding of these terms. This in itself should be enough to defuse arguments which make the mere presence of the language of causality in a given theology sufficient grounds for positing the presence of a strong Aristotelian content.

Second, if, for the sake of argument—and only for the sake of argument—we allow that Owen did consciously choose to use

---

23. For example, see Trueman, *The Claims of Truth* (forthcoming), ch. 1.

24. See Schmitt, "Towards a Reassessment of Renaissance Aristotelianism" in *Studies*, 163 ff.

25. For example, Richard Muller's study of Arminius shows quite clearly that both Reformed Orthodox and Remonstrant depended upon Aristotelian and scholastic terminology. See his *God, Creation and Providence in the Thought of Jacob Arminius* (Grand Rapids: Baker, 1991).

Aristotelian language because of a basic sympathy for peripatetic philosophy, we must ask if such a sympathy would have been unexpected or unacceptable in his own day, given that he could, presumably, have opted for a tradition of philosophy stemming from the alternative classical tradition of Plato.[26]

This question is important precisely because those who criticize what they see as the Aristotelian commitments of the Reformed Orthodox, including Owen, have consistently failed to ask what alternative approaches may have been on offer in the seventeenth century and have thus failed to set the perceived philosophical choice of their subjects within the wider pedagogical context. Part of that context—indeed, the most important and decisive part—has been dealt with above: the prevalence of the language of causality etc. within the scholarly discourse of the time. This in itself should be sufficient to answer the question concerning Owen's language, but, at the risk of overkill, it is worthwhile just glancing at why Platonism could never have been a suitable alternative, even had such been possible within the university context.

It is obvious from the history of theology that Christian theologians from Augustine to Bultmann have chosen a variety of philosophical vocabularies, from the Platonic to the Heideggerian, to articulate their message. A critical appropriation of the language of secular philosophy by Christian theologians is thus very common, and it is clear that this demonstrates the flexibility of philosophical terminology when baptised into a Christian setting. One should beware, therefore, in a dogmatic context of any *a priori* association of the appropriation of any particular philosophical terms with any given theological outcome. Nevertheless, there are times when the general perception of particular philosophical traditions by particular theological traditions is such as to rule anyone using the language of that philosophy as guilty by suspicion. The classic example is, of course, the problems surrounding the Aristotelian renaissance of the later Middle Ages where the church took some time to be persuaded that Aristotelian concepts could be successfully used in the

---

26. The subsequent argument should not be read as implying that Owen was indeed an Aristotelian—whatever that might mean in a seventeenth-century context—but simply as indicating the suspicion with which the other broad philosophical paradigm, that of the Platonic tradition, was viewed by Puritans at the time. I raise the argument in this way because those such as Clifford who misread the situation have read it in this fashion, not because I regard Platonism and Aristotelianism as either monolithic or discrete movements, or even as in themselves particularly meaningful terms in the university context of the seventeenth century.

expression of orthodox theology.[27]

When this is taken into account, the question which Owen's use of Aristotelian language raises becomes: was there something in the prevailing Puritan attitude to Platonism which made his Aristotelian leanings inevitable? The answer to this is provided by the work of William Twisse entitled *A Discovery of D. Jacksons vanitie* (London, 1631). Twisse, a leading Reformed theologian and the first Prolocutor of the Westminster Assembly, was a vigorous defender of Reformed doctrine against Arminian assaults, and in this treatise he focuses on his contemporary, Thomas Jackson. In his polemic, Twisse sees the debate with Jackson as working on three different levels: a clash between Reformed Orthodoxy and Arminianism; a dispute between dialectic and rhetoric;[28] and an argument between a Christian Aristotelian and a Christian Platonist.[29] These are not three separate levels but all part and parcel of the overall problem as Twisse sees it: Arminianism, rhetoric, and Platonism are all inextricably linked in Jackson's attack on Reformed Orthodoxy, with the last two providing crucial support to the theological agenda of the former.

While the attack on rhetoric is of interest, again pointing to the need to set Puritan theology within the wider linguistic context, it is the attack on Platonism which, after the direct attacks on Arminianism, is the most prominent aspect of the text and of most interest to us here. From the introduction onwards, the approach to Platonism throughout the work is uniformly hostile, with Twisse pointing to the superiority of Aristotle over Plato on a number of key issues, such as the nature of time and creation, on the latter of which he cites Zabarella, a Renaissance Aristotelian, in support.[30] Indeed, for Twisse, Aristotle came to as great a knowledge of the truth as any pagan can.[31] As he says, it is surprising to find Platonic teaching coming from the pen of a man educated at his own *alma mater*, Oxford:

27. See, for example, the problems surrounding the teaching of Aristotle in the Faculty of Arts in Paris in the thirteenth century: F. C. Copleston, *A History of Medieval Philosophy* (Notre Dame: University of Notre Dame Press, 1990), 199–212.

28. For example, see Twisse, *A Discovery*, 237.

29. For a discussion of Twisse's Aristotelianism as opposed to Jackson's Platonism, see S. Hutton, "Thomas Jackson, Oxford Platonist, and William Twisse, Aristotelian" in *Journal of the History of Ideas* 39 (1978): 635–52.

30. See Twisse, *A Discovery*, 62 (creation) and 150 (time).

31. See Twisse, *A Discovery*, 65. Earlier, he cites *Metaphysics* 12 as the best discourse on the nature of God of which he is aware, *A Discovery*, 60–61.

> I muse not a little to see Platonicall and Plotinicall Philosophy, so much
> advanced by an Oxonian: as if Aristotles learning left Logicians perplext
> in a point of sophistry, and only Plotinicall Philosophy would expedite
> them.[32]

The precise reasons for Twisse's objection to Platonism in the theological
realm are not explicitly given and the reader has therefore to look
between the lines for his objections. When this is done, it would seem
that he dislikes Jackson's Platonism partly for the way it makes eternity
the fundamental category for discussing God and cuts out the explicit
causal priority of God to his creation. This would appear to lie behind
Twisse's uncharacteristic approval of Aquinas at one point:

> As for eternitie, I had rather rest upon Aquinas his definition of it, then
> on yours. For it hathe no parts formally; and as for an eminent
> conteyning of all parts of duration, that is in respect of activitie to
> produce them. Now time, and the duration therin, is rather produced
> by the *counsayle* and *will* of God, then by his *eternitie*. And therefore all
> durations doe flowe rather from Gods will, then from his *eternitie*.[33]

This is a theme which runs throughout the work, where Twisse prefers
to speak of God's relationship to the world in terms of faculty psychology
and his will rather than in terms of eternity, a position reinforced by his
nominalistic emphasis upon the noetic priority of God's acts over his
being.[34] More generally. However, what we seem to have in Twisse is the
manifestation of a general dislike and mistrust of a philosophical
tradition which he has been led to believe is incompatible with a
Reformed understanding of predestination. The rejection of Plato is so
blunt and so sweeping that it is difficult not to see cultural prejudice
rather than deep, philosophical reflection, at work here.

In this respect, it is somewhat irrelevant whether Twisse's
presentation of Jackson is a fair one, or whether, as seems even less

---

32. See Twisse, *A Discovery*, 179–80.

33. Twisse, *A Discovery*, 231. The approval of Aquinas here is uncharacteristic
because of Twisse's general, though not exclusive, preference for Scotus: see, for
example, *A Discovery*, 170–71, where he cites Scotus in opposition to Aquinas.

34. "We say, that God in doing what he will cannot sinne, because hee hath no
superiour Lord to give him lawes, to binde him; his owne wisedome alone can and doth
direct him, and it becomes his wisedome to manifest his owne glorious nature; and
therefore whatsoever hee can doe, in case hee doth it, it shall be wisely done, for as
much as his power therein is manifested." *A Discovery*, 435.

266

likely, the connection he seeks to make between Arminianism and Platonism is a necessary one: the point is that he made the connection and thus indicated that there was a link in the Reformed, Puritan mind between these two schools of thought, a connection which would inevitably drive Reformed Puritans away from a Platonic approach to theology and towards an Aristotelian one on the grounds of their desire to avoid heterodoxy. If Twisse is a sound guide to the cultural preferences of English Reformed Orthodoxy, there were no compelling reasons for Puritans to break with the means of expression used by medieval and Renaissance scholastics—Reformed thought could easily be expressed using the accepted vocabulary, even where such drew on the various Aristotelian traditions then available; moreover, alternative Platonic traditions were viewed with suspicion as carrying with them implications of Arminianism.

When one comes to Owen, it is apparent that this tendency to equate Arminianism with Platonism is present also in his works. In his early polemical piece, *A Display of Arminianism* (1642), he makes an explicit correlation in the treatise between the idea of a non-determining decree and Platonic philosophical tendencies:

> To apprehend an election of men not circumscribed with the circumstance of particular persons is such a conceited, Platonical abstraction, as it seems strange that any one dares profess to understand that there should be a predestination, and none predestinated . . . Now, such an election, such a predestination, have the Arminians substituted in the place of God's everlasting decree.[35]

Such an accusation misrepresents the position of Arminius, but, more important for our purpose here, clearly echoes some of Twisse's own sentiments by making explicit the connection that exists in Owen's mind between particular philosophical commitments and corresponding theological outcomes. Earlier in the same treatise, he had singled out Jackson as teaching precisely this heretical view of the decrees, though without explicit reference to Jackson's Platonism.[36] Then, later on, he cites the influence of Platonic philosophy on the early church as being the reason that some patristic authors felt able to argue for salvation for those who lived without knowledge of Christ but according to "right

---

35. Owen, *Works*, 10:57.
36. Owen, *Works*, 10:17.

reason."[37] Again, the connection between Platonism and heretical theology is explicit.

This supposed link between Arminian theology and Platonic philosophy would clearly have made it very difficult for Owen to have opted for a Platonic philosophical paradigm or even a vocabulary dominated by Platonic philosophical terms. This is not to argue that either man was an Aristotelian—medieval and Renaissance Aristotelianism was a pluriform phenomenon, rendering the general term unhelpful; and as is typical of theologians using (as opposed to slavishly following) secular philosophy, they were both quite capable of criticizing philosophical traditions.[38] It is, however, to point to one further reason why the Aristotelian contribution to the medieval and scholastic vocabulary would not have been obnoxious to English Puritan thinkers. Use of such language, including the Aristotelian terminology of causes, ends, and means, substance and accidents etc., is not sinister; it is simply indicative of the fact that Puritan intellectual culture developed within the context, and the normative traditions, of Renaissance universities which drew heavily on the legacy of medieval scholasticism.

In short, therefore, a study of the wider linguistic culture of Owen's thought points to three basic conclusions: first, given the dominance of the scholastic tradition within university discourse, along with its concomitant means of expression, Owen's use of Aristotelian language and argumentation is neither innovative nor surprising; second, given the close identification that existed in at least some Puritan's minds between Platonism and the hated theology of the Arminians, there are strong reasons internal to the intellectual culture of Puritan thought which would make a critical break with that dominant tradition at the points where it appears to draw on Aristotelian terminology inconceivable; and, third, given the almost universal use of scholastic language in the seventeenth-century as a means of expression for a whole variety of different, and often contradictory, thought systems, there can be no necessary link between the theological position of Owen and his choice of scholastic vocabulary, including those parts which might be characterized as Aristotelian in ultimate origin. In other words, careful linguistic analysis of Owen's thought in its contemporary setting serves to tear away a very important dimension of the arguments which stem from the influential equation made by Armstrong between

37. See Owen, *Works* 10:110–11.
38. See, for example, Twisse, *A Discovery*, 122.

Aristotelianism and a certain type of theology.

Given the above, it is clear that Owen's use of scholastic language is not, in fact significant as a gauge of his theological intentions. What he is doing is utilizing the accepted linguistic forms of the educational establishment of his day to argue his particular theological case—in much the same way as his opponents are doing. Set within the broad context of European education and theological discourse of the time, his Aristotelian language of causes, ends, and means is not indicative a sinister, hidden agenda, but rather of the generally accepted vocabulary of seventeenth century universities.

What this all points to, of course, is the need for the student of Puritan thought to take careful account of both the synchronic and diachronic contexts of linguistic usage. The latter allows us to locate Puritan thought within the contemporary intellectual culture. Here, it is not the differences between Puritanism and, say Arminianism or Roman Catholicism which are so significant. Indeed, it is the shared background of scholasticism which is so interesting and which, when acknowledged, allows to truly see where Puritan and Reformed theology is making a distinctive contribution. The former, the diachronic context, allows us to set Puritanism within a much longer linguistic tradition than that suggested by the narrow terms of the "Calvin against the Calvinists" debate, a tradition which stretches back well before the Reformation and points again not to the fundamental discontinuities between Puritanism and the rest of the Western tradition but to the basic continuities, continuities which once again have first to be acknowledged in order to understand where Puritanism is making a distinctive contribution.

A fine example of this kind of study is provided by an examination of John Owen's attitude to the medieval distinction between God's antecedent and consequent wills. These terms are used, for example, by Thomas Aquinas in the *Summa Theologiae*, particularly in 1a.19.6 and 1a.23.4. In the first, he is asking the question, "Whether the will of God is always fulfilled," which he answers in the affirmative, on the basis that God's will is the universal cause of all and cannot be frustrated in its effects. This, of course, creates an obvious problem with the text chosen for Aquinas first objection, 1 Tim. 2:4, "God will have all men to be saved, and to come to a knowledge of the truth." Aquinas offers three answers to this: one can follow Augustine and refer "all" to the elect; one can understand the term as applying to all classes of human beings, not every individual; or one can borrow a distinction from John of Damascus and understand the statement to refer to God's antecedent, not consequent, will. On this reading, the text effectively says that God wills all to be saved antecedently, but only those to whom grace is given to be saved consequently. These thoughts are essentially echoed in the second appearance of the terms in 1a.23.4, where the question is "Whether the predestined are chosen by God?" Here, Aquinas declares in his reply to Objection 3 (a citation of 1 Tim. 2:4) that "God wills all to be saved by his antecedent will, which is to will not simply but relatively; and not by his consequent will, which is to will simply."

There are a couple of important things to note at this point. First, the terms are being used to overcome exegetical problems raised by Aquinas' vigorously anti-Pelagian understanding of predestination, effectively allowing him to interpret universalist passages in a way which preserves the particularity of God's predestination. Second, and more important, is the fact that the terms themselves, though used here by Aquinas to support an anti-Pelagian theology of grace, are not in themselves inherently anti-Pelagian: they facilitate a conceptualization of God's will which is strongly predestinarian but they do not determine it—it is the relationship between the two, a relationship determined by Aquinas's understanding of God as First Cause and of the exegetical priority he gives to certain biblical verses, which is what makes his thinking anti-Pelagian.

In the light of this, it then becomes interesting that, in the 1647 treatise, *The Death of Death*, John Owen refers to the distinction as being "Arminian," a comment which he qualifies by noting that this represents an abuse of its purpose.[39] To impute such semi-Pelagian tendencies to Aquinas's use of the term is clearly illegitimate, so this raises the question of precisely what kind of abuse Owen has in mind. The key would appear to be the modification of the term which took place, in the Protestant tradition, at the hands of Arminius himself.

Arminius's clearest use of the terms appears in *Disputatio Privata* 19:6, where he makes the following statement:

> The will of God is either absolute or relative (*respectiva*). The absolute will is that by which he simply (*simpliciter*) wills something without respect to the will or action of the creature, such as the salvation of the faithful. The relative will is that by which he wills something with respect to the creature. This is either antecedent or consequent. The antecedent will is that by which he wills something with respect to a following volition or action of the creature, such as God willing that all should be

39. Owen, *Works* 10:323.

saved if they believe. The consequent will is that by which he wills something with respect to an antecedent volition or action of the creature, such as "It would have been better for that man through whom the Son of Man is betrayed if he had not been born." Each depends on the absolute will and is regulated in accordance with it.[40]

Arminius's distinction is identical to that of Aquinas, and it seems more than likely that it is this to which Owen is referring when he rejects it. What is significant, of course, is the fact that in Arminius' theology, the distinction is not being used to overcome exegetical difficulties entailed by a strongly anti-Pelagian doctrine of God but as a means of articulating a soteriology which allows that salvation is not, in one important sense, caused ultimately by an absolute predestinarian decree as Owen would have understood it, but is decisively influenced by the human response of faith.[41] In other words, the distinction functions in a manner not dissimilar to the *pactum* soteriology of the late medieval nominalists. This is particularly clear in his treatment of predestination and the decrees, as laid out in his *Declaration* of 1608. Arminius argues for four decrees: in the first he appoints Christ as mediator; in the second he resolves to receive into grace those who repent and believe; in the third he resolves to administer sufficient means for repentance and faith; and in the fourth he resolves to save the particular individuals who believe and persevere in faith and damn those who either do not believe or do not persevere.[42] The pattern is thus parallel to that between the absolute and consequent will: Christ's appointment as mediator is the work of God's absolute will, a connection he makes explicit elsewhere; and his resolution to save x and damn y is the result of his consequent will. The crucial key is the relation between the absolute and the consequent—a relation determined not by God's own sovereign causal will but by his foreknowledge of who would and who would not believe.[43] Thus, the framework used by Thomas has been replaced by one which is, at least in

40. Arminius, *Opera Theologica* (Leiden, 1629), 347.

41. On Arminius and God's decrees, see Eef Dekker, "Was Arminius a Molinist?," *Sixteenth Century Journal* 27 (1996): 337–52.

42. Arminius, *Opera Theologica*, 119.

43. "Hinc sequi quartum decretum, quo decrevit singulares et certas quasdam personas salvare et damnare. Atque hoc decretum praescentia Dei innititur, qua ab aeterno scivit, quinam iuxta eiuscemodi administrationem mediorum ad conversionem et fidem idoneorum, ex praeveniente ipsius gratia credituri erant et ex subsequente gratia perseveraturi; quive vero etiam non erant credituri et perseveraturi." Arminius, *Opera Theologica*, 119.

this respect, significantly different, and the soteriology of which the distinction between absolute/antecedent and consequent divine wills is now a part has a distinctly synergistic flavor, at least from the perspective of a Reformed Orthodox thinker such as Owen. As was the case with the use of scholastic language noted above, the linguistic and theological genealogy of the terms is no safe guide to the nature of the theological purpose to which it is now being put. Indeed, the theological tension between Aquinas's anti-Pelagian understanding of salvation and the exegetical issues raised by 1 Tim. 2:4 do not exist in the same way at all within Arminius's understanding of salvation.

This, then, provides part of the background to Owen's rejection of the distinction. But is this all there is to Owen's argument? If this were so, it is surely surprising that Owen himself did not seek to salvage the terminology by stressing its use in a thinker, such as Aquinas and pointing to its later abuse, rather than just rejecting it on the basis of its use by Arminians. This is where a careful comparison of the underlying purpose of the distinction as it used in Aquinas with the theological agenda of Owen is useful, revealing as it does the fact that, even in its original context, it represented a theological position which Owen himself was keen to avoid and which arguably provides a second significant layer in his rejection of it.

It will be remembered that Aquinas used the distinction as a way of dealing with the obvious exegetical problems which his vigorous predestinarianism raised for 1 Tim. 2:4. His answer was to allow a universality to a conditional will within God. If one examines Owen's exegesis of this same passage, it is interesting to note the complete absence of the hypothetical universality of God's will to save which Aquinas is willing to allow. Indeed, Owen is keen to exclude precisely such a possibility because of the unacceptable theological implications which it has:

> For God's willingness that all should be saved, from 1 Tim. 2:4, taking *all men* there for the universality of individuals, then I ask, . . . Is it in an antecedent desire that it should be so, though he fail in the end? Then is the blessed God most miserable, it being not in him to accomplish his just and holy desires . . . For our parts, by *all men* we understand some of all sorts throughout the world, not doubting but that, to the equal reader, we have made it so appear from the context and circumstances of the place, the will of God there being that mentioned by our Savior, John 6:40.[44]

44. Owen, *Works,* 10:381.

What Owen is effectively doing is picking up on part of Aquinas's thought with approval—that exegetical tradition which understands the "all men" of 1 Tim. 2:4 to refer to "all kinds of men" while explicitly rejecting another part of Aquinas's solution, his allowance for an antecedent universality in God's will to save.

Seen in this light, the relationship of both Owen and Arminius to the medieval distinction becomes more complex. On the one hand, if Owen rejects the antecedent/consequent distinction because of its Arminian abuse, it is quite clear that he also sees this abuse as being inherent in what he would clearly regard as, at best, a nonsensical and illusory distinction in God's will. On the other hand, Arminius's rejection of the predestinarian dimension of Aquinas's theology does not make his use of the distinction entirely equivocal—he is, in fact, trying to do justice to the universality of God's will to save which was precisely the reason for which Aquinas adopted the distinction.

What emerges from this analysis of the differing attitudes of Arminius and Owen to the Thomist distinction is the clear need to set their adoption/rejection of the terms in context. In the former case, the use of the term represents neither a wholesale endorsement nor a complete abuse of the tradition. It offers instead insights into the way in which scholastic terminology could be transformed within a new historical and theological context to achieve a new set of theological goals. In the latter case, the rejection of the terms does not rest simply upon their contemporary abuse but upon a rejection of the very theological concept which they were originally designed to safeguard. In other words, Owen's statement about the Arminian abuse of the distinction can only be fully understood in terms of its status as a seventeenth-century theological statement once its synchronic and diachronic linguistic contexts are taken into account. Attempts to understand its significance without reference to the wider picture, synchronic and diachronic, are doomed to failure from the outset.

IV. Conclusion

A number of points suggest themselves by way of conclusion. First, Skinner's plea for a linguistic approach to the history of ideas offers an excellent way into the study of Puritan thought as a phenomena which precludes the temptation to treat Puritan theological works as primarily dogmatic and abstracted from the wider historical context. Owen and company wrote works that were linguistic events within a historical context—and, as any other category of historical event, they must be understood in terms of both what went before them and what was happening in the wider context at the same time. When this is done, the mistakes of previous scholarship—whether that driven by the grinding of anachronistic theological axes, or the silliness of reifying "national" theologies—English, Scottish or otherwise—will be avoided. Intellectual culture in the seventeenth century was shaped by its medieval and Renaissance antecedents and was, for the most part, an international phenomenon, having no respect for national boundaries. Careful attention to Puritan use of language points quite clearly to the fact that English Puritanism was no exception to this and must indeed be located within the wider linguistic context of European theology of the time, and within the wider tradition of theology which looked back to the development of scholastic pedagogical apparatus in the later Middle Ages and Renaissance for its basic vocabulary and framework. This arises from the simple fact that the English Puritans, like their Roman Catholic and Reformed Orthodox contemporaries, were shaped in their basic outlook not just by their dogmatic convictions but also by the European University culture of which they were all a part. The historical categories and methods used to study Puritan theology must, therefore, reflect these facts if they are to function as useful heuristic tools rather than as useless Procrustean beds.

Puritan theology is indeed ill served if it is divorced from this context and treated as an independent entity. If Puritanism is one part of this wider culture, and this wider culture is that which provides much of the shape and vocabulary with which it works, then it is important that it be first located within this context before sweeping claims about its distinctive contribution to theology can be made. What is distinctive about, say, Owen's doctrine of atonement is not his use of the Aristotelian language of causality or scholastic argumentation, both of which were shared and used even by his opponents, but the ordering of intratrinitarian decrees, as I have shown elsewhere.[45] Such a point will be lost, however, if it is not first realized that his use of the language of causes, ends, and means is not distinctive but typical of the age. It is only when the basic continuities between Puritan thought and the wider cultural framework are understood that any of its distinctives become truly visible.

Finally, in focussing on the common linguistic basis of Puritanism and other seventeenth century theological movements, this kind of analysis

---

45. See Trueman, *The Claims of Truth*, Chapter Five and Appendix One.

points inevitably to the ecumenical dimension of Puritan thought. Puritanism is not an isolated aberration but one expression of the Western tradition. The language which it uses, the theology upon which it builds, and the issues with which it engages, from the Trinity to predestination, are of the essence of Western Christianity. Puritan theology needs to be studied as one of the voices within the developing story of that tradition; only then will its image as a sectarian and destructive force give way to one which emphasizes the constructive theological dialogue with the patristic, medieval and Reformation authors which thinkers such as Owen saw themselves as engaged.

12

Scholasticism and Contemporary Systematic Theology

Luco J. van den Brom

I. Introduction

Most of the systematic theologians of the dawn of the 21st century are not even interested in scholasticism, let alone a scholastic approach to theology. The rare exceptions are often theologians with a background in historical theology. The general education of theologians requires that they are at least informed about historical theology, or the history of theology, as it is often called today. A quick glance at the systematic theological textbooks shows, however, that scholasticism, like so much of the pre-Enlightenment theological tradition, remains a closed book. Where interest is shown in scholasticism, it is usually expressed very apologetically. For instance, a good excuse for studying scholastic theology is that one needs to take cognizance of the pre-history of a theological concept, or that one should be sufficiently informed about a certain ecclesiastical or theological tradition in order to address the contemporary context adequately. Apart from some rare exceptions, people who show any degree of congeniality towards scholastic theology are not easy to find. In systematic theology, the term scholasticism shares the fate of the term "dogmatics": many associate these terms with rigidity, inflexibility, traditionalism, a-historicity or timelessness, lifeless logic, or hair splitting, forced systematization etc. It certainly does not serve to encourage theologians to turn to scholasticism in search of a theological method.

It has often been pointed out that "scholasticism" is ambiguous. On the one hand, it is used in a general way to refer to a medieval type of theology, of which Thomas Aquinas is the model. It is often accompanied by a caricature in the form of an example of how some scholastic theologian had pursued some wholly unimportant detail of a theological question at great length. I shall not comment here on whether we are really dealing, in such cases, with truly unimportant or even futile issues.

On the other hand, the term scholasticism is sometimes used to refer to a particular scientific methodology, which has certainly not been limited to the Middle Ages. This latter meaning is of some importance in the discussion about the significance of scholasticism. The reason is quite simple. It remains a serious question whether there is any point in speaking of scholasticism, let alone whether theologians even know what they are talking about when they use the term in a pejorative sense. Talk of scholasticism seems to imply that we are dealing with a single thought pattern, as if all scholastics adhered to a single theology and philosophy. It is often suggested that this alleged uniformity could hold several advantages.

One advantage of a uniform scholastic theology and philosophy is that one can easily employ it to formulate a standard. On the one hand, such a uniform standard can be easily criticized, for if one has criticized one thinker on a particular point, then it is assumed that all have been countered on that point. In this way, scholasticism has effectively been made into an ideal-typical or strict theoretical model, which does not exist in reality. It is more like a way of thinking, which is presented to students as an exercise, or a classificatory concept used to group together some typical representations and ideas. On the other hand, such a uniform standard can also easily be employed as a means of criticizing other, perhaps offensive, teachings. In a theological or religious tradition, for instance, such a standard makes it much easier to identify and point out deviations from the commonly accepted views. Moreover, it could be that scholasticism as a univocal theological tradition was expressly invented or designed for that purpose, assuming that the great theologians have always thought that way. Thus for example, in Pope Leo XIII's encyclical *Aeterni Patris* (1879), it is assumed that a common kernel is to be found in the teachings of Albert the Great, Thomas Aquinas, Bonaventure and Duns Scotus, which has best been formulated by Thomas.[1] This kernel is valid for all time. This example shows that the idea of the unity of scholasticism seems to be (not only, but also) a 19th-century construction, partly inspired by the unitary thought so typical of post-Enlightenment developments.[2] If this last observation is correct,

1. See Denzinger, *Enchiridion*, 3139s. This operation formed part of a broader movement of thought attempting to use a Christian philosophy as the basis of societal renewal juxtaposed with the rising influence of modernist thought.

2. See F. C. Copleston, *Aquinas* (Harmondsworth, 1977), 246 f. He is of the opinion that, with this choice for Thomas, Leo XIII did not so much intend to set limits to philosophical reflection in the Roman Catholic tradition, as to stimulate precisely such

then the repugnance with scholasticism is understandable, since it appears to involve forced systematization.

From this brief discussion, it should be clear that a distinction ought to be made between the scholastic methodology on the one hand and the content of orthodoxy's theology on the other. Thus Van Asselt points out, quite rightly, that one could be a scholastic without being recognized as orthodox, and vice versa.[3] Scholasticism is also not bound to an ecclesiastical denomination: Lutheran theology showed as much skill in employing it for the development of its own points of view, as did Reformed and Roman Catholic theology. In what follows, I would like to argue that, methodologically speaking, scholasticism is not an outdated option for systematic theology. In order to show this, I shall consider the following questions: Of what, broadly speaking, does the scholastic method actually consist? Can it still be fruitfully employed, as a comment of Karl Barth seems to suggest? Are there examples of contemporary theologies that do not despise scholasticism? There are striking similarities between Voetius and the contemporary "Utrecht school," but the relevance of scholasticism is not limited to that, especially when it comes to questions of method.

II. Karl Barth and Scholasticism

After the account just given of the reigning distaste for scholasticism as a school of thought, one may wonder whether, in our time, not a single word has been spoken in favour of scholasticism. It certainly comes as a surprise to hear the following from the lips of a 20th-century Protestant church father, of all people, and from no less than Karl Barth himself: "Abhorrence of scholasticism is the mark of the false prophet."[4] In Barth's work are to be found countless references to the Protestant scholasticism of the 17th and 18th centuries, which he regarded, next to the Reformers, as part and parcel of his reformational theological tradition. Of course I do not mean to claim that Barth's statement

---

reflection for the sake of thinking through Thomas' work more thoroughly with an eye to contemporary intellectual concerns.

At the same time, I imagine that we may be dealing here with an actual interpretation of Vincentius of Lérin's classic rule: "quod ubique, quod semper, quod ab omnibus creditum est" (in his *Commonitorium*, 2).

3. Willem J. van Asselt, "Studie van de gereformeerde scholastiek. Verleden en toekomst," *Nederlands Theologisch Tijdschrift* 50 (1996): 290–312, esp. 291f.

4. Karl Barth, *Die Kirchliche Dogmatik*, 4 vols. in 13 parts (München: C. Kaiser, 1932–67), I/1, 296 (hereafter cited as *KD*).

justifies the reintroduction of any kind of scholasticism into theology. After all, in that statement he formulates his view negatively: he is speaking of a typical characteristic of the false prophet—fear for scholasticism. However, he leaves open the question of the mark of the true prophet. What he does say on this matter remains limited to the attitude of the true prophet: "The true [prophet] will, in the final analysis, be prepared to submit his message also to this test." According to Barth, it would seem, the attitude of the true theologian with regard to scholasticism is the same as the one she ought to have with regard to any baptism of fire. Apparently, he does not view scholasticism as a suitable climate for systematic theology. I shall return later to Barth's final declaration on this matter.

In his foreword to the reissue of Heppe's summary[5] of the most important doctrines of Protestant orthodoxy, Barth recounts how he had been deeply impressed by the beauty and perspicacity of that orthodoxy, which had made use of what had been "in any case a reliable method." He admits that—also with respect to the minute details—a relentless questioning can be very rewarding for theology, particularly with an eye to the existential implications of the truth question. Apparently, he is not only impressed by the intellectual rigor of orthodoxy, the Protestant variety of scholasticism, but also expresses warm appreciation for it by emphasizing its beauty. Moreover, Barth here expresses confidence in the methodological approach characteristic of 17th and 18th-century theology. The latter should be kept in mind in taking cognizance of Barth's subsequent remarks to the effect that he had come to the realization that the theology of orthodoxy had suffered from the same disease that he had already diagnosed in the case of neo-Protestantism. In appropriating the tradition, Barth declares, orthodoxy attempted to subordinate revelation in all its mystery to a system, with the eventual aim of making it into a useful, reasonable principle, which could be possessed by the believer, or by theology. This is the point at which he raises his objection to Protestant scholasticism. Barth is not so much concerned about scholasticism's method as with the purpose which this method was employed to serve. The aim is not justified by the means.

In Protestant orthodoxy's doctrine of Scripture, revelation came to be regarded as a principle of reason—a reason enlightened by revelation; in the 18th century, theological reason came to hold sovereign sway even

---

5. Heinrich Heppe, *Die Dogmatik der evangelisch-reformierten Kirche*, 2d ed. (Neukirchen, 1958), VII–X.

over that principle itself, but now *without* the light of revelation. Barth's claim that a transfer of authority from Scripture to reason took place is quite accurate. That had already been given with the idea of the Scripture principle itself. In the 17th century, as long as the Scripture principle[6] still functioned as a criterion for the framework within which theology had to be practiced, it meant that theology had to orient itself to Scripture as the place where divine revelation had come to expression. What God wanted to communicate is *identical* with that which had come to be expressed in Scripture. Therefore theology as reflection upon the salvific acts of God is bound to Scripture. That seems to imply a dismissal of the possibility that any new revelations might be expected from God. During the Enlightenment period, the reverse was the case, so that reason was precisely that which determined the place of Scripture within the whole of theology. This actually meant that the fundamental and final character of the Protestant Scripture principle was relativised. Elsewhere, Barth shows how this domination of revelation by reason is particularly evident from the fact that Protestant orthodoxy gave much room to a theology based on a revelation other than, and next to, the revelation of God in Jesus Christ, namely natural theology.[7] This freedom of choice with regard to revelation is theologically problematic because it suggests that people can actually choose which revelation they will take to heart: Scripture or nature. However, revelation cannot be something we do or do not choose: it is something that "happens to us"

6. The Scripture principle states that Holy Scripture (as the canon of the Old and New Testaments) is to be unconditionally accepted as the final source and rule of preaching, religious experience and knowledge. See Otto Weber, *Grundlagen der Dogmatik* (Neukirchen, 1955), 1:135f. As such, this principle is constitutive for Christian theology, but it does pose a problem for theology in the sense that God as actor becomes bound to the past. After all, even if mention is made of His great deeds of long ago, what perspective can the principle provide upon God's action in the present? The Scripture principle, taken over by the Reformers from medieval theology, does constitute a problem for Christian theology. The Jewish tradition is also familiar with the Scripture principle, by which revelation becomes fixed in the past, but is simultaneously viewed as relevant to the present and future. However, within the Jewish thought-world, the early Christian acknowledgement that divine revelation had occurred in Jesus Christ, is a revolutionary idea. By admitting the person of Christ, and the Gospels and Epistles, the early Christians broke open the closed Jewish canon, and with it the Scripture principle of their day. This has consequences for the question of the open canon, and the legitimacy of a rigid Scripture principle within the Reformed tradition.

7. *KD*, II/1, 140f.

whether we like it or not.[8] I would like to add here that Barth is right to argue in this way. It is conceptually impossible for one to prepare for revelation, for then one would have to know what such a revelation will consist of, in order to prepare for it. A revelation, of which one knows beforehand what it will be like, cannot logically be called revelation anymore, because the adoption of such an attitude suggests that God is predictable. By doing so, one regards God as being subject to the natural law, so that any element of surprise disappears from revelation. That certainly seems to entail a refusal to let God be God.

This brief analysis of some of Barth's comments makes it clear that one should distinguish between the scholastic method on the one hand, and the theological content of Protestant orthodoxy on the other. As long as this theology kept its inquiry within the confines of the Scripture principle, Barth viewed the latter as a kind of "litmus test" for this theology. However, as soon as the Scriptural criterion begins to regulate divine revelation, so that theologians may manage, organize or possess it in some way, the scholastic method becomes an instrument in service of a bad cause. Barth's argument can be further strengthened by pointing to the possibility that the extreme regulative function given to the rational Scripture principle by orthodoxy may lead to the idea that God may be experimented upon. Thus this methodology does not preclude failure to take God's transcendence seriously. However, a virtuous method is by itself never a guarantee of sound theology, so that the above comments do not yet prove that the scholastic method as a whole is profitable for theology. Before that can be said, some material comments must be made about the scholastic method itself.

III. The Method of Scholasticism

The term scholasticism is often associated with the medieval period, and taken to denote the theology and philosophy of that period. Although scholasticism did flourish during that period, the term should not be understood as referring to a phase in the history of human thought, but rather as denoting a *style* or form of thought. It concerns a style of thought that was prevalent both in antiquity and in the 18th century. The 19th century also witnessed the development, within the Roman Catholic tradition, of a kind of neo-scholasticism as one reaction to the historicising thought of the Enlightenment—a development sanctioned

8. *KD*, II/1, 154f.

by Pope Leo XIII, as has already been mentioned. Furthermore, the term refers to a scientific approach followed not only in theology and philosophy, but also in the study of law.

Typical of the latter is the use of *authorized* textual sources from the scholarly tradition that have been the subject of research and elucidation by legal practitioners. Authority is not arbitrary, but is rather an originally legal concept with which one expressed the conviction that one was dealing with a reliable witness. That does not mean that the scholastics approached their sources uncritically, or simply accepted them as they stood without further discussion. When one investigates the structure of the treatment of a question in Thomas Aquinas' *Summa Theologiae*, it strikes one that Thomas deals with both the denial and the affirmation of a statement (in that order). He then gives his own judgement, supported by reasons, and discusses the objections in the light of the reasons that he has put forward as pro-arguments. If one compares this scholastic method with the approach of the natural sciences, it seems rather rationalistic and also primitive in the sense that it is unfamiliar with experimentation as a source of knowledge. In that respect the Franciscan Roger Bacon (1214–1292) appears much more "modern" than Thomas, since it is said of Roger that he defended experimentation as the criterion for the truth of all factual statements, whether they derive from Scripture or from Aristotle.[9]

Yet Dampier notes that scholasticism had trained people so well in inductive and deductive reasoning that they could learn to formulate and test their hypotheses with observations and experiments. Even so, he makes the observation that "experimental investigation would have been foreign to their ideas." The appeal to authorities from the past is particularly objectionable to Dampier, who views it as an obstacle to the development of an experimental method. Before rushing to construct a contradiction here, one ought to realize that these "ideas" concern their metaphysical ideas about the world, rather than their views regarding methods. The forms of reasoning in which the scholastics had trained themselves are obviously not of the same order as experiments in natural science, but these reasonings do not therefore exclude the idea of an experiment. The scholastic method juxtaposes different opinions about a certain question, including the arguments in favor of them, in order to

---

9. See W. C. Dampier, *A History of Science*, 4th ed. (Cambridge, 1968), 90–93, 95f; John Losee, *A Historical Introduction to the Philosophy of Science*, 2d ed. (Oxford, 1980), 29–32, 34–36.

debate the issues, thus approaching a solution to the problems that have arisen. What occurs in this procedure is in many ways reminiscent of a thought experiment. By means of pro- and contra-argumentation, a final statement is sought, which can stand the test of the contra-arguments. In this respect, Thomas' procedure, the development of which was much stimulated by the work of Abelard, is very similar to the falsification procedure regarded by Karl Popper as the demarcation criterion for science. The issue of authority, which can easily be raised by the modern scientist as an objection against scholasticism, in order to expose its lack of scientific qualities, also plays a role in the natural sciences. But the natural sciences have shifted the issue of authority from the classic witnesses from the past to the contemporary observations of those who carry out experiments. However, the witness of the observers now has authority, as long as no one shows that the interpretations of the observations under discussion are mistaken. Then once more, we shall be dealing with reasoning in the form of pro- and contra-arguments that look suspiciously like the *Sic et Non* technique as we have it from Abelard.[10] It seems to me that one should be wary of simply dismissing the scholastic method as unscientific. It would be more prudent to enrich and reappropriate it.

As strange as this may sound to our twentieth century ears, the scholastic method, since the 12th century, was far from traditional, and the theological results could certainly not be labeled as such. Until that time, the aim had often been to read traditional texts with a literary interest (like the humanistic reading method), and then to provide a traditional interpretation of the ethos and experience of one's own world. Now, however, the traditional texts were being questioned about their meaning and truth-value from within the contemporary frame of mind of the scholastic theologian and philosopher. In order to encourage these kinds of discussions concerning the question of truth, collections were edited of so-called *sententiae*, of which that of Peter Lombard has become most famous. *Sententiae* are authoritative statements about an aspect of Christian doctrine, ranging from Holy

---

10. See e.g. F. C. Copleston, *A History of Medieval Philosophy* (London, 1972), 83; Julius R. Weinberg, *A Short History of Medieval Philosophy* (Princeton, 1964), 74. That this whole method of pro- and contra-arguments is not in the least regarded as dated in the science of argumentation, is sufficiently clear from the much used and translated book by Arne Naess, *Kommunikation und Argumentation* (Kronberg, 1975). This book employs both *pro-et-contra* and *pro-aut-contra* schemas in order to inventarise arguments, and to make argumentative structures explicit.

Scripture to the councils and church fathers.[11] The idea behind it was to formulate a problem from the Christian doctrinal tradition (*a quaestio*), which was then to be tackled with the help of pro- and contra-arguments collected from theological authorities, in order to assist students in arriving at their own judgement about the question. Although theology was regarded as direct exegesis of Holy Scripture, such a collection of *sententiae* formed the basic text of the theological curriculum from the 13th century onwards (Alexander of Hales).

What strikes one again and again is the debate about the *truth* of the authoritative texts, in which the texts are subjected first of all to an inquiry into their internal *coherence*. If a text is not coherent, we cannot grasp its meaning and can therefore not easily determine what truth claim it may contain. After all, an incoherent text can be reconciled with any number of statements or interpretations. If the latter turned out to be the case, that also spelled the end of the authority of the text under discussion. The aim of such an inquiry into coherence was to arrive subsequently at commentary on the actual content of the text. Such a commentary could be anything from an exegesis of the content of the text, to a detailed analysis, but always with the aim of answering the question of the truth of the central claims in the text. The text could also serve as the occasion for—or a first step towards—addressing certain material problems.

Next to the question of internal coherence, the *quaestio*, with its accumulation of arguments for and against, constituted the typical methodological approach of scholasticism in seeking to gain insight into the nature of the problem posed by a certain question, and subsequently to find a successful, consistent solution. A successful solution had to be rationally defensible. To achieve that, cognizance had to be taken of both semantics and logic, in order to be able to investigate authoritative statements carefully with regard to their consistency. The result was that much attention was given to the further development of logic (*logica modernorum*), in respect of which the Middle Ages may certainly be regarded as a highpoint in the intellectual history of humanity.

All this could give the impression that the *ratio* and the *auctoritas* of a materially reliable witness provide sufficient grounds for answering the questions of theology. However, that is not quite accurate. For

---

11. L. M. de Rijk, *Middeleeuwse wijsbegeerte*, 2nd ed., (Assen, 1981), 117f (French trans. *la Philosophie au Moyen âge* (Leiden, 1985), 89f); Copleston, *A History of Medieval Philosophy*, 100f.

theological knowledge one could appeal to both reason and authorities. At the same time, however, medieval thinkers did not regard the action radius of authority and reason as unlimited. The relativity of the authorities (like the church fathers) is clear in the prevailing methodological approach of the time, specifically at those points where attempts were made to give an account of revelation and faith. In other words, there was a strong awareness of the limitations of the scholastic method.

With regard to *revelation*, scholastic theology realizes that God transcends the possibilities of human thought, so that no matter how strong the impression may be that theology can map God in a myriad of distinctions, in the final analysis what must be said of Him is that He "is that than which no greater can be conceived" (thus Anselm[12]). In saying that, Anselm was not only expressing his existential awareness of God's transcendence, but was providing the theology of his day (and of later ages) with a conceptual-analytical clarification of the use of the term "God," and therefore of the role of the concept of God in the Christian religion. On the one hand it means that a certain hesitancy should characterize our dealings with revelation, given our human finitude; on the other also that, in speaking of God on the basis of revelation, this rule must be taken into account. With this expression (God is "that than which no greater can be conceived") insight is provided into both the logical and the existential function of the word "God" within the Christian community of faith. Apparently, the scholastics did not think of these two functions in terms of a strict separation, as was later often done. Kierkegaard's idea of the "infinite qualitative difference" between God and humanity and Barth's description of God as the "wholly other" were therefore existentially and functionally very much alive in the minds of the early scholastic thinkers.

Also with regard to *faith*, the theology of that period was thoroughly aware of the fact that faith is by no means merely a conclusion following from good grounds. Later the idea became popular that at that time faith had been understood as a purely cognitive and reasonable matter, to the extent that the element of revelation had actually become superfluous. This line of thought, however, fails to recognize the function of the scholastic method: in this objection the method of thought has been confused with the content of thought. A caricature of scholasticism is thus easily created! Take for example someone like Thomas Aquinas,

12. Anselm of Canterbury, *Proslogion*, II.

someone not known for underestimating the importance of reason. Thomas declares that theology puts its trust in the principles revealed by God Himself.[13]

Therefore, while reason does possess a certain universal applicability, the same cannot be as easily said of the authorized texts. After all, from the point of view of the method, these texts put forward *opinions*, of which it only needs to be made clear that a certain truth claim is not introduced into the debate solely for the sake of intellectual exercise, but because apparently it is also regarded as a serious and live option. Furthermore, in the scholastic method it is important to analyze the text in order to determine in which sense truth is being claimed. Thus the last word in a particular *quaestio* cannot be that of an authorized text. It must always consist of a coherent argument in support of the statement, which is being defended, taking into account that the truth claim in question must also be reconcilable with other accepted claims. It is, moreover, a simple matter to see that an authorized text can never have universal authority, because "authority" is a relational concept, and is as such in need of recognition. At most, the rejection of an authority can sometimes mean that a certain tradition is implicitly being rejected or left behind, particularly in cases where a specific authority is constitutive of the tradition.

It is accurate to characterize scholasticism first of all as a reasonable methodology. The aim of scholasticism is the effort to explicate critically both the meaning and the rationality of Christian faith. In doing so, possible inconsistencies must be sought out and eliminated as far as possible in order to achieve maximal clarity with regard to the role of Christian statements of faith. As such, it seems to me a laudable aim, to which no reasonable person can object. What then are the problems associated with a scholastic method, that have caused so many people to develop a distaste for it? It comes across as rather distant, and it allows no associative reasoning. But can that be regarded as a serious objection? After all, the scholastic inquiries, seeking as they do to clarify what Christian faith actually states, and what it concerns itself with, are themselves not the faith they express, but are rather reflections of faith on lived faith. A related objection is that scholastic arguments often come across as very impersonal. That is probably true, but that is also not a

13. Thomas Aquinas, *Summa Theologiae*, 1a.1.2. For scholastic Protestantism we could argue the same, i.e. that it understands reason as *instrumental* in theological argumentations. Reason does not replace revelational notions or statements of faith, but argues for their coherence. Cf. Richard A. Muller, *PRRD*, vol. 1, chapter 7.

very convincing argument against the scholastic method. Here once again a rational argument is confused with a homily, while these are obviously very different genres. That love of a coherent argument need not lead to forced systematization and the degeneration of the method into a procrustean bed can moreover be well illustrated by means of the "local method" of Protestant orthodoxy.

For instance, in Heppe's anthology of classical Reformed Protestant dogmatics, the author treats the material according to "loci." Thus he speaks of a *locus de proprietatibus Dei*, and a *locus de homine*. This division of the theological material into *loci* became characteristic of Reformed Protestant dogmatics, especially under the influence of Melanchthon in his *Loci communes*. With the term *locus*, this classical Protestant theologian means a cluster of concepts that have been developed around a central theme in Church teaching in order to explicate that theme more clearly. The heart of these *loci* is formed by those themes that concern the doctrine of salvation, and which are structured according to a salvation-historical sequence. In the local method, these different themes are not assembled under one all-embracing structure, but are treated more or less one after the other. Horst Georg Pöhlmann's textbook is a good contemporary example of this local method.[14] The fact that the different *loci* are not forced into an all-embracing system, so that every *locus* retains its own structure and thematic focus independently of the other *loci*, gives to this kind of dogmatics a unique character. Even if the classic views of life are criticized in post-modern circles for presenting themselves in "grand narratives," the one thing that cannot be said of a systematic theology, modeled on the local method, is that it offers some grand narrative, which is intended to represent the unity of the Christian view of life. The local method is therefore *by definition* the very opposite of forced systematization. The local method is rather the opposite of the universalizing tendency of the Enlightenment, which sought to reduce everything to a single theory or origin.[15]

One of the most problematic aspects of scholasticism is the fact that various material insights of Aristotle were also appropriated. These appropriations have also often been labeled scholasticism. One example is the epistemology that was taken over, and which was based on reason and experience alone, so that room came to be made for natural

14. Horst Georg Pöhlmann, *Abriss der Dogmatik,* 3d ed. (Gütersloh, 1980).
15. Perhaps the pre-moderns were more post-modern than the post-moderns would ever expect.

theology. This need not have happened, if Voetius' and Barth's distinction between method and metaphysics was consistently adhered to.[16] This applies not only to Aristotelian philosophy, but also equally to the various Platonic ideas that were taken over during the Middle Ages by humanism, among other movements. All this does not seem sufficient reason to discard scholasticism as a method. Rather, it serves as an argument in support of the thesis that scholasticism is first of all a method that is still undergoing development. This is also suggested by the realization that the scholastic thought-world provided the ideal methodological context that made possible, for the first time, the great flowering of the experimental approach, as we have already heard Dampier arguing. A more balanced picture of scholasticism is further achieved once one realizes that, at the height of scholasticism's influence, the theological and philosophical discussions continued unabated. Realism, nominalism and voluntarism existed side by side while their proponents all availed themselves of a similar methodology. Thus all the evidence seems to point towards a characterization of all the various efforts at deepening the analysis of human speech and thought as, in principle, a continuation of the scholastic method.

IV. Scholasticism's Significance for Contemporary Theology

Can the scholastic method still be made fruitful and serve as a good testcase for our own contemporary theology, as Barth suggests in his remark: "The true [prophet] will be prepared, in the final analysis, to subject his message also to this test?" It all depends. We can learn from critical thinkers to think critically ourselves, which is different from merely imitating them. The endeavor to achieve clarity about the meaning of texts by questioning them critically seems to be as much an imperative in our time as it was eight hundred years ago. In the final analysis, we can appeal for this to the fathers who, in their time, attempted with the conceptual apparatus available at that time to elucidate the Gospel. At the same time, they serve as a glaring example that we ought to be careful not to allow metaphysics inconspicuously to develop a life of its own within theology. The alternative is for us to learn

---

16. With regard to the Protestant appropriation of the scholastic tradition of thought, it is important to note that Voetius understood scholasticism in the strict sense as a method for theology, which he distinguished sharply from its material contribution. See on this W. J. van Asselt and E. Dekker, "Rond Voetius's *Disputationes Selectae*," in their publication *De scholastieke Voetius* (Zoetermeer, 1995), 23 ff.

merely to recite the texts of Scripture, and of councils or holy synods. Would we then know, however, what they might mean for our understanding of our own lifeworld? The latter at least was one of the aims of the scholastic movement. That is perhaps its real significance for contemporary theology: a kind of rational laboratory for the testing of the extent of the relevance of theologoumena and dogmata.

The posing of critical questions with regard to faith, tradition and inherited texts is never a traffic in one direction only. It would be naive not to take a continual critical look at the analytical apparatus itself. There are at least two points at which the classical inquiry into texts would have to be updated. One is the *question of truth* as it emerges from the discussion with natural science, and which poses to theologians the challenge of giving an account of their worldview; an analogous challenge issues from the human sciences, from which angle theologians are being questioned with regard to their view of humanity. The analytical apparatus can be enriched with these kinds of questions. On the other hand, new insights have been developed within theology regarding *exegesis* and the *making of theology*. After all, the question of truth is not the only thing that Christian faith is concerned about, even though that is what positivism sometimes tends to make us think. There are also things like praise, commandments and repentance, that is to say the expressive, commissive and prescriptive dimensions of language in general, and the language of faith in particular. Thus during an earlier period, dimensions of language were left unaccounted for in the scholastic inquiries, which, since Wittgenstein, we would certainly not want to neglect now. In addition to the multi-layered character of the language of faith, we have now also become more aware of the metaphorical nature of language as it is used in theology. At the same time, we should not forget that the scholastics realized very well that God transcended their systems, as we have noted earlier, so that they, too, did not think of their language as strictly covering reality, so to speak. In this regard, one only needs to mention the discussions about the concept of analogy.

In the Netherlands, there is a new interest in scholasticism as a method in systematic theology, especially in the so-called "Utrecht school." Just as, in the U.S.A., people speak of a "Yale school," the Netherlands also has its "Amsterdam school" and "Utrecht school" when it comes to theology; the former is an exegetical, and the latter a systematic-theological group. Since 1980 a number of studies have come from the pens of people attached to the theological faculty at Utrecht, each of which took one aspect of Christian talk about God and His deeds as its subject matter. The titles give a programmatic impression.[17] These studies have in common that they offer systematically *argued* analyses of the language of Christian faith. After a number of them had appeared, people began to speak of the "Utrecht school." Some theological commentators qualified this movement as a kind of Protestant neo-scholasticism. After all, it seemed as if these Utrecht theologians were trying once again to speak of God in terms of the formulations of classical dogmatics. Some spoke jokingly of the tendency in Utrecht "to attempt a mapping of God." Indeed, several titles do invite such remarks. Even so, these studies cannot be dismissed in such a fashion. The different authors have not always stuck to the study of the doctrine of God in their more recent publications; yet their style of argumentation has remained unchanged.

The existence of this group of theologians is for a great part due to the influence of the philosopher of religion Vincent Brümmer, whose teaching in Utrecht was structured systematically rather than historically. Students also learned *how* to analyze and tackle a particular question. The studies that have been mentioned are examples of such systematic-theological analyses that look for understandable images or useful alternatives, which will also be recognized by the believing community. It will not do to characterize this line of research as apology or repristination, because they are concerned with finding a contemporary understanding of the foundations Christian language. Both the doctrine of God and Christology have been subject to much modern criticism. If it can be shown that Christian talk of God as the Father of Jesus Christ is incoherent, and full of contradiction and paradoxical ambiguities, then theologians and believers face a problem because no content has actually been conveyed. Then it would be pointless to have recourse to an antique map of God; rather the question must be squarely faced whether we are (still) able to believe within the framework of the Christian tradition without withdrawing to a sphere of esoteric or mysterious

17. A. Vos, *Kennis en Noodzakelijkheid* (Kampen, 1981); L. J. van den Brom, *God Alomtegenwoordig* (Kampen, 1982), expanded as *Divine Presence in the World* (Kampen, 1993); Vincent Brümmer, *What Are We Doing When We Pray?* (London, 1984); F. G. Immink, *Divine Simplicity* (Kampen, 1987); H. Veldhuis, *Een verzegeld boek* (Sliedrecht, 1990), on the concept of nature in J. G. Hamann; M. Sarot, *God, Possibility and Corporeality* (Kampen, 1992); G. van den Brink, *Almighty God* (Kampen, 1993); Vincent Brümmer, *The Model of Love* (Cambridge, 1993); E. Dekker, *Rijker dan Midas* (Zoetermeer, 1993), on the relation between predestination and freedom in Arminius.

language.

A look at this group of theologians also shows clearly that what is at stake here is a method of analysis, because the movement did not result in a unitary theology; all those involved went their own ways and remain in discussion with one another. These differences should not be exaggerated, for what binds them together is their love of the beauty of a coherent argument. Furthermore, a notable consensus has emerged with regard to the significance of the Enlightenment for Christian faith. Although it is undeniable that the Enlightenment has shaken much that Christians take for granted, the Enlightenment is for these theologians no insurmountable obstacle, as it is for many of their colleagues, precisely because they think in such ideological, reductionist-positivist terms. On the other hand, although they have some sympathy for the odd post-modern theologian, generally they regard that thought-world as too relativistic.

All this research is strictly systematic in nature: ideas are analyzed with respect to their embeddedness in, and coherence with, a broader, overarching framework, such as the tradition of Christian faith, their presuppositions and implications, the criteria appealed to and their rationality. Attention is also given to the question of how far the Christian tradition of faith can be reconciled with other convictions that believers might want to believe. Can that be done in a consistent fashion? Concretely, what is at stake in this inquiry is whether and how the *believer*, who at the same time believes in God the Creator and accepts certain insights of the natural sciences, can arrive at an authentic integration of both frameworks into a single form of life.

These are the questions to which theologians have always felt compelled to find answers. One could mention the fathers, Augustine, Anselm, Thomas Aquinas, Duns Scotus, Melanchton, Calvin, Kepler, Descartes, Newton, Schleiermacher, but also someone like Bavinck. The argumentative work of such authors is also consulted because they, too, approach the teachings of the Church by means of conceptual analysis, and there is no point in reinventing the wheel. Yet, the main emphasis is on the work of those contemporary theologians who approach theological questions in a comparable way, like Wolfhart Pannenberg, Ingolf Dalferth, Colin Gunton, and Christoph Schwöbel.

One may justifiably speak here of a new theological contribution. It is in any case theological: the basic assumption is the idea that God is personal, and that one should speak of Him in relational terms. This relational character of the language of faith expresses trust in God's faithfulness as it has been formulated in the witness regarding God's dealings with Israel, and His self-expression in Jesus Christ. God's personhood implies that the world has been given meaning—that human beings may live in a personal relationship with God. The idea of God's faithfulness signifies a certain continuity on His part in His relation to our world. On the basis of this continuity, one may expect to recognize something of it in creation: faithfulness excludes arbitrariness and capriciousness. The last observation implies at least the legitimacy of posing questions with regard to the reasonableness of God's policies. Even if that threatens to further sharpen the existential problems of Christian faith, such as the problem of suffering or of human responsibility. This may give rise to some tension in relation to certain traditional interpretations of Christian faith, and may also serve as the occasion for certain new developments, such as a new appreciation of the classical Trinitarian dogma.

13

Scholasticism and Hermeneutics

Bert Loonstra

This chapter tries to weigh the significance that Reformed Scholasticism might have for the present-day hermeneutical debate about the interpretation of the Bible, and for the current practice of Reformed dogmatic theology.

It is important to stress beforehand, that an historical appreciation of scholastic hermeneutics is not intended. The historical treatment has been performed in an exemplary manner by Richard A. Muller, in the second volume of his *Post-Reformation Reformed Dogmatics*.[1] In an historical approach, of course, scholastic theology has to be measured by the historical standards of its own time. With Muller this leads to a strikingly more positive appraisal of Protestant scholasticism than with many others who have examined the same issue. He shows that many of the negative reviews fall short because they measure the historical phenomenon by their own anachronistic standards and thus the judgment they express is based upon present-day hermeneutical considerations and terminological distinctions.[2]

What I have in mind, however, is *not* an historical appreciation of Reformed Scholasticism. Instead, I intend to ask whether Reformed Scholasticism can make any relevant contribution to contemporary hermeneutical reflections. As a result, I will deliberately use considerations and criteria which are taken from our present-day insights into the origin and the interpretation of biblical texts. This corresponds to the occasion in which this paper was read initially: a workshop on the significance of Reformed Scholasticism for present-day theology.

At first sight the hermeneutical significance of Reformed Scholasticism for the interpretation of the Scripture would seem to be

---

1. Richard. A. Muller, *Post-Reformation Reformed Dogmatics*, 2 vols. to date (Grand Rapids: Baker, 1987–), hereafter cited as *PRRD*.
2. Muller, *PRRD*, 2:470, 528.

minimal, since many of the hermeneutical positions taken by 17th century scholastic theologians are superseded by new insights. In what follows, I will first give some examples of outdated conceptions about the Bible and its interpretation. On their own, these provide insufficient grounds for dismissing the scholastic approach to the Bible. Therefore, I will then invite the reader to examine with me the most important presuppositions of the Reformed scholastic use of the Scripture. Finally, I will compare these hermeneutic presuppositions with important premises of modern hermeneutics, and point out some elements in scholastic hermeneutics that are of contemporary interest.

Much of what is said about Reformed Scholasticism may be true of Lutheran Scholasticism as well, but I limit my scope to the former.

I. Untenable Hermeneutical Positions

A first glance at the hermeneutical reflections of Reformed Scholasticism might make us rather skeptical about its significance. Many of its opinions about Scripture and its interpretation appear to be the results of an aprioristic way of thinking, which is out of step with our modern analytical approach. To demonstrate my point, I will give some examples. Our sources are Andreas Rivetus, Amandus Polanus a Polansdorf, Gisbertus Voetius, Melchior Leydekker and Franciscus Turrettinus.

The first example refers to the idea that even the vowel points in the original Hebrew text of the Old Testament have been inspired by the Holy Spirit. According to this view they cannot have been added by the Jewish Masoretes in the 5th century A.D. As late as 1627 a less rigorous position was held by Rivetus, in line with the views of Calvin, Zwingli and Piscator. He maintained that the force of the arguments for a later Jewish vocalisation of the Hebrew text could not be ignored, although there was no reason to be afraid that this assumption would cause uncertainty about the meaning of the original text.[3]

As early as 1609, however, Polanus had defended the position that the vowel points could not be of Masoretic origin, but must have been added by Moses and the prophets themselves. His arguments are as follows: God made use of the prophets to hand down the Old Testament Scriptures, not only with regard to their message, but also with regard to the very words used, which included the vowel points. Obviously he

---

3. A. Rivetus, *Isagoge seu Introductio generalis, ad Scripturam Sacram Veteris & Novis Testamenti* (Leiden, 1627), 100–5.

considered his position a logical implication of the verbal inspiration of the Bible.

His second argument is, that our faith is not built on the foundation of the Masoretes, but on the foundation of the prophets.[4] Apparently he believed that the absence of vowel points would affect the univocality of the Hebrew text. Not without reason, I would add.

Voetius, too, defended this view in the first volume of his *Selected Disputations*, edited in 1648. According to him it would be absurd to suppose, that the authority of the Scripture partially depended on Jewish critics and fallible rabbis. And without vowel points many sentences in the Old Testament would be unclear and ambiguous, and that would be unacceptable.[5] Later observations and conclusions, however, have falsified the position of Polanus, Voetius, and many others. Their aprioristic argumentation appears in retrospect to be inadequate.

The second example of aprioristic argumentation relates to the tradition of the biblical texts, to the *Textgeschichte*, as it is called. Here, too, Rivetus was the one who dealt with the data in the more relaxed way. He took seriously the text criticism that was practiced particularly by Roman-Catholic theologians. At the same time he held the view, that only minor points of the textual differences under discussion could not be solved with certainty.[6]

On this subject Voetius proceeded more rigidly. In his view, it was out of the question that texts would be rendered defectively during the whole era of the text tradition. Mistakes in some manuscripts can always be adjusted by comparison with better manuscripts. Differences that still remain are at worst variations in spelling, which do not alter the meaning. For this he again adduces highly preconceived arguments: God has preserved his Word by his admirable providence; without this purity of the text tradition the door would be opened wide for atheists, pagans, Jews, and enthusiasts to submit the Word of God to their own human opinions and interests. Voetius could not see how in such a case the authority of the Scripture could be defended. If conjectures were allowed, the fences would be down.[7] In the same way Turrettinus, in the second half of the 17th century, excluded in advance the possibility that real mistakes had corrupted the text witnesses to the point where they

---

4. A. Polanus a Polansdorf, *Syntagma theologiae christianae* (Frankfurt and Hanau, 1655), I.xxxvii (p. 138f).

5. G. Voetius, *Selectarum disputationum pars I* (Utrecht, 1648), 34.

6. Rivetus, *Isagoge*, 116.

7. Voetius, *Sel. disp. I*, 50f.

could not be corrected by better manuscripts or parallel scriptural places.[8] Here, too, later inquiry has superseded this position.

The third example of outdated hermeneutical views refers to the relation between theology and science. Voetius and his partisans simply ruled out the possibility, that in the Bible descriptions of earthly phenomena deviated from the actual state of affairs. In that case the Holy Spirit would have taught us falsehoods. Therefore, the new ideas put forward by Copernicus, Galilei, and Kepler had to be rejected.

In this conflict the Reformed scholastics combated the privatization of reason from faith. In other words, they combated the independence of philosophy (including science) from theology. This very independence was pleaded by Descartes. However, this separation seemed to imply, as Leydekker put it sharply, that in natural affairs philosophy was the interpreter of the Holy Scripture. Here we seem to leave the principle that Scripture is its own interpreter (*Sacra Scriptura sui ipsius interpres*).[9] On this issue, too, from the 17th century onward a bulk of analytical evidence has proved the weakness of the scholastic position.

The last example which demonstrates the problematic character of scholastic hermeneutical decisions is the most far-reaching one. The Reformed scholastics were of the opinion that biblical texts were apt to function as logically exploitable arguments in a systematic discourse. In this conception logical conclusions, drawn from a scriptural passage, have the same authority as the passage itself. Here Scripture texts are taken as proof-texts, from which by logical inference universal truths can be gathered. The main difficulty with this is not, that biblical texts are advanced to support a theological position, but that these texts are handled within a logical framework.[10] The historical context and the specific historical scope of the texts are left out of consideration too

8. F. Turrettinus, *Institutio theologiae elencticae* (Leiden and Utrecht, 1696), I.V.iv-v (p. 79).

9. Voetius, *Thersites heautontimorumenos, hoc est, Remonstrantium hyperapistes* (Utrecht, 1635), 256, 266; M. Leydekker, *Fax veritatis, seu Exercitiones ad nonnulas controversias quae hodie in Belgio potissimum moventur* (Leiden, 1677), 29 ff.

10. Muller, *PRRD*, 2:525, fights the objection that 17th-century "proof-texting" neglects the context and the results of exegesis. He shows that, from a historical point of view, this objection is not correct. My systematic objection, however, is slightly different and is actually expressed by Muller himself, when he states about the 17th-century method of exegesis, 2:521: "its emphases on the occasion, scope, and context of the passage are, . . . directed toward the specifically theological occasion, the dogmatic scope, the doctrinal context. . . . this Protestant exegesis . . . does not focus on the original, historical situation of the text as its primary locus of meaning."

easily.

Let me give some illustrations. As we have seen, Voetius opposed the view that in the course of the history of the Scripture-text irreparable text corruptions could have happened. For support, he appealed for instance to Matthew 5:18: "Till heaven and earth pass away, not an iota, not a dot, will pass from the law until all is accomplished," and to 1 Peter 1:25: "The word of the Lord abides for ever."[11] In my view, this is an improper appeal to the Scripture, because the application is incompatible with the scope of the text. This is not to say that Voetius missed the scope of these words. Rather it reveals his opinion, that within this scope the words express a general truth which can be traced out by logical inference.

The impact of logical reasoning upon proof-texts can also be noticed in relation to the doctrine of God, particularly in the discussion of what we call His incommunicable properties. Expressions in the Bible that speak of God's almightiness and faithfulness in His relation to people, were understood as proof passages for His absolute independence and immutability. In other words: interrelational qualifications of God were transferred into an ontological framework.

Biblical statements, like "I am God Almighty" (Genesis 17:1), "I am the first and I am the last" (Isaiah 44:6), and: "who is and who was and who is to come" (Revelation 1:4), were advanced as immediate testimonies of God's self-existence, that is, His being from Himself. And God's explanation of the Name: "I am who I am" (Exodus 3:14), as well as statements like: "I the Lord do not change" (Malachi 3:6), and: "with whom there is no variation or shadow due to change" (James 1:17), were transformed from testimonies of God's unchangeable faithfulness to declarations of God's substantial, that is, ontological, immutability, which includes for instance the idea that God is without emotions.[12]

Here we get the impression of an inappropriate appeal to the Bible. A difference can be noted with the use of the Bible by the Reformers. The difference is *not*, that the Reformed scholastics would be less careful in doing exegesis. The opposite has been demonstrated convincingly by Muller.[13] The real difference is, that with the Reformers, notably with Luther and Calvin, the Scripture-appeal came about within a kerygmatic setting. Here the biblical texts have their natural room. For the scholastic

---

11. Voetius, *Sel. disp. I*, 51.

12. For example M. Leydekker, *Synopsis theologiae christianae* (Utrecht, 1689), 52, 60. See also *Westminster Confession*, 2nd Article: "without passions."

13. Muller, *PRRD*, 2:525–40.

theologians, however, the text-references were placed within a logical-systematic setting. This setting is foreign to the texts. Yet, the scholastics were not very sensitive to this shift.[14]

II. The Hermeneutic Presupposition of the One Truth

Let us now try to penetrate the presuppositional level of the discussion. In order to trace the specific hermeneutic presupposition of Reformed Scholasticism, it is important to have a keen eye for the stated task of Reformed scholastic theology. This special task arises from its connection with the Reformation on the one hand, and from its connection with Medieval Scholasticism on the other. Let us first look at its relationship to the Reformation.

The Reformation was an ecclesiastical movement; its strength lay in the preaching of the Word of God. The Word had to have the first and final word. To achieve this goal, the very meaning of the biblical texts had to be elicited. Scripture could only really be authoritative, if it was interpreted according to its own purport. As a result, all exegetical traditions within the church had to be submitted to the authority of the Bible itself. Moreover, Scripture could only be interpreted according to its own intentions, and these could only be gathered from the texts themselves. The assumption of the single, literal, historical sense of Scripture was rooted in this principle. Thus, Medieval notions of a plural sense of Scripture and of a deeper, hidden meaning of the text fell apart.

This ecclesiastical Reformation movement required elaboration on the academic level. The basic considerations for this were the principles of *sola scriptura* and of the clarity of Scripture in the demonstrable single Scripture sense. On the ground of the *sola scriptura*-principle an ecclesiastical and confessional theology had to be developed, which could meet the academic standards of univocity and logical consistency. The clarity of the Scripture had to be demonstrated by the systematic perspicuity of the dogmatical exposition, and, in return, the truth content of dogmatics had to be justified by appeals to the Scripture.

On this point there was a clear shift in the task of theology with respect to Medieval Scholasticism. For the latter, Scripture did not in

---

14. C. Graafland, "Gereformeerde scholastiek V," *Theologia Reformata* 30 (1987): 11–25. Muller, *PRRD*, 2:521 f., 531, 539 f., also accounts for this logical setting of Bible exegesis. He even notices its consequence for preaching, 2:509. Yet, he seems to minimize the difference with the kerygmatic setting of the Reformers' theology and preaching.

practice occupy the predominant place of the only and ultimate authority. Often it could content itself with an appeal to the interpretation of Scripture as it was given in the tradition of the church. So in Medieval Scholasticism the ultimate theological account came down to demonstrating the continuity of an opinion with the theological tradition of the church. Protestant Scholasticism, however, was set the task of defending the traditional doctrines of which it could approve, solely on the basis of the biblical evidence itself.[15]

Surveying the positions mentioned, we can see that the 16th century Reformation and the scholastic theology that grew out of it, have much in common. They both confront important parts of the Roman-Catholic traditions of doctrine and theology; they both accept the Holy Scripture as the ultimate authority for faith and life; and they both hold to the principle of the clarity of Scripture, as it expresses itself in the single literal and historic sense of the texts. Thus, Reformed Scholasticism has to be understood as the academic elaboration of the Reformation principles.

Nevertheless, there is a remarkable shift in accent between a reformer like Calvin on the one hand, and the scholastic theologians on the other. This shift in accent refers to the account of the single sense of Scripture. It has to do with the difference that we found already, between the kerygmatic context of the reformers' appeal to the Bible, and the logical-systematic context of the scholastic approach to the Bible.

In accounting for the single sense of the Scripture, Calvin links his conviction about the clarity of the Scripture with humanistic views about *rhetoric*. The interpretation of a text had to focus on discerning the intention of the speaker or writer. This led to an explanation *e mente auctoris*, that is, from the author's mind. With what he writes, the author has an end in view, and with his words he tries to achieve this one end.[16]

The scholastic theologians, on the other hand, link their conviction about the clarity of the Scripture in its single sense not so much with

15. Muller, *PRRD*, 2:465f.; 2:466: "Doctrines like the Trinity, the Person of Christ, the fall, and original sin, which had developed over centuries and with the assistance of an easy mingling of theological and exegetical traditions and of an exegetical method designed to find more in a text that [read: "than," B.L.] what was given directly by a grammatical reading, would now have to be exposited and exegetically justified—all in the face of a Roman Catholic polemic against the sole authority of Scripture as defined by the Reformers over against the tradition and the churchly magisterium."

16. John Calvin, "Letter to Grynaeus," antecedent to his Commentary on Romans, CO 10/2, column 402f.; T. F. Torrance, *The hermeneutics of John Calvin* (Edinburgh, 1988), 112 ff., 121 ff.

rhetoric, but with *logic*.[17] The major argument for the single sense of Scripture refers to the nature of what is true: there is only one truth. The truth is not ambiguous, but univocal and logically consistent. Hence the biblical text does not have more than one meaning. This is summed up in a characteristic expression, which I found in Polanus as well as Rivetus: *unum et verum convertuntur*, that is, unity and truth apply to each other.[18]

One can expect that this logical defense of the single sense has consequences for the method of Scripture interpretation. The scholastic method of interpretation is partly in agreement with the procedure which was followed and argued for by the reformers, but it is also in part different.

The points of agreement refer to the concentration on the text in the original language, with ample attention paid to grammar and semantics. For the rest they concern the view on the Bible as a unity, the principle of comparing Scripture with Scripture and interpreting obscure places with the help of clear places. This leads to the acceptance of the grammatical meaning as the proper meaning of the text, if the text itself does not point clearly in another direction.

Some exceptions on the literal grammatical interpretation can be noticed. Sometimes it is evident that a text is meant metaphorically, for instance Jesus' parables, and His words: "I am the good shepherd" (John 10: 11). In other cases the evidence for a metaphorical interpretation is inferred from the supposition that the literal meaning includes an absurdity, as in the institutional words of the Lord's Supper: "This is My body" (Marc 14: 22). Finally the exegesis of a text can make clear that a text is not only fulfilled literally, but also metaphorically, as in Jesus' announcement of the destruction of Jerusalem as an image of the end of the world (Marc 13).[19]

In those cases the proper sense of the texts is not (only) the grammatical, strictly literal one, but (also) a more metaphorical one, according to the intention of the text itself. Although some tension in the concept of the single, literal sense of the text can be noted here, the main

17. With Polanus and Turrettinus any argument referring to the author's intention is lacking. In W. à Brakel, *Redelijke Godsdienst (Reasonable Religion)* I.II.xviii, we read as the final argument: "The sincerity of the speaker demands, that he expresses his opinion simply, univocally, and that he does not confuse or mislead the hearer by ambiguous words."

18. Polanus, *Syntagma*, I.xlv (p. 181); Rivetus, *Isagoge*, 218.

19. Rivetus, *Isagoge*, 220.

thing is, that it was focussed on the evident meaning of the text, as this could be discerned by careful analysis, in accordance with the prevailing insights into the structure of the language in question. On this point, then, there is no difference between Reformation theology and Reformed Scholasticism.

On another point, however, scholastic theology moves away from the kerygmatic theology of the reformers. The emphasis on the unity of the truth leads to the opinion that the biblical testimony is the perfect expression of an immutable and unequivocal truth system. Hence the logical framework within which the Scripture is interpreted and also the inability to interpret utterances about, say, the revolution of the sun otherwise than as adequate information. And hence the need for an inspired vocalization of the Hebrew text and for a pure text tradition. Without these properties the univocity of the Scripture and consequently the unity of the truth were held to be affected.

Our question is: can we in one way or another take profit from these hermeneutical presuppositions of Reformed scholastic theology?

III. Present Significance

In modern hermeneutics the assumption of one single truth has been totally abandoned. After Hans-Georg Gadamer truth is conceived as the result of a process of understanding to which both the text and the interpreting reader contribute. The understanding of a text is affected by a kind of pre-understanding on the reader's part. This is not only inevitable, it is legitimate, even indispensable. Only on the basis of a certain interest and a certain question can any understanding of a text be achieved. A text can only communicate, if there is a previously given frame of understanding, within which it can be interpreted. So the interpreter is not only receptive, but in his effort to understand he is also active in shaping the meaning of the text. Only in this way can the truth of the text be put into the interpreter's own words.

This view implies, however, that one single objective truth does not exist. It implies, on the contrary, that truth is as diverse as the variety of encounters between the text and its readers. Instead of objective truth, being absolutized by Scholasticism, now relational truth is absolutized by modern hermeneutics. In the framing of hermeneutic theory the scholastic premises have lost their common acceptance. How should we judge this development?

In the first place we have to admit that modern hermeneutic theory is in a manner right in that our understanding is always historically and culturally confined. This cultural-historical impact can be recognized in the Bible itself. Older traditions are passed on by means of application and actualization. In the New Testament the interpretation of Old Testament texts is influenced by the situation and the conviction of the interpreter. Also the logical framework in which the Bible was interpreted by the scholastics, is a cultural-historical presupposition which affects the understanding of the texts. With it emphasis on the validity of its logical method of interpretation Reformed Scholasticism does not meet with approval any more.

On another point, however, we should give credit to the scholastic truth concept. On this point it is of lasting significance, as a correction to modern hermeneutics. Credit should be given to scholasticism in its assumption that there exists an objective, immutable truth, that this truth is one, and that it is accessible to the human mind. Sure, the truth of any proposition, confession, hymn, or thesis, always has a personal side, for it expresses a personal conviction, which can vary from person to person. And the shape in which it comes about depends on the cultural-historical situation of the person in question. This is what Scholasticism did not take into account sufficiently. But a conviction also has a factual side, so that one can ask: is it true or false?

If the substance of a confession is true, this substance agrees with a reality which exists independently of my experience. If, on the contrary, truth would be dependent on our personal understanding in all respects, then there would be as many truths as there are ways of understanding. That would end in sheer subjectivism, which opposes the spirit of the Gospel. For this reason I say that truth is not only personal, it is also superpersonal. In that superpersonal dimension it is one, that is, neither ambiguous nor self-contradictory.

So there is the single, universal truth on the one hand, and a wide range of truth experiences and ditto expressions on the other. Given the multiplicity of truth experiences, a question occurs. How can the single truth be put into words adequately? Just *talking* about one universal truth, isn't it a contradiction in itself, because every word about it is an utterance of a contingent truth experience? In other words: if this universal truth exists, is it accessible indeed to the human mind?

The real question at stake here is the question of the relation between the epistemological and the ontological aspect of revealed truth. Epistemology refers to the way in which the truth is experienced and expressed in a text, and to the way in which the text is understood and experienced again as truth by the reader. Ontology refers to the universal truth that the text wants to express by its formulations. Epistemologically, in the interaction between revelation and experience, truth is always relational, but ontologically, revealed truth is true objectively, in the sense of independent of all human understanding. The truth about God, Christ, and the Holy Spirit is independent of my faith in Him and of my knowledge of Him.

Here is no logical contradiction at all. This can be explained in two steps. Firstly, the assumption of a universal, objective truth fits within modern hermeneutical theory. This assumption is a kind of pre-understanding, and of this modern hermeneutics recognizes the legitimacy. Characteristical for this pre-understanding is the claim that this independent truth really exists.

Secondly, the cultural-historical nature of a truth-claim does not exclude the possibility that it is a true claim, in the sense of an objectively valid claim. The view on objective truth will be *limited* by cultural-historical factors, but limited knowledge of the outside reality is also true knowledge of it.

The weakness of both Reformed Scholasticism and modern hermeneutics is, that they mix up epistemology and ontology. Reformed Scholasticism concluded from the ontological unity of the truth, that both the revelation and the experience of this truth participate in its logical uniformity. Biblical texts were interpreted by the scholastics as unequivocal expressions of doctrine. They were insufficiently aware of the fact that generally the structure of written revelation is not analytical-logical, but emotive-rhetorical.[20]

Modern hermeneutic theory approaches the matter from the other side. From the historical nature of texts and their interpretation it concludes, that truth itself is a historical variable phenomenon, and therefore lacks ontological constancy.

Over against these mixtures I advocate a clear distinction between the ontological and the epistemological aspects of truth. Our knowledge of the truth is always a limited knowledge. True knowledge is knowing in part. So in the Bible truth is expressed in a limited and varied way.

---

20. This awareness was not entirely absent. Utterances of God's emotions were explained as accommodations to the comprehension of the ordinary people. This can be regarded as a rhetorical motif. However, God is said to have emotions only by way of concession to the incomprehension of the ordinary people's minds. That God would identify Himself with these accommodations, and really would act emotionally, is denied on logical grounds. So in this accommodation-concept the logical pattern is predominant.

Obviously the Holy Spirit has conformed to the personal and cultural-historical potentials and limitations of the speakers and writers. Moreover, our understanding of these historically stamped testimonies are partly dependent on our cultural and personal situation too. These limitations and potentialities lie on the epistemological level.

On the ontological level, however, the truth and validity of the Gospel transcend these limitations. It is possible to have knowledge about universal truth in a limited, cultural-historically dependent way. Our knowledge-filter transmits only a part of the eternal light, but what it transmits is true light.

What does this imply for the nature of dogmatic theology and for its appeal to Scripture? It implies that dogmatic theology occupies itself with universal truth, on the ground of historical texts, with the help of logical reasoning. The texts do give doctrinal information about the truth, but in a different way from what was thought in 17th century Scholasticism. They do not give this doctrinal information within a logical framework; rather, they give it through images borrowed from the changeable experiential world of man. Logical reasoning extrapolates the contingent expressions about God and His deeds, and verifies the results by comparing them with the texts. This means that dogmatic theology has to produce a coherent and consistent truth system in which the historical statements in the Bible about God and His deeds can be interpreted fruitfully.

So just like 17th century Scholasticism present-day dogmatic theology has to lay claim to universal validity of what it wants to say, and it has to justify its claim by appeal to the Scripture and by sound reasoning. It differs however in that it is more aware of the cultural-historical nature of human language and understanding, and so its formulations are less definite and its appeal to Scripture is less direct. The theologian realizes that the logical-dogmatic assimilation of the biblical message does not proceed immediately from the text, but that is a separate act, based on culture-dependent assumptions. The theologian has to be aware of the cultural conditions of his own reasoning. Logical reasoning is just our academic way to attest to universal truth, tied to our historical context. This knowledge makes us modest and prevents us from the delusion that, with our systematics, we could hold the message of the Bible in our grasp.

Index